CREATIVE DANCE
FOR ALL AGES:
A CONCEPTUAL
APPROACH

by
ANNE GREEN GILBERT

photos by
HELEN P. SMITH

National Dance Association
an association of the
**American Alliance for Health, Physical Education,
Recreation and Dance**

Dedicated to David, Huw, Bronwen and Griffith,
who put up with a lot when I am writing, and to
Sandra Robertson Norton and Suzanne Keating Wente,
two modern dance teachers who allowed me to be creative.

Printed in the United States of America

First printing 1992
Second printing 1994
Third printing 1995
Fourth printing 1996
ISBN 0–88314–532–4

The National Dance Association is dedicated to promoting the development and implementation of sound philosophies and policies in all forms of dance and in dance education at all levels. By providing leadership for improvement in programs, materials, and methods, NDA is active in identifying resources and in gathering and disseminating pertinent information on dance to Association/Alliance members, other organizations, governmental bodies and agencies, and the general public. In cooperation with other arts and education organizations and structures in the Alliance, NDA strives to cultivate, facilitate, and promote the understanding and practice of dance.

Membership in NDA includes dancers, choreographers, dance educators, therapists, dance science and medicine specialists, arts administrators, and Alliance members interested in dance. NDA sponsors programs by leaders in the field at state, district, and national conventions and through special conferences and workshops, some of which are presented in cooperation with other arts and education organizations. Through its publications, the NDA provides information on dance research, career opportunities, current information on the arts, curriculum guidelines, teacher preparation/certification, and a directory of dance programs, resources, and scholarships. Each year awards honor those members who have made special contributions to the field of dance. The NDA Scholar Award recognizes a member who has a scholarly/creative record extending over ten years and is a significant contributor to NDA and its goals. The NDA Heritage Award honors a member who has made outstanding contributions of national or international significance and provided meritorious service to NDA, other dance organizations, or to dance in general. Other awards honor dance students and educators throughout the country.

To meet its goals, the NDA promotes increased cooperation with other dance, education, and arts organizations to pursue common goals; continued efforts to establish and elevate standards; development of curriculum and methodology to augment instructional materials; and increased communication and influence with educators, administrators, and local/state/federal bodies and agencies.

To enhance the role of dance as an integral and vital part of education and the human experience, the National Dance Association continues to be a significant force in promoting the quality of dance for individuals of all ages, skill levels, and cultures.

National Dance Association
an association of the American Alliance for Health, Physical Education, Recreation and Dance
1900 Association Drive, Reston, VA 20191-1599
703-476-3436

Purposes of the American Alliance for Health, Physical Education, Recreation and Dance

The American Alliance is an educational organization, structured for the purposes of supporting, encouraging, and providing assistance to member groups and their personnel throughout the nation as they seek to initiate, develop, and conduct programs in health, leisure, and movement-related activities for the enrichment of human life.

Alliance objectives include:

1. Professional growth and development -- to support, encourage, and provide guidance in the development and conduct of programs in health, leisure, and movement-related activities which are based on the needs, interests, and inherent capacities of the individual in today's society.

2. Communication -- to facilitiate public and professional understanding and appreciation of the importance and value of health, leisure, and movement-related activities as they contribute toward human well-being.

3. Research -- to encourage and facilitate research which will enrich the depth and scope of health, leisure, and movement-related activities and to disseminate the findings to the profession and other interested and concerned publics.

4. Standards and guidelines -- to further the continuous development and evaluation of standards within the profession for personnel and programs in health, leisure, and movement-related activities.

5. Public affairs -- to coordinate and administer a planned program of professional, public, and governmental relations that will improve education in areas of health, leisure, and movement-related activities.

6. To conduct such other activities as shall be approved by the Board of Governors and the Alliance Assembly, provided that the Alliance shall not engage in any activity which would be inconsistent with the status of an educational and charitable organization as defined in Section 501(c)(3) of the Revenue Code of 1954 or any successor provision thereto, and none of the said purposes shall at any time be deemed or construed to be purposes other than the public benefit purposes and objectives consistent with such educational and charitable status.

Bylaws, Article III

CONTENTS

PREFACE

**WARNING: The incorrect use of this book may be hazardous
to your students' health!**

This book is filled with exciting, educational activities. It will be tempting, because of your busy schedule, to thumb through the pages selecting activities here and there to present in a random fashion. With this approach, you do yourself and your students a disservice. PLEASE READ THE THEORY SECTION before planning a creative dance class.

I have tried to be succinct in explaining how to teach creative dance and have included many helpful hints that will make lesson planning and teaching successful. By taking the time to plan a sequential and comprehensive dance curriculum, you will be giving your students a strong foundation for a lifetime of understanding and enjoyment of the wonderful world of dance!

INTRODUCTION

I started dancing at the age of two around my living room. Like most mothers who have children who do this, my mother enrolled me in dancing class when I was three. I have to admit that I never really liked most of my dance classes, although I LOVED to dance! I took ballet, jazz, and tap and most of my teachers ignored me because I had a stout little body. When I was about 10, a new instructor came to town and she taught modern dance. I learned many of the same skills and techniques that I had learned in previous classes but, always at the end of class, she turned off the lights, turned on some very dramatic music, and let us dance anyway we wanted. This was heaven! I was finally able to express MY inner feelings rather than my teacher's!

I was fortunate to go to New Trier High School in Winnetka, Illinois where modern dance classes were an everyday occurrence and student choreography was encouraged. I discovered that what I liked most about dance was choreographing. I continued to choreograph throughout my college years, always anticipating I would join a dance company, but never really wanting to because I wanted to do my own work.

I never thought I would teach, especially children, because I had not enjoyed my early dance training very much. It eventually occurred to me, however, that I didn't have to teach the way I had been taught. I could teach a combination of modern dance and choreography. The two did not have to be taught separately. I started to devise creative dance classes that combined skill development with exploration and improvisation. I also wanted ALL my students to feel good about themselves so I encouraged everyone, no matter what their shape, size, or sex was, to try class.

For four years I simultaneously taught children's dance classes for Bill Evans and "Creative Dance for Children" to physical education and education majors at the University of Washington. This was a time of great growth and experimentation. From these experiences I developed a sequential and comprehensive dance curriculum based on exploring the concepts of dance. In 1981 I founded the Creative Dance Center where I have continued to develop this curriculum. I also started a dance company of children called Kaleidoscope, because I don't believe in formal recitals, but wanted children who desired to, to have the opportunity to perform and have their choreography performed.

My students' appreciation and love for dancing has encouraged me to share my curriculum and ideas with you. Everyday at the Creative Dance Center and in the public schools where I teach, I see miracles. I see toddlers jump and leap for the first time. I see chubby children feeling wonderful about themselves and their creativity and beginning to become healthier human beings. I see boys feeling confident in their masculinity, yet caring and cooperative with both sexes. I see whole classes of initially uncooperative children learning to solve problems together. I see adults who said they could never dance, choreographing and sharing these works with others. I see everyone becoming stronger, healthier, and happier humans because the joy of creative dance has touched them.

You can be responsible for more miracles. Creative dance should be a part of everyone's life. Enjoy the ideas in this book. Please let them open your mind to new ways of exploring and sharing dance with others.

Many of the ideas in this book were generated in faculty meetings at Bill Evans Dance Center Seattle and the Creative Dance Center. Every quarter (and sometimes more frequently), the faculty meets to share ideas and to dance together. I give the faculty a concept to explore, a problem to solve, or part of a lesson to share. We teach each other, discussing the many possiblities that occur to us as we explore new ideas through dance. We grow and so does our curriculum. These meetings are very special and have been occurring for the past fifteen years.

I wish to thank the dance teachers who have taught with me and who have taught me so much in the process: Gail Heilbron, Jesse Jaramillo, Marilyn Dubitsky, Meg Robson Mahoney, Lassie Webster, Helen Lewis, Ingrid Hurlen, Eric Chappelle, Krista Gemmel Harris, Robin Greer Martinez, Lynn Beasley, Phillip Lewis, Debbie Gilbert, Joanne Petroff, and Dina Kushnir. A special thanks to Barbara Lacy for sharing so much over the years and to Helen Heitmann who got me started on the path to teaching creative dance. A big thank you to Price photo for developing the photos. A very, very special thank you to Helen P. Smith for her outstanding photographs, her generosity and williness to stay with the project all these years!

The students, children and adults alike, that I have taught during the past fifteen years in Seattle have also taught me. I wish to thank them all for allowing me to share with them my love of dance and through their joy encouraging me to continuously explore and expand my own creativity.

I would like to gratefully acknowledge Alina Rossano for proofreading my book and offering comments; Marcia Lloyd for her encouragement; Ruth Emerson for her feedback and friendship; Martha Glover and Katie Anderson for their administrative support at CDC, which gave me time for writing; Teri Conti for all the messages and massages; Ellen Meyer and Nancy Rosenberg, for constructive attention to the details of editing and production; and Luke Kahlich, Rebecca Hutton, and the National Dance Association for believing in this work.

Anne Green Gilbert

PART ONE
THEORY

CHAPTER 1

What Is Creative Dance?

For me, creative dance combines the mastery of movement with the artistry of expression. It is this combination, rather than a separation of the two, that makes creative dance so powerful. I have seen creative dance taught as merely an acquisition of dance skills on the one hand or unbridled expression on the other. I have also seen creative dance classes which consist solely of imitating nature or dancing stories or an activity in which only children too young to study "real" dance take part. I feel that when creative dance combines skill development and self-expression, it can be learned at any age level and enjoyed throughout a lifetime.

I approach creative dance from a conceptual standpoint. More and more people in the educational world are realizing the importance of teaching concepts rather than just facts. More people in the dance world are realizing the importance of teaching dance concepts rather than just steps. If a dancer is to truly understand dance and be able to create and view dances, he or she must learn and explore the elements or concepts of dance. It is not enough to learn a teacher's steps and movement phrases. You should be able to create your own steps and phrases, enlarging not only your own expressive world but also the world of dance.

There might be a misconception that creative dance means turning on music and letting the students dance the way the music makes them feel. This is like giving an American student a book written in Chinese and expecting them to read it. Most people are not familiar enough with the dance concepts to improvise dance movement. Could a student create a piece on the piano without some knowledge of notes and rhythm? We feel that dance is natural. Therefore, simply turning on music should make people dance. It is true that young children respond to music with movement. But without knowledge, one's movement responses cannot develop and grow. Creative dance consists of more than just exploring dance concepts. Skills must be developed, in relation to the concepts. The development of skills will improve the compositions and increase the level of creativity.

The knowledge to dance freely, with skill and creativity, comes from a thorough study of the dance concepts listed on the following page. These concepts are fully defined at the beginning of each chapter in the section "Exploring the Concepts: Ideas and Lessons." A good creative dance program must be based on the study of these concepts.

Creative dance can open up for you and your students new worlds of knowledge, creativity and self-expression. Creative dance can be a powerful tool toward peace because people learn to solve problems, express feelings, cooperate, accept and value individual differences, gain an awareness of their own and other's cultures and engage in an activity that increases, rather than decreases, self-esteem.

I hope this book opens many doors for you and provides new knowledge to help you open the minds, strengthen the bodies, and feed the souls of your students. ENJOY!

Dance Concepts -- The Elements of Dance

THE CONCEPT OF SPACE

Place	self space/general space
Size	big/small, far reach/near reach
Level	high/low
Direction	forward/backward, right/left, up/down
Pathway	curved/straight/zigzag
Focus	single focus/multi focus

THE CONCEPT OF TIME

Speed	fast/slow
Rhythm	pulse/pattern/breath

THE CONCEPT OF FORCE

Energy	sharp (sudden)/smooth (sustained)
Weight	strong/light
Flow	free/bound

THE CONCEPT OF BODY

Parts	head, neck, arms, wrists, elbows, hands, fingers, pelvis, spine, trunk, legs, knees, feet, toes, ankles, heels, shoulders, etc.
Shapes	curved/straight, angular/twisted, symmetrical/asymmetrical
Relationships	body parts to body parts, individuals to groups, body parts to objects, individuals and groups to objects: near/far, meeting/parting, alone/connected, mirroring/shadowing, unison/contrast, over/under, above/below, around/through, beside/ between, on/off, gathering/scattering, in/out, etc.
Balance	on balance/off balance

THE CONCEPT OF MOVEMENT

Locomotor	basic: walk, run, jump, hop, leap, gallop, slide, skip, crawl, roll combined: step-hop, waltz run, schottische, two-step, grapevine, jop, prance, slither, creep, etc.
Nonlocomotor	bend, twist, stretch, swing, push, pull, fall, melt, sway, turn, spin, dodge, kick, poke, lift, carve, curl, lunge, slash, dab, punch, flick, float, glide, press, wring, shake, rise, sink, burst, wiggle, etc.

THE CONCEPT OF FORM

Recurring Theme	theme in variation, canon, round
ABA	a = one phrase, b = different phrase
Abstract	a geometric form, not representational
Narrative	in the form of a story, representational
Suite	moderate beginning, slow center, fast end
Broken Form	unrelated ideas, often used for humor

CHAPTER 2

Why Learn Creative Dance?

Learning Outcomes

Cognitive Outcomes

1. Dancers increase their knowledge and vocabulary through an understanding of the elements and principles of dance.

2. Dancers learn to solve movement problems that are both simple and complex, honing their problem-solving skills.

3. Dancers gain an understanding of the dance histories and cultures of the world's peoples.

4. Dancers increase their listening skills and learn how to follow directions.

5. Dancers sharpen their skills of observation and learn how to make informed judgements regarding dance performances and choreography.

6. Dancers increase their learning in other curricular areas as dance is integrated into the curriculum.

7. Dancers expand their creative skills through choreography and improvisation.

Affective Outcomes

1. Dancers express their feelings through movement, becoming more attuned to the inner self.
2. Dancers experience contrasting movements which help them define their feelings.
3. Dancers express their feelings verbally about their own and other people's dances, helping them to put feelings and thoughts into words.
4. Dancers increase their self-esteem through self-expression and the mastery of movement concepts while being engaged in a positive and noncompetitive dance form.
5. Dancers learn self-discipline as they develop skills and create dances.
6. Dancers learn to take risks by mastering movement challenges and learn trust through activities that engage in weight-sharing, partnering and group cooperation.
7. Dancers gain an appreciation for other cultures.

Physical Outcomes

1. Dancers lessen health risks through movement and exercise.
2. Dancers apply the concepts and principles of dance as they develop dance skills.
3. Dancers learn body awareness, control, balance and coordination.
4. Dancers gain physical strength, flexibility, stamina and agility.
5. Dancers release stress through positive physical activity.
6. Dancers increase their personal movement vocabulary as they work with other dancers and learn from other cultures.
7. Dancers respect the role dance has in life-long well being.

Social Outcomes

1. Dancers learn to cooperate with others through partner and group work.
2. Dancers bond with one another through positive physical contact and the sharing of ideas and space.
3. Dancers learn poise before a group through informal showings or formal performances.
4. Dancers increase leadership skills through partner and group work.
5. Dancers learn appropriate ways of touching others through gentle physical contact and weight-sharing.
6. Dancers discover the value of individual differences through creative exploration, problem-solving and the study of other dance forms and cultures.
7. Dancers attend and support a variety of dance functions and events.

CHAPTER 3

Where Is Creative Dance Taught?

Places and Spaces

Where does dance belong? In the private studio? On stage? In the school gymnasium? In the classroom? In preschool? In elementary school, middle school, high school, college, graduate school? In the workplace? In the home?

Dance belongs everywhere! In America, however, dance is rarely found anywhere except private studios and recreation centers. In most cities, we have made dance an art form that often only the gifted, talented and well-off can enjoy. And yet dance is an essential part of every person because we ARE the dance. Our body is our tool for communication. We express ourselves through movement. As soon as schooling begins, however, we ignore and often squelch that basic need to move expressively. Because our schooling does not include appropriate dance activities, we do not continue dancing after school. As adults, our lives would be healthier and richer if dance were a part of it.

Much argument about whether students need the art of movement (dance) or practical movement (physical education) has also kept dance out of the schools. Of course, students need instruction in both to be healthy in a holistic sense. Creative dance and physical education can become strong partners in the school curriculum at all levels. This does not mean that creative dance is delegated to a two-week unit within a year-long physical education class but rather is taught on alternate days of instruction throughout the school year. At the secondary and college level, athletes and physical education majors should be encouraged, if not required, to take creative dance classes and dancers should study kinesiology and other movement related courses.

Fortunately, research is teaching us that one of the essential ways we learn is through the kinesthetic (body) intelligence (Gardner, H., *Frames of Mind -- The Theory of Multiple Intelligence,* New York: Basic Books Inc., Publishers, 1985). We also know that students must be emotionally involved in order to learn. Creative dance combines kinesthetic learning with emotional involvement, which makes it a very powerful educational medium.

It is the right of every person to feel comfortable with his or her body, to be able to express feelings through movement and to develop the kinesthetic intelligence to the fullest. Creative dance, taught everywhere sequentially, comprehensively and in a noncompetitive environment, will provide opportunities for all participants to learn, to create and to enjoy!

Dance in the Classroom Setting

Creative dance CAN be taught in the classroom. Students quickly increase their spatial awareness when moving around desks and chairs. All the concepts introduced in this book can be explored, all the skills can be developed and dances can be choreographed and performed in the classroom setting. Dance class is a special time, just like math, reading or physical education class. Set the tone for the class by creating a ritual for beginning. Perhaps you will begin class with deep breathing to focus and center minds and bodies. Perhaps you will start with a simple mirroring exercise or a few dance exercises. Perhaps your beginning is to create the space by pushing desks aside. Whatever you choose, a special beginning helps the students prepare for the excitement ahead.

Hints

Ask the dancers to push unattached chairs close to the desks to allow for more empty space when they are moving through general space.

Use the aisles for leaping and free dancing. Push some desks together to create wider aisles.

Use the most open space, usually in the front or back of the room, to perform choreography.

Keep the groups small when doing group work, so they can work in the aisles.

Do partner activities where one person is moving in self space while the other is moving in general space.

Use a scattered formation for most activities. Even creative folk dance can be done individually or in pairs scattered around the room. Leaping and other skills could be done in lines down the aisles or in a scattered formation.

If you have the time and the manpower, occasionally move all the desks to the sides of the room to clear a large space for special activities.

Above all, try it! Your students will love moving in the classroom and they will soon discover wonderful and creative ways of adapting their movement to fit the space and the space to fit their dancing!

Dance in Open Spaces

Open spaces are any places that are not filled with furniture. They might include gymnasiums, lunchrooms, libraries, multi-purpose rooms, empty classrooms, playrooms, dance studios and even athletic fields. Many times a teacher will choose an empty space over a classroom space because that seems more desirable for dance. However, some open spaces are actually less desirable than spaces filled with furniture.

Hints

Consider the acoustics. If you are in a huge gymnasium or outdoors where your instructions or the music cannot be heard clearly you will have a difficult time teaching successfully.

Consider the floor surface. It is not always possible to dance on a floor that has spring or give, but it is very desirable. Dancing on a cement surface can cause injury to the joints and leg muscles. A carpet, sponge mat or good gym shoes help absorb the shock a little. However, I would choose a classroom with a springy floor over a gymnasium with a cement floor. Very often wood flooring is laid directly over cement so do not be fooled. When you jump up and down on a floor in your bare or stocking feet, you can tell whether the floor is laid on cement or is sprung -- has some give. If you have to dance on cement, cut down on the leaping, jumping and hopping activities.

Consider the size. A space can be too large for the number or size of your students. You may have trouble maintaining control with young children in a very large space or they may feel overwhelmed. Perhaps you can think of a way to divide the space, using cones, benches or curtains. A very small space, often found in preschools and high school classrooms, can also be difficult. Try to rearrange or remove some furniture. It is worth taking the extra time and trouble.

Creating a Dance Environment

If you are lucky enough to have a good dance space, think about how you can make it even better. Be sure the elements of dance are prominently displayed. Create a space for pictures and posters of famous dancers, announcements of dance events and classes in the community, and a spot for your own students to post their dance pictures, news articles, stories, etc. If you are a studio teacher, have dance magazines available for parents and toys or drawing materials available for waiting siblings. Create a friendly, open and informative atmosphere where learning, creativity and self-expression can flourish. Welcome your students and tell them how pleased you are to see them. Make each one feel special and excited to be coming to dance class. Do this each time you see them as they enter the class. Say goodbye and try to give each a special compliment as they leave so that they will be eager to return. Do this for students of ALL ages!

If you do not have the perfect dance space, do not wait for it. Start your dance program in whatever space is available to you. Try to create the best environment from what you have. Use the ideas in the preceding paragraph to create a positive environment. By teaching well and informing others of the values of creative dance, you can help make the need for a dance space for your excellent dance program become apparent to building administrators. Your enthusiastic and educated dance students will be your best publicity.

CHAPTER 4

When Is Creative Dance Taught?

Times and Lengths of Lessons

The following times will give you a basis from which to begin to plan your classes. The best times and lengths of lessons are not always possible in certain settings, but perhaps these ideas will give you something to work toward.

In School Settings

In Preschools and Daycare Centers a 20-30 minute lesson twice a week works well for this age level, when taught by a teacher based in the school. When the dance class is taught by an independent dance specialist, a 30-45 minute lesson once a week is appropriate. Dance specialists can work on a ten-week schedule. This allows a few weeks break each quarter to gather new music sources and movement ideas.

For Primary Grade children a 60 minute lesson once a week or a 30 minute lesson twice a week is recommended. You may want to plan three ten-week units or conduct classes weekly throughout the school year.

Intermediate Grade children need longer periods to work on choreography and evaluation. A 45 minute lesson twice a week or three 30 minute lessons weekly are optimum. If this is not possible, the primary grade plan can be used. With the physical education, music or dance specialist and the classroom teacher working together, more time can usually be found to allow the students to share and evaluate their dances.

At the Junior High and High School level there are many options. Dance elective students can take class daily during their 50-60 minute periods. Dance technique and concept exploration can be taught three days a week and choreography taught the other two days, or vice versa. Another plan is to teach technique two days, choreography two days and use the last day for dance history, dance production, anatomy, etc. If a dance elective is not currently available, creative dance can be included in the physical education, drama, music or language arts program once or twice weekly. It is recommended that technique be taught only by a qualified dance specialist, but the other lesson areas can be explored by classroom teachers until a dance specialist is available at your school.

College Students should take creative dance classes just as they do other courses, on a daily basis for several quarters or semesters.

In Studio Settings

Plan an 8, 10 or 12 week quarter depending on your situation. I prefer a 10 week quarter because this allows me time between quarters to discover new music and movement ideas and to catch up on other work.

For toddlers and preschoolers, a 45 to 60 minute lesson once a week is appropriate. Most parents do not want to bring children to a class that lasts only 30 minutes. If you include a relaxation/alignment time after 30 minutes, children this age do well in a 60 minute class.

For ages 5-7, a 60 minute class weekly works well.

Children ages 8-12 can be in a weekly 60 minute class. What I prefer, however, is a 75 minute class which gives me time to include choreography. Even better is a 90 minute class or a two hour class. In a two hour class a teacher can work on technique and concept exploration for one hour and composition skills for the second hour.

Teenagers and Adults need more technique, so a 90 minute or two hour class is preferable. One might teach an hour of technique and concept exploration and 30 minutes of improvisation or choreography. Other options are to teach 60 minutes of technique and 60 minutes of improvisation and choreography or 90 minutes of technique and 30 minutes of choreography.

For Seniors, a 45 minute class works nicely. Once your seniors start feeling comfortable with choreography you may want to move to a 60 minute class. This will give them time to work on their dances and time to view and discuss their creations.

CHAPTER 5

Who Experiences Creative Dance?

Age Groupings, Developmental Stages, Special Populations

Age Groupings

In School Settings the age groupings are already defined. However, you can certainly mix different age groups together as is done in the studio setting or in open or nongraded classrooms. Creative dance can be taught at all levels, from preschool through college.

Outside the School Setting, teachers and administrators of recreation centers, private arts organizations and dance studios define their own age groupings. I have tried grouping ages in many different ways and have found that grouping children in ages close together, especially in the early years, works best. Some possibilities follow.

1 1/2 - 2 1/2 year olds with parent	2 1/2 - 3 year olds
3-4 year olds	4-5 year olds
5-6 year olds	6-8 year olds
7-8 year olds	9-12 year olds
9-11year olds	Teens
12-14 year olds	Adults
15-17 year olds	Seniors
Adults	
Seniors	

Many organizations group 3, 4 and 5 year olds together. I find that there is such a difference in skill ability between a three year old and a five year old that this grouping is not very successful on a long term basis. It would be fine for a special class. 8-12 year olds is another favorite grouping. I feel that 8 and 12 year olds are too far apart in terms of skill level and interests to have this be a successful class. It is possible but not at all optimal. I feel that one of the reasons classes fail is because we try to reach too many age groups in a single class. You will find more success when grouping ages closer together. Studio classes can also be grouped in terms of levels of experience: Beginning, Intermediate, Advanced or Level I, II, III, IV, etc.

Developmental Stages

Ages 2-4
Learns through imitation - copying teacher or parent
               manipulation - being physically moved/molded
               observation - watching and listening
               exploration - exploring the elements of dance
Concerned mainly with self
Easily distracted
Short attention span
Sometimes unfamiliar with school/class setting
Needs practice following directions
Needs structure and repetition
Enjoys lively music and enjoys stories
Enjoys exploration more than skill development
Emotional, moves quickly from happy to sad to angry to happy
Might have trouble separating from parent
Loves to move
Responds to praise, positive reinforcement and smiles

Ages 5-7
Learns through imitation - copying teacher and peers
              observation - watching and listening
              exploration - exploring the elements of dance
              creation - improvising and choreographing
Able to concentrate a little longer
Loves to move; enjoys self-expression
Enjoys practicing skills for short periods of time
Often likes to have his/her own way
Sometimes "tests" the teacher
Needs structure
Feelings easily hurt by peers and teachers
Responds well to positive reinforcement, praise and smiles
Enjoys a variety of music
Able to manipulate props
Enjoys some repetition, but also enjoys new challenges
Vocabulary and understanding of concepts increase
Enjoys choreographing and performing for peers

Ages 8-12
Learns through exploration - exploring the elements of dance
        verbalization - verbalizing feelings and concepts
        execution - practicing skills
        creation - choreographing and improvising
        observation - watching dance
Changing from self-centered to peer-centered activities
Wide range of individual differences and physical maturity
Ages 10-12 starting preadolescent growth spurt -- may appear tired, clumsy,
    inhibited, insecure
Enthusiastic learner if well motivated
Enjoys variety of learning experiences
Able to be good listener, observer and contributor
Interests become better defined
Enjoys experimentation and creating dances
Enjoys performing if part of a group
Motor coordination and endurance increase
Enjoys developing and practicing skills
Needs action, excitement and opportunites to participate fully
Emotional needs must be met or will drop out
Needs individual praise and positive reinforcement
Enjoys variety of music and dancing with props
Responds well to respect, fair treatment and understanding
Enjoys taking responsibility and feeling grown-up

Teens
Learns through execution - practicing skills
        verbalization - verbalizing feelings and concepts
        exploration - exploring the elements of dance
        creation - choreographing and improvising
        observation - watching dance
Pays more attention to peers than teachers
Works hard if motivated
Some prefer practicing skills to creating, others prefer creating
Emotions similar to 2-4 year olds
Experienced dance students differ greatly from inexperienced students
Wide range of individual differences and physical maturity
Responds well to respect, fair treatment and understanding
Needs encouragement and positive reinforcement
Enjoys fun activities
Loves to chat
Very social age
Needs structure
Feels comfortable with familiar activities but can be very creative
Able to take responsibility if motivated
Appreciates being involved in decision making

Special Populations

Infants and Toddlers should be paired with parents. It is very difficult to teach dance to children under the age of two without parents, because young children need to be carried and manipulated much of the time. However, this is a wonderful age to begin creative dance. Infants and toddlers find music and movement stimulating AND relaxing. Through manipulation they discover new movements and rhythms. Infants and toddlers who take creative dance consistently learn gross and fine motor movements more quickly, are often more flexible and have better coordination at an earlier age than do young children who have not had the benefit of creative dance.

Suggestions for Class: Encourage parents to say the dance words as the children are doing the movements. In this way the children will connect the movement with the appropriate vocabulary.

Do simple rhyming exercises, having the parents move the children through the movements.

Use the lesson plan format for 2-4 year olds, choosing activities that are fun and playful.

Many partnering activities can be done with the parent and toddler as partners or with two parents and infants as partners.

Use a variety of music that both parents and children will enjoy. Activity songs work well at this age as does lively music with a strong beat. Nursery rhymes, body part songs, finger plays and feet stories are fun.

After 30 minutes provide a rest time for parents. Turn on soothing lullaby music, have the parents lie down on their backs with children on or near them. Ask them to take three deep breaths, then turn off the lights and allow them to relax for the duration of the song. Remind them to do this at home when they are stressed out. It works miracles! I always sit against a wall and keep my eye on the

children, who are allowed to move quietly around, while the parents rest. Many children come over and sit by me. It is a peaceful time. Resume class feeling refreshed!

Rhythm instruments are a must! Do two songs -- one sitting and playing, one moving through space and playing. Encourage parents and children to try many different instruments. Encourage parents to play steady rhythms and uneven rhythms.

Props are fun. Infants and toddlers can be pulled on or swung in big pieces of material (old sheets and tablecloths work well). They love the feel and movement of scarves. Different sized balls can be used to roll between parent and child or on top of. Beanbags can be tossed. Stretchy rubberbands (made of jersey loops) help strengthen muscles. Streamers encourage arm movements. Milk cartons can be used for jumping or leaping. A parachute has a wonderful feel and adds excitement!

Remind parents that young children learn through manipulation, imitation, observation and exploration. Infants and toddlers may not be able to attend for the full hour. Some may need to be nursed or have diapers changed, others may simply need to watch a spell. Encourage the parents to keep dancing themselves and to continue to encourage their children. The children are learning, even when they are not moving. Consistency is important at this age. After five classes parents will see changes. After ten classes they will be surprised at their child's growth. After a year of classes they will be amazed! Use the sample lesson plans to get started. Have fun and feel good about what you are offering young children and their parents.

Preschool Classes offer certain challenges but also many, many rewards. 3-4 year olds are a special group unto themselves. Creative dance is an absolutely essential part of their education. They

grow and develop so much through movement that it seems like magic. Many of the lesson plans you develop for toddlers can be used with 3-4 year olds but remember, there will be no parents to help you. This means you will put a lot of energy into class management, so read the sections on developmental stages and management hints carefully. You must maintain control while being loving and playful. Plan your lesson carefully, know it well, then try to push through it but also be prepared to move in other directions if need be. This is my favorite age to teach but it also takes the most energy!

Repetition is very important at this age. Children will ask for their favorite exercises and activities over and over again. While repeating familiar explorations, change them slightly by focusing on different elements of dance. This way the children will be happy and you will be expanding their movement vocabulary, helping them grow and develop. Choose music that is structured in such a way as to help you with class management. Music that has pauses or alternates contrasting rhythms or qualities helps motivate and control very young children. Check the "Activity Music List" for music appropriate to this age group.

In private studios or recreation centers parents should not be sitting in the dance class watching, except on special visiting days. At this age, children are too distracted and torn between teacher and parent. If children are not ready to leave a parent they should be in a parent/toddler class. Provide a waiting area for parents so that the children will know they are nearby. I start class in a small circle, chatting with the children as we wait for all to arrive. They are eager to tell me their many stories and this provides a warm, friendly atmosphere.

Parent/child Classes are fun on a regular basis or for special events. Parent/child classes can encompass any age but seem to work best on a long term basis with ages 5-10. In these classes, focus on partner and small group activities. Choreography works well because parents are there to help guide younger children. It is fun to watch children begin to bond to different adults and to see parents develop dance skills along with their children. Several sample lesson plans are provided for this type of group.

Seniors can benefit greatly from creative dance. It is an excellent form of exercise for senior citizens because they can move at their own pace and do movements that feel comfortable and safe for their own bodies. It also gives them an opportunity to express themselves creatively while stimulating their brains through a problem-solving approach. Creative movement helps seniors to relax better, have more energy and to feel graceful once again.

Be responsive to their cues of fatigue, confusion, disinterest and of pleasure and joy. Go with their needs, not yours. Choose music more for pleasure than for accompaniment. Old waltzes and ragtime are fun but seniors also enjoy more modern music. Ask your students for suggestions and share some of YOUR favorites with them.

Be careful when working on different levels and in different directions. You should avoid any work on the knees, or movements which change directions quickly. Your senior students should dance barefoot, if they feel comfortable, or wear a non-slippery shoe such as a gymnastic slipper or aerobic shoe. Never allow your students to dance in footed tights, nylons or socks.

Seniors love choreography, although they may appear shy at first. Start with simple problems and give them lots of reinforcement. Soon they will be wanting to start their own dance company! When possible, combine children and seniors for special classes or events. They love to dance together and learn so much from one another!

Special Education Students love creative dance! I have found much success in mainstreaming these students in my private studio classes and in classroom situations. If you are going to teach a class that contains a large number of special education students, you will want to have teacher aides or students helping you. Some special education students thrive in a mainstreamed class while others do best in a homogeneous class. Hopefully, your school provides both opportunities. If not, do the best you can with your situation as you try to educate your community about the need for mainstreaming AND special classes.

Encourage *students with mobility impairments* to do all the movements that they can. If only their eyes can move, have them move them! Encourage them to stretch beyond their normal movements. Make them responsible for figuring out how to solve the problem THEIR way! Let them know you have faith in their creativity and ability to do so. Offer a suggestion or two if necessary and give them lots of reinforcement for their solutions. Be encouraging but never patronizing. Challenge them, provide a lively atmosphere and soon they will be going beyond what even they thought possible.

Students in wheelchairs can dance with any body parts that move and can also be manipulated and moved creatively in their wheelchairs by students who are not in wheelchairs. Special lightweight sport wheelchairs are available that have a very fine balancing point. These wheelchairs are wonderful for dancing and might be made available to schools through foundation or grant money.

Students with emotional concerns often find creative dance very therapeutic because of the emphasis on self-expression. Through the exploration of contrasting movement concepts, these students are able to get in touch with feelings that have become stifled or hidden. By carefully observing your students you will be able to spot their movement preferences. Their body language -- tight, lanquid, hunched, nervous, etc. -- gives cues to their emotional distress. Through physical exercise and creative problem-solving, individuals with emotional concerns begin to slowly loosen, strengthen, open and relax their bodies. As the students gain control of their bodies, they gain control of their feelings. By strengthening their ability to communicate nonverbally, they become more adept at appropriate verbal communication. With students who display hyperactive or aggressive behavior, focus on slow motion mirroring activities where they follow you. Do "Space Between" activities where they move together through space *never touching*. Work with negative and positive shaping, again reinforcing students who work together without touching. Practice leaping, running and jumping combinations alternated with stretching and melting combinations.

Hearing impaired and deaf students respond very well to creative dance. Signing itself is somewhat like dancing. If you are not familiar with sign language, encourage your students to follow your lead, but not imitate your movements. Point out the dance vocabulary, used throughout the lesson, on your charts or word cards. You might create a special sign or shape to signal the change from one activity to another or you could flick the lights on and off. Moving to a new formation also gives the cue that a new activity is about to begin. When working with a signer, stay next to the person and do not move all over the room. Hearing impaired students find creative dance fun because they are not so dependent on moving to a specific beat or keeping time to the music. They can respond to their own internal rhythms rather than becoming frustrated with imposed rhythms.

Visually impaired and blind students usually derive great pleasure from music but are inhibited in their movement. Overcoming the fear of moving freely through space can be an incredible boost to these students' self-esteem. Use music, rhythm and rhyme as a motivator. Start with simple

20

rhythmical exercises in self space that help open the chest area, lengthen the spine and relax the muscles. Do movements on a low level that move in different directions. Your students will feel more grounded, supported and safe sitting, crawling or slithering. Eventually, encourage movement in different directions while standing. Do tactile partnering activities such as connecting body parts, mirroring with hands pressed together, sculptor and clay or weight sharing activities. Props add a different tactile dimension and are fun to manipulate during any creative dance activity. Work on specific nonlocomotor movements with isolated body parts, slowly adding parts until the whole body feels comfortable dancing. If your students can do a sharp and smooth arm dance while sitting, they will eventually be using their whole body to create sharp and smooth movements. Start your students in self space, having them slowly increase the size of their space until they begin to explore movement into general space -- a few steps at a time. When working with mainstreamed classes, pair blind and sighted students together for movement that travels through space. When dancers are performing for each other, let sighted students quietly describe the movement for their partners.

Students with developmental disabilities increase their learning through dance. Practicing sliding, swinging, hopping, jumping, leaping, crawling and exploring a variety of movements with body halves helps to integrate the mind and body and reinforces cross-lateral and bilateral movements. Movement combinations increase memory, order and sequencing skills. Creating dances increases self esteem which is necessary for learning to take place. Give clear, simple, direct instructions. Demonstrate the activity. Repetition is important. Do simple creative folk dances to reinforce social skills and shaping activities for increased body awareness.

Be positive, encouraging and enthusiastic

Special education students are NOT that different from regular education students. It is our attitude that so often gets in the way and makes the possible seem impossible. EVERYONE has the right and need to engage in creative dance. EVERYONE reaps the benefits outlined earlier when involved in quality, ongoing creative dance classes. Remember these points when teaching any type of individual:

Try anything, challenge your students, be silly, be active.

A modulated voice, eye contact and sensitive physical contact are important.

Plan your lessons carefully but remain adaptable.

Be prepared to energize your students or calm them down.

Music is essential -- find a good accompanist or use music you AND your students like.

Give constructive, objective criticism -- don't accept any old solution but don't impose your own aesthetics upon your students.

Be positive, encouraging and enthusiastic!

CHAPTER 6

How Are Creative Dance Classes Structured?

STARTING OUT

Nondancers

If you are a classroom teacher, physical education teacher, music or drama specialist, recreation leader, preschool teacher, high school language arts teacher or anyone other than a trained dance specialist you CAN include dance in your program. START SIMPLY. START SLOWLY.

Use the ideas under "Exploring Concepts" or "Shaping" in the dance elements chapters as a warm-up activity at the beginning of each day or class. Start with the first concept of Place and continue through the other concepts, then start again with Place, finding a new way to explore each concept. You will find that movement stimulates the brain and prepares your students for active learning. Try using movement throughout the day to relieve stress; to energize yourself and your students; as a tool to teach academic concepts, arts concepts or physical education concepts; for motivation and enjoyment.

As you become more familiar with the dance concepts and more at ease with movement, try expanding your dance time to include more exploration, then skill development and finally choreography. Use the sample lesson plans at the end of each chapter to guide and support you. DO NOT CRITICIZE YOURSELF OR BLAME YOUR STUDENTS if a lesson or activity fails. Analyze the situation and try to discover what went wrong and how to solve the problem. TRY AGAIN. I have worked with many nondancers over the years who have successfully integrated dance into their curriculum. They have started with a single exploration, they have had successes and failures, but they have continued to try because of all the benefits they see their students reaping through creative dance.

Whatever you do, do not give up after one or two lessons. Every time I start a new dance residency in a school, I wonder how I will survive! How will I help these students understand space, time and energy when they seem to be bouncing off the walls? At the end of six classes I wonder how I will ever be able to leave these students who have become such beautiful dancers, such cooperative and creative human beings! If I had given up after the first class, we all would have lost so much.

My method of teaching creative dance will provide the structure, the progression and the understanding that will help your students gain control of their bodies while giving them the skills to express themselves creatively. Read the material on lesson planning thoroughly. Creativity comes out of structure and skill development, so do not hesitate to carefully plan and structure your lessons. A sound structure will help both the hyperactive student and the inhibited student gain control and freedom.

Dance Specialists

If you are a dance specialist I invite you to try using a conceptual approach to teaching dance. If you have been teaching steps and routines, you may well find the conceptual approach more rewarding and enjoyable. It is certainly a more appropriate way to teach young dancers and you will find that this approach lays an excellent foundation for dance techniques that should only be taught after the age of seven.

It is a wonderful approach for the nonprofessional and professional dance student. The conceptual approach accommodates all body types and levels, providing a positive and successful experience for all your students. Through this approach, professional dance students and older students will benefit from an increased knowledge of the dance concepts which will lead to greater skill in composing and performing dances.

I highly recommend that you follow the lesson plan format as closely as possible rather than selecting ideas to explore at random from the various dance concept chapters. A hit and miss approach will bring little success. A structured, well-planned lesson and a sequential and progressive curriculum, as outlined in the following pages, will provide your students with the knowledge and skills to dance with grace and creativity.

If you are an experienced dance teacher, trying a new teaching approach can at times be frustrating. After so many years of teaching you may feel like a novice again! DO NOT GIVE UP. Your students, and in the long run yourself, will benefit greatly from a conceptual approach to teaching dance.

START SIMPLY. START SLOWLY. Each week choose an element of dance to introduce to your class. Use an idea under "Exploring the Concept" or "Shaping" as a warm-up activity at the beginning of class to introduce the element and another one at the end of class to review the element. Slowly begin to focus your entire lesson on a dance element.

Use the lesson plans at the end of each chapter to guide and support you. Read the material on the following pages carefully. It will help you understand the conceptual approach and how to plan a strong, cohesive lesson.

If you are a new teacher you are likely to teach the way YOU were taught. If the conceptual approach is new to you, be brave! Take a risk! The benefits far outweigh the nervousness at trying something new and unfamiliar. No doubt you may already be nervous about your new career. You will soon find great comfort in the structure, lesson plan ideas and sequential curriculum found in this book. You will enjoy teaching and you will be giving your students a great gift -- the knowledge and skills to express themselves through dance!

CREATIVE DANCE CLASS COMPONENTS

Planning a creative dance class is like writing a story or choreographing a dance. You need a beginning, a middle and an ending. Activities must build upon each other to create a meaningful lesson, one that entertains and educates, and that reaches all learning styles. All five LEARNING PROCESSES should be present, to some degree, in every class you teach, no matter what the age level. Using the LESSON PLAN FORMAT will help assure that this takes place. The processes and the format appear on page 25.

Choosing a different element of dance from the list of dance concepts (see below and also page 5) as the focus of each lesson, helps you teach much more than just steps and routines. By including all the components, you give your students the skills to create their own dances and to enjoy dance for a lifetime! Please note that although the learning processes are written in a linear fashion to coincide with the lesson plan format (on page 25), they may occur several different times throughout the lesson.

Dance Concepts -- The Elements of Dance

THE CONCEPT OF SPACE

Place	self space/general space
Size	big/small, far reach/near reach
Level	high/low
Direction	forward/backward, right/left, up/down
Pathway	curved/straight/zigzag
Focus	single focus/multi focus

THE CONCEPT OF TIME

Speed	fast/slow
Rhythm	pulse/pattern/breath

THE CONCEPT OF FORCE

Energy	sharp (sudden)/smooth (sustained)
Weight	strong/light
Flow	free/bound

THE CONCEPT OF BODY

Parts	head, neck, arms, wrists, elbows, hands, fingers, pelvis, spine, trunk, legs, knees, feet, toes, ankles, heels, shoulders, etc.
Shapes	curved/straight, angular/twisted, symmetrical/asymmetrical
Relationships	body parts to body parts, individuals to groups, body parts to objects, individuals and groups to objects: near/far, meeting/parting, alone/connected, mirroring/shadowing, unison/contrast, over/under, above/below, around/through, beside/ between, on/off, gathering/scattering, in/out, etc.
Balance	on balance/off balance

THE CONCEPT OF MOVEMENT

Locomotor	basic: walk, run, jump, hop, leap, gallop, slide, skip, crawl, roll combined: step-hop, waltz run, schottische, two-step, grapevine, jop, prance, slither, creep, etc.
Nonlocomotor	bend, twist, stretch, swing, push, pull, fall, melt, sway, turn, spin, dodge, kick, poke, lift, carve, curl, lunge, slash, dab, punch, flick, float, glide, press, wring, shake, rise, sink, burst, wiggle, etc.

THE CONCEPT OF FORM

Recurring Theme	theme in variation, canon, round
ABA	a = one phrase, b = different phrase
Abstract	a geometric form, not representational
Narrative	in the form of a story, representational
Suite	moderate beginning, slow center, fast end
Broken Form	unrelated ideas, often used for humor

CREATIVE DANCE CLASS COMPONENT CHART

LEARNING PROCESSES

LESSON PLAN FORMAT

Understanding
Defining, understanding and exploring dance concepts and terms.

Warming Up
Warming up the body and mind through warm-up activities and/or exercises; introducing a dance concept. (Any of these activities might be included.)

Exploring the Concept
Understanding the concepts and elements of dance through guided exploration.

Developing Skills
Developing and refining dance skills through exploration and practice.

Developing Skills
Practicing and refining locomotor and nonlocomotor skills, dance steps and technique through the dance concepts.

Creating
Improvising and choreographing movements, phrases and dances.

Creating
Improvising movements and phrases and choreographing studies/dances based on the dance concepts.

Perceiving
Viewing professional and/or student dance works (live and on video or film) inside and outside the school setting.

Cooling Down
Viewing improvisation or choreography; evaluating improvisation or choreography; relaxing and alignment; stretching and reviewing the dance concepts. (Any of these activities might be included.)

Evaluation
Expressing feelings and making observations about one's own work and the work of others.

PLANNING LESSONS

Plan your creative dance lesson using the following steps:

1. Choose an element of dance for your weekly lesson focus from the list of Dance Concepts on page 24). It is easiest, in the beginning, to start at the top of the list and progress down. Week 1 - Place, Week 2 - Size, Week 3 - Level, Week 4 - Direction, etc.

2. On the page titled Lesson Content (page 27), find the column that best describes the age and length of your class (5-7 years/30 minutes). Using a blank Lesson Plan Form (page 30), circle the Lesson Plan Areas that you need or want to include after studying the Lesson Content page, such as Warm-up Activities, Introducing Concept, Exploring Concept, Developing Skills and Free Dancing. The Lesson Plan Areas are described and defined on page 28. Sample lesson plan formats for various age groups and lesson lengths appear on pages 31-34.

3. Locate the chapter on the dance element you chose as your weekly focus. Each element chapter is arranged in the order of the lesson plan form, starting with "Introducing the Concept" and ending with "Choreography." "Warming Up" and "Cooling Down" activities are found in separate chapters in this book. For each lesson plan area that you circled on your blank form, select an activity from the chapter that you would enjoy teaching and feel would be appropriate for your class. Write that activity next to the lesson area on your blank Lesson Plan Form. Continue until your lesson is complete.

4. Look at the sample lesson plans on pages 36-37 for help. At the end of each element chapter are two sample lesson plans with more detail and Chapter 26 contains additional samples for various age groups.

5. Remember, you will be teaching creative dance for a long time. Start slowly. Choose only one element for each lesson. Do not confuse your students by trying to focus on more than one concept. Each element chapter has many, many ideas for exploring each concept. Choose only one activity for each lesson plan area you circled. You will have time during the year to explore each concept in many ways. (See page 35 for sample ten week curriculums.) Each time your students explore a familiar concept, they will bring to it new knowledge based on what they have discovered since they explored that concept earlier. I call this a layering effect. Each week a new concept is layered on the previous week's concept. By making the lesson focus very clear, each concept is explored in depth then layered upon the next concept. What occurs, in time, is a deep understanding of the concepts and an ability to use the concepts in a clear and integrated fashion.

6. BE PATIENT! Teach ten concepts over a period of ten weeks before evaluating your program. You will be surprised, if you use this method correctly, at how much your students have learned, how much they enjoy dancing and how well they use the elements of dance in their dancing. Instead of a few steps they will soon forget, you are giving them the building blocks with which to create dances throughout their lives.

LESSON CONTENT

	2-5 Years		5-7 Years		8-12 Years		Teen/Adult	
	30 m	60 m	30 m	60 m	30 m	60 m	45 m	90 m
WARMING-UP								
Warm-up Activities	●	❑	●	❑	●	❑	❑	❑
Dance Exercises	●	✔	●	✔	●	✔	✔	✔
Introducing Concept	✔	✔	✔	✔	✔	✔	✔	✔
EXPLORING THE CONCEPT								
Exploring Concept	✔	✔	✔	✔	✔	✔	✔	✔
Shaping	●	✔	●	●	❑	❑	❑	❑
Rhythm Instruments	●	✔	●	●				
DEVELOPING SKILLS								
Developing Skills	✔	✔	✔	✔	✔	✔	✔	✔
Turning	●	✔	●	●	●	●	●	●
Combining Movements	●	✔	●	✔	●	✔	✔	✔
Leaping	●	✔	●	●	●	●	●	●
CREATING								
Free Dancing/Improvising	✔	✔	●	●	●	●	●	●
Choreographing			●	●	●	●	●	●
COOLING DOWN								
Good-bye Dance	●	❑	●	❑				
Relaxation/Alignment	●	✔	●	●	●	●	●	●
Stretching/Review Concept			●	●	●	●	●	●
Sharing and Showing Dances			❑	✔	❑	✔	❑	✔

✔ = do each class   ● = choose one option   ❑ = do if there is time

LESSON PLAN AREAS DESCRIBED AND DEFINED

WARMING UP

Warm-up Activities: Any 2-5 minute activity that warms up the mind and muscles such as mirroring the leader; stretch, curl, swing and shake; jogging alternated with nonlocomotor movements; simple activities from "Exploring the Concept." The warm-up activity could review the concept previously taught or introduce the concept for the current lesson.

Dance Exercises: Safe, correct exercises that lengthen and strengthen the muscles, increase flexibility, and encourage proper alignment. Use rhyming exercises for young children. See the bibliography for a selection of dance books containing technique for older dancers.

Introducing the Concept: Explain the concept, which is the dance element that you have chosen for the lesson focus, briefly through words and movement. It also helps the dancers to see the words (written on cards or a blackboard) and to say the words, e.g., "Level -- high, medium, low."

EXPLORING THE CONCEPT

Exploring the Concept: Dancers become familiar with the dance element through guided exploration individually, in pairs or groups.

Shaping: Dancers explore the dance element while creating stabile and mobile body shapes.

Rhythm Instruments: Dancers explore the dance element while playing instruments in self and general space. They can also explore keeping a beat or other rhythm concepts.

DEVELOPING SKILLS

Developing Skills: Dancers are introduced to and practice locomotor and nonlocomotor skills through the dance element.

Turning: Using the dance element, dancers develop various turning skills.

Combining Movements: Using the dance element, dancers put locomotor and nonlocomotor movements together into dance phrases. Dancers focus on the transitions between the actions using flow from one action to another.

Leaping: Using the dance element, dancers develop and practice leaping skills.

CREATING

Free Dancing/Improvising: Improvisation is unplanned movement. In free dancing young dancers improvise their own movements showing an understanding of the dance element/s. The teacher should provide a simple structure for young students such as: dance high when the music is loud and dance low when the music is soft. Teachers can provide a more complex structure for older students' improvisations which will help prepare them for choreography.

Choreographing: Choreography is planned movement. Dancers create their own dance phrases or pieces, spending time to set specific movements relating to the dance element and then performing these pieces for peers or others.

COOLING DOWN

Good-bye Dance: Dancers move across the floor individually or in pairs, trios or groups using the dance element. This activity is a time to evaluate each dancer's understanding and ability to use the dance element introduced at the beginning of class. (Idea from Mary Joyce.)

Relaxation/Alignment: Relaxation, visualization and alignment exercises are used to reduce stress and become atuned to the body.

Stretching/Reviewing Concept: Dancers stretch muscles to gain length and prevent cramping. While stretching, the dancers can verbally review the lesson's concepts and the dance element used in the class.

Sharing and Evaluating Choreography: Dancers positively evaluate each other's dance compositions. Statements could be made about the use of the dance element, other elements used, transitions, performance skills, or movements and relationships that made the piece exciting or different.

LESSON PLAN FORM

Age or Grade_____   Length of Lesson_____

Circle this lesson's concept:

Place   Level   Size   Direction   Pathway   Focus   Speed   Rhythm   Energy   Weight

Flow   Body Parts   Body Shapes   Relationships   Balance   Other_____

Circle and fill in the lesson plan areas you are teaching:

WARMING UP

Warm-up Activity:

Dance Exercises/Technique:

Introducing the Concept:

EXPLORING THE CONCEPT

Exploring the Concept:

Shaping:

Instruments:

DEVELOPING SKILLS

Developing Skills:

Turning:

Combining Movements:

Leaping:

CREATING

Free Dancing/Improvising:

Choreographing:

COOLING DOWN

Good-bye Dance:

Relaxing/Alignment:

Stretching/Reviewing Concept:

Sharing/Evaluating Choreography:

SAMPLE LESSON PLAN FORMATS FOR CREATIVE DANCE CLASS

1/2 HOUR CLASS FOR 2-5 YEAR OLDS

4 minutes -- **Warming Up**
    Quick Warm-up
    Introducing the Concept
10 minutes -- **Exploring the Concept**
    Exploring the Concept
    Shaping
10 minutes -- **Developing Skills**
    Developing Skills
    Combining Movements
5 minutes -- **Creating**
    Free Dancing
1 minute -- **Cooling Down**
    Goodbye Dance

1 HOUR CLASS FOR 2-5 YEAR OLDS

15 minutes -- **Warming Up**
    Exercises
    Introducing the Concept
15 minutes -- **Exploring the Concept**
    Exploring the Concept
    Shaping
    Instruments
5 minutes -- **Relaxation/Alignment**
15 minutes -- **Developing Skills**
    Developing Skills
    Combining Movements
    Leaping
5 minutes -- **Creating**
    Free Dancing
5 minutes -- **Cooling Down**
    Goodbye Dance

CONTINUED

SAMPLE LESSON PLAN FORMATS FOR CREATIVE DANCE CLASS, continued

1/2 HOUR CLASS FOR 5-7 YEAR OLDS
(Alternate the two formats within the week if you teach twice a week and weekly if you teach once a week.)

10 minutes -- **Warming Up**
　　Exercises
　　Introducing the Concept
5 minutes -- **Exploring the Concept**
　　Exploring the Concept
10 minutes -- **Developing Skills**
　　Developing Skills
　　Leaping
4 minutes -- **Creating**
　　Free Dancing
1 minute -- **Cooling Down**
　　Relaxation/Review Concept

5 minutes -- **Warming Up**
　　Quick Warm-up (from Exploring the Concept)
　　Introducing (or reviewing) the Concept
5 minutes -- **Exploring the Concept**
　　Shaping
5 minutes -- **Developing Skills**
　　Combining Movements
10 minutes -- **Creating**
　　Choreography
5 minutes -- **Cooling Down**
　　Sharing and Evaluating Choreography

1 HOUR CLASS FOR 5-7 YEAR OLDS
(Alternate the two formats.)

15 minutes -- **Warming Up**
　　Exercises
　　Introducing the Concept
15 minutes -- **Exploring the Concept**
　　Exploring the Concept
　　Shaping
　　Instruments
5 minutes -- **Relaxation/Alignment**
15 minutes -- **Developing Skills**
　　Developing Skills
　　Combining Movements
　　Leaping
5 minutes -- **Creating**
　　Free Dancing
5 minutes -- **Cooling Down**
　　Goodbye Dance or Review Concept

15 minutes -- **Warming Up**
　　Exercises
　　Introducing the Concept
10 minutes -- **Exploring the Concept**
　　Exploring the Concept
　　Shaping or Instruments
5 minutes -- **Relaxation/Alignment**
10 minutes -- **Developing Skills**
　　Developing Skills
　　Combining Movements
10 minutes -- **Creating**
　　Choreographing
10 minutes -- **Cooling Down**
　　Sharing and Evaluating Choreography

CONTINUED

1/2 HOUR CLASS FOR 8-12 YEAR OLDS
(Alternate the two formats within the week if you teach twice a week and weekly if you teach once a week.)

10 minutes -- Warming Up
  Exercises
  Introducing the Concept
5 minutes -- Exploring the Concept
  Exploring the Concept or Shaping
10 minutes -- Developing Skills
  Developing Skills
  Leaping
4 minutes -- Creating
  Free Dancing/Improvising
1 minute -- Cooling Down
  Relaxation/Review Concept

5 minutes -- Warming Up
  Quick Warm-up (Exploring the Concept)
  Introducing (or reviewing) the Concept
5 minutes -- Exploring the Concept
  Shaping
5 minutes -- Developing Skills
  Combining Movements
10 minutes -- Creating
  Choreographing
5 minutes -- Cooling Down
  Sharing and Evaluating Choreography

1 HOUR CLASS FOR 8-12 YEAR OLDS
(Alternate the two formats.)

20 minutes -- Warming Up
  Exercises
  Introducing the Concept
10 minutes -- Exploring the Concept
  Exploring the Concept
  Shaping
18 minutes -- Developing Skills
  Developing Skills
  Combining Movements
  Leaping
7 minutes -- Creating
  Free Dancing/Improvisation
5 minutes -- Cooling Down
  Stretching and Reviewing Concept

20 minutes -- Warming Up
  Quick Warm-up (Exploring the Concept)
  Exercises
  Introducing the Concept
5 minutes -- Exploring the Concept
  Shaping
10 minutes -- Developing Skills
  Developing Skills
  Turning
15 minutes -- Creating
  Choreographing
10 minutes -- Cooling Down
  Sharing and Evaluating Choreography

CONTINUED

50 MINUTE CLASS FOR TEENS AND ADULTS

(Alternate the two formats when teaching once or twice a week. When teaching daily classes, spend three days a week focusing on developing skills and technique and two days a week on exploration and choreography.)

20 minutes -- **Warming Up**
    Exercises
    Introducing the Concept
10 minutes -- **Exploring the Concept**
    Exploring the Concept
    Shaping
10 minutes -- **Developing Skills**
    Developing Skills
    Leaping/Turning
5 minutes -- **Creating**
    Improvising
5 minutes -- **Cooling Down**
    Stretching/Reviewing Concept

20 minutes -- **Warming Up**
    Quick Warm-up (Exploring the Concept)
    Exercises
5 minutes -- **Exploring the Concept**
    Shaping
5 minutes -- **Developing Skills**
    Combining Movements
10 minutes -- **Creating**
    Choreographing
10 minutes -- **Cooling Down**
    Sharing and Evaluating Choreography

90 MINUTE CLASS FOR TEENS AND ADULTS

35 minutes -- **Warming Up**
    Quick Warm-up (from Exploring the Concept)
    Exercises
    Introducing the Concept
5 minutes -- **Exploring the Concept**
    Shaping
20 minutes -- **Developing Skills**
    Developing Skills
    Combining Movements
    Turning and/or Leaping
20 minutes -- **Creating**
    Improvising
    Choreographing
10 minutes -- **Cooling Down**
    Sharing and Evaluating Choreography

SAMPLE TEN WEEK CURRICULUMS

FALL QUARTER	WINTER QUARTER	SPRING QUARTER
Place	Place	Place
Size	Speed/Rhythm	Size/Level
Level	Relationships	Body Parts/Focus
Direction	Size	Direction/Pathway
Pathway	Level	Shapes
Speed	Energy	Weight
Energy	Pathway	Energy/Speed
Weight	Direction	Rhythm
Flow	Focus	Relationships
Body Parts/Balance	Balance	Flow

FALL QUARTER	WINTER QUARTER	SPRING QUARTER
Place	Relationships	Focus/Relationship
Direction	Energy	Shapes
Pathway	Weight	Balance
Level	Place	Flow
Size	Pathway/Direction	Body Parts/Weight
Speed/Rhythm	Shapes/Body Parts	Rhythm
Relationships	Level/Balance	Direction
Weight	Size	Energy
Energy	Focus	Level/Size
Flow	Speed or Rhythm	Place/Pathway

CREATE YOUR OWN

FALL QUARTER   WINTER QUARTER   SPRING QUARTER

SAMPLE LESSON PLAN

Age/Grade _5-7 years_   Length of Lesson _30 minutes_

Circle the lesson concept: Place (Level) Size Direction Pathway Focus Speed Rhythm

Energy Weight Flow Body Parts Body Shapes Relationships Balance Other_____

Warming up
Warm-up Activity:

Dance Exercises/Technique: *four rhyming exercises sitting, four standing.*

Introducing the Concept: *LEVEL: high, middle low - make a few shapes in each level.*

Exploring the Concept
Exploring the Concept: *LEVEL, Exploring the Concept, #1 "Rising and Sinking."*
                        Dancers rise and sink in 8 counts, 4, 2, 1!
Shaping:

Instruments: *LEVEL, Instruments #2 "Highland and Lowland."*
                        Play instruments on low level in one half of room and on a
                        high level in other half of room.

Developing Skills
Developing Skills:

Turning:

Combining Movements: *LEVEL, Combining Movements #6 "Cinquain."*
                        Dancers improvise to five line poem about level.
Leaping:

Creating
Free Dancing/Improvising: *LEVEL, Exploring the Concept #11, "Back to Back."*
                        Dancers connect body parts with a partner at different levels
                        and then dance away on different levels.

Choreographing:

Cooling Down
Goodbye Dance:

Relaxation/Alignment: *Dancers close eyes and rest. Review the vocabulary : Level - high,*
                        middle, low.

Stretching/Concept Review

Sharing/Evaluating Choreography:

SAMPLE LESSON PLAN

Age/Grade *3-4 years old*   Length of Lesson *60 minutes*

Circle the lesson concept: (Place) Level Size Direction Pathway Focus Speed Rhythm

Energy Weight Flow Body Parts Body Shapes Relationships Balance Other_____

Warming up
Warm-up Activity:

Dance Exercises/Technique: *four rhyming exercises sitting, four standing.*

Introducing the Concept: *PLACE: self space, general space - dancers say the words and
demonstrate the different places.*

Exploring the Concept
Exploring the Concept: *PLACE, Exploring the Concept #1 "Spots."*
*Practice nonlocomotor movements in self space and locomotor
movements in general space.*

Shaping: *PLACE, Shapes #5 "Three Shapes."*
Make three shapes in self space, move the last shape in general space. Repeat.

Instruments: *PLACE, Instruments #5 "Freeze."*
Play and dance through general space, freeze in silence in self space.

D0 RELAXATION/ALIGNMENT HERE

Developing Skills
Developing Skills: *PLACE, Developing Skills #4 "Foot Story."*
Tell a story about two feet, dancers do actions with feet while sitting in self space.

Turning: *PLACE, Turning #1 "Create a Turn."*
Dancers explore turning in self and general space.

Combining Movements: *PLACE, Combining Movements #6 "Activity Song."*
*Play song "Moving Game" from Hap Palmer and do movements
in self and general space.*

Leaping: *PLACE, Leaping #1 "Scattered."*
*Place milk cartons around room in scattered formation, leap
over cartons then leap over only your own carton. Alternate.*

Creating
Free Dancing/Improvising: *PLACE, Exploring the Concept #4 "Find a Friend."*
Dance with a friend in self space, dance alone in general space.

Choreographing:

Cooling Down
Goodbye Dance: *Do if time allows.*

Relaxation/Alignment: *Do relaxation/alignment exercises after the Instruments.*

Stretching/Reviewing Concept:
Sharing/Evaluating Choreography:

SAMPLE LESSON PLAN

Age/Grade _8-12 years old_ Length of Lesson _30 minutes_

Circle the lesson concept: Place Level (Size) Direction Pathway Focus Speed Rhythm
Energy Weight Flow Body Parts Body Shapes Relationships Balance Other _Math and Science_

Warming up
Warm-up Activity: _3'Rs, Math #1_
Stretch and Release body parts for sums of 12.

Dance Exercises/Technique:

Introducing the Concept: _Size: Dancers say and demonstrate words: SIZE- big, little_

Exploring the Concept
Exploring the Concept: _SIZE, Exploring the Concept #6 "Shrinking Space."_
Dancers shrink movements as room shrinks.
Shaping:

Instruments:

Developing Skills
Developing Skills:

Turning: _SIZE, Turning #1 "Big and Little."_
Dancers explore at least five different big and small turns.
Combining Movements:

Leaping:

Creating
Free Dancing/Improvising:

Choreographing: _SIZE, Choreographing #7 "Molecules."_
Groups create molecule dances using different sized movements.

Cooling Down
Goodbye Dance:

Relaxation/Alignment:

Stretching/Concept Review

Sharing/Evaluating Choreography: _Show group dances and discuss the use of size and other elements used to create interesting molecule dances._

PLANNING APPROPRIATE ACTIVITIES

When planning a creative dance class you must take into account your students' ages AND experience. Your students' ages are important because certain motor and social skills are more appropriate for one age than for another age. Experience is important because third graders who have had no dance experience will obviously need a different lesson from third graders with three years of dance experience. This section will address both age and experience appropriate activities using an overview of the general lesson plan.

THE LESSON PLAN

Warming Up

Quick warm-ups can be very similar for different age groups and levels of experience. The object of a quick warm-up is to get moving quickly in order to warm up the blood and muscles. Therefore, the activity should be simple and even familiar. The suggestions under "Quick Warm-ups" can be used with all levels and age groups.

Technique and exercises should differ with age and experience. 2-7 year olds can do "Rhyming Exercises." As these dancers gain more experience or increase in age you can add new exercises and spend more time focusing on alignment, arm movements, balance and rhythm (counting). 8-12 year olds, teens and adults can spend a longer time doing technique. More advanced exercises can be introduced if time allows and a dance specialist is teaching.

Exploring the Concept

Beginning level students, regardless of age, can enjoy doing the same activities to explore the concepts. Experienced students can explore the concept:
> with partners, trios or small groups
> with a prop
> adding another element of dance
> combining two explorations.

Developing Skills

Developing skills is the area that needs to be most carefully looked at in terms of what is appropriate at certain age levels. Dancers with experience, who have already mastered skills in their age group, can be introduced to skills described in an older age group.

2-4 year olds should be practicing basic locomotor and nonlocomotor skills (see "Movement" chapters for appropriate skills). The focus might be on practicing old skills while developing new ways of doing them such as backward, faster, bigger, etc. Hopping and skipping can be introduced to 4 year olds and more experienced 3 year olds. Coordination of arm and leg movements is also developed. Simple movements are put together to form short combinations.

5-7 year olds can practice different ways of skipping and hopping, along with more advanced locomotor skills such as the step-hop and chainee turn. Experienced students combine locomotor and nonlocomotor movements to create more advanced movements such as a slashing skip or floating turn. Familiar movements can be done with a partner. Combinations of movements are done within a simple time frame or rhythmical phrase.

8-12 year olds perfect the basic locomotor and nonlocomotor skills while learning more advanced movements such as the polka, piqué turn, etc. Experienced dancers can change and combine familiar movements using the elements of dance to make them more challenging Complex combinations are learned and often done with a partner or small group.

Teens and adults practice combined locomotor and nonlocomotor skills using the elements of dance to vary them and to create more involved movements. Skills are performed with varying speeds and rhythms. Movements that require using opposite elements in the body simultaneously are practiced (upper body smooth/lower body sharp). Complex combinations, which make use of spatial and rhythmic patterns, performed in pairs and small groups, are learned or created.

Creating

2-4 year olds should improvise dances using the skills and elements of dance learned in class. The "Free Dance" should have a simple structure which allows the young dancer to show the teacher he or she understands and can use the dance concept introduced at the beginning of class. More experienced dancers can use props or dance with partners during the free dance.

5-7 year olds begin developing composition skills through more structured and complex improvisations. Young choreographers are asked to work in pairs to create simple AB or ABA dances (a high/low dance or a high/low/high dance). More experienced dancers can work in trios and small groups, add props, or use different choreographic forms. Dancers perform for each other and comment on the dances.

8-12 year olds create more complex dances using one or more elements of dance. Experienced dancers use a variety of forms, are given more time to create longer pieces, are asked to develop themes and make positive critical comments about the dances performed in class. Structured improvisation is used as a foundation for choreography.

Teens and adults continue to use improvisation as a tool to discover new movements and to become familiar with the elements of dance. In choreography, dancers experiment with different forms, styles and music. Full use of props can add variety and complexity to the dances. Group and solo works are done. Students can take turns setting pieces on each other. Positive comments on dances could take the form of written critiques, if desired.

Cooling Down

2-4 year olds relax while the teacher uses visualization or manipulation to work on alignment and release of tension. For variation, simple mirroring movements could be done or a verbal review of the lesson's concept could take place.

5-7 year olds can relax as above or discuss any choreography that was shared.

8-12 year olds can relax as above, discuss choreography or do simple stretching and lengthening exercises.

Teens through adults can work in pairs doing alignment exercises, discuss choreography, write critiques or engage in stretching exercises.

HELPFUL HINTS

Partners

Many of the most important benefits from creative dance come from partner and small group work. Therefore, teachers are always asking me for ways to encourage children to work cooperatively with each other.

The best advice I can give you is to focus on the dance activity instead of on the act of finding a partner. First, always describe the dance exploration briefly, using a student to help you demonstrate. This will solve many problems because the students will understand that 1) each person will be a leader or 2) they will be changing partners frequently or 3) they will be connecting different body parts, not holding hands or 4) the activity looks like a lot of fun or 5) all of the above. In other words, finding a partner is secondary to engaging in an exciting activity.

After demonstrating the activity, challenge your students to find a partner before you count to a certain number. Ask students who don't have a partner to come to the "lost and found" in the center of the room. There they can find a friend or you can put them together with another group. Some partnering challenges might be:

"I will give you 5 counts to connect your elbow to a friend's elbow."
"You have 6 counts to stand back to back with another dancer."
"By the count of 4 form a high/low statue with someone of the opposite sex."
"You have 8 counts to form a triangle with two other friends (a trio)."
"Connect thumbs with a partner by the time I count to 5. Now, connect toes with another pair so that you form a quartet by the time I count to 6."

Again, the fun is in the different ways you can connect with a partner quickly, instead of agonizing over with whom to dance.

Turn the music on and begin the activity, reviewing the directions as your students start dancing. People slow to find partners will soon realize that you will not wait for them. The fun is beginning and they will want to join in.

I will often begin practicing partnering skills by asking the dancers to find a partner in the middle of a dance exploration. For example: the dancers have been moving in different pathways through general space. When the music pauses they have been asked to make a special shape. Toward the end of the music you ask them to make a curved shape with a friend during the pause, before the music begins again. They have a sense of the music, they know that the pause is short, you help out by quickly connecting slower dancers together. Then you may or may not ask them to dance together when the music resumes. This is a good way to work in partners briefly without a lot of fuss.

Learning to work with others is a skill that is learned through practice. One of the greatest gifts you can give your students is the chance to practice that skill until they are very adept at working with others in a variety of situations.

Formations

The use of different formations can be very helpful in managing your class. Try to use circles, lines and scattered formations in your classes. Moving through different formations gives variety to your lesson.

A circle is one of the hardest formations to make. Try taping a circle on the floor or use an existing circle on a gymnasium floor to help guide your students. Some other ideas follow.

> Mark an X in the center of the floor. Ask students to put their toes on the X while sitting on the floor and sit very close together like a big pizza. Then blow into the middle of the circle and each person scoots backward with each blow until the circle is the right size.

> Have students stand with their hands on their hips so that their elbows stick out, then ask them to come together so that they touch each elbow to someone else's elbow forming a circle.

> Ask students to stand with legs apart and connect toes together to form a circle.

> If students need to hold hands in a circle, introduce the "magic ring." The circle is magic and will not be broken because everyone cooperates, sharing the space and weight so that no one individual pulls or pushes too much. Strongly reinforce the magic and compliment all who keep the ring unbroken.

Lines are useful when practicing locomotor skills, although a scattered formation may also be used.

> Choose 4-6 leaders and ask the remaining students to arrange themselves equally behind the leaders. You will need to help young students initially. The 6 leaders constitute the first line, the second line is the dancers directly behind each leader, etc. For fun, lines could be given names instead of numbers.

42

If you use squads in your classes, every month or so choose new squads and squad leaders. Dancers can line up in squads shoulder to shoulder instead of back to stomach and move across the room by squads.

Ask your students to make a shape near to a friend. Now direct them to move far from that friend, half forming a line against one wall and half against the other wall. You now have two lines facing each other. The dancers can move toward and away from each other or the head couple can move together between the two lines to the end of the line and the other dancers follow a pair at a time.

Direct the dancers to divide in half and move to opposite corners. The dancers can move on diagonal lines past each other, along the opposite wall and to the other corner to begin again. Dancers may also be divided into four corners or all come from one corner. Diagonal lines are better for older or more experienced dancers because of the potential for collisions in the middle.

Scattered formations can be used to save time. They are good for young children (and older ones). They are useful for exploring concepts and movements.

Ask the dancers to find a "perfect spot." That means a place with lots of empty space around it. No one or thing should be near them. They are like an island or inside a bubble. Once you have explained and practiced this concept, dancers will find "perfect spots" quickly and efficiently.

You may want to use a prop, such as a circle made of carpet padding, to create a visual spot for each dancer. Challenge the dancers to find a perfect spot by a certain count.

"Blow" the dancers into a perfect spot.

Ask them to make a shape they have never made before in a perfect spot.

Exercises can be done in a scattered formation. Try to rotate your position during the exercises so that you stand in front of different students. In other words, the same students do not remain "in front" for the whole class. If you are unable to rotate your position because of handling the music, request that the students rotate their positions.

Changing Activities

If you teach your young students to freeze when the music ends, you can always give a brief direction while they are frozen that will direct them to the next activity, before you lose control. You might say: "That was terrific! Now come and sit on the white line (or back to your seats)." "Super dancing! Please form a circle in the center of the room." "Excellent partner work! Come to the box and choose a scarf." "I loved your shapes! Now connect knees with a partner by the count of 5."

Your students will know that more fun is ahead. They will move to the next activity ready to listen to new directions. However, if you turn off the music and take time to set up the prop or change music or read your notes before directing the next activity, your students may start to chatter and dance around undirected. You may find it more difficult to gain their attention at this point than at the point of freezing.

Boys Dancing

Creative dance is an excellent way to engage boys in dancing. With the focus on the exploration of contrasting elements of dance, boys are able to experience many types of movements -- strong and light, sharp and smooth, fast and slow, etc. This makes dance athletic and exciting. In fact, it has been my experience that boys often like creative dance more than girls! Girls sometimes have a preconception of dance as soft, light, and balletic. They do not immediately understand that dance can be strong, powerful, and asymmetrical. When I teach in schools, it is often the boys who find great delight in exploring new movements in a noncompetitive arena and in creating their own dances. It is preconceptions on the part of many adults that foster the idea that boys don't like or cannot dance. Try creative dance in your class and you will see a very different picture.

Imagery

Imagery, imitation, and themes can actually be detrimental in teaching creative dance. This is not to say that you should never use imagery, but you must be very careful HOW you use imagery. An exploration and a grasp of the elements of movement must come before imagery is introduced.

The elements of dance are the meat, the "stuff" of dancing. Pretending to be something (imitation) does not allow your students the opportunity to fully explore or understand all the wonderful ways the body can move! If you ask your students to "jump like a kangaroo" they will only think of one way to jump. If you ask them to "jump in different directions, on different levels, with changes in size, speed, energy and weight, with and without a partner" they will think of many, many ways of jumping!

If you want to use imagery to stimulate movement ideas, be sure you use a variety of images coupled with the elements of dance if possible: "burst like a little bubble," "burst like a big balloon," "burst like a firecracker," "burst like a ripe tomato." The emphasis here is on exploring different ways to "burst." You are not asking the students to imitate a balloon or tomato.

Ironically, teachers often think that young children need imagery the most. They ask them to do story dances about holidays and to pretend to move like animals or objects. Young children have the least experience with the world and the strongest sense that an animal or object moves in a very particular way. Imagery for young children can be especially limiting and prevents them from fully exploring the many ways one can do a particular movement. As your students become more experienced with the world and the elements of dance, they may find imagery less inhibiting.

Even with experienced dancers, the dance vocabulary should come first -- the imagery second. When discussing choreography, you might say, "What does that remind you of?" "How does that movement make you feel?" "What image or picture does that make you think of?" And "WHY?" In other words, what dance elements were used that brought forth a particular image? Then the students will learn to use the elements to create specific images.

A thorough understanding mentally and physically of the dance elements empowers the dancers. They will be far more articulate and expressive coming from an element based curriculum than from an image based curriculum.

Many schools today are using a theme approach to teaching. If your theme is dinosaurs you might want to ask your students to do a dinosaur dance. However, if your students are not familiar with the elements of dance they will simply pretend they are dinosaurs instead of creating an interesting dance. You will end up with a boring product and your students will have learned little.

If you really want to do a dance about dinosaurs you must begin with the dance elements. "On what level do dinosaurs move?" (It depends on the dinosaur. Already you will have many levels in your dance.) "What speed do dinosaurs move?" "What kind of energy and weight do dinosaurs use?" "What shapes are dinosaurs?" "What pathways do dinosaurs move in?" "What are some relationships between dinosaurs?" By focusing on the elements of dance, your students not only learn a great deal about dinosaurs, their dinosaur dance will be much more expressive and creative, also.

Your students will take great joy in discovering the many exciting ways they can move when you introduce them to the elements of dance. They will craft wonderful dances using these elements. Imagery should be used carefully to support their ideas, not to stifle them.

Demonstration

One of the best ways to get your ideas across to your students is through demonstration. Always use a demonstration to explain the activity you are introducing. Involve one or more students in your

demonstration. It is much easier to understand a movement activity by seeing it than by hearing about it. Also, use a demonstration to show your students how they can do a certain skill in a better way.

For example, demonstrate leaping with your focus down and your arms flopping around; then demonstrate leaping with your focus out and your arms controlled. Ask your students which way looked better and why. By demonstrating two ways skills can be done -- one way and then a better way -- your students have a clear picture of what to work toward. The dancers learn faster and remember more than if you just made verbal suggestions, because they are involved in figuring out why one way looks better and how to achieve that quality of movement.

Discussion of Feelings

It is important to help your students make connections between movement and feelings. This will help your students make better movement choices in their compositions, understand better the different meanings of movements, and express themselves with more feeling in their dancing. Remember, dance is an expressive and transforming art, not just a series of technical movements.

Take time throughout your lesson to ask your students how this or that movement makes them feel; how moving to certain music makes them feel; how contrasting movements create different feelings; how people feel differently doing the same movement; how people react differently watching the same set of movements and so on. There really is no time during the dance class that you cannot ask them to share and discuss their feelings. Think about your lesson objectives and use your discussion questions to help you achieve those objectives. Remember to be accepting of all the students' answers about how they feel and share your own feelings, too.

Say What You Want To See

To encourage correct behavior, creative exploration and use of the dance elements, say what you want to see: "I see dancers skipping and doing fancy arm movements. I see people moving in different directions. I see high and low level movement. I see children moving in empty spaces, being aware of the others around them. I see dancers sharing the space. I see many different strong and light movements. I see turning, galloping, floating and gliding movements."

46

Although you may not actually be seeing those movements, as soon as you mention them they miraculously appear! The dancers are very busy moving through space, often unaware of what is going on around them. All a dancer is aware of is that he/she may or may not be doing the movements you mentioned. The dancers appreciate the positive reminders of ways to move, elements to explore and behavior to adopt. Remember, it is often your job to teach them how to behave in a dance class as well as how to dance. Stressing the desired positive behavior is very effective.

This is the single most important technique I have discovered to increase acceptable behavior and creative exploration.

Be Personal

Learn your students' names as quickly as possible or use name tags. If you are an arts or physical education specialist in a school teaching 600 children this seems like a monumental task! But I highly recommend you give it a try. Studio teachers and classroom teachers should have no difficulty. When you have learned your students' names, use them! Try to use each child's name at least once during the class. Make sure you are not always repeating the same names over and over.

> "I like the way John is sitting quietly, waiting for directions. Thank you, John. Thank you, Paco. Thank you, Rachel. Thank you, Kyung. Thank you all!"

> "Teri is really using her stomach muscles instead of her shoulders to move. So is Shaun and Lissa and Brian and now everybody is trying!"

> "Toby is really watching where he is dancing. He is moving through space carefully but freely. So are Melissa and Fatahya and LeToya and Jesse. Thank you everybody for dancing in the empty spaces!"

> "Interesting arm shapes, Sheryl. Tom, good leg extension. Susan, excellent alignment."

Be Positive

Always stress the positive and try to ignore the negative. Calling attention to negative behavior increases that behavior. Calling attention to positive behavior will increase appropriate behavior. Be personal whenever possible. Try to make a positive statement every minute.

This may seem like a lot, but you will notice a great difference in the atmosphere of your class when you start mentioning all the positives and stop dwelling on the negatives. Even if only one person is doing something right -- mention it. Soon another will follow (mention it) and another (thank them) and another, etc., etc. Make sure you personally compliment the negative attention getter when they engage in appropriate behavior. Let go of your anger.

> "I am so proud of the way you are following directions."

> "Your shapes are terrific!"   "Super listening today!"

> "Group number one is doing a wonderful job of cooperating."

"Susan and Marcus, Jim and Tanya, Heather and Motoko did an excellent job of finding a partner quickly and quietly."

Always end class on a positive note. With young children this may mean stamping hands or feet with a special stamp for being such good dancers and listeners. Compliment older students for their attention, creativity, cooperation, hard work, etc. Ending class on a positive note will make everyone eager to return to dance class -- even you!

Keep Directions Simple

Your dance students are in your class to MOVE, not to listen to a lecture. Keep your directions very simple. If you have to say too much, reevaluate the activity. How can you make it simpler, or do it in two parts? As much as possible, give the directions as the students are moving or repeat them as they move through the activity. The quickest way to lose students, young and old, is to talk a dance exploration to death.

Ask a student to help you demonstrate the idea -- a picture speaks a thousand words. Then start the music and talk the students through the activity or skill. If there is mass confusion, stop and quickly reevaluate. Either explain the activity in a different way, simplify the activity or drop it and go on. Do not be angry at yourself or the students. Figure the problem out later. Be positive.

If you are using props or rhythm instruments, plan ahead how you will distribute and collect them with minimal effort or confusion. Practice your directions before class. Are they clear, simple and to the point?

Use Music

Music can motivate your students and help maintain control. Use a variety of music styles. Read the section on accompaniment for ideas. Mark your records or tapes clearly. Have them set out in an order so that you are not fumbling with the sound system with your back turned to the students. Five minute cassettes are very helpful because you do not have to search for music or rewind tapes.

Music that has pauses and/or clear changes of tempo, volume or style is very helpful. During the pause you can have students freeze and give a quick direction if necessary. Pauses stop the flow and allow you to change movement.

Music containing changes motivates the students to concentrate on the music and kind of movement they are doing. When the music changes, you can direct a change in movement or use of another dance element such as changing from general space to self space. Music with changes allows the students to explore the contrasting elements of dance without spending too long on one element (such as fast or strong) which might lead to exhaustion or disruptive behavior.

Use Props

Props can be helpful with young children ages 2-5 as an attention getting mechanism. With older students they add variety and spice. Over-use of props, however, may lead to a dependence on them, boredom, or not using the body fully. Find the happy medium. Each element chapter gives ideas for using props to help explore different concepts. If your students are playing with props instead of dancing with them or wearing them instead of exploring concepts with them, put them away for awhile.

Stretchy rubberbands (circles made of lycra or jersey) are one of my favorite props. The students are very creative when using this prop. They are focused and concentrated in their dancing. Foam

spots help young students find their self space, cones can be used to delineate pathways and to divide the room in half, benches can be used as balance beams, bridges or tunnels. Other props, such as streamers, plastic, scarves and balloons can be used to explore the elements of dance. Please review the section on props for more ideas and where to procure these items.

Use the Dance Elements

Make charts for your room containing the elements of dance (see page 5). The dance vocabulary should always be on view for you and your students. Besides the charts, I have a "Word Corner" in my dance room where I display the week's concept.

When I introduce the concept (such as Level -- high and low), I have the students say the words, sometimes spell them with their bodies or write them in space, and describe the words through movement. It is not enough for the teacher to say the dance words. If you want your students to internalize the words, they must say and do the vocabulary -- even 2 year olds and adults.

Using the dance elements throughout your lesson provides the structure needed to motivate your students to learn and cooperate. Inexperienced dancers often feel inhibited or embarrassed and so will act out in class. They are unfamiliar with the dance vocabulary and do not have the knowledge to dance. You need to impart this knowledge to them in a structured way that makes them feel secure to try new ideas.

If your students are acting out, add more structure by calling out many different ways of moving using the dance vocabulary from your dance elements charts: "Try moving at a low level ... high level ... slowly ... quickly. Are you moving many different body parts ... try dancing with just your head ... your arms ... your legs ... your shoulders ... your feet. Move in different directions ... forward ... backward ... sideways. Can you gallop ... float ... roll ... slash?" Pause for about 10-15 seconds between each suggestion to allow your students to explore the elements you mention.

When teaching inexperienced dancers you will find yourself talking a great deal during the class. You will be suggesting ways of moving, giving positive reinforcement and saying what you want to see. As the students become more familiar with the material and more comfortable dancing, you will be talking less and less.

The ideas in the lesson chapters are fairly structured and of course relate directly to the dance elements. Using these ideas in your lesson planning should help greatly.

Use the Lesson Plan Format

The lesson plan format is carefully devised to provide experiences in all the learning processes and a balance between creative exploration and skill development. Try to follow it as closely as possible. As you become familiar with the structure, then feel free to experiment.

Planning a lesson is like choreographing a dance. You need a beginning (Warming Up and Introducing the Concept), a middle (Exploring the Concept and Skill Development), and an end (Creating and Cooling Down).

You need to think about SPACE. Use a variety of spatial formations to maintain control: start in a circle, move to a scattered formation, move in lines, end in a scattered formation. This is but one example.

Think about TIME. Alternate fast activities with slower activities. After moving quickly your students will not mind sitting and listening for a minute or taking turns. After taking turns or moving in lines, the dancers are ready for group movement again.

Think about FORCE. Alternate high energy movements with lower energy movements. For Exploring the Concept you can choose an activity that allows the whole class to move with full body movement through general space. This might be followed by a Shaping activity that is done in self space and requires less energy. This could be followed by practicing a locomotor skill such as leaping, moving in lines across the floor. Then the dancers could rest a minute as you explain the final Free Dance or Choreography problem.

Think about RELATIONSHIPS. The wonderful thing about creative dance is all the opportunities it provides for working together, touching appropriately, sharing and cooperating. Make sure you have at least one activity where the dancers are relating to one another. Explore the lesson's concept in partners, trios, quartets or small groups at least once during each class.

Think about FLOW. Try to keep the class flowing from one part to another. Don't get bogged down in your directions, putting on your music or attending to disruptive behavior. Keep the flow going! Planning these elements carefully will prevent you from either boring your students or exhausting them.

Evaluate the Situation

When you are successful, ask yourself why. What works? When you are not successful, ask yourself why. What's wrong? Here is a checklist that might help.

Music: appropriate to the age and activity? a variety of styles?

Lesson Plan: are you using one? do you know it well?   are the activities appropriate to your students' age, level and experience? are you providing a variety of experiences both directed and free?

Directions: are they simple? clear? have you practiced them?

Environment: are the dance element charts on your walls?   is the floor clean? is the space the right temperature, the right size?

Attitude: are you positive? confident? having fun?   smiling?   using your students' names? do you believe in the value of dance education and expect your students to take part, learn and have fun?

Be Confident

Students can sense hesitancy, nervousness and fear very quickly. Some like to take advantage of such a situation. Breathe deeply, believe strongly in what you are doing, smile, start slowly, know your lesson plan. Remember all the tips in this chapter and you will be successful!

Behavior Problems

Most behavior problems can be prevented by good teaching and a positive attitude. A well-planned lesson with a variety of music and appropriate activities will keep your students involved and feeling successful.

Your attitude about dance class is very important. Studio teachers need to remember to emphasize self-expression and creativity as well as skill development. Classroom teachers need to feel that dance is an important part of the curriculum. All your students should be expected to take part, just as they do for math or physical education. Creative dance should be called dance, not movement. Calling dance by another name does not make dance more acceptable. Everyone loves creative dance, when it is well taught. Why do we think our students won't like it? Because we feel uncomfortable? If you had creative dance as a child, you might not feel this way today!

Sometimes, no matter how well planned your lessons are, you will encounter special problems. I have touched upon some of the more common behavior problems below.

The Shy or Inhibited Student: Some young children may feel timid about dancing around with so many other children. They may be used to small spaces, more restricted movements or being alone. It is particularly important for these children to experience gross motor movements and feel comfortable moving through space with others. Give them time. Hold their hands, from time to time, and gently encourage them to participate. Do not nag or give them undue attention. Keep the class going, smile, enjoy yourself. Eventually, they will join in. Once I had a student who stood in my class, not moving, for ten weeks. The following ten weeks this student only participated in the leaps. The third quarter this student participated fully and is now one of my best students! This is an extreme case. Usually a shy student will participate after a few classes. Some older students may feel inhibited at first. If you feel inhibited, they may take their cue from you. I love dance and expect everyone to join in and have a wonderful time. I always choose my favorite activities when teaching inexperienced students their first class. I make it especially fun and nonthreatening. Within minutes, everyone else is having as much fun as I am. It would never occur to me that my students would not love dancing. Attitude is key!

The Manipulative Child: Some children, even by the age of three, have become very good at manipulating adults. These children seek attention through negative or manipulative behavior. They may talk constantly or keep interrupting the lesson with questions. They may lie down in the middle of the floor, complaining of being tired. They may try to distract other children. They may ask for a drink or to use the bathroom several times during class. Their behavior is not awful but they are like a little thorn in your side. It is easy to give them attention without meaning to. Ignore their behavior! State your rules clearly at the beginning of class: drinks and bathroom before class, everyone participates, save talking for question and answer period, etc. Give lots of positive reinforcement to those following the rules, making sure you reinforce the manipulative child when he/she follows the rules. Pretend the child is invisible (even if they are talking) when they do not behave. If this means you have to dance around them, do so. In time, the manipulative child will see that he/she cannot manipulate you.

The Severe Negative Attention Getter: This child is similar to the manipulative child, except that the negative behavior is more severe. This child might knock other children down, throw temper tantrums, refuse to follow rules, etc. If you teach in a private studio, you have the right to ask that this child not return to class. You have the safety of your other students to consider. If you teach in a school

52

setting you may not have this option. Set clear limits for this student. Let this student know that you will not allow dangerous, disruptive behavior. Time out is one option. Behavior modification is another option. Everyone who listens and dances appropriately might receive stamps or stickers. It takes a lot of time and energy to change these children's behavior, but I have done it a number of times using positive reinforcement and creative dance. For me, it has been well worth the effort.

The Hyperactive Child: The hyperactive child never seems to slow down. He/she is always on the go -- running, falling, sliding, bumping. Creative dance is an excellent way to help these children. Through an exploration of the elements of dance, hyperactive children experience opposite qualities of movement. For the first time their muscles may move slowly instead of quickly, lightly instead of strongly, smoothly instead of sharply. Activities such as slow motion mirroring, sculptor and clay, and shadowing are particularly good for hyperactive children. The more they experience and practice slow, controlled movements the better they will be at using these movements.

The Bibliography (Appendix H) contains a selection of some useful books on changing children's behavior.

PERFORMANCES

I feel strongly that formal recitals are not appropriate at any age level. In many schools a major portion of the child's dance class is devoted to preparation for a recital. In this setting, children learn A dance but do not learn HOW to dance. Class time should be spent learning and exploring the elements of dance, not just learning a few steps for a recital piece. I spent my youth learning "cute," often inappropriate routines. It was not until I took modern dance in high school that I really began to understand and utilize the principles of dance. I was finally able to express my own feelings through movement, rather than just mimic my teacher's steps.

However, there is little sense in developing skills and learning to express yourself if you never have the opportunity to share these skills with others. A few alternatives to recitals are described below.

Informal Showings or the Informance

An informal showing is an excellent way to share your students' knowledge and skills with parents, friends and the community. Creative dance has a dual focus -- developing skills and learning to use these skills to express yourself creatively. Without spending a lot of class time, you and your students can create a simple combination of movements that displays skill development and creativity. The combinations, structured improvisations and choreography done in class can easily be translated to an informal performance setting. Choose a favorite exploration and share it with the audience. One of the best parts of informal showings is that all the students have the opportunity to see each other and to learn from each other. They are not stuck behind stage waiting for their turn to dance.

The word "informance" has a dual meaning. It is an informal performance AND you are sharing information. The best way to share information is to briefly explain to the audience the concepts your students have explored and are using in their dancing. Explain the benefits of creative dance and the learning process behind the product. You have an opportunity to educate not only your students but the community as well. In the long run this will benefit your program.

Have the students wear their dance clothes or a special dance outfit, if they desire. Fancy costumes are unnecessary, it is their dancing you are showing off, not their clothes! If the students ask for costumes, a simple costume can be created by wearing similar or contrasting colors, school T-shirts or by adding an accessory such as matching belts, sashes, scarves, etc.

Explorations for Informances

The following structures work well for informal showings. Full descriptions can be found in the Methods Section.
Shape Museum
Poetry: Cinquain, Haiku, Rhymes
Back to Back
Mirroring
Shadowing
Shape Story
ABA Structure
Finger/Body/Finger
Creative Folk Dances
Props
Chance Dance
Line designs or art motivated dances
Alternate half the body dancing, half freezing
Alternate whole body dancing with isolated body parts dancing
Alternate locomotor/nonlocomotor skills with improvisation
Alternate movement combination with improvisation
Simple pair or group compositions joined together by movement transitions, performance
   in different stage areas or entering and exiting the center space.

Choreography Concert

Students working on their own choreography may want to show their pieces in a more formal setting. Dance clubs that meet before, after or during school give more time for interested students to work on choreography and to polish their pieces. In private studios, a special rehearsal time might be provided for students who have a particular interest in performing. The teacher in both settings serves as a facilitator, helping students to strengthen composition skills and use the elements of dance to create well-rounded works. Students can help create simple costumes and design lighting, if available. Involve students in as much production work as possible, from designing programs to pulling curtains. Their self-esteem will grow tremendously. Remember, time should not be taken away from regular dance class for program rehearsal. Without the knowledge learned in class, your student's choreography will not be worth performing.

Performance Skills

Performance skills are acquired through classwork and experience. During class, when your students are sharing their choreography or improvisation, remind them to use appropriate focus; encourage them to express their ideas not only through movement, but also through appropriate facial expressions; remind them to hold their ending shapes until the music stops and applause begins;

remind them to relate to each other on stage; encourage the use of their technical skills, reminding them to perform with clear, clean movements and full extensions. If your students are performing in a stage setting, remind them about being quiet and calm backstage; warming-up before performing; visualizing their next piece so that they are focused when they enter the stage.

I tell my students before performances to concentrate on three things: the HEAD -- remember to THINK about the dances, remember the spacing and the movements; the STOMACH -- remember to pull in the GUT and keep centered so that the technical skill will show; the HEART -- remember to EXPRESS the ideas in the dances, to enjoy the movements, to share the joy of dancing with others! When the head, stomach and heart are used equally, in an integrated fashion, the magic of dance is truly apparent.

Audience Skills

Audience skills are also taught during class as your students watch and discuss their peers' dance studies. Encourage your students to be polite, quiet and attentive. They should watch the dances carefully so that they can discuss them intelligently. No student is too young or too old to talk about the interesting use of the dance elements in a particular study. Your students need to hone observation skills as well as movement skills. You and your students should applaud when a study is completed. Practicing audience skills in class will ensure appropriate behavior outside of class.

CHILDREN'S PERFORMING COMPANY: A MODEL

In 1981 I founded Kaleidoscope, a modern dance company of young people between the ages of eight and fifteen. So many people have asked me about the company, I would like to share the model I use in hopes that more companies like Kaleidoscope will be formed. The dancers take class at my studio, the Creative Dance Center, one day a week. We have three levels of modern dance - ages 7 1/2 to 9, 10-12 and 12-15. The company dancers take class with noncompany dancers in their age group. The class consists of one hour of modern technique followed by forty-five minutes of choreography. On Fridays all the Kaleidoscope dancers, between 20 and 35 children, meet together for a two hour rehearsal. The children do not audition for the company but are invited to join. A positive, cooperative and hard working attitude can take preference over technical skill.

During the Fall Quarter, the dancers choreograph their own pieces which may be solos, duets, trios or group dances. These pieces are performed for the community in December. We also rehearse the school concert that we take on tour to schools in Washington State. Winter and Spring Quarter rehearsals are spent learning new dances from adult choreographers in the Pacific Northwest to be

presented at our May concert. The company is divided into two or three groups at a time so that two to three choreographers can be teaching dances simultaneously. Each dancer learns three to four new dances for the May concert. During the school year, we travel to about ten different schools and perform our 45 minute school concert. We also perform at community events and arts fairs during the year. Every two to three years we travel during the summer. We have been to Wolf Trap, Japan, Canada and the Dance and Child International Conference in Utah. We hope to go to Hungary, China and Russia in the future.

Our goal is to provide an opportunity for children to choreograph their own dances for performance and to also work with professional choreographers. We are not a preparatory program for professional dancers. We wish only to provide a quality educational experience. Our mission is to inform the public about modern dance and to make modern dance accessible to and enjoyable for people of all ages.

READ, EXPLORE, RE-READ

The material in this book is meant to open your mind, not to close it. If you do not understand some of the activities, let those be a springboard for you to create your own ways of exploring the concepts. As you read about one concept, you may decide that a certain activity would be great for exploring a different concept. You may try an activity under "Shaping" that you think would be a wonderful way to "Develop Skills" or use as a "Choreography" problem. Mix and match activities with lesson plan areas and different concepts. Be creative! Have fun!

If you are feeling overwhelmed, go back and read the chapter on "Why Learn Creative Dance." People learn so much through movement. It is so important that we feel comfortable with our body. How we relate to others and how we react to situations is reflected in how we feel about ourselves. You have the ability to change people's lives through positive movement experiences.

Remember that only by teaching creative dance will you become a better creative dance teacher. You need to practice and become familiar with the material just as your students do. It takes time to become familiar with all the material in this book. Be patient. Move slowly. With each lesson you plan, whether it is successful or not, you will learn more and more about creative dance.

Re-read the theory section from time to time. You will be reminded of important concepts, management ideas and lesson planning hints that will help you plan and teach successful lessons. Be positive and encouraging with yourself and your students. Creative dance can bring so much joy and fun into your life!

PART TWO

METHOD

CHAPTER 7

Warming Up

QUICK WARM-UPS

The following ideas are excellent ways to warm up at the beginning of a 30-minute dance class, if you do not have time to present a longer exercise period. The activities can also be used at the beginning of a 60 or 90 minute dance class to introduce the lesson's concept and warm up the muscles before exercising. A third option is to present one of these activities at the start of the day to energize your students and prepare them for active learning; do one before a test to wake up the brain; do one before or after a stressful situation to relax yourself and your students. Do one any time for exercise, fun and learning.

BACK TO BACK

"When I say 'Back to Back' stand back to back with the person nearest you. Now turn around and touch elbows together, now touch toes together, now touch knees together. When the music starts, dance away from each other emphasizing knee movements .... Back to back! If you don't have a partner, go to the center of the room and find one. Now, touch toes together, touch shoulders together, touch arms together ... dance away emphasizing arm movements. Back to back!" Continue in this way, alternating partner connections with free movement in general space.

This is a great warm-up activity and ice breaker because you do not have to choose a partner face to face. You quickly stand back to back with someone -- the emphasis is on backs not partners. Students should be back to back with different people each time. Instead of a body part focus, choose another dance element -- perhaps level. "Make a low shape together, make a medium level shape, make a high shape together ... now dance away at a high level." Any dance element can be the focus of this quick warm-up.

GROUP MIRROR

"Stand in a perfect spot so that you have empty space around you but you can focus on me. Mirror, or follow, my movements. If I move my arm that is nearest the windows, you move your arm that is nearest the windows. If I move my head toward the clock, you move your head toward the clock. Keep your eyes on me at all times and be my mirror reflection."

This can be an energizing activity or a calming activity depending on the speed and quality of your movement. Use lively music and high energy movements for warming up muscles. Use peaceful music and smooth, slow movements for cooling down muscles. Try to move each body part and joint. Start with your head and move down to your toes or vice versa. Use familiar, but safe, exercise movements or basic locomotor and nonlocomotor movements such as running in place, twisting, stretching, swinging, bending, turning, etc.

If you feel uncomfortable as leader ask a student with a movement background to be leader. You can help them by naming body parts and movements from the dance elements chart. For variation, you can have the students mirror you and then dance freely in general space. Alternate mirroring with free movement several times.

GROUP ECHO

"Find an empty spot where you can focus on me. I will move for 4 counts then you echo, or copy, my movement for 4 counts. We will never be moving at the same time. I move, you echo, I move, you echo. When I freeze, you move. You have to remember what I did and copy my movement."

Four counts seems to work best, but you can vary this warm-up by trying 8 count phrases and even 2 count phrases. Remember to move different body parts so the whole body is warmed up, not just the arms. Try different nonlocomotor and locomotor movements. Ask a student to be the leader if you feel uncomfortable as leader. Use music with a strong beat. (This activity is difficult for students ages 2-5. Try mirroring instead.)

SELF AND GENERAL SPACE

"When the music starts I will call out a locomotor movement. Do that movement through general space. When the music pauses, I will call out a nonlocomotor movement. Do that movement in self space. As you move in general space, keep your eyes open for empty space to move through. When you move in self space, be sure you have plenty of empty space around you. Remember to try the movements with many different body parts. Walk ... stretch ... jog ... swing ... skip ... bend ... gallop ... poke."

A WALK THROUGH THE ELEMENTS

"Start walking around the room. As you are walking, I will call out different dance elements. Just listen to me and respond through movement.

"Walk forwards ... backwards ... sideways. Walk way up high on tip toes ... walk way down low ... walk at a medium level. Move with great big steps, stretching your legs and arms far away from each other ... move with little steps, bringing arms and legs close to each other.

"Move through the room drawing curvy pathways with your arms and legs .. .draw the letter 's,' the letter 'o,' a number '8.' Draw straight pathways using straight movements ... try a straight pathway backwards ... a straight pathway with big steps sideways ... try a zigzag pathway with knees and elbows ... move forward and backward ... left and right ... up and down ... draw big zigzags and little zigzags.

"Walk focusing on your hand ... your foot ... someone's back ... the ceiling ... straight ahead. Move as slowly as you can, you have all the time in the world ... now move quickly, hurry up ... slow down ... move slowly backward in a curvy pathway with little steps ... move quickly in a zigzag pathway with big steps.

"Move to the beat of my clapping ... take a step on every clap so that you are moving to an even rhythm ... try changing directions, level and size. Now create your own rhythm, mixing up slow and fast steps ... sometimes slow, sometimes fast. Move with strong powerful movements ... push through the space ... try light movements as if there was no gravity ... you are an astronaut in space ...weightless... strong movements again in different directions ... light movements, floating effortlessly.

"Move with smooth, continuous movements ... never stopping, always flowing ... now try sharp movements ... movements that move and stop ... move and stop ... sharp! sharp! sharp! ... smoooooooooth ... sharp! Make a curvy shape ... try a straight shape ... a twisted shape ... an angular shape ... a big curvy shape ... a little curvy shape on a high level ... a big, strong twisted shape. Stay

in your self space and move just your head in different ways ... your arms ... legs ... elbows ... knees ... shoulders ... hips ... feet ... your whole body ... now let yourself move through general space, remembering all the different ways you can move!"

Your students will really be warmed up after this activity! They will also have a new awareness of the dance elements -- the many exciting ways they can move. This is a good beginning activity for any age and level because they begin by walking and end dancing! New Age music by Ray Lynch, Dave Grusin or Shadowfax is great background for this exploration.

STRETCH, CURL, TWIST AND SWING

Stretch and curl different body parts and then the whole body. Twist different parts and then the whole body. Swing different parts and then the whole body. These movements should be done gently, smoothly and continuously until the muscles are warm.

FINGER-BODY-FINGER

"Make a shape focusing on your index finger. When the music begins, move just your finger ... now add your hand ... your arm ... your head ... your other arm ... a leg ... your other leg so that you are moving through general space ... add your torso ... spine ... pelvis ... your whole body should be dancing through space ... now take away one leg ... your other leg ... your arm ... your head ... just your hand is dancing ... now just your finger ... now freeze."

James Galway has an excellent song called "Brian Boru's March" that works well for this idea because the music starts softly, increases in volume and then recedes again. However, any lively music could be used with you increasing and decreasing the volume as body parts are added and subtracted.

16 COUNTS

"Find a partner. One of you will move in self space first and the other in general space. I will call out a way to move and count to 16. The self space dancers will move on their own spot for 16 counts and the general space dancers will travel through space and back to their partners in 16 counts. Then you will change roles. Keep switching back and forth from self space to general space after each set of counts. Here we go -- 16 counts high and low movement (count to 16 out loud) ... 16 counts stretching ... 16 counts swinging ... 16 counts fast and slow movement ... 16 counts jumping."

Continue using different movements and concepts from the dance elements charts. If you wish, vary your counts anywhere from 5 to 30.

Encourage the general space dancer to really travel through the space, not hang around their partner. Remind the self space dancer to keep moving through all the counts. Dancers can make a connected shape on the last count. (This is an idea adapted from Mary Joyce.)

AEROBIC SHAPE MUSEUM

"When I call your name, form a shape in an empty space in the room. (Call half the class.) Now move that shape in self space, perhaps by jogging in place, twisting, stretching, bending. When I turn on the music, the museum will open and the rest of you will enter and dance around, under or over the statues. When you copy a statue and its movement right in front of it, the statue will then move through general space doing a new type of movement until she/he copies another statue. Dancers copy statues, statues move in self space until they are copied and then change their movement to travel through general space."

Encourage a variety of nonlocomotor and locomotor movements and use of different body parts to warm up the entire body. Remind the dancers to keep moving continually while they are in self or general space.

SHADOWING

"Find a partner and stand with one person in front and one behind. The leader will move through general space with the shadow, or follower, following behind and copying the leader's movements. When the music stops, move as I direct. When the music resumes, change leaders and continue moving freely through space."

On the pauses you might call out a nonlocomotor movement -- bend, stretch, swing, twist, slash, etc. This will keep their muscles warming up. You could call out a body part and the dancers would move that part any way they wanted to. This would encourage full body participation instead of just legs and arms moving.

With novice dancers you may have to suggest ways of moving on the shadow section if the dancers run out of ideas. Refer to the dance elements chart.

TOGETHER/APART

"Find a partner. (This can also be done in trios or other groupings.) Move slowly around, under and over each other. When I call out 'apart,' move away from each other with lively movements. When I call out 'together,' find your partner (or change partners) and move slowly together again."

Encourage a change of pace when together and apart. This will allow students to "rest" when together and move full out when apart. Remind students to move at all times, however. Novice dancers may need you to call out some directed ways of moving -- run, gallop, slide, skip, etc.

DIRECTED AND FREE

"I will call out a certain type of movement. You may do that movement in self or general space. Then I will say 'free' and you will dance any way you choose. We will alternate directed and free movement. Slide with a fancy arm ... free ... run in a curvy pathway ... free ... jump and shake ... free ... spin and poke ... free." Your directed movement calls can be very simple or quite complicated, depending on the age or experience of your students.

ACTIVITY SONGS

Activity songs from the "Activity Music List" can be used as warm-ups with students ages 2 - 7.

EXPLORATIONS

Certain ideas under "Exploring the Concepts" and "Shaping" lend themselves as warm-up activities. Look through the list of ideas under the particular concept on which your lesson is based. Choose an idea that is familiar or needs few directions and provides a fair amount of continuous movement.

EXERCISES

Starting Class

Exercises can be done in a circle; a scattered formation in the studio, gym or classroom; or, if necessary, seated at a school desk. A circle is good for small to medium sized classes that have access to an open space. A scattered formation is better for large classes or spaces filled with desks or tables. Below are a few ways to begin dance class.

FIND YOUR SPACE: (For scattered formations.) "By the time I count to 5, I want you to be frozen in a special shape in a perfect spot. Remember, a perfect spot is one that has a lot of empty space around it."

BLOWING A CIRCLE: (For circle formations sitting down.) "Come close together with your feet pointing into the center of the circle like pieces of pizza. Let's do four blows into the center of the circle as if we were blowing up a balloon. With each blow we will push ourselves backward with our hands, until our circle is like a perfectly round balloon. Be aware of the dancers next to you. Do not move out more or less than they do. Everyone should have empty space between them when our balloon is blown up. 1 (blow), 2 (blow), 3 (blow), 4 (blow). Now POP! and scoot quickly back into the circle. Let's try 3 blows (or 5 or how many you need to create the right sized circle for your class and space)." Blow and pop several times. This is a fun warm-up and space awareness game.

PEANUT BUTTER AND JELLY FEET: (For starting exercises sitting down with the soles of the feet together.) "Put a big scoop of peanut butter on one foot, now put a big scoop of jelly on the other foot. Sprinkle some raisins in between and stick your feet together and make a foot sandwich!" Try "slicing" bananas, "squishing" marshmallows, or "chopping" peanuts between feet for variety. Make peanut butter and jelly knee sandwiches before doing sitting exercises with the legs straight in front.

RHYMING EXERCISES FOR AGES 2-7

The following exercises are done to rhymes which provide rhythm, fun and structure. You can create your own rhyming exercises using familiar rhymes like "One, Two, Buckle My Shoe" or rhymes you and your students create. Several sitting exercises are followed by some standing exercises.

Sitting Exercises

BOUNCE RHYME

This exercise can be done sitting with the soles of the feet together (Peanut Butter and Jelly Feet) or the legs straight in front. "Bounce, bounce, bounce like a ball (bounce gently and look at your tummy while you bounce), stretch your arms and back and neck very tall, put your hands in your lap, look back toward the wall (actually look at the ceiling), reach for your toes and curl up small, balance on your seat and fall!" While balancing on their seats, dancers can relate to the lesson's concept, e.g., balance in forward, backward and sideways shapes; balance in big and little shapes; balance in curvy and zig zag shapes; balance and move smoothly and sharply, etc.

Note: Dancers should bounce very gently and slowly and should look more toward the ceiling than the wall. Do not pinch neck muscles but rather open chest area. If you do not want the students to bounce, simply have them stretch over the legs.

TOES TO THE CEILING

Legs should be straight in front. Feet are flexing and stretching. "Toes to the ceiling, toes to the ground, toes to the ceiling, run your feet around. Knees and toes to the ceiling, knees and toes to the ground, knees and toes to the ceiling, move smoothly all around. Fingers, toes to the ceiling; fingers, toes to the ground; fingers, toes to the ceiling; shake everything around. Head, fingers, toes to the ceiling; head, fingers, toes to the ground; head, fingers, toes to the ceiling; dance everything around!"

Try many different movements or relate the movement to your lesson's concept such as "move smoothly all around, move sharply all around." You can keep it simple and move only feet or add other body parts to make the exercise more complex. Remind the dancers to flex and stretch the whole foot -- do not just bend the toes up and down while the foot stays flexed.

TOUCH MY TOES

Legs are straight in front. "I touch my nose, I touch my toes, I spin around on my seat! I touch my nose, I touch my toes, I say 'hello' with my feet! I touch my nose, I touch my toes, I turn my legs in and out! I touch my nose, I touch my toes, I turn my head all about! I touch my nose, I touch my toes, I stretch my arms way up high! I touch my nose, I touch my toes, I stretch my feet to the sky ... and I wave 'goodbye'!" (Wave with the feet.)

SHAKE YOUR FEET

"Shake your feet up high, shake your feet down low, shake your feet above your head, shake them below, shake them to the left, shake them to the right, shake them all around and shake with all your might!" Try other movements such as poke, stretch, kick, etc. This can be done with other body parts.

I ASKED MY MOTHER

Soles of the feet together or legs crossed. "I asked my mother for fifty cents" : touch nose to knee, alternating knees. "To see the elephant jump the fence": stretch arm over head to right side, left, right, left. "It jumped so high, it touched the sky": stretch one leg at a time toward the ceiling -- right, left, right, left. "And never came back til the 4th of July!": spin around on your seat. Repeat with this verse: "I asked my daddy for five cents more, to see the elephant climb the door. He climbed so low, he stubbed his toe, and that was the end of the elephant show!"

TWINKLE LITTLE STAR

Soles of the feet together or legs crossed. "Twinkle, twinkle little star, how I wonder what you are": stretch arms up -- left, right, left, right, left, right, left, right. "Way up in the world so high": stretch legs up left, right, left, right. "Like a diamond in the sky": form diamond shapes with arms and legs. "Twinkle, twinkle little star": turn around on your seat. "How I wonder what you are!": stretch arms and legs out to form star shape.

ROW YOUR BOAT

This is a modified sit-up for stomach muscles. "Sit in a little boat, with your knees bent and your feet flat on the floor. Put on your life jacket and zip it up so your back is nice and tall." "Row, row, row your boat, gently down the stream": easy curl down and up, knees bent. "Merrily, merrily, merrily, merrily": swimming arms or twisting action in torso. "Life is but a dream": stretch up in a slide shape, legs extended, strengthening arm and shoulder muscles.

For variation say "In my submarine" and make a shape as if you were about to do a push-up. Repeat several times.

THE CAT

"Get on hands and knees, making sure the hands are away from the knees so that you are not sitting on your heels. Be a mad cat and arch your back, pulling your stomach in and make a hissing sound. Now relax your stomach and make a meowing sound." Repeat several times. Make sure your students are looking at their thighs as they contract and hiss so that the back of their neck is long. For a variation have them lift their leg up like a tail when they relax. Try big, mad cats: "Hiss and stretch your hips in the air so that your knees come off the ground and your calf muscles stretch. Now relax and meow." Repeat.

FRUIT SALAD

"Sit with your legs folded or soles together. Somebody give me the name of a favorite fruit (strawberry). We are going to pick some strawberries (gently bounce or round the back over the legs), pick them up, pick them up, pick them up, pick them up (reach high with alternating arms), now put them in your lap and toss them back in your salad bowl (mime motions)."

Continue with different fruits and different actions such as "pick them sideways, pick them out and across, pick them forward and backward," etc. Do stretching actions in many directions and with different body parts. Then stir the salad up by turning around on your seat using your feet. You can also make Halloween stew or vegetable soup.

Exercises Standing

BOUNCE RHYME

Do the bounce rhyme described under "Exercises Sitting" except do it standing in parallel, first, and/or second position. Instead of "balance on your seat" say "balance on your feet."

THE BIG SPIDER

"The big hairy spider went up the water spout": climb your hands up your legs from your toes to the ceiling. "Down came the rain and washed the spider out": rub your hands down your body from your chest to your toes and stretch up two or three times. "Out came the sun and dried up all the rain": Stretch your arms open. "And the big hairy spider went up the spout again": climb your hands back up your body.

PLIÉS or KNEE BENDS

"Bend and straight, bend and straight, bend and straight. Toes take the weight (relevé or tiptoe)." Bend and straighten the knees, keeping the knees over the toes. Remind the dancers to push down and pull up rather than just bending, which does not strengthen the muscles very much. Or perform to "London Bridge." Instead of "my fair ladies" say "my fair dancers" and relevé.

REACH UP HIGH

"I reach up high, I reach down low, I touch the ceiling, I touch my toe, I stretch to the left, I stretch to the right, I spin around fast and curl up tight." Dancers follow the motions as you say the rhyme.

SHAKE MY HANDS

"I shake my hands up high, I shake my hands down low, I shake my hands above my head, I shake them below. I shake them to the left, I shake them to the right, I shake them all around and I shake with all my might!" Try other movements such as: stretch, punch, swing, etc.

MISS MARY MACK

"Miss Mary Mack, Mack, Mack, all dressed in black, black, black": keeping legs straight, hang over and stretch or bounce gently looking at your knees so that your neck is relaxed. "With silver buttons, buttons, buttons up and down her back, back, back": stretch the arm over the head alternating R,L,R,L. "She asked her mother, mother, mother for fifty cents, cents, cents": lift the knees up to the chest alternating R,L,R,L. "To see the elephant, elephant, elephant jump over the fence, fence, fence": swing the body forward and backward four times. "He jumped so high, high, high he touched the sky, sky, sky": jump. "And he never came back, back, back til the Fourth of July, ly, ly!": spin around.

71

SWING YOUR LEG

"Stand up tall, pull your stomach in, relax your chest and hug the circle with your arms. Swing and swing and swing your leg, swing it way up high. Swing and swing and swing your leg, now wave your foot goodbye." (Flex and point the foot while balancing on one leg.) Change legs and try waving the foot behind and to the side.

MOP THE FLOOR

Swing with the whole body forward and backward -- arms brushing the floor. "Mop and mop and mop the floor, mop the floor some more. Now make the number 4." (Balance on one leg with the other foot resting on the standing leg at the knee.) "Now make the number seven." (Extend the leg to the side.) "Make the number three." (Extend both arms and a leg forward.) Repeat on the other side. Try other numbers.

WASHING MACHINE

Twist the whole body gently from side to side. "Twist and twist in the washing machine, twist and twist til you're all clean. Twist and twist in the washing machine, twist and twist, now we're all clean! (Jump up.) Twist and twist in the drying machine, twist and twist til you're dry and clean. Twist and twist in the drying machine, twist and twist now we're dry and clean!"

UP AND DOWN

"Shoulders up and down, up and down, up and down and around and around. Arms up and down, up and down, up and down and around and around. Chin up and down, up and down, up and down and around and around." Body parts move up and down and then slowly circle on "around and around." Continue on with other body parts such as knees, fingers, hips, toes, legs, eyeballs, whole body!

JUMP IN AND OUT

Jump from 2nd to 1st position or from wide to narrow. "Jump in and out, in and out, in and out, now spin about. Jump out and in, out and in, out and in and the other way spin."

JUMP AROUND

"Make a special shape with your arms. Jump and jump and jump around (slowly). Jump and jump around (faster). Jump and jump and jump around (fastest) and make a shape on the ground!"

Try to relate the arm shape, jump and last shape to the lesson's concept: big and little arm shapes and jumps and end in a big shape; high and low arm shapes and jumps and end in a low shape; strong and light arm shapes and jumps and end in a strong shape, etc. Instead of jumping, try hopping.

CHAPTER 8

Dance Technique

When and Where to Teach Dance Technique

Dance technique is primarily taught in a private studio setting. Dance classes in public schools are rarely long enough to include time for serious dance technique. Only trained dance specialists should teach technique and at the present time there are few of those to be found in public education. However, it is appropriate to teach technique in public schools if done by a trained dance teacher and class time allows for technique AND creative exploration.

Nondance specialists can introduce beginning technique through "Rhyming Exercises," "Quick Warm-Ups," and "Developing Skills," all found in this book. Serious technical training should not begin before the age of seven. Students ages one to six should be introduced to dance and alignment exercises through simple rhyming exercises such as those found in Chapter 7.

Teaching Technique Through Concepts

Dance technique can be taught by trained dance specialists to best advantage through a conceptual approach. Studying dance technique through concepts allows the student to gain a deeper understanding of the technique. The student begins to dance from the inside out, rather than simply imitating the teacher's exercises. Learning technique through concepts increases the student's understanding of correct alignment, leads to a greater awareness of why proper technique is important and provides the knowledge to use the body in an integrated fashion. The dancer moves with ease, grace and strength through space. When technique is learned by rote, with little understanding of the movement concepts underlying the technique, dancers use more peripheral movements and appear stiff and mechanical. As with any subject, a greater understanding of the concepts underlying the subject leads to a fuller use of that material.

Let me provide you with an example of teaching technique through concepts. Whatever concept you choose as your lesson focus for a particular class is also the concept you focus on in technique. Each week, although you may repeat exercises, you will be focusing on them in a new way through the different concepts. This will give more clarity and depth to the technique.

I have used the plié as an example of how to teach an exercise through different dance concepts. As you move through the other exercises and skills that constitute your dance technique, use the concepts to explore fully the technique you are teaching. Rather than have your students mechanically move through exercises with their minds on other matters, engage their minds through the conceptual approach and they will train their bodies fully.

PLIÉ
(You do not have to follow this order of concepts.)

Week 1   Concept - Directions: "Plié in parallel position. Knees should be bending directly FORWARD over the toes. Now rotate your feet out in first position. Your feet should not be pointing directly SIDEWAYS, but pointing DIAGONALY toward the front corners of the room. Your knees should be bending directly over the toes, not FORWARD, but in a SIDEWAYS direction. Think about rotating the legs in the hip sockets BACKWARDS. This will help your rotation. When you stretch your legs straight, think about going DOWN and when you plié, think about stretching UP. This will help your back to stay long." Use DIRECTIONAL cues for any arm movements you wish to add.

Week 2   Concept - Level: Add grande plié and relevé if your students are ready. "Perform a demi-plié in first position. Knees are at a MEDIUM LEVEL. As you plié lower, let your heels come off the ground and your knees stretch to a LOW LEVEL. Try to keep your gut lifting HIGH. Now, go back to demi-plié at a MEDIUM LEVEL and then stretch the lower half of your body HIGH into relevé while you imagine your tailbone sinking LOW." You may wish to phrase things differently but the object is to use the words HIGH, MEDIUM and LOW to teach plié and relevé instead of having the students mindlessly bend and straighten their legs in poor alignment.

Week 3   Concept - Size: "When you perform a demi-plié, your legs are at MEDIUM REACH from each other. Now do a grande plié and feel your knees REACH FAR from each other. Return to MEDIUM REACH demi-plié then relevé by bringing your legs to NEAR REACH. You have gone from MEDIUM to WIDE to MEDIUM to NARROW. Let us think of all the positions. First position is near reach (legs close together), second position is far reach (legs apart), third position is near reach, fourth position is far or medium reach and fifth position is near reach." Using these terms helps beginning students to remember the positions -- they alternate near and far reach. Use the concept of size when working with arm movements to create full extension of the arms, instead of arms that are always sagging in medium reach shapes.

Week 4   Concept - Pathways: "When you plié, what pathways do you draw in space? Your back creates long straight pathways, your legs create zigzag pathways, bending and straightening and your arms can create beautiful curved pathways. That is a lot of different pathways happening simultaneously, but if you think of drawing pathways in space your movements will be much clearer."

Week 5   Concept - Focus: "Think about putting two eyes on your knees, two eyes on the front of your hip bones and two eyes on the inside of each heel. When you plié in first position, the eyes on your knees should FOCUS out to the front corners of the room, not forward at the wall facing you. The eyes on your hip sockets are FOCUSING directly forward and the eyes on your heels are FOCUSING directly forward also. When you relevé, feel the eyes on your heels peering forward, do not let them turn in to focus on each other." You may wish to put imaginary eyes on hands, back, etc. to emphasize where you want those body parts to focus. Alignment will increase dramatically if you remind your students to FOCUS correctly with their imaginary eyes.

Week 6   Concept - Speed: "Try doing your pliés very SLOWLY. Think about all the concepts we have explored while doing the pliés. Try to remember directions, level, size, pathways and focus. Concentrate on each element (you will have to help them remember) while you move slowly through the plies. We will gradually INCREASE the SPEED of the pliés. Try to do the pliés QUICKLY as well as you performed them SLOWLY. Keep your correct alignment even though you are dancing FASTER."

Week 7   Concept - Rhythm: "We will do our pliés in 4/4 time, then 3/4 time. (You might also try 2/4, 6/8 and 5/4.) How does the rhythm make you feel different? Do you perform your pliés differently?" The 3/4 rhythm often creates a greater emphasis on the first beat making the initiation of the plié stronger with a lighter follow-through. The 4/4 rhythm produces a more even, sometimes monotonous, series of movements. A change of RHYTHM often helps put life back into a plié!

Week 8   Concept - Weight: "When you perform your pliés, the lower half of your body should feel very STRONG and POWERFUL. The upper half should feel LIGHT and SOFT. Your gut and legs are working very hard, but your torso and arms and neck are barely working at all. They are simply floating above your lower half. If you feel your chest and lungs extending out, bulging or tightening, take a deep breath and let the STRENGTH leave your upper body as you exhale. Your torso should feel hollow and LIGHT, your arms hollow and floating. LIGHT is not the same as 'weak.' Your torso and arms are not limp, they are LIGHT but extending fully, floating without gravity pulling them down. Your legs should be pushing out and pulling in as STRONGLY as possible, not just bending." This concept is extremely important. The ability to use strong gut and legs beneath light torso and arms creates beautiful alignment and grace. If your dancers are using their shoulders and arms instead of their gut and pelvis to move them through space, go back to this concept and explore and practice it thoroughly.

Week 9   Concept - Quality: "Try performing pliés with SHARP movements. How does that feel compared to the SMOOTH way we usually do pliés? When you use sharp movements you are just bending and straightening instead of stretching and strengthening. You are in danger of injuring yourself when using sharp movements. Sharp movements are needed for other exercises like degagé (day-gah-zhay), but they are not appropriate for pliés."

Week 10   Concept - Balance: "To help you BALANCE in grande plié and relevé, think about being suspended in space. You are being equally pulled front and back, side to side and up and down. If one direction pulls too much, you are pulled off balance. As you sink, think about rising. As you rise, think about sinking. Remember your sagittal and horizontal pulls as well as your vertical pulls to help you maintain balance."

Week 11   Concept - Relationships: "Think about all the RELATIONSHIPS your body parts have to other body parts when you plié. Legs reach apart and together and hang long from the hip sockets. Knees bend directly over the feet. The back feels long and hollow. The tailbone reaches to the floor. The 'sits' bones are directly above the heels. The shoulders reach down, the head floats on the spine, the arms reach away from the center of the back in many directions. Each body part has a special relationship to another. Each has its place and when all the relationships are correct the body moves with ease and grace and power."

Exploring the Elements of Dance:

Ideas and Lessons

CHAPTER 9

PLACE
Self and General Space

INTRODUCING THE CONCEPT

"Self Space is the space your own body takes up. It is also called your kinesphere. Think of being inside a giant bubble. When you move around, this bubble travels with you. If you move too close to someone your bubble will pop. That is why dancers are very aware of the space around them. They can move quickly through space without bumping into other people. Being in control of your body can be very exciting. A dancer's tool or instrument is the body. A painter can buy new brushes, a violinist can buy a new violin, a writer can buy a new typewriter but a dancer cannot buy a new body. Learning about moving in space helps learn body control. Within your self space you can grow, shrink, rise, sink, twist, turn, balance and do many more exciting movements. We will explore some of these today. When I ask you to find a PERFECT SPOT I am asking you to find a place where your self space or bubble is in an EMPTY SPACE. You should be away from people and objects and walls. Remember when you move around the room you take your bubble with you."

"General Space is the space we travel through as we move around the room. We usually share the general space with other people which is why we always remember to travel in our bubble to avoid bumping into each other. If you do bump into someone both of you can freeze for 5 counts. That will help you remember to look for the empty space."

EXPLORING THE CONCEPT

1. **SPOTS:** "Find a spot (real spot such as carpet padding or imaginary) and try twisting different body parts on your spot in self space. Twist your neck gently, your arms, try twisting your legs. Now gallop around the spots through general space and back to your spot. Shake on the spot. Shake different body parts and then your whole body. Now slide through general space around the spots and back to your spot." Continue alternating nonlocomotor movements in self space and locomotor movements in general space. This alternation keeps the dancers from becoming too tired. Try alternating high and low energy movements, also: float/run, shake/walk, twist/gallop, slash/crawl, stretch/jump.

2. **PAUSE:** "Every time the music stops, I want you to freeze in a shape. If I say 'self space' dance in one place when the music starts again. If I say 'general space' dance all around the room until the music stops." Call out self and general space and locomotor and nonlocomotor words to encourage new ways of moving.

3. **GLUE:** "Glue two hands and a foot to the floor. Now, can you find ways of moving in that shape in self space. Become unglued, and slide through general space to a new spot and glue your stomach to the floor. Can you roll through general space to a new place in the room?" Continue in this manner using different body parts and other locomotor movements. Instead of gluing body parts to the floor, try gluing to the wall, an object or a person! Keep alternating self space (nonlocomotor) and general space (locomotor) movements.

4. **FIND A FRIEND:** "Dance through general space (or skip, hop, glide, etc.). When the music changes (or I give a signal) find a friend as quickly as possible and connect in a shape. Now dance together, connected or unconnected, in self space until the music changes again. Say good-bye to each other and dance through general space." You can direct the movement or the dancers can dance freely, depending on their experience. The dancers can keep the same partner or find new partners each time. Spots or cones can be used to help define self spaces. The dancers would then find a spot (use half as many spots as dancers) and a friend at the spot.

5. **GESTURES:** "Dance through general space. When the music stops I will call out an everyday action. Do that action in self space. Make the action big, using your whole body or do the action with different body parts. When the music begins again, dance through general space in a new way." Give specific general space movements such as fly, skip, wiggle, gallop if working with inexperienced dancers. Some gesture suggestions: wave hello, brush teeth, comb hair, iron clothes, put on shoes, write your name, eat food, polish the table, mix a cake, bounce a ball, juggle beanbags, etc.

6. **TRAVELING ACTIONS:** "Start shaking in self space. Now shake through general space. Freeze. Swing in self space. Can you swing through general space? Freeze. Float in self space. Float through general space." Continue, asking the dancers to start an action in self space then move it through general space. It is fun to use spots, moving on the spot until the action moves off the spot,

through space around the spots and back to the original spot. This can be done with locomotor or nonlocomotor movement. Jump in place, jump around the room. Poke in place, poke around the room. More advanced classes can try this exploration in pairs, trios, small groups or the whole group which will require cooperation and spatial awareness.

7. **WORD CARDS:** "Choose a card from the card pile (write locomotor words on cards of one color and nonlocomotor words on cards of another color). Find a perfect spot and put the card face up on the floor in front of you. We will read each dancer's card and perform that action in self or general space. Now find a friend with a different colored card and put your two cards in front of you on the floor. This time we will combine the two cards to create a special dance word. If one card says 'run' and the other card says 'float' we will try to do a floating run!" Some of the combinations are difficult, but every one is possible. The dancers will discover many new and exciting ways of moving.

8. **16 COUNTS:** This exploration can be done with a partner, a spot or an object (shoe, desk, etc.). The directions are given in terms of partners. Just substitute desk or spot for partner. When working with partners only half the class is moving through general space at one time so it is a good activity for large classes or small spaces. Very young dancers work best without partners. "Find a partner and decide who will dance in general space and who will dance in self space first. The self space dancer will dance in a perfect spot. The general space dancer dances around the room but must be back to his/her partner by the time I stop counting. If I say, '16 counts jumping,' the self space dancer jumps in different ways on the spot while the general space dancer jumps away from his/her partner and back to the partner by count 16. Try connecting in a shape on count 16. Now roles reverse. The self space person will travel through general space while the general space person dances in self space. Remember, self space dancers, keep moving in self space for all the counts. General space dancers, be brave and use all the space. Don't hang around your partner."

Change the number of counts and the movement frequently. Explore locomotor and nonlocomotor movement. Floating in self space and floating through general space creates different feelings and uses some different muscles, as does hopping in place or hopping from place to place. When doing this without partners, have the dancers alternate self and general space. Call out 16 counts jumping in self space ... 16 counts jumping in general space.

9. **CORNER-MIDDLE-SIDE:** "Dancers, make a shape in the MIDDLE of the room, skip through general space to any SIDE wall, shake in self space when you get there. Skip to a CORNER. Float in the corner. Jump backward to the middle, twist with a friend in the middle. Turn quickly to a side wall, wriggle at the sidelines. Slide to a new corner, swing in the corner. Creep to an opposite corner, stretch in all directions in the corner." Continue in this fashion alternating corner, middle and side directions and locomotor and nonlocomotor movement. Use simple or complex movements depending on the dancers' abilities. Keep the action moving and the commands creative.

10. **FOLLOW THE LEADER:** "Follow my movements in self space when the music is slow. When the music is fast, dance any way you wish through general space. When the music is slow again, follow my movements." Alternate following and free dancing several times. Instead of slow/fast music use soft/loud music or songs with a verse and chorus or just give a signal to change from self to general space.

11. **MIRROR/SHADOW:** "Find a partner. Choose a leader. The leader moves through general space while the partner follows or 'shadows' the leader's movements. When the music changes, face each other and the shadow will now mirror (copy) the leader's movements in self space. When I give the signal, change leaders and do shadowing through general space and mirroring in self space with the new leader." Give the dancers specific movement ideas if they are inexperienced. Instead of changing music, give a clear signal of when to change from shadowing to mirroring.

12. **BACK TO BACK:** "Stand back to back with a partner. Make a shape touching knees (you can turn around and face each other), then elbows, then thumbs. Now, skip away from each other through general space. Come back to back with your partner again. (Or they can find new partners.) Connect hips, now fingers, now shoulders. Dance any way you like through general space away from your partner." Continue until the music ends. This is a wonderful way to get the dancers to know each other and feel a connection as a group. The body part connection can be simple -- three basic body parts -- or more complex such as connecting a high body part of one dancer to a low body part of another dancer or connecting two body parts to partner's two body parts or connect in an opposite shape, etc.

13. **SPACE BETWEEN:** "Find a partner. Try to move around the room keeping the space between your hands always the same, perhaps one foot apart. There is no real leader. (With young dancers you may want to designate leaders.) The leadership can change anytime. Cooperate! Alternate moving in self space and general space. Try having other body parts as the invisible connection point such as noses, shoulders, stomachs, backs!" With more advanced dancers work in trios and small groups.

14. **SEVEN JUMPS:** This exploration uses the music for the folk dance called "Seven Jumps." "Move through general space any way you like for 16 counts. On the 'hum' freeze in a shape. The hums get longer and longer so on the longer hums we will do nonlocomotor movements in self space." On the locomotor section practice different movements or practice the same movement different ways -- gallop low, strong, backward, etc. On the self space "hum" section practice different nonlocomotor movements.

15. **SOLOS:** "Dance in self space any way you like (or you can call out a specific movement). When I call someone's name that person can dance a solo through general space. Then I will say 'self

space' (or name a movement such as shake) and we will all dance together again until I call another name." Continue until all dancers have had a chance to do a solo through general space. If dancers are shy and/or the class is large, call two or three names at one time. Try the opposite - solos in self space and group dancing in general space.

16. **PROPS:** Use props with the activities above. Dancers move with their props (plastic, scarves, streamers, balloons, rubberbands) in self space: hold it, dance on, over, under, beside it, put it on different body parts. Dancers move their props through general space: throw it, kick it, hold it, use different body parts to 'hold' it. Dancers can dance individually or work with a partner. Alternating self and general space makes a nice exploration.

17. **ACTIVITY SONGS:** Check the "Activity Music List" for songs to use with 2-7 year olds that help explore self and general space.

SHAPING

1. **MOVING SHAPES:** "Make a shape. Move that shape to a new place in the room. Shake out the shape and try a new shape. Now move the new shape to a different place in the room." Continue. You can ask the dancers to gallop the shape, turn the shape, etc. or have them figure out their own movement. Encourage them to hold the shape as they move.

2. **BODY HALVES:** "Freeze the lower half of your body in a shape. When the music starts, dance with the upper half of your body in self space. When the music stops, freeze the upper half in a shape and dance with the lower half through general space." Alternate upper and lower halves dancing. More experienced dancers can also alternate right and left halves.

3. **GEOMETRIC SHAPES:** "Make a triangle shape with your body in self space. Can you move that shape through general space while tracing a triangle on the floor? (Young dancers can relax the shape before tracing the shape through space.) Try making a circle body shape, then tracing a circle on the floor. Now try a square, a figure eight and a rectangle." This can also be done in pairs or groups. The groups can create a large shape and move it through space.

4. **XEROX SHAPES:** "Make a shape. Remember the shape by closing your eyes and feeling the shape in your muscles. Open your eyes and gallop through general space to a new spot and make the same shape. That is shape #1. Shake out the shape and make shape #2. Close your eyes, feel the shape, open your eyes and skip to a new spot and remake shape #2." Continue this way for 4 or 5 shapes. Can anyone remember their shape #1! It helps the dancers if they make very different shapes. Encourage level changes, use of different body parts, size and directions. More experienced dancers can dance any way they like through general space.

5. **THREE SHAPES:** "Make three shapes in self space -- shape! shape! shape! Gallop that shape through general space to a new place. Make three new shapes -- shape! shape! shape! Turn the last shape to a new place." Repeat, practicing different locomotor movements through general space. This can also be done in partners -- dancing with the partner through general space or away from the partner.

6. **COPY CAT:** "Find a partner. #1 makes a shape. #2 copies the shape. #1 comes alive and dances through general space. #2 changes the shape when #1 leaves. #1 returns to #2 and copies the new shape. Now #2 dances away while #1 changes into a new shape." Encourage use of levels, size, directions, etc. Continue until the music stops.

7. **SHAPE MUSEUM:** Half of the students make different shape statues spread around the room in self space. The other students dance around the shapes and copy the shapes. Only one dancer at a time should copy a statue. When a statue has been copied, the statue can come alive and become a dancer. Statues stay frozen until copied by a dancer. Dancers dance around, then copy a statue when they feel like doing so. Dancers should be encouraged to use different movements while dancing from statue to statue. They can move under and over statues if possible. As a variation, statues could change shapes at any time. This is a good exploration for large classes or small spaces because only half the dancers are moving at a given time. This is a favorite activity and has many variations in subsequent chapters.

8. **SCULPTOR AND CLAY:** "Find a partner. Mold your partner into a shape (statue). Move your statue's body parts very gently. Statue, hold your shape. Sculptor, remember to mold your partner into a shape that will be comfortable to maintain." Reverse roles. With inexperienced students, be more directed -- ask the sculptors to mold specific shapes such as big and little, high and low, strong and light or verbs, adjectives, emotions, letters, numbers, etc.

9. **GROUP SCULPTOR AND CLAY:** "Half the class will stand, sit or lie in a neutral shape. The other half will move around the shapes and mold or move one body part, then move to the next shape. The shapes are continually being changed by the sculptors who are moving quickly from one shape to the next. Statues are in self space. Sculptors are dancing through general space." Reverse roles. This is great fun to watch. Large classes can be divided into audience and performers. Be sure to change roles.

10. **PREPOSITIONS:** "Dancers, find partners. One of you make a shape while the other moves through, under, over or around you to create a new shape. Continue taking turns." Chinese jump ropes or rubberbands can be used to add dimension to the shapes.

11. **SHAPE CHAIN:** "One dancer will make a shape starting in the corner of the room. The next dancer will make a different shape, connecting to the first dancer. Each dancer connects to the next with a different shape. Dancers hold your shapes until all are connected." With small classes the line can begin again with the first dancer connecting to the last and starting the process over.

INSTRUMENTS

1. **GENERAL SPACE/SELF SPACE:** Dancers alternate playing instruments through general space and putting the instrument down and dancing around it.

2. **SELF SPACE/GENERAL SPACE:** Dancers play instruments and move in self space, then put the instrument down and dance away. Remind dancers to dance around or leap over instruments and keep eyes open.

3. **PARTNERS:** Dancers dance to a partner and try to make music together, then dance away and make music alone. Alternate together and apart.

4. **CONTINUOUS:** Alternate self and general space dancing while continuously playing an instrument. Use a folk dance tune to provide phrases of music or use Ella Jenkins "Play Your Instrument..." dancing in self space when a specified instrument plays and general space when everyone plays together.

5. **FREEZE:** Play and dance in general space until the music pauses, then freeze in self space and be silent. Alternate playing and freezing. Try reversing this idea so that you move and play in self space and then move silently through general space.

DEVELOPING SKILLS

1. **IN PLACE:** Dancers walk through general space until they hear a signal to stop, then they walk in self space. On the go signal they walk through general space again. Alternate self and general space. Try different locomotor movements from the movement chart. Galloping, skipping, sliding and leaping are hard to do in place but possible. Dancers can move for any duration the teacher specifies. More advanced dancers could move to counts. Try using nonlocomotor movement -- twist in self space then twist through general space. A discussion could focus on how locomotor movements tend to be easier to do traveling, while nonlocomotor movements are usually easier to do in self space. Of course, this is why these movements are categorized this way. It is more meaningful for the dancers to experience this before they discuss it.

2. **8 COUNTS:** Direct dancers to walk for 8 counts then twist for 8 counts. Run 8 counts, punch 8 counts. Jump 8 counts, stretch 8 counts. Try different combinations and different counts. Have the dancers create their own locomotor/nonlocomotor sentences.

3. **BODY HALVES:** Direct dancers to do locomotor movements with their legs while doing nonlocomotor movements with their arms: skip legs/swing arms, jump legs/punch arms. More advanced dancers can try the reverse: punch legs/jump arms, swing legs/skip arms. It sounds silly and maybe impossible but it is possible and leads to unusual movements and feelings and often laughter!

4. **FOOT STORY:** Dancers sit in a circle with their feet in front of them. Teacher tells a story about two feet and the dancers help tell the story with their feet. They have to describe all the actions with their feet without standing up. This is a great activity for small spaces. It can be a real workout.

"Once upon a time there were two feet. These two feet were just walking down the street and who should they meet, these two feet? (Dancers are walking feet in place in front of them.) These two feet met a juggler! The feet asked the juggler if they could juggle and the juggler said sure, so the feet started to juggle (feet juggle). The juggling balls went higher and higher and higher (feet go higher) until they disappeared." The story continues with a growl chasing the feet, the feet hiding, hopping down to a river, going for a swim, shaking the water off, balancing across a log, galloping on horseback, tiptoeing home, eating dinner and going to sleep. (The feet curl up under the legs and disappear.) The story always begins with "Two feet were walking down the street..." and ends with "...so the feet went to sleep and that was the end of the feet!"

Dancers love to help make up new adventures and movements for the feet!

5. **PROPS:** Use objects with younger children to make practicing skills more interesting. For example: slide to a cone, slide around the cone, slide to a spot and jump or hop on the spot; gallop to a spot, punch or float on the spot, turn to another spot; skip to a milk carton, make two shapes over the carton, skip with fancy arms to another carton.

6. **DANCE STEPS:** More advanced dancers can explore and practice steps such as: the step-hop, schottische, grapevine, lunge, two-step, or waltz-run. (See the "Movement" chapters for ideas.)

TURNING

1. **CREATE-A-TURN:** Explore at least five different ways of turning in self space and then through general space. Then alternate self space and general space turns.

2. **COPY CAT:** Ask dancers to create their own self or general space turns. One at a time have dancers show their turns, then have everyone learn or copy each turn. Dancers could also work in pairs and teach their turns only to each other to save time.

3. **CHAIN REACTION:** Have dancers find perfect spots. One dancer begins turning across the floor to another dancer. When #1 reaches #2, #2 takes off to #3. #1 continues to turn in self space on #2's spot. If dancers are too dizzy they can freeze in a shape on their new spot. With a small class it is fun to reverse. When reversing, turners freeze in a shape after they move to a new spot for the second time.

4. **BALLET TURNS:** More advanced dancers can explore and practice chaîné and piqué turns (general space turns) and pirouette and attitude turns (self space turns).

COMBINING MOVEMENTS

1. **SENTENCES:** Using words from the movement chart, create a short movement sentence such as " walk, turn, run, stretch, melt." Make sure to use a combination of locomotor and nonlocomotor words. Do the combination across the floor or in a scattered formation, repeating it several times.

2. **CINQUAIN:** Create a cinquain using the word SPACE or PLACE, such as:

Space

Self, general

Turning, twisting, tiptoeing

Dancers move through space

Place

Perform the cinquain as you say each word out loud. It could be further explored in the composition section of the lesson. Dancers can be asked to help create parts of the cinquain.

3. **WORD CARDS:** Have dancers choose 4-5 movement word cards from a pile and put them into a combination. Ask them to think about logical beginnings and endings and transitions.

4. **CREATIVE FOLK DANCE:** Use a simple folk dance form that has two sections. Make up general space movement for one section and self space movement for another section.

5. **TRADITIONAL FOLK DANCE:** Use an authentic folk dance that has general and self space sections in it. Seven Jumps, Doudlebska Polka, Troika, Mayim, Shoemaker are a few suggestions.

6. **ACTIVITY SONGS:** Choose a song from the "Activity Music List."

LEAPING

1. **SCATTERED:** Each dancer places a milk carton in a perfect spot. They practice leaping, jumping and hopping over their own carton in self space. At a signal they leap through general space over everybody's cartons. RULE: when two dancers approach a carton they both turn away. This avoids collisions. Alternate self and general space.

2. **SHAPES:** Each dancer places a milk carton in a perfect spot. Everyone leaps over milk cartons traveling through general space. At a signal they stop at the nearest carton and make a shape over it and catch their breath. They could make several shapes or do slow movement around the carton. Alternate self and general space movement.

3. **NUMBERS:** Milk cartons are scattered around the room. 1 drum beat signals leaping movements, 2 beats signal jumping movements, 3 beats signal hopping movements, 4 beats signal resting in a shape. Dancers use one type of movement until they hear a new signal.

4. **GROUP SHAPES:** Arrange the milk cartons in a line, several lines or a horseshoe. Place several spots between cartons or at the end of the line. Dancers leap over the cartons and make shapes on the spots or do a nonlocomotor movement on the spots. Group shapes can be formed on the last spot, as each dancer takes a place in the shape at the end of the leaps.

5. **WITHOUT OBJECTS:** Practice leaping through empty space. Suggest different arm movements and shapes. Try repeating patterns such as run, run, run leap or run, run, leap or run leap, run leap or leap, leap, leap.

FREE DANCING/IMPROVISATION

Choose an activity under "Exploring the Concept" that is not too directed. Some ideas under "Combining Movements" and "Choreographing" can be adapted for structured improvisations.

CHOREOGRAPHING

1. **WORD CARDS:** Use #3 in "Combining Movements" but divide dancers into groups and have them compose a phrase and perform for each other. It is fun to give each group the same word cards and see the different dances. Talk about the use of space in the compositions.

2. **CINQUAIN:** Have groups write their own cinquains and perform. Discuss use of space.

3. **ABA:** Have dancers create or improvise a dance based on ABA form. They could do self/general/self or general/self/general. This could be done as solos, duets, trios or groups. Have the audience guess in what order the elements of place were used in each dance.

4. **PROPS:** Have dancers create self and general space dances using props. Props could be used for one kind of place and not the other or for both self and general space.

5. **DANCE BY CHANCE:** Assign numbers 1-4 to four movements such as 1 = walk, 2 = roll, 3 = shape, 4 = slash. Each dancer picks four cards from a group of cards with numbers 1-4 written on them. The order picked should be the order performed. A dancer might pick 2,2,4,3. That would mean they would do roll, roll, slash, shape. They would create a dance based on those words and that order. When several dancers perform simultaneously a wonderful dance may appear. Have dancers discuss what is exciting and why. Always pull the discussion back to the use of self and general space and how its use affects our feelings about dance. Also discuss the use of freezes, shapes and stillness.

6. **WORD CARDS:** Have all the dancers perform a phrase created from the movement word cards. Let them move at their own tempo. Experiment with time until a dance emerges. Different forms such as canon, theme and variation, relationship to others could be used. This is a case of group improvisation turning into a set piece. This process could take several weeks.

7. **FLOCKING:** Start in a group in a corner of the room. One dancer initiates a movement in self space, lets the movement grow and moves into general space then brings the movement back to the group and into self space. Two more dancers join the first dancer. As the trio moves back to the group they pick up the whole group and, like a flock, they travel through space and back to self space together. The movement builds in size and intensity. Try another leader and another movement. Divide the class into groups and let the groups each set a piece based on this improvisation.

8. **MOVEMENT MAPS:** This can be done individually or in groups. Draw three shapes on a piece of paper (triangle, circle and square). Connect the three shapes with three lines (perhaps curvy, straight and zig zag). Now choose a movement to do in self space in each shape and a movement to do for each line which travels through general space. Perform the dance, using the map to tell you what to do and how and where to travel.

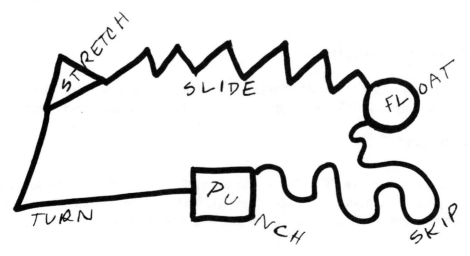

LESSON ON PLACE

Age: 3, 4, 5, or 6 year olds   Length: 60 minutes

WARMING UP

Dance Exercises/Technique: Select four rhyming exercises sitting and standing from "Warming-up."

Introducing the Concept: PLACE: self space and general space. See, say and do the words.

EXPLORING THE CONCEPT

Exploring the Concept: "Follow the Leader" #10
Follow the teacher's movements in self space when the music is slow, dance your own way through general space when the music is fast. Music: "Slow and Fast" - *Feel of Music*.

Shaping: "Body Halves" #2
Freeze the legs and move the upper half in self space, then freeze the upper half and dance with the lower half through general space. Music: "Pause" - *Movin'*.

Instruments: "Continuous" #4
Play and march through general space; swing/sway/turn in self space while playing; jump/hop/kick in self and general space while playing. Music: "Lead the Band" - *Play Your Instruments*.

COOLING-DOWN

Relaxation/Alignment: While the dancers rest on their backs, the teacher manipulates arms and legs. Music: "Gentle Sea" - *Movin'* or any lullaby or quiet song.

DEVELOPING SKILLS

Developing Skills: "Foot Story" #4
While the teacher tells a story about two feet doing many different movements, the dancers act the story out with their feet while sitting in self space.

Combining Movements: "Activity Song" #6 or "Word Cards" #3
"Wake Me, Shake Me" - *Time After Time* : On the chorus, dance through general space; on the verse do the suggested gestures (comb hair, brush teeth, etc.) in self space. OR do a simple combination such as: Run, turn, stretch, three shapes. Repeat several times.

Leaping: "Shapes" #2
Dancers leap over scattered milk cartons, freezing in shapes when the music pauses. Music: "Wildwood" (with stops) - *Homemade Band* repeated several times.

CREATING

Free Dancing/Improvising: Exploring the Concept - "Seven Jumps" #14
Dance different ways through general space when the music plays. Dance different ways in self space on the "hums." Music: "Seven Jumps" - *Rhythmically Moving 2*.

COOLING-DOWN

Good-bye Dance: If time allows, dancers dance across the room individually or in pairs demonstrating self and general space.

LESSON ON PLACE

Ages: 4-Adult as an introductory class in creative dance
Length: 30 minutes

WARMING UP

Dance Exercises/Technique: Do ten minutes of exercises appropriate to age level.

Introducing the Concept: PLACE: self and general space. See, say and do the words.

EXPLORING THE CONCEPT

Exploring the Concept: "16 Counts" #8
Ages 6 and up can do "16 Counts" with a partner. Ages 4-5 can use a "spot" instead of a partner and alternate moving in self and general space. Music: counts or drum beat.

Shaping: "Xerox Shapes" #4
Suggest different movements for young students to do between shapes such as galloping, turning, jumping, etc. Older dancers can think of their own movements.

DEVELOPING SKILLS

Developing Skills: Practice walking and running through general space "eating up" as much space as possible - really travel. Practice jumping and hopping in different ways in self space. Music: drum beat or "Funky Penguin" - *Movin'*.

CREATING

Free Dancing/Improvisation: Exploring the Concept - "Follow the Leader" #10
Mirror the teacher's movements in self space during the slow music and dance different ways through general space on the fast music. Music: "Inima" - *Solitude*.

CHAPTER 10

LEVEL
High, Middle, Low

INTRODUCING THE CONCEPT

"Our new word is level. We can move many ways on different levels. Let's divide our body into three parts. From our hips to our toes can be one part. That is what we call the low level space. Can you make a shape with all your body parts at the low level -- the space in which your legs usually move? Our second section goes from our hips to our shoulders. When you are standing, the space between your hips and shoulders is called the middle level. How many body parts can you move at a middle level while balancing on two legs...one leg? The third section is everything above our shoulders. The space we move in above our shoulders is called ...? (high level) How many body parts can you move at a high level? How much of your body can you get into the high level space? (Dancers experiment with different types of jumping.) Let's explore other ways of moving at different levels."

EXPLORING THE CONCEPT

1. **RISING AND SINKING:** "Start in a low level shape. I will count to 8 while you rise slowly to a high level shape. You should be frozen in a high level shape on count 8, not before or after. Then I will count backwards to 1 as you slowly sink down to make a new low level shape. On what count should you be making a middle level shape? (On count 4.) Remember to move slowly and smoothly and to change your shape each time." Continue doing this with 6 counts, 4 counts, 2 counts. With 2 counts they will be moving quickly and sharply! With more experienced dancers try moving during 16 counts and then only 1 count.

2. **SCALES:** "I am going to play music that moves up and down the scale -- the music goes from low to high and back down to low. (*Feel of Music* contains a scale song or play a recorder, penny whistle, harmonica, piano, etc.) Move your body to the rise and fall of the music. As the notes go up the scale, let your body rise. As the notes go down the scale, let your body sink. Listen also to the speed of the notes. Sometimes the notes rise and sink slowly, sometimes quickly. Follow the speed of the music with your body." Try this first in self space then travelling through general space. You can have a lot of fun changing the speed of the music.

3. **ELEVATORS:** "Think of your body as an elevator. Start in the basement, rise slowly to the first floor, second floor and the top floor. Now come back down. I am going to push imaginary buttons at a high, middle or low level. Watch carefully and take your elevator to the level at which I push the button. If I make a knocking motion, freeze and let some people out (by opening arms or however individual dancer decides), then watch for which button I push next." Push the buttons slowly at first, then speed up to provide more challenge and fun. This may be done in pairs, with an elevator and an operator. You can encourage different shapes by asking for creative elevators or alien elevators.

4. **HIGH/LOW BODY PARTS:** "I am going to name a body part and a level. Make a shape or do a movement with that part at that level. Hands high, hands low, hands high, hands middle. Dance your hands through space at a middle level. Now freeze. Feet low, feet high, feet middle, feet low. Dance your feet through space at a low level. Freeze. Elbows middle, elbows high, elbows low, elbows high. Dance your elbows through space at a high level." Continue on in this fashion.

5. **CLAP HANDS:** Sing the song "Clap Your Hands Together" changing the words to focus on level. "Clap, clap, clap your hands, clap your hands up high. Clap, clap, clap your hands, clap your hands down low. Shake, shake, shake your feet, shake your feet up high. Shake, shake, shake your feet, shake your feet down low." Continue with other parts and movements. Try moving through self and general space. Ask the dancers for ideas.

6. **BODY PARTS:** "Can you put three body parts on the floor and move at a low level? Can you put three parts on the floor and move at a middle level ... a high level? Try two parts touching the floor and moving low...two parts moving at the middle level ... two parts moving at a high level. Can you put five parts on the ground and move low? Can you put ten parts on the ground and move high ... middle? (Ten toes?) Who can put 20 parts on the ground and move at a middle or low level? (Ten toes and ten fingers!)" Continue with other challenges.

7. **LEVEL BOOGIE:** "Find a partner. I want partners to dance around each other but you can never have your heads on the same level. You will have to watch each other the whole time, change

levels and try to keep your partner off guard." This can be done with a group of young dancers playing against the teacher. With experienced dancers try trios and small groups. This can be a tiring exploration so watch the time. Jazzy music helps support the boogie element.

8. **LOUD AND SOFT:** "When the music is loud, dance at a high level. When the music is soft, dance at a low level. When the music is normal, dance at a middle level. Now, dance low when the music is loud and high when the music is soft. Mix up levels when the music is normal. Which level music made you feel most like dancing at a high level ... which at a low level?" Feelings will vary. Discuss the fact that we react to music in different ways.

9. **SPOTS:** "Stand on your spot. Can you shake at a high level...try shaking at a middle level...now, shake at a low level. Can you shake to a new spot moving from high to low, so that you end in a low shape on the new spot? Try punching at a low level...middle level...high level. Punch to a new spot moving from high to low, ending in a new low shape on a new spot. Can you stretch at a low level...high level...middle level? Now stretch to a new spot moving in a wave-like motion from high to low to high to low." Continue in this fashion using different movements while changing levels in self space and through general space.

10. **ROCKS AND BRIDGES:** "I would like half of the class to each form a bridge shape in an empty space. The other half of the class will dance under the bridges. When going under a bridge you will be dancing at a low level. Between bridges you may dance at any level. The bridges may change shapes when dancers are not going under them." Change roles after 30 to 60 seconds. "This time I would like the shapes to be rocks. The dancers will dance over the rocks moving at a high level. The rocks may change shapes when dancers are not going over them." Change roles after 30 to 60 seconds. More experienced dancers may change from a bridge shape to a rock shape at any time, thus making the dancers move high and low. Discuss safety. Be careful when moving under or over people. Be careful when changing shapes.

11. **BACK TO BACK:** "Find a partner. Touch low level parts together. Touch high level parts together. Touch middle level parts together. Now dance away on a middle level. Come back to your partner (or a different one) and touch a different high level part together ... a middle level part ... a low level part. Now, dance away at a low level. Dance back together and one of you connect a high part to your partner's low part (shoulder to knee) ... now the partner connect a high part to your low part (head to foot). Now dance away moving high and low (rising and sinking)." Continue with similar challenges, always having dancers dance away at the last level named.

12. **MIRRORING:** "Find a partner (or copy the teacher or group leader). The leader will do slow movements in self space changing levels (you can direct the levels or let the dancers choose on their own). When I give the signal, change leaders. Try to make your movements rise and sink slowly in space." For more challenging variations try these ideas: leader moves on high level while the follower tries to mirror these movements at a lower level. Or the leader could move arms while the follower has to mirror with legs and vice versa.

13. **SHADOWING:** "Find a partner. The leader will dance through space slowly at a high and middle level. The follower will move on a low level on the floor, as a real shadow does, trying to copy the leader's movements." This is really difficult but can be challenging and fun with the right class! The leader needs to move slowly. Remember to change leaders. Young dancers can follow the leader on the same level, then pause, make a connected shape and change leaders and levels.

14. **PROPS:**

BENCHES -- Dance over and under benches.
CONES -- Stretch Chinese jump ropes or rubber bands around two cones. Dancers can move over and under these props.
PLASTIC/SCARVES -- Dance at different levels with your prop or dance at opposite levels from your prop. Put your prop on the floor and dance high on top of it. Dance under it. Leap over it
BALLOONS -- Bat it high while moving low. Kick it low while dancing high. Move at a middle level while holding it.
STRETCHYBANDS -- Stretch in a high shape, dance with it high, tossing it. Stretch in a low shape, roll with it. Stretch in a middle level shape, twirl with it.
STREAMERS -- Move the streamers at different levels. Move your body at different levels with the streamers or opposite the streamers. Hold the streamers in your hands or toes. Try to move two streamers on different levels simultaneously. Toss them. Leap over them.

15. **ACTIVITY SONGS:** Choose a song from the "Activity Music List" for ages 2-7 that explores level.

SHAPING

1. **SHAPES:** "Make a twisted shape on a high level ... make a curved shape on a low level...try a straight shape on a middle level ... can you make an angular shape on a low level? Can you make low level body parts angular, middle level body parts straight and high level body parts twisted? Can you make three different twisted shapes on three different levels? Can you make a similar curved shape on three different levels?" Continue with similar challenges.

2. **BODY PARTS:** "Can you put a high body part on a low level and a low body part on a middle or high level and freeze in that shape? (Head low and foot high.) Can you put two high parts low, two low parts low and a middle body part on a middle level and freeze? (Hands and feet on floor with tummy or back to ceiling.)" Continue with other body part challenges.

3. **BLANKET SHAPES:** "Can you make a shape under this big piece of material? Decide on which level you will make your shape. We will try to guess your level and shape. Then I will take the blanket off - stay in your shape and we will see how well we guessed. Then we will copy your shape exactly." Continue until all have had a turn, then try two or more dancers under the blanket. If the class is large have 2-3 dancers under the blanket initially.

4. **SHAPE STORY:** Create a story about a shape which is always changing levels such as this one: "Once upon a time there was a high shape. One day high shape went for a walk in the forest. All of a sudden he heard a strange noise so he started to run. As he ran, a strange thing started to happen. He started getting shorter and shorter. Soon high shape was low shape. He could no longer run so he slithered into a hole. The strange noise came to the hole and said 'Come out, low shape or I will twist you into a pretzel!' Low shape came out and curled into a ball and rolled away from

the noise. He rolled away until he hit a magic rock. The rock made low shape grow into high shape again. High shape was so happy, he skipped around in circles. Skipping in circles made him so dizzy that he became a middle level shape. Middle level shape started to creep through the forest looking for his way home. Soon he came to the edge of the forest and saw his house in the distance. He stretched so hard to see it that he grew into tall shape. He galloped to the river, lept over it and ran through the door of his home, at last. He gobbled up a piece of cake sitting on the table. Unfortunately this was shrinking cake and tall shape sunk into low shape once again. But he didn't care. He was safe at home. He curled up on the floor and went to bed."

5. **MOVING SHAPES:** "Make a high level shape, move it to a new place. Shake it out. Make a low level shape and move it to a new place. Shake it out. Can you make your high level shape sink to a low level while traveling through space? Try to keep the form of the high shape as similar as possible to the low shape. Make a different low level shape and let it rise to a high level. You will have to make some changes but try to keep it similar to the low level shape. It is like taking a short shape and stretching it into a tall shape." Continue with similar questions. Encourage the dancers to move their shapes through space.

6. **MELTING SHAPES:** "Make a high level shape. Melt slowly to a low level, changing your shape completely. If you started in a twisted shape, maybe you will end in a straight shape. If you started in a big shape, maybe you will end in a little shape. If you started in a backward shape, maybe you will end in a forward shape. Now, let your low level shape get stretched slowly to a high level shape. Change the shape completely." Continue in this way. You may play with time, melting and stretching quickly and/or slowly.

7. **OVER/UNDER:** "Find a partner. One of you make a low shape. The other make a high shape over your partner. Now the high person will slowly sink while the low person rises to form a shape over their partner. Continue rising and sinking to form shapes over or under each other. Move slowly, being aware of each other's space and movements. Hold the over/under shape for 5 counts before changing levels."

8. **PICKET FENCE:** "I would like one person to make a high shape in an empty spot. The next person I call will make the same shape right next to the first person but on a middle level. The third

person will make the same shape (or as close as possible) next to the second person but at a lower level. Let's begin again with high, middle and low shapes (they can repeat the first set or begin a new set of shapes) and continue until we have made a fence with the whole class."

9. **SCULPTOR AND CLAY:** "Find a partner. You will mold your partner into a low level shape. Remember to move your partner's body parts gently. Remember, 'clay,' to hold the shape into which you are molded. Then your partner will mold you into a high level shape. Now, try molding a shape on a level you didn't do last time. Take turns being the sculptor. Pick the two different level shapes you both like the best and show them to the class."

10. **SCULPTURES IN THREES:** "Find three friends so that you form a quartet. If you are the sculptor first, mold your three friends into a tri-level statue. Use different shapes to create an interesting look. Let your shapes be connected in some way. Make the level differences clear. When you are finished, we will briefly show the statues and then another member of the quartet will become the sculptor."

11. **GROUP SCULPTOR AND CLAY:** "I would like half of the class to each stand, sit or lie down in an empty space. The other half will dance around the statues, moving different body parts to create new statues. Remember to move quickly from one statue to another. Besides changing body parts, gently move the statues to different levels by lifting them to their feet or sitting them down or slowly laying them down." This takes a lot of care and trust and should only be done with responsible dancers. Remember to change roles, but first, let the sculptors view their museum of statues.

12. **MACHINES:** "One at a time make a shape, connecting to another shape, but at a different level. Add a little movement to your shape that doesn't make you change level. Add sound to your shape. If you have a low shape, make a sound low in pitch. High shapes should make sounds high in pitch. Do machines make different pitched sounds? Does this machine look like any particular machine?" This can be done in small or large groups or the whole class. For variation: make the movement cause the shape to change level. The sound should go high and low, also.

13. **HIGH/LOW:** "Find a partner. Make a connected shape at the opposite level from your partner. Now, slowly change levels but keep connected. Continue to move to opposite levels from each other while staying connected. Hold your shapes for at least 5 counts before changing. Change your point of connection after 3-4 shapes. You will feel a pull on each other. Share the weight, try not to pull more or less than your partner. Keep the shapes changing slowly like sand shifting on the desert."

14. **SHAPE MUSEUM:** "I would like half (or name a number) of the class to make a shape on any level in an empty space. The other half will dance at different levels around, over or under the statues. Dancers, copy a statue, but make a similar shape at the opposite level. If you copy a high shape you will try to copy it at a low level. Remember when you are copied, you are free to dance around until you copy a new shape. When you are copied, be sure to give the dancer time to copy your shape. Don't dance off too soon. It is hard to try to make the same shape at a different level!" Dancers and statues continue to change places until the music ends.

15. **PROPS:** Make shapes holding props on the same level or make shapes with props at opposite levels.

INSTRUMENTS

1. **SOFT AND LOUD:** "Play your instrument soft and dance low. Play it loud and dance high. Play it at a normal volume and dance at a middle level." Try other combinations of volume and level.

2. **HIGHLAND/LOWLAND:** "This half of the room is Highland. All the people dance at a high level here. This half is Lowland and all the people dance at a low level here. You and your instrument may go visit any land, at anytime, but remember to move at the appropriate level. Try to change the sound of your instrument to accompany your movement."

3. **SCALES:** "When you hear the high sounds, play and dance high. When you hear the low sounds, play and dance low."

4. **MIRROR:** "Mirror your partner's high and low movements and loud and soft sounds."

5. **SONGS:** Use the instruments to accompany different activity songs from the "Activity Music List" that are listed under LEVEL. Move the instrument on different levels as you dance on different levels.

DEVELOPING SKILLS

1. **LOW MOVEMENTS:** Practice slithering on stomach and back, scooting, creeping, crawling, rolling different ways, crab walk, dinosaur walk (on hands and feet with buttocks up), buttocks walk, lame puppy dog walk (three body parts touching the floor), and other low movements the dancers create and name themselves.

2. **HIGH MOVEMENTS:** Practice tiptoe walks, jumps, leaps, hops, spanking runs (feet kick back to spank buttocks), hitch kicks, heel clicks, high stepping march, high skips, high movements the dancers create and name themselves.

3. **HIGH/LOW:** Practice movements on a low level that are normally done on a high level and vice versa. Try rolling on a high level. (The dancers will discover a solution even if you do not have

one.) Try jumping at a low level. Try leaping at a middle level. Try crawling at a high level. Try tiptoe walking at a low level. Discuss the difficulties.

4. **NONLOCOMOTOR MOVEMENTS:** Practice nonlocomotor movements at different levels. See the "Movement" chapter for ideas. Start with body parts then use the whole body. "Shake your arms up high, shake them down low, shake them on a middle level. Shake your legs down low, shake your legs up high, shake them on a middle level. Shake your head carefully at a high level..low level...middle level. How high can you shake your hips...how low..now on a middle level? Shake your whole body high, shake it low, shake it on a middle level."

5. **LOCOMOTOR MOVEMENTS:** Practice different locomotor movements with a sense of rising and sinking as you travel through space. See the "Movement" chapter for ideas. "Start at a low level. As you WALK forward, rise slowly. When you reach your peak, start to sink slowly as you advance through space. Feel as though you are climbing up a mountain and back down." Try this with other movements such as running, galloping, jumping, sliding and skipping. Be careful not to put too much strain on the knees. You might practice these movements travelling backward through space while rising and sinking.

6. **FALL/MELT:** Practice different ways of falling safely (see *On the Count of One*). Practice different ways of melting. Vary the speed, size, direction and shape of your movements.

7. **WALTZ RUN:** The waltz run consists of three steps moving forward -- down, up, up. The first step is taken on the right (or left) foot with a bent knee (plié). The second two steps are left tiptoe and right tiptoe (or two steps in relevé). The step is done in 3/4 time or waltz rhythm. The cues are "down, up, up; down, up, up." It helps to emphasize one middle level step and two high level steps. As the dancers become more adept, you can increase the tempo and add creative arm movements. See the "Movement" chapter for more detail.

8. **LIFTS:** Lifts are an exciting part of dance. More experienced, older dancers (age 10 and up) can practice simple lifts at first and then explore more complex lifts. Young children can be lifted by the teacher, teacher aides or older students. I try to lift all my very young dancers several times during the year. This is a favorite part of any lesson, but a particularly good activity for the concept of levels. But be careful! Lifting 60 seven year olds one day gave me a sore arm for a year. Pace yourself! *On the Count of One* has a good section on lifts. The most important concept to teach the dancers doing lifts is that it takes both dancers to perform a lift. The dancer being lifted has to use the stomach muscles and feel light and lifted, not go limp and be dead weight. The dancer doing the lifting has to find a comfortable and secure way to hold his/her partner and then bend the knees and stretch up. Both have to work together to time the take-off and lift.

9. **JUMPS, HOPS, LEAPS:** Practice many different ways of doing movements that take flight. Practice different leg shapes with the leg(s) that are in the air - straight, curved, angular shapes...forward, backward, sideways directions...big and little movements. After practicing different ideas with the legs, try different arm movements that match or oppose the leg movements.

10. **OBJECTS:** Use objects such as benches, cones and spots to motivate the young dancers (ages 2-5) to practice skills. For example: roll to a bench, move under the bench, stretch up and slide to a cone, balance in a high shape beside the cone. Repeat several times.

TURNING

1. **SPIRAL:** Practice spiral turns. A spiral turn rises and sinks around the axis of the body. These turns can be done in self or general space. Some helpful images: the stripe around a candy cane or barber pole, sea shells that have spirals, spinning tops with spiral designs painted on them. If you have any of these objects, bring them in. A visual spiral helps produce a kinesthetic spiral.

2. **COPY CAT:** "Explore three different ways of turning at a low level. Now, pick your favorite one and teach it to the class. We will copy you." If you have a large class, ask everyone to do their favorite turn at the same time, then choose several turns for the class to copy or have the dancers teach their turn to another dancer. Do this with medium and high level turns. These turns can later be used in the "Combining Movements" section of your lesson plan.

3. **KNEE ROLLS:** Practice turns curled in a round shape and rolling on your seat, then knees, then seat, then knees. Placing your hands on the floor by your hips helps propel you through space.

4. **RISE AND SINK:** Practice turning through general space as you change levels. Start turning on a high level, then gradually sink to a low level as you turn and then rise again to a high level.

5. **ARMS:** Practice turns with different arm movements. Try arms in a high shape, on a middle level and on a low level as you turn. Try turning as your arms move from high to low or low to high.

COMBINING MOVEMENTS

1. **WORD CARDS:** Choose actions that move on different levels and arrange them into a combination. "Roll, crawl, walk, jump, walk, crawl, roll." (This combination rises and sinks.) "Low shape, spiral turn up and down, roll, jump, fall, stretch." (This combination goes low, high, low, high, low, high.)

2. **TURNS:** Create a combination using three turns on different levels. Choose three particular turns that all the dancers know but have the dancers create their own transition from one turn to another. Give them 8 or 16 counts to design the movement between turns.

4. **SEVEN JUMPS:** This folk dance involves seven shapes that move from high to low. You could do the specific shapes or have dancers create their own multi-level shapes.

5. **LOOBY LOO:** Instead of putting body parts into the circle, put shapes on different levels: "put a high shape in, put a high shape out, give your shape a shake, shake, shake and turn yourself about."

6. **CINQUAIN:** Create a cinquain using levels. Read the poem as the dancers perform. For variation, ask the dancers for three different action words for the third line.

Levels
High, low
Reaching, bending, rolling
We can rise and sink
Levels.

7. **STORY:** Put words together that make you move on different levels and create a sense of a drama or story. "Creep (you're scared), run low (you hear a noise), jump, jump, jump (somebody yells boo), fall (you faint)."

8. **ACTIVITY SONGS:** Choose an activity song from the "Activity Music List" for ages 2-7 that focuses on level changes.

LEAPING

1. **CARTONS:** Stack milk cartons one, two, and three high. Dancers leap low, middle and high. Add arm shapes. Vary leg shapes. Stack the cartons as high as safety will allow.

2. **ARMS:** Add arm shapes that move low, middle, high, middle, low or combinations of this.

3. **BENCHES:** Leap over cartons, crawl under and jump off of benches.

4. **SPOTS:** Leap over low, middle and high cartons then make a low, middle or high shape on the spot.

5. **FOCUS:** Encourage the dancers to focus out at a middle to high level rather than down low at the cartons or floor when leaping. Focusing out gives the dancer a sense of more height.

6. **TUNNELS:** Create a tunnel by putting a sheet over two benches placed side by side and a few feet apart or put material over chairs, etc. Have the dancers leap high over cartons, then crawl low through the tunnel. Younger dancers love this!

7. **EMPTY SPACE:** Practice leaping over empty space. Try low leaps and high leaps. Practice low, middle and high level arm shapes and movements.

FREE DANCING/IMPROVISATION

Choose an activity under "Exploring the Concept" that is not too structured. There are also several activities under "Combining Movements" and "Choreographing" that could become excellent improvs for ages 8-adult.

CHOREOGRAPHING

1. **IMAGES:** Give images on cards (or let dancers make up their own) that dancers could use to create a short study on levels. Some examples: smoke rising, snow falling, enchanted cobras rising, trees falling, sun rising, feathers falling, balloons rising, leaves falling.

2. **ABA:** Individuals or groupings of dancers create a high/low/high dance or a low/high/low dance. Mouth sounds that rise and sink in volume or pitch could add an interesting dimension.

3. **ABC:** Create a dance in three sections using the three different levels in any order. The dancers might choose three different areas of the "stage" in which to perform each section. A suite form could

be used so that the first section is performed at medium speed, the second section is slow and the third section is fast.

4. **TRIOS:** Trios create a dance based on three levels. They could each focus on a different level or they could all do all three levels. They could each take a turn dancing, they could dance simultaneously or they could dance in canon.

5. **FLOCKING:** See the chapter on DIRECTIONS. Have dancers move on different levels.

6. **STATUES:** The dancers stand around the edges of the room. One at a time, three dancers dance on any level into the center of the room and freeze in a shape on a certain level. The three dancers in the statue should all be on a different level. Then the dancers dance out on a different level. Three more dancers dance into the center and the dance continues. This is called structured improvisation. You may want to call the names of the young dancers. Older dancers can choose when to enter the space. They need to watch each other and have a feel for the group as a whole. If four dancers start to move, one will have to stay back.

7. **WORD CARDS:** Assign five word cards to each group of dancers. Have them put the words into a logical sequence. Then have the group add level words so that the dance will change levels. "Run, swing, twist, gallop, freeze." "Run LOW, swing MIDDLE, twist HIGH, gallop MIDDLE, freeze LOW."

8. **PROPS:** Create a dance that changes levels and uses one to three props. These props could be three objects that are the same (three balloons) or three different objects (balloon, scarf, chair). The class could be divided into individuals, pairs, trios or small groups.

9. **CINQUAIN:** Have pairs or groups create their own cinquain about levels or give each group the same cinquain and discuss the difference in the final dances.

LESSON ON LEVEL

Ages: 4, 5, 6, 7, or 8   *Length: 30 minutes*

WARMING UP

Dance Exercises/Technique: Do 5-10 minutes of dance exercises.

Introducing the Concept: LEVEL: high, middle, low. See, say and do the words.

EXPLORING THE CONCEPT

Exploring the Concept: "Rising and Sinking" #1
Dancers rise and sink to counts or scales. Music: drum beat, flute, piano, etc. or "Celestial Soda Pop" - *Deep Breakfast.*

Instruments: "Soft and Loud" #1
Play softly and dance on a low level, play loudly and dance on a high level and then reverse. Music: "Soft and Loud" - *Feel of Music.*

DEVELOPING SKILLS

Developing Skills: Exploring the Concept "Body Parts" #6
Dancers move on different number of body parts. Music: "Move Around the Room" - *Ideas, Thoughts and Feelings* or "Far East Blues" - *Movin'.*

CREATING

Free Dancing/Improvisation: Combining Movements #6
Ask dancers for three ways of moving on different levels and use these actions for the third line of the poem. Say the poem and have the dancers improvise their own interpretation. Music: "Children's Dance" - *Windham Hill Sampler 81.*

COOLING DOWN

Good-bye Dance, slow breathing or mirroring.

LESSON ON LEVEL

Ages: 9-Adult   *Length: 30-60 minutes*

WARMING UP

Dance Exercises/Technique: For a 30 minute class do 10 minutes of exercises. For a 60 minute class do 20 minutes of exercises. Emphasize the concept of level as you do the exercises.

Introducing the Concept: LEVEL: high, middle, low. See, say and do the words.

EXPLORING THE CONCEPT

Exploring the Concept: "Level Boogie" #7
Do this in trios and encourage movement through general space as well as in self space. Music: "Javanaise" - *Suite for Flute and Jazz Piano.*

Shaping: "Group Sculptor and Clay" #11
Emphasize changing levels carefully. Encourage dancers to move on different levels around the statues. Music: "Far East Blues" - *Movin'.*

DEVELOPING SKILLS

Developing Skills: "Waltz Run" #7
Experienced dancers can add arm movements that move from low to high, slash from high to low, or move in and out at a middle level. Music: "Dreamgift" - *Emerald* or any waltz.

CREATING

Free Dancing/Improvisation: For a 30 minute class do Choreographing "Statues" #6. For variation, allow 3-6 dancers to enter the space. Each dancer must make a statue on a different level. Music: "Baroque and Blues" - *Suite for Flute and Jazz Piano.*

Choreographing: For a 60 minute class do Choreographing "ABC" #3. Small groups choreograph a dance in three sections using the three levels (high/middle/low OR middle/low/high OR low/high/middle, etc.). Music: different selections from *The Essential Jarre.*

COOLING DOWN

Sharing/Evaluating Choreography: For a 60 minute class share and evaluate the ABC studies.

CHAPTER 11

SIZE
Big, Medium, Little
Near Reach, Far Reach

INTRODUCING THE CONCEPT

"Today our special word is SIZE. SIZE (or range) means how close or far apart one thing is to another. Can you make your arms and legs stretch far away from your stomach? What SIZE shape are you? (BIG) Now bring your arms and legs near to your stomach. What SIZE shape are you? (LITTLE) Try stretching your arms and legs half way between big and little. What SIZE are you? (MEDIUM) Is SIZE the same as LEVEL? (No, but people often confuse the two.) Show me a BIG shape on a low level. Show me a BIG shape on a high level. Show me a LITTLE shape on a low level, a LITTLE shape on a high level. Remember, LITTLE doesn't mean short, it means close together. BIG doesn't mean tall, it means far apart." The words "near reach" can be used for "small" and "far reach" for "big."

"We have been exploring different sized shapes in our self space. Let's try different sized movements through general space. How far apart can you make your legs while walking? Are these

BIG (far reach) steps? (Yes) How close together can you make you feet while walking? Are these LITTLE (near reach) steps? (Yes) Add big and little arms to your big and little steps. Now walk in a normal way. Does this feel like medium sized movement?"

EXPLORING THE CONCEPT

1. **BALLOONS:** "Start in a small shape on any level. Blow your shape up like a balloon. Fill your stomach with air, your arms, legs. Keep blowing until you are a big shape. Feel like a giant balloon, stetched until you feel you might pop. Now, POP! Let all the air out and shrink up into a small shape again. Start to blow yourself up again but make a new shape. Balloons come in many shapes and colors. Choose one. Now instead of popping, you have a small leak. Let all the air out very slowly until you are a little shape again. Put a patch on your leak and blow up again. Choose a new shape and level. This time we will float around the room in our big shape. The wind is getting faster, you are swirling and leaping in your big shape. POP! You fly through general space shrinking as you go until you are a little shape once more." Continue in this way adding speed, level, direction and energy for more experienced dancers.

2. **GROWING:** "Start in a little shape. As I count to 8, I want you to grow so that just on the count of 8 you are in the biggest shape possible. Now as I count backwards to 1, I want you to shrink up to form the smallest shape possible. Let's try that in 4 counts, 2 counts, 1 count!" Encourage continuous movement. The dancers will be moving from smooth to sharp energy as the counts get smaller. Try this on different levels and in different directions. Try 16, 20, 24 counts if you want to practice sustained movement and balance. Try growing and shrinking as you move through general space. Sprinkling children with shrinking powder and using a growing and shrinking voice can add smiles to this exploration when using it with young children.

3. **BODY PARTS:** "Someone name a small body part (finger). Move just your finger with the biggest movements possible. Now move it just a little. Someone name a big body part (leg). Try moving your leg with the biggest movements possible, now move it just a little." Continue with more body parts. Try two body parts at a time so that your movements could take you through general space. More experienced dancers could try moving a big body part with little movements at the same time they are moving a little body part with big movements and vice versa!

4. **NEAR/FAR:** "Move your foot as far from your nose as you can. Move your foot as close to your nose as you can. Move your shoulders near your ears, far from your ears. Move your wrists near your ankles, far from your ankles. Move your stomach as close to your spine as you can, far from your spine." Continue this way with many different body parts. Solicit ideas from the dancers. This exploration is good for stretching.

5. **GIANTS AND ELVES:** "When you hear the loud music you will be giants dancing in the forest. Move with big steps and shapes -- leap, jump, stretch, slash. When you hear the soft music you will shrink into little elves dancing through the forest -- scamper, tiptoe, flick, spin. Change your character and movements everytime you hear the music change." Encourage the use of different movement elements -- level, speed, direction, etc. Add as much imagery as you want to -- a witch's spell, dancing under the midnight moon, etc., but remember to also focus on the elements of dance. Sometimes I end with the dancers awakening from a dream, being themselves and dancing with medium movements.

6. **SHRINKING SPACE:** "Dance all around the room until you hear my signal (or music changes). Use the biggest movements you can. When you hear my signal, the space will shrink and you will only be able to dance in one-half of the room. At the next signal the room will shrink again -- only 1/4 of the space can be used. The next time the room will shrink so that you must dance in this little circle (or designated area). Adjust your movement each time so that you can keep your self space bubble intact. Think about what you are doing and how you feel each time the room shrinks." After the last time, I like to use all the room space once more, so that the dancers can experience open, free space again. I keep this as a surprise so that the open feeling is all the more appreciated. A discussion of space, size and environment always follows this exploration. "How did you feel? How should you move when in a crowded classroom? How can you move in an open space like the gymnasium? Do you still need to be careful in open places? Do you need to estimate the size of the space you are moving through and adjust your body size accordingly? How do people move in crowded cities? How do people move in open country? How do you feel in these places? Can a place be too small or too big?"

7. **FINGER/BODY/FINGER:** "Start in a shape focusing on your index finger. When the music starts, dance just with your finger. At my signal add your hand, then your arm, your head, other arm, trunk, a leg, your other leg. Now you are dancing through general space using all your body parts and dancing with big movements. At my signal stop moving an arm, a leg, the other leg, your trunk, your head, just move your arm, hand, now just your finger again and freeze as the music ends." With young children, sometimes I start with the lights off, turn them on as the movement gets bigger and turn them down as the movement shrinks again.

8. **MIRRORING:** "Find a partner (or mirror the teacher). If you are the leader, start with one body part and add parts until the whole body is dancing. Remember to stay facing your partner. At my signal change leaders. The second leader can start with the whole body moving and subtract body parts until only one part is dancing." You can also have dancers alternate big and little movements as the music changes from loud to soft or changes qualities. Remind dancers that moving body parts far away from each other creates big movements, body parts dancing close to each other creates small movements.

9. **SHADOWING:** "Find a partner. The first leader will dance through general space with big movements, while the follower copies the leader's movements. When the music stops, freeze together in a little shape. Now the same leader will move with little movements and you will both freeze in a big shape." Change leaders and repeat.

10. **PARTNERS:** "Find a partner and make a little shape together. Dance near to each other, either connected or separate, with little movements. Now dance far away from your partner with big movements. Dance back to your partner (or find a new partner) and do the opposite: dance near your partner with big movements (be careful) and dance away from your partner with little movements." Try this in trios and in small and large groups with more experienced dancers.

11. **SPACE BETWEEN:** "Find a partner. Move in and through space together keeping the space between you always the same (about 1 foot). Now try shrinking the space between you so that you are moving very closely together. Cooperate, sense each other and continuously change leadership. Try moving far apart from each other but still move as though you were connected." With inexperienced dancers you might have pairs alternate the leadership on your signal. This will be easier for them to handle.

12. **SEVEN JUMPS:** Use the folk dance music "Seven Jumps." "Dance with big movements for 16 counts. When you hear the hum, slowly shrink into a small shape during the hum, until the music begins again. Now, dance with little movements for 16 counts. On the second hum, grow from a little shape to a big shape. Everytime you hear the hum, shrink or grow in your self space. When you hear the music, dance with little or big movements." Repeat until the song ends. The 16 count phrase could be directed as above or free, allowing the dancers to use any size movement or change size at anytime.

13. **TREES AND GIANTS:** "Half of the class will be trees and half will be giants. Then we will reverse roles. The trees should find a perfect spot with a lot of empty space around them. Trees, create an unusual shape. Giants will dance around the trees. Watch your space. If you bump into a tree or another giant you become a tree. At my signal the forest will shrink a little. The trees will take two steps toward the center of the room. The giants will have to adjust their movement. Soon the forest will be very small and the giants will have to shrink into elves." This works well with a large class because only half are moving at one time. Older dancers prefer to create statues in a museum instead of trees.

14. **THROUGH THE HOLE:** "Find a partner. One of you will make a big shape with empty space created by legs and/or arms. The other dancer will move through the 'holes' in the shape using small movements then grow into a big shape with empty space. Now the first dancer moves through the second dancer's shape with little movements. Keep taking turns being the big shape and the little dancer. Try to make the transitions from moving little to making the big shape smooth, using the image of growing and shrinking. Try to keep moving until you freeze in a shape."

15. **TOGETHER/APART:** "Dance through space using big and small movements. When I give the signal, find a partner and dance together. Dance away finding new ways to move big and little. Now find two or three friends to dance with. Hold hands and come close together and then move away. Can you move together and away without letting go of hands? Dance away. Now find five or six friends to dance with. Try coming together and moving apart in new ways without letting go. Dance away. Now, I want the whole class to come together. Come in close and stretch out into a big circle. Do that a new way. Try it again. Now let the circle burst open and dance away with big movements."

16. **PROPS:** Use props with any of the explorations above or try these ideas:
   STRETCHYBANDS -- make big and little shapes and movements, use with "Seven Jumps," have friends move through shapes.
   PLASTIC -- move with it spread wide, crumple it up and dance small, hide it when you dance little and show it when you dance big.
   BALLOONS -- hold the balloon and dance little with it, then bat the balloon with big movements. Try holding the balloon using big movements and then batting with little movements.
   STREAMERS -- do large movements with a streamer, then small movements.

17. **ACTIVITY SONGS:** Check the "Activity Music List" for songs that explore SIZE to use with 2–7 year olds.

SHAPING

1. **ADD-A-PART:** "Put your hand somewhere and freeze it. Keep it there while you put your head somewhere and freeze. Add a knee to the shape. Add an arm, a leg, your tongue. Hold it. Now shake it out." Try adding different body parts and watch the shapes grow!

2. **SCULPTOR AND CLAY:** "Find a partner. Mold your partner into a big shape. Remember to move your partner gently and to provide a good base of support for your statue. You could start with your partner lying down, sitting or standing. Create an interesting statue by using the movement elements of direction, level and shape. When you are finished, let your partner mold you into a big statue. Then each of you sculpt the other into an interesting little statue." Show the statues if time allows.

3. **SHAPE MUSEUM:** "Half of you will make a big or little shape in a perfect spot. The other half will dance around the statues. If you want to copy a big shape, you must form a small, contracted version of that big shape. Then the big shape will be free to dance big or little through space until it copies another shape. If you copy a little shape, you must form a big, expanded version of that shape. Remember, big is not the same as high and little does not mean low. Think of expanding and contracting." Less experienced dancers can simply copy the big or little shape exactly, then when they are copied and become free, they can dance big or little to another shape.

4. **NEGATIVE SPACE:** "Find a partner. One of you will make a big shape with lots of negative (empty) space. The other person will fill the negative space with a little shape. Change roles. Try different levels. Try moving smoothly from shape to shape." Try this in trios, small and large groups.

5. **MACHINES:** "We are going to make a small machine. When you connect on to the next person in the machine, connect in a shape that is close to another shape. Make your machine movement small. Can you make a small sound? Now let's try a big machine. Make a big shape and connect to another person. Stretch as far away from that person as you can while staying connected. Make a big machine movement and a big sound. Let's compare the two machines. What could they be doing?" Try a machine that combines big and little shapes, movements and sounds.

6. **BALLOON SHAPES:** "Blow yourself up into a big shape. Now, that shape has a small leak. Shrink slowly to a little shape." Try many different shapes, on different levels, blowing and popping with different speeds.

7. **MAGNETS:** "Make a shape with all your body parts far apart. Think of your stomach as a big magnet. Let your stomach pull all your body parts close together until you are curled into a small shape. Now let the walls be big magnets and let them pull all your body parts out into a big stretched shape again." Try this on different levels, pulling in different directions. Have a hand be the magnet and all the body parts pull and curl around the hand. Then the magnet can travel to the foot and the body parts stretch away from the foot and then contract around the foot. This takes a lot of control and is appropriate for more experienced dancers.

8. **PROPS:** Use many different props with the explorations above or make big and little shapes with, under and over props. Ask dancers (one, two or three at a time) to make big and little shapes under a large piece of material or sheet. Have the other dancers try to copy the shape without seeing it. Try to guess whether the shape under the material is big or little. Remove the material and see how well they guessed.

9. **SHAPE CHAIN:** "One person will make a big shape, now the next dancer connects on with a little shape, the third dancer with a big shape, the fourth dancer with a little shape, etc. until we have a chain of shapes across the room." Encourage the dancers to connect on with different body parts, to use different levels and directions.

INSTRUMENTS

1. **LOUD AND SOFT:** "When the music is loud, play loudly and dance with big movements. When the music is soft, play softly and dance with little movements." Also try the opposite.

2. **FAR AND NEAR:** "Play and dance. Then put your instrument down and dance far away from your instrument. Dance back to your instrument and dance with your instrument. Now put your instrument down and dance near to your instrument." Keep alternating near and far.

3. **BIGLAND/LITTLELAND:** Half of the room is Bigland, the other half is Littleland. Travel from one to the other, changing the volume of your instrument and size of your movement. Use benches, cones or spots to mark the boundary.

4. **GROWING:** "As the volume of the song increases, increase the size of your movement and the volume of your instrument. Then decrease the volume and let your movement shrink." You could increase the volume of a song or simply use a hand signal for growing and shrinking.

DEVELOPING SKILLS

1. **LOCOMOTOR MOVEMENTS:** Practice locomotor movements with big and little strides. Review the "Locomotor Movement" chapters for ideas. Try big walks alternating with small walks, big and little jumps, skips, gallops, etc.

2. **NONLOCOMOTOR MOVEMENTS:** Explore nonlocomotor movements using far and near reach. Most nonlocomotor movements can be done both ways but their quality changes. Try a big and little punch, swing, twist, bend, etc. Discuss how an action becomes bigger or smaller.

3. **LUNGE:** A big step becomes a lunge because you must bend your forward leg as you step on it. This is a nice way to introduce lunges. Your front leg is bent and bearing your weight. The back leg is straight. Your body is leaning forward over the front leg. The back is straight. You can do a lunge in any direction. See the "Locomotor Movement" chapter for more information on the lunge.

4. **TIPTOE:** When you tiptoe (or relevé on both feet) you usually bring the legs closer together and take smaller steps. A nice combination for big and little is to do two lunges and four tiptoe steps, alternating.

5. **OBJECTS:** Do locomotor movements with big strides to an object (cone, spot, desk, etc.), do small steps around the object, do medium sized steps away from the object. Repeat. Practice a particular step or try several different steps.

6. **GROWING AND SHRINKING:** Practice a locomotor and/or nonlocomotor movement moving from near reach to far reach and back to near reach. Practice going from far reach to near to far reach.

7. **TOGETHER/APART:** Start far away from each other moving with big movements. As the dancers come closer together, let the movements become smaller. As they return to their places, let the movement expand. Reverse the process. This can be done in pairs, trios, small or large groups.

8. **DANCE STEPS:** With experienced dancers, practice combined locomotor movements discussed in the "Locomotor Movement" chapter.

TURNING

1. **BIG/LITTLE:** Explore many different turns big and little. Ask the dancers for ideas. Have dancers try each other's ideas. Try different sized turns in self space and general space. Try turns growing and shrinking. Try turns that burst and pop. Try big and little turns on different levels. Try big and little turns fast and slow. (It is easier to do big turns slowly and little turns quickly -- discuss this.) Try using big and little arm movements.

2. **OPEN/CLOSE:** Practice turning through general space (chaîné turn) while opening and closing your arms, changing from a wide to narrow shape. This might help you turn.

3. **LEAP TURNS:** If you increase your speed and really open wide when doing the turn described above, you will be doing a leap turn. You move from wide (leap) to narrow (step and turn). You are moving in a sideways direction.

4. **BARREL TURNS:** Do the above turn but add an upward direction on the wide, opening leap and a downward direction on the narrow, closing step turn.

COMBINING MOVEMENTS

1. **SENTENCE:** Choose words from the movement chart that have a feeling of size such as flick (little), slash (big), walk (medium), leap (big). Put these together into a movement phrase and perform.

2. **WORD CARDS:** Choose five to seven nonlocomotor and locomotor word cards. Put them together into a movement phrase and practice it a few times. Now, add word cards that have big, little and medium written on them to designate the size of the actions, perform the new phrase and discuss the differences. For example: "run, jump, turn, swing, melt" might change to "SMALL run, BIG jump, BIG turn, MEDIUM swing, SMALL melt."

3. **CINQUAIN:** Ask the dancers to write a cinquain, together in groups or individually, about SIZE. Read the poem as the dancers move.

SIZE
Big, little
Leaping, flicking, lunging
We grow and shrink
RANGE

4. **STEPS AND ACTIONS:** Create a combination alternating big steps through general space and little actions in self space. Try the reverse. "4 lunges, 8 flicks, 4 lunges, 8 flicks." "8 tiptoe steps, 4 stretches, 8 tiptoe steps, 4 stretches."

114

5. **THREES:** Create a combination of three big movements, three small movements and three big movements. The movements could be directed by you or the dancers or they could be free, improvised movements. "Jump, slash, leap -- flick, hop, poke -- stretch, fall, jump." "Big, big, big -- small, small, small -- big, big, big." Why not try "big, small, big -- small, big, small -- big, small, big" for more experienced dancers!

6. **LOOBY LOO:** Do the dance "Looby Loo" but instead of putting a body part into the circle, put in a big or little shape. "I put a big shape in. I put a big shape out. I give my big shape a shake, shake, shake and turn it all about." Try practicing different locomotor movements on the chorus "Here we go looby loo."

7. **GROWING:** Use a familiar combination and ask the dancers to increase the size of all the steps. How big can they make the movements? Then have them do the same combination with small movements. How small can they do the combination? Discuss the difficulties and feelings.

8. **OBJECTS:** With young children, use objects such as benches, spots and cones in different combinations: gallop with big movements to the spot, flick on the spot, turn in a medium shape away from the spot. Repeat several times.

9. **ACTIVITY SONGS:** Choose a song from the "Activity Music List" that will help 2-7 year olds explore SIZE.

LEAPING

1. **BIG RUNS:** "A leap is a run that is so big it takes off from the ground so that both feet are in the air. You take off from one foot, both feet are in the air and then you land on the other foot. Try increasing the size of your running until you are leaping."

2. **CARTONS:** "Leap over two or more milk or egg cartons placed next to each other, so that your legs are stretched far apart. Leap over one carton so that your legs can be close together." Create a leaping course starting with one carton, running space, two cartons in length, running space, three cartons and then reverse down to one carton, etc. The dancer's leaps can grow bigger and bigger and then shrink.

3. **SPOTS:** Dancers do big and little leaps until they reach a little spot where they make a little shape. On a big spot they make a big shape.

4. **ARMS:** "Stretch your arms wide when you leap wide, make a narrow arm shape when you do a little leap. Now, try narrow arms and wide legs and wide arms and narrow legs!"

5. **NEAR AND FAR:** Place about six cartons or spots near each other on one side of the room about two to four feet apart, depending on the length of your students' legs. Perhaps, two feet for ages 2 - 3, three feet for ages 4 - 7, four feet for ages 8 - adult. On the other side, place two cartons far apart. The dancers can do six small continuous leaps over the cartons near to each other and two big leaps with runs in between over the cartons far apart.

6. **EMPTY SPACE:** Practice leaps over empty space. Try different combinations such as leaps without runs, three runs and leap, two runs and leap, step and leap. Discuss the size of the leaps.

116

FREE DANCING/IMPROVISATION

Choose an activity from "Exploring the Concept" that is not too directed or try adapting an activity from "Combining Movements" or "Choreographing."

CHOREOGRAPHING

1. **ABA:** Individuals, pairs, trios or small groups create a big/little/big dance or a little/big/little dance. Ask the dancers in the "audience" to guess the order of the elements and name other elements they saw in the dance.

2. **WORD CARDS:** Create a dance in small groups using a phrase made by combining actions with the elements of size as in #2 from "Combining Movements." The dancers need to decide how they will create transitions from one action to another, whether they want recorded music or will create their own sounds, a beginning and ending shape, how they will use the stage space, etc. Each audience member should make one positive comment about the dances, if time allows.

3. **GIANTS AND ELVES:** Groups create a story dance based on the Giant and Elf exploration. Talk about setting a scene (where, when, what, who and how) before sending the dancers off to work together.

4. **FAR AND NEAR:** Use the images of far and near, growing and shrinking, expanding and contracting, or gathering and scattering to create a dance.

5. **EXPLOSIONS:** Create a dance using the whole group. Use the imagery of a star exploding -- tight mass moving closely together; explosion; little particles bursting far apart and continuing to dance.

6. **MOTIFS:** Have the group create a simple movement motif. Then let them change the size of the movement -- increasing and decreasing the movement and putting this into some kind of form, perhaps a canon.

7. **MOLECULES:** Create a dance based on a solid (bodies close together), changing into a liquid (bodies farther apart), changing into a gas (bodies very far apart). One group could be the molecules and the other group could be the agent that causes the molecules to change from a solid to liquid to gas. The dance could also move from a gas to a solid. For example, one group could do a dance about a volcano which goes from a solid to liquid to gas and then perhaps back to liquid and solid. Another could do a dance about a glacier melting because of the sun heating it. The ice turns to water and then steam and then when the sun leaves, the water turns back into ice.

8. **PROPS:** Use props in any of the previous dances.

9. **VOLUME:** Create a dance based on size and music volume. Try different combinations such as: loud and big/soft and small, loud and small/soft and big. Discuss how the dancers and the audience felt with each variation.

10. **CINQUAIN:** Have pairs or groups create their own cinquain about SIZE.

11. **SUITE:** Use the suite form to create a dance about size. The first section is medium speed (what size?), the second section is slow speed (what size?), the third section is fast speed (what size?). Each group will make different choices.

LESSON ON SIZE

Ages: 4, 5, 6, 7, or 8   *Length: 30 minutes**

WARMING UP

Dance Exercises/Technique: Do rhyming exercises emphasizing the concept of SIZE.

Introducing the Concept: SIZE: big, medium, little; near reach and far reach. See, say and do the words.

EXPLORING THE CONCEPT

Exploring the Concept: "Balloons" #1
Dancers grow and shrink like balloons on different levels and with different speeds. Music: "Celestial Soda Pop" - *Deep Breakfast.*

Shaping: "Sculptor and Clay" #2
Partners mold each other into big and little shapes or upper and lower case letters. Music: "Gentle Sea" - *Movin'.*

DEVELOPING SKILLS

Developing Skills: "Lunge" #3 and "Tiptoe" #4
Practice lunging and tiptoeing then do a combination of two lunges and four tiptoes, repeating. Music: "Funky Penguin" - *Movin'.*

Leaping: "Cartons" #2
Leap over milk cartons set up in narrow and wide configurations. Music: "Rakes of Mallow" - *Rhythmically Moving 2.*

CREATING

Free Dancing/Improvisation: Exploring the Concept "Finger-Body-Finger" #7
Do a dance with your little finger, gradually add more body parts until your whole body is dancing, then subtract body parts until just your little finger is dancing. Music: "Brian Boru's March" - *James Galway's Greatest Hits.*

*For a 60 minute lesson: Do 15 minutes of dance exercises, add an activity from Instruments, do Alignment after Instruments, do an activity from Combining Movements after Developing Skills and do a Goodbye Dance for Cooling Down.

LESSON ON SIZE

Ages: 9-Adult   *Length: 30-60 minutes*

WARMING UP

Dance Exercises/Technique: For a 60 minute class do 20 minutes of exercises emphasizing the concept of SIZE.

Introducing the Concept: SIZE: big, medium, little; near reach and far reach. See, say and do the words.

EXPLORING THE CONCEPT

Exploring the Concept: "Shrinking Space" #6
For a 30 minute lesson use this exploration as a warm-up activity. Music: "Slow and Fast" - *Feel of Music.*

Shaping: "Shape Museum" #3 and "Negative Space" #4
Do shape museum but instead of copying the shape, the dancer makes a big shape around a little shape or a little shape within a big shape. Then the original statue comes alive and moves to relate to a new statue in the same fashion. Music: "Another Country" - *Dreams of Children.*

DEVELOPING SKILLS

Turning: "Open and Close" #2
Practice turning through space while opening and closing your arms. Music: "Turning" - *Turning: Turning Back.*

CREATING

Choreographing: "ABA" #1
Give each group three movement word cards. They put the words in an order and then decide in what size they want to dance each word. For example: skip big - crawl little - leap big; turn little - jump big - poke little. More experienced dancers can be encouraged to do more difficult movements. For a 30 minute class, decide on the words together and let the dancers improvise the movement.

COOLING DOWN

Sharing/Evaluating Choreography: For a 30 minute class, let half the class show and then the other half. Briefly discuss the dances. For a 60 minute class, let each group show their study and then discuss each group's dance.

CHAPTER 12

DIRECTION
Forward, Backward
Right Side, Left Side, Up, Down

INTRODUCING THE CONCEPT

"Today we will explore moving in different DIRECTIONS. There are six directions: forward, backward, right side, left side, up and down. When you move forward what part of the body leads you through space? (Front surface.) When you move backward what leads you through space? (Back surface.) When you move sideways what leads you through space? (Right side leads you right and left side leads you left.) When you move up what body part leads? (Usually the head or top surface.) When moving down what part leads?

"Let's try moving forward through space. When we get to the other side of the room, do we have to stop moving forward? No, if we remember that our front leads us forward we can continuously move through space in a forward direction. Walls can't stop us. We simply turn away and let our front lead us to a new place in the room. (Young dancers often confuse body direction with room direction. When you say move forward, they may move to the front of the room and stop.) Let's try moving backward. Remember to look behind you as you move so that you can find the empty spaces to move into." Continue on with sideways and up/down.

DIAGONAL: Students often think of diagonal as a separate direction. However, diagonals in the body involve the use of three directions simultaneously: up/side/forward, down/side/forward, up/side/back, down/side/back. The diagonal begins in the center of the body and stretches out through fingers and toes. Your body does not make an X because that is a flat, two-dimensional shape. Diagonals create three dimensional shapes because the body stretches in three directions. They can be done with the right side, left side, upper and/or lower body. The term "diagonal" can be introduced to and explored with ages six through adult. Diagonals in space, moving through space from corner to corner, can be explored in the chapter on pathways and introduced at the age of four or five.

BODY PLANES: There are three body planes. The vertical plane, sometimes known as the frontal plane, is often described as the "door plane" and includes the directions up/down and right/left. The sagittal plane is called the "wheel plane" and includes the directions up/down and forward/backward. The horizontal plane is described as the "table plane" and includes the directions right/left and forward/backward. The concept of planes is rather abstract for young children. It is best to explore this element with experienced dancers.

EXPLORING THE CONCEPT

1. **MOVE AND STOP:** "Dance in a direction until you hear the music stop (or my signal). When the music stops, freeze in a shape pointing in the direction in which you were moving. If you were dancing backward, your shape should be reaching back. When the music begins again move in a different direction. Try to dance in each of the six directions." More experienced dancers can combine directions or mix them up. Their shapes should reflect two or more directions, also.

2. **MAGIC STRINGS:** "I am going to tie invisible strings to all your body parts. When the music starts, I will call out a body part and a direction. The string attached to that part will magically pull you through space in the direction I named." You will need to demonstrate being "pulled" through space. "Here we go! Your stomach string is pulling you forward ... your back string is pulling you backwards -- watch where you're going. Your hand strings are pulling you forward ... backward ... to the right ... to the left ... up ... down. Your knee strings are pulling you forward ... your heel strings are pulling you backward ... your toe strings are pulling you forward ... sideways ... backward ... up ... down." Continue in this fashion. You may want to have a discussion after this exploration about which body parts can move in many directions and which can move in only one or two. For example, the arms and legs can move in all directions because they have joints which allow them to rotate. The chest and buttocks can only move in one direction because they are fixed body parts.

3. **STRETCHES:** "Stretch your arms forward, now move forward to a new spot. Stretch one of your legs forward and move forward to another spot. Now, stretch as many body parts as you can

forward and move forward to a new spot. Stretch your body parts forward and move backward. How does this feel?" It usually feels better (more coordinated and balanced) to move in the opposite direction from which you are stretching. "Try stretching to the right and moving right. Now, stretch right and move left. Remember when you are stretching sideways your body parts must come from the sides of your body. Don't turn sideways and stretch parts from the front of your body. (A common error.) Try stretching forward and moving sideways ... stretching up and moving down ... stretching down and moving sideways." Try many different combinations.

4. **16 COUNTS:** "Find a partner. One of you will travel through general space in a designated direction for 16 counts and return to your partner on count 16. The other dancer will stretch different body parts in the designated direction for 16 counts. On count 16, pairs should be in a connected shape reaching in the designated direction. The next time you will change roles (self and general space) and I will change counts and directions. Here we go -- 16 counts backwards. (Count to 16.) Remember to change places now. 12 counts sideways. (Count to 12.) Change places. 24 counts up and down." Continue on in this way.

Young dancers can do this without a partner. Specify self or general space along with the counts and direction. More experienced dancers can combine three directions -- 20 counts forward, side and down. They will move, changing directions at will.

5. **MAGNETS:** "Find a partner. Imagine your hands are magnets. If you are the leader you will 'push or pull' your partner through space in different directions. Do not touch your partner. Let the magnetic force be strong between you. Move slowly at first so that your partner can follow you. Remember the six different directions. When I give you the signal, change leadership." When the dancers become adept at sensing each other, encourage them to vary their speed, range of movement and locomotor movements. When working with very young children, the teacher can be the magnet and the whole class can follow him or her.

6. **TRAFFIC COP:** "Find a partner. One of you will be the traffic cop. (With very young dancers the teacher can be the traffic cop.) Make a shape that points strongly in a certain direction. You can use many different body parts to indicate the different direction. Don't use your voice. Be clear in your movements. Your partner will copy your shape and then move around the room in the direction you indicate. When your partner returns to you, he or she will make a new directional shape for you to copy and then you can move through general space." Instead of holding a shape, the dancers could do movement in their self spaces that indicates a direction, while their partners move through general space in that direction. Experienced dancers can make a shape that indicates two or three directions. Then the partner must move in all those directions through space! This activity helps dancers to enlarge their movement vocabulary and to clarify their shapes.

7. **MIRRORING:** "Find a partner and face each other. (Or follow the teacher.) The leader will move slowly in self space reaching in different directions with different body parts. Your partner will mirror your movements. When the music becomes faster (or you give the signal) the leader will travel through general space in different directions and your partner will continue to mirror your movements. Remember, leaders, you must always face your partner as you move in different directions. Change leadership on my signal."

8. **SHADOWING:** "Find a partner. If you are the leader you will dance through general space, changing direction as you move. Your partner will shadow your movements. Be careful when you

move backwards not to step on your partner, who should be right behind you. When the music stops, form a shape with your partner reaching in a direction. When the music begins again your partner will become the leader and you will be the follower." Repeat.

9. **PARTNERS:** "Find a partner. Make a forward shape with your partner, now a backward shape ... sideways shape ... up shape and down shape. Now, dance away from your partner any way you want to. Return to your partner (or a new one) and begin the shapes again ... forward, backward, sideways, up and down. Dance away." Repeat. Encourage dancers to move smoothly from one shape to another and to dance in different directions through space.

10. **BACK TO BACK:** "Make a shape with your partner, back to back. Now, dance forward away from your partner. Dance forward toward your partner and make a shape front to front. Dance backwards away from your partner. Dance sideways toward your partner, make a side to side shape and dance away leading with the other side. Come towards your partner moving up -- rising, make a shape reaching up with your partner and dance away sinking." Next, ask the dancers to move toward each other in opposite directions and form opposing shapes -- forward/backward, right/left, up/down. This activity is for experienced dancers.

11. **STEERING:** "Find a partner. If you are the driver you will stand behind your partner with your hands on his/her hips. Carefully steer your partner in different directions through general space. Cars should close their eyes and tell the drivers in what direction they are moving. Remember the speed limit. Move slowly." This exploration requires trust and cooperation. After practice, the dancers can speed up a little and work toward moving their partners smoothly and quickly through space while changing direction.

12. **PROPS:**
PLASTIC/SCARVES - - "Make a shape with the plastic in front of you, now dance forward moving the plastic in front of you." Repeat in other directions.
SPOTS -- "Move forward to a new spot, dance backward to another spot, slide sideways to a spot far away, move down to the next spot, slowly dance up to a spot you haven't been to."

STREAMERS -- "Put the streamers in front of you and move backwards, put them behind you and move forwards, put them to the left of you and move right, to the right and move left. Hold one in each hand and move side to side. Stretch them above your head and melt down. Hold them in your toes and jump up." Continue with variations.

STRETCHYBANDS -- "Make a shape stretching the band in front of you, to the side, back, up, down. Now try two directions - forward and back, up and down, right and left, forward and left, up and back. After making your shape move in a direction with your band."

BALLOONS -- "Jump up with your balloon, roll down, stretch in different directions holding on to it, hold it with your feet and stretch up while lying down, bat it in front and behind you, toss it from your left hand, over your head to your right hand. Try batting it with different body parts while moving in different directions. Hold it in different directions and dance through space in different directions."

13. **ACTIVITY SONGS:** Check the "Activity Music List" for songs to use with 2-7 year olds that help explore moving in different directions.

14. **DIAGONALS:** "If we combine three directions we will create a diagonal shape. Stretch your right arm up, back and side. Do you feel the diagonal pull? Now, stretch your left leg down, forward and side. Add your right diagonal arm and you have a strong diagonal shape from your toes to fingertips. Try moving through space feeling a strong diagonal pull. Do the same with the left arm and right leg. Now try a different diagonal -- right arm up, forward and side and left leg down, back and side. Do this with the left arm and right leg. Try this diagonal -- right arm down, forward and side and left leg up, backward and side. How many other diagonal shapes can you create? How can you move these diagonal shapes through space while maintaining the diagonal pulls? Share your ideas with others." Try diagonals in the whole body and with body halves.

15. **VERTICAL PLANE:** "Make a big X shape, stretching right and left and up and down. Move this shape from side to side and up and down. Feel as though you were a solid door or pressed between two panes of glass, one in front of you and one behind you. Begin to explore different arm, leg and head movements that you can do while remaining in this plane such as reaching and bending, tipping and rocking, small circular movements, poking, jumping, sliding. Remember you can only move up/ down and right/left."

16. **SAGITTAL PLANE:** "Remember, this is the 'wheel plane.' It helps to keep that image in your mind or you can use the idea of panes of glass on each side of you. You can only move up/down and forward/back. What kinds of movement can you do in this plane? Perhaps, galloping forward and backward; swinging forward and backward with body parts and then the whole body; many different locomotor movements forward and backward; arm circles which grow larger and lead the body through space forward or backward. Explore some movements and share them with others."

17. **HORIZONTAL PLANE:** "This is perhaps the most difficult to experience. The whole body cannot move on a horizontal plane at one time unless you are being held by someone or lying on a table or flat surface. You might think about cross sections of the body and move only your arms in the horizontal plane or as many body parts as possible. Think about being pressed between two panes of glass above you and below you. Remember to move forward/backward and right/left. Using arms, legs, pelvis or torso do movements that feel as though you are 'wiping a table top.' How many body parts can you move in the horizontal plane at once?"

18. **COMBINED PLANES:** Circling movements work well for combining planes. "Do a circling arm movement which leads the body through general space in the sagittal plane, add a head circle in the vertical plane and change to a circling arm movement in the horizontal plane while still moving the legs in a sagittal plane. Explore movements moving in a figure eight that travel through the three planes. What other movements can be done in two or three planes simultaneously? Share your ideas with others."

Moving in more than one plane makes the dance movement exciting and alive. The movement becomes three dimensional. Encourage your students to think about planes as they choreograph. Use the planes to help your students increase their movement potential.

SHAPING

1. **BODY PARTS:** "Form a shape with all your body parts reaching forward. Try a different forward shape. Another forward shape...backward...sideways...up and down. Think carefully about your shapes. If you are lying on your side but your arms and legs are reaching out of the front of your body, this is a forward shape, not a sideways shape. To make a sideways shape your arms and legs need to reach out of the sides of your body. Your right arm and leg can stretch right while your left arm and leg stretch left. (A wide shape.) Both arms and legs can stretch to the left or right. (One side will stretch across the body to reach toward the other side.) Your arms and legs can stretch to the opposite side. (A narrow shape.)"

2. **BODY HALF:** "Make a shape with the top half of your body parts moving forward and the bottom half moving backward. Now reverse -- top half backward and bottom half forward. Try left half forward and right half backward. Now reverse -- left half backward and right half forward. Try half up and half down, half right and half left." Try several different shapes using all the different body half combinations. This is an excellent coordination exercise. After body halves, work with quarters -- right arm and left leg forward, left arm and right leg backward (opposition).

3. **ADD-A-PART:** "Make a shape with one body part stretching forward, one down and one backward. Try that using three different body parts. Add a fourth body part reaching sideways. Add a fifth part reaching up. Add a sixth body part reaching to the other side. Remember you can use your fingers, eyeballs, hips, head .... Now, shake your shape out and we will try another shape." Continue in this manner asking dancers to add parts in specific directions.

4. **PARTNERS:** "Find a partner. Make a forward shape together. You can face each other or connect in another way as long as your body parts are reaching forward. Try a connected backward shape ... sideways ... up ... down. Now try opposing shapes. One of you will create a backward shape, the other will connect on in a forward shape. You may use different levels. Try an up/down shape and a right/left shape. Now find a smooth way of moving from one shape to the other with your partner."

5. **SCULPTOR AND CLAY:** "Find a partner. Mold your partner into a statue that we could give a directional title to such as 'backward.' Make your statue interesting by using different body parts and curved, straight and angular lines. When you are finished, your partner will mold you into a different directional statue. Remember to mold each other gently and to always have a strong base of support. Your clay can start on any level." Later you can ask the dancers to work in two or three directions.

6. **GROUP SCULPTOR AND CLAY:** "Half of the class will find a perfect spot and stand, sit or lie down. The other half will dance around the statues continually molding the statues' body parts in different directions. The statues will always be changing, sort of like the scarecrow in The Wizard of Oz. After you mold a body part in a direction, dance in that direction to a new statue."

7. **SHAPE MUSEUM:** "Half (or a quarter) of the class find a perfect spot in the room. Each of you will make a shape pointing in a direction. The other half (or quarter) will dance around the shapes. Copy one of the shapes exactly and hold that shape until someone copies you. When someone copies you, you will dance around the statues but you MUST dance in the direction that your statue was pointing. If you were in a backward shape, you must dance backward to a new statue. Perhaps that statue will be in a sideways shape. You will copy it, hold the shape until someone copies you, then dance sideways to a new statue." If you have a large class, half can do the shape museum while the other half watches. Then reverse roles.

8. **MIRRORING:** "Find a partner (or mirror the teacher/leader). Move slowly from one directional shape to another. Try to use all the directions. When you hear the signal, change leadership. Next time try moving in two directions at once but keep your movement clear. You can use just two body parts or your whole body."

9. **YOGA SHAPES:** "Try this yoga shape (bee, bird, tree, etc.). In what directions are your body parts pointing? Are they stretching in one or more directions? Name them. Let's try another shape." You might ask dancers to create their own shapes and give them a name (like the yoga shapes). Then let the other dancers try to copy the shapes. Talk about the directions used in each shape.

INSTRUMENTS

1. **LEADING:** "Place your instrument in front of you and move forward. Now put your instrument behind you and move backward as you play. Change direction every time I give you the signal."

2. **OPPOSITES:** "Place your instrument in a direction and move in the opposite direction. Play your instrument in front of you and dance backward. Play your instrument behind you and move forward. Play your instrument on your left side and move to the right. Play your instrument above your head and move down."

3. **MIRROR:** "Mirror your partner's (or a leader's) rhythm and direction."

4. **SHADOW:** "Shadow your partner through space. Try to copy your partner's rhythm, movement and direction."

DEVELOPING SKILLS

1. **LOCOMOTOR:** "Can you walk forward, backward -- watch where you are going, sideways right, left, stretching up, down? Try running in all those directions." Practice each of the locomotor movements. Hopping, galloping and skipping are difficult to do backward and sideways but possible. See the "Locomotor Movement" chapter for more ideas.

2. **NONLOCOMOTOR:** "In what directions can you poke your arms ... bend ... stretch ... glide ... push ... twist ... swing? (all directions) Show me the same actions with your legs." Explore all the nonlocomotor movements with different body parts in different directions. See the "Nonlocomotor Movement" chapter for more ideas.

3. **SLIDING:** Sliding is galloping sideways, which makes it the one locomotor movement that naturally moves in a sideways direction. This is an excellent locomotor skill to practice when exploring directions. It is also an excellent skill for developing both sides of the body. Most people have a dominant leg, just like their dominant hand. When galloping or leaping their dominant leg leads. When practicing sliding, work in both left and right directions and you will force the non-dominant leg to get exercise and take the lead. This will help when skipping because both legs take turns leading with this movement.

Have dancers hold both hands, facing stomach to stomach, with a partner and slide across the room and then return. Strong 6/8 music will help with the rhythm of a slide. Encourage different arm movements when sliding alone. Add size, level and speed, etc.

4. **RUNNING BACK:** Practice moving in a backward direction smoothly. Increase the speed from walking to running.

5. **JUMPING:** Practice a combination of jumps that move forward, backward, side left, side right. Repeat several times increasing range or speed. Add some special arms.

6. **FANCY SKIP:** Instead of bringing both knees forward and up in alternation, the dancer brings one knee forward and up then stretches the other leg back and down. The same leg always goes

forward and the other goes back. After the dancers understand the movement, change legs. Add arm movements that reach forward with the front leg and stretch backward with the back leg.

7. **ARMS:** Practice arm movements that work in opposition to the leg movements -- when the right leg moves forward, the left arm moves forward. Practice arm movements that swing forward and back or side to side. These work well with skipping, galloping and sliding movements. Practice arm movements that poke, slash, carve, push, stretch, and glide in different directions while doing different locomotor movements.

8. **GRAPEVINE:** The grapevine is a common step used in folk dances. The step moves sideways in this fashion -- right foot side, left foot back, right foot side, left foot front (side, back, side, front, side, back, side, front). The legs move sideways to the right or to the left while the upper body remains facing front, thus the hips twist and the step has a twisty, viney quality, hence the name grapevine.

I have found a simple way to teach this step using direction. Moving in a sideways direction the dancers take two steps forward and two steps backward (always continuing in the same sideways direction, right or left). "Forward, forward, backward, backward, forward, forward, backward, backward. Keep the chest facing front and your hips will twist right and left." Soon the dancers' feet are moving side, back, side, front naturally.

9. **FALLS:** More experienced dancers can practice falls in different directions. See On The Count of One for descriptions on the front fall, side fall, back fall and split fall.

10. **PLANES:** Practice different locomotor and nonlocomotor movements moving in only one plane, then in multiple planes.

TURNING

1. **RIGHT AND LEFT:** Practice many different turns moving right and then left.

2. **QUICK CHANGE:** Practice a turn that moves right two steps then left two steps, right two, left two. The dancers will have to bend their knees when they stop, in order to change directions quickly.

3. **ARMS:** Change familiar turns into new ones by adding arms that move in different directions (up and down, in and out, forward and backward, side and forward). Try turns with arms frozen in different directions.

4. **SPIRAL TURNS:** Practice turns that spiral up and down or that change levels as you turn.

5. **FORWARD AND BACKWARD:** Practice turns that move forward through space or that turn in toward the center of the body. Practice turns that move backward in space or that turn away from the center of the body.

COMBINING MOVEMENTS

1. **FOLK DANCES:** Many folk dances move in a variety of directions. My favorites include Mayim, Te Ve Orez (Tea and Rice), Pljeskavac, Ve'David, and Virginia Reel. These dances travel in multiple directions. Teach the authentic version or adapt the movements to fit your students' level of experience.

2. **LOOBY LOO:** When moving around the circle on "Here we go looby loo," specify certain movements in different directions such as walk backwards, slide sideways, jump up and down, hop forward.

3. **CINQUAIN:** Create a cinquain. The dancers could help by making suggestions for different words. Read the cinquain as the dancers do the movements.

Directions
Forward, backward
Sliding, jumping, rolling
We travel many ways
Directions

4. **WORD CARDS:** Choose cards with words that travel in different directions - slide (side), gallop (forward), melt (down), leap (up), pull (back). Put them into a logical sequence and perform.

5. **SEQUENCE:** Choose any word cards, put them into a logical sequence, then add direction cards -- run, turn, shake, stretch, freeze. Run (backwards), turn (down), shake (sideways), stretch (forward), freeze (up).

6. **ADVANCE/RETREAT:** Create a combination of movements that advance (move forward) and retreat (move backwards). Perhaps: creep forward 8 counts, jump up 2 counts, run backwards 8 counts, curl into a shape 6 counts. Repeat.

7. **ZIGZAGS:** Create a combination that travels side to side in a zigzag pathway. Perhaps: slide right 4 counts, stretch right 4 counts, slide left 4 counts, stretch left 4 counts. Repeat. Have the dancers add special arm movements.

8. **RISE/SINK:** Create a combination that rises (up) and sinks (down). Perhaps: stretch up 8 counts, turn 4 counts, melt 4 counts, roll 8 counts. Repeat. Have dancers add arms or create their own combination. Combine this with the "Advance/Retreat" combination for experienced dancers.

9. **ACTIVITY SONGS:** For ages 2-7, choose a song from the "Activity Music List." Numbers 1-5 above are also good activities for this age.

LEAPING

1. **ARMS:** "When you leap over the cartons, stretch your arms in a different direction with each leap -- forward, backward, sideways, up and down."

2. **BENCH:** "Leap over the cartons moving your arms in a different direction. When you reach the bench (or line) travel across it in a specific direction. Then continue leaping and make a special directional shape on the spot."

3. **DIAGONALS:** "Leap over the cartons from one corner to another, travel in a specific direction across the end of the room to the other corner and continue leaping to the opposite corner. Get back in line to begin again. You will be moving in a figure 8. Change your travelling movement and direction when you start again."

4. **PARTNERS:** "You and your partner will leap together over the cartons placed down the middle of the room. When you reach the end, split up and find a way to travel up the sides of the room back to the beginning of the leaping line. Change your direction each time you dance back to the line. You may mirror your partner or dance differently."

5. **SIDEWAYS/BACKWARD:** "Try leaps to the side. You must step across with one leg and leap with the other. If traveling sideways right you step across with the left leg and leap with the right leg. Try leaps moving backward (difficult but possible).

6. **CONES:** "Leap over the cartons (or spots) reaching your arms in different directions. When you come to a cone move backwards (or sideways) until you reach the next cone, then turn around and continue leaping."

7. **PROPS:** Have dancers hold scarves, streamers or plastic in each hand. As they leap over the cones they stretch the prop in different directions.

8. **EMPTY SPACE:** Experienced dancers can do all of the above activities without the use of objects to leap over.

FREE DANCING/IMPROVISATION

Choose an activity under "Exploring the Concept" that is not too directed. Also, any activity under "Combining Movements" could become a structured improvisation.

CHOREOGRAPHING

1. **WORD CARDS:** Assign 5 word cards to pairs or small groups and have them create their own dance focusing on changing directions.

2. **ABA:** Work with solos, pairs, trios or groups. Dancers create a dance using only two directions - up/down/up, forward/backward/forward or side/front/side, etc. Sometimes it is fun to assign each group a different combination and have the audience guess the words. Sometimes it is interesting to assign each group the same words and discuss the differences between each dance.

3. **ABACAD:** Have the dancers choose 4 directions, a main one and three secondary ones. The dancers create a dance such as side/backward/side/up/side/forward. They return to their main theme in between each new section.

4. **THREES:** Dancers choose three words from the following list: advance, retreat, rise, sink, open and close. They create a dance using their three words in any order (advance, open, sink). The audience will try to guess the three words and talk about the feelings evoked by the combination of the three words. This can be done in solos, pairs, trios, groups.

5. **TRAFFIC COP:** Dances can be created in pairs or groups using the "Traffic Cop" idea from "Exploring the Concept." The traffic cop is the choreographer, moving his or her group in different directions. The dancers must follow the choreographer's lead. This could be structured improvisation or a set piece.

6. **FLOCKING:** Divide the class into three or four groups. Each group should decide on an order within their group. The groups themselves should have an order and place themselves in the corners

of the room. The first leader, from the first group, moves to the center of the room with a rhythmical and simple step and freezes in a shape. The rest of the first group copies the leader's steps in unison and makes his or her shape. The group remains frozen while group two moves in a similar way with a different step and shape. As group three takes its turn, group one slowly melts backward to their corner. As group four moves, group two melts backwards. As group one begins again with a new leader, group three melts and so on until all dancers have had a chance to be leader of their group. This may be structured improvisation or each group could set their movements. Encourage use of different levels, speed, size and most of all, directions.

7. **ENTER/EXIT:** Dancers can work in pairs or groups. They enter the stage area in a certain direction, move on the stage in a direction and exit in a third direction. Pairs could come from opposite sides. Groups could work in canon. Stress variation and use of stage space and time. Anything is possible. Discuss what has the most impact and what works the best. This can be done with young dancers as a chance dance. Each dancer is given three different direction words such as side, back, down (or forward, up, backward, etc.) and is asked to create a solo. One word is used for the entrance, the second word is used to move around on "stage," the third word serves as the exit, e.g., enter sideways, dance backward and exit down. Have five to six dancers perform their solos simultaneously and watch for magic moments.

8. **FEELINGS:** Assign different groups tasks and have them create a dance to perform for each other. Tasks might include: group dances down all the time; group dances up; group advances and retreats always facing the audience; group uses only sideways movement always facing the audience; group advances and retreats with back always to audience; group dances with all body parts reaching

down except for one which reaches up; group does the opposite of last idea. There could be many more tasks along this line. Each dance will make a strong statement. Discuss the results and have the dancers express their feelings while watching these dances. When would a choreographer want to use certain directions? What do certain directions say to the audience? Which ones are strong? Which ones are weak?

9. **DIRECTION BOOGIE:** Divide the group into trios. Each dancer in the trio chooses a level (high, medium or low) and independently creates a dance phrase that moves forward, backward, side, side, up, down on the chosen level. Decide whether each movement will take one count, six counts, four counts, etc. Once the phrases are set, the dancers form their trios and perform their phrases moving in different directions on different levels. Let the dancers discover relationships as they move together and expand on these. Also experiment with time. This dance could be worked on for several weeks adding different dance elements as they are explored.

10. **CINQUAINS:** Have the dancers create their own cinquains using directional vocabulary. Their poems could be about diagonals, planes or the simple directions. Let them choose how the poems will be verbalized -- by the teacher, one dancer, several dancers, all the dancers, etc.

LESSON ON DIRECTION

Ages: 3, 4, 5, 6, 7, or 8   *Length: 60 minutes**

WARMING-UP

Dance Exercises/Technique: Do rhyming exercises standing and sitting.

Introducing the Concept: DIRECTION: forward, backward, right side, left side, up, down. See, say and do the words.

EXPLORING THE CONCEPT

Exploring the Concept: "Magic Strings" #2
Invisible strings attached to different body parts pull you through space in different directions. Music: "Pause" - *Movin'*.

Shaping: "Partners" #4 - variation
With your partner make a forward shape, backward shape, up shape, down shape and side shape then dance away from your partner in a sideways direction. Return to partner and try a new set of directed shapes. Dance away from partner in the direction of the last shape. Keep the same partner with ages 3-5, change partners with ages 6-8. Music: "Another Country" - *Dreams of Children*.

Instruments: "Leading" #1
Put instrument in front of you and move forward while you play. Put instrument in back and move backward as you play, etc. Music: "Homemade Band" - *Homemade Band.*

COOL DOWN

Relaxation/Alignment: Dancers rest as teacher manipulates body parts. Music: "Midnight Moon" - *Movin'* or any lullaby/quiet song.

DEVELOPING SKILLS

Developing Skills: "Sliding" #3 or "Grapevine" #8
Practice sliding right and left with ages 3-5. Add an interesting arm movement for 5 year olds or let them create their own arm movements. Practice the grapevine step with ages 6-8. Try it in lines then in a circle formation. Music: "Funky Penguin" - *Movin'*.

Combining Movements: "Folk Dances" #1
For ages 3-5, do a simple version of Mayim from Israel - slide left 8 counts, slide right 8 counts, go forward 8 counts, go backward 8 counts, jump up and down 4 counts, turn right in self space 8 counts, turn left 8 counts. This can be done in a circle or scattered formation. Older children can do the real Mayim - grapevine left 16 counts, forward 4 counts with arms lifting up, backward 4 counts with arms going down (like a wave, Mayim means "water"), repeat forward and backward, run left four small steps, hop on the right foot in place as the left toe touches forward and side 8 counts, repeat on the left foot (hands can clap in front as the toe touches front). Repeat the entire dance until music ends. Music: "Mayim" - *Rhythmically Moving Series.*

Leaping: "Cones" #6
Leap over cartons, move backward or sideways between cones (or spots). Music: "Blackberry Quadrille" - *Rhythmically Moving 2.*

CREATING

Free Dancing/Improvising: Exploring the Concept "Props" #12
Put your prop (streamer, scarf, plastic) in different directions and then dance in those directions. Name different directions during the music for ages 3-5; ages 6-8 can think of their own directions. Music: "Beautiful Day" - *Jump Children.*

* For a 30 minute lesson: Exclude Shaping, Instruments, Relaxation and Leaping.

LESSON ON DIRECTION

Ages: 9-Adult   *Length: 30-60 minutes*

WARMING UP

Warm-up Activity: For a 30 minute lesson do Exploring the Concept "Move and Stop" #1. Play a variety of world music and have the dancers change direction when the music changes. Encourage use of other elements as well as Direction. Music: selections from *Music from Distant Corners of the World.*

Dance Exercises/Technique: For a 60 minute lesson do Warm-up Activity and 15-20 minutes of exercises. Remember to emphasize the concept of DIRECTION as you perform each exercise.

Introducing the Concept: DIRECTION: forward, backward, right side, left side, up, down. See, say and do the words.

EXPLORING THE CONCEPT

Exploring the Concept: "Back to Back" #10
Dancers form shapes together and then travel through space in different directions. Encourage the dancers to use different arm movements as they travel through space. Music: "Word from the Village" - *Dreams of Children.*

DEVELOPING SKILLS

Developing Skills: "Fancy Skip" #6
Practice this skip in lines across the floor or in a scattered formation. Focus on the different directions that the legs, arms and head move in. Music: "Brian Boru's March" - *James Galway's Greatest Hits.*

CREATING

Choreographing: "Threes" #4
Ask each dancer to choose three direction words and create his or her own short dance phrase. For a 60 minute class, have three to six dancers perform their solos simultaneously. For a 30 minute class, divide the class in half and have each half show their dances.

COOLING DOWN

Sharing/Evaluating Choreography: Watch for the magic moments created by chance and discuss the words chosen and the elements used by the performers.

CHAPTER 13

PATHWAY
Straight, Curved, Zigzag

INTRODUCING THE CONCEPT

"When you walk in wet sand or snow what do you create with your feet? Yes, footprints that form a path. In dance we make PATHWAYS with our feet and our whole body. We move through general space in different pathways and we can create pathways in the air in self space with different body parts. If you painted your feet red and walked around the room, what kinds or shapes of pathways could your red footprints make on the floor? Yes, you could move in a STRAIGHT line or pathway. You could create CURVED, circular lines or pathways. You could move in sharp, angular or ZIGZAG lines or pathways. Let's explore moving in different PATHWAYS more fully."

EXPLORING THE CONCEPT

1. **PAINTING:** "Put 'paint' on your hands in a color that you would like to use for drawing straight lines. In your self space draw straight lines in front of you, behind you, up high, down low, to the sides. Now put paint on your nose. Draw straight pathways in different directions with your nose. Can you draw little straight pathways ... big straight pathways? Can you draw straight pathways with your elbows quickly ... slowly? Let's try other body parts (knees, shoulders, head, legs, arms, wrists, toes, torso, pelvis, feet, etc.). Put paint on your whole body. Let's travel through space in straight pathways. How many different ways can you move through space in a straight pathway? (Change levels, directions, speed, force, size, locomotor movements.)" Do this same exploration with curvy pathways and zigzag pathways. Remember to change the color of paint for each type of pathway. Dancers can choose their own color or the class can choose a color.

2. **MUSIC:** "Listen to the music. If the music makes you feel like moving in curved pathways, dance that way. If the music makes you feel like dancing in straight pathways, show me movement in straight pathways. If the music moves you to dance in zigzag pathways, do that. I will play short sections of music. Dance in your special pathways when the music plays. Freeze in a special shape when the music stops between selections. You will not all react to the music the same way. Everyone has different feelings. Remember to use the other dance elements you have explored to make your movement more interesting. Change levels, direction, size, speed, force, etc."

3. **PICTURES:** "I am going to hold up a piece of paper with a design on it. (Draw simple line designs made of curved, straight and zigzag lines.) I want you to draw that design through space with your whole body. Look at the color I used for the design. Paint your body that color and think of the space as a huge piece of paper. If the design uses curved lines you will dance in curved pathways. Draw curved pathways on the floor and in the air with your body. When the music stops, freeze in a shape you see in the design. Then I will hold up a new design. Look at that, paint your body a new color and draw the new design through space using pathways from the new picture." Continue with several different types of straight, curved and zigzag designs. Music that complements the different pathways will help support the dancing.

4. **DRAWING:** "I am going to give you a piece of paper. Pick three different colored pens (or crayons). Pick a color for zigzags, a color for curves and a color for straight lines. On a third of your paper (fold the paper for young dancers), let your hand dance curvy on the paper. You will create a curved design. Don't draw a picture. Just let your pen move in curved pathways on the paper. Now pick up the pen you chose for straight lines. Draw straight pathways on the paper -- up, down, right, left, corner to corner, little, big. Now pick up your last pen and draw zigzag pathways. The designs may look like mountains, lightning, monster teeth, crowns. Now, turn your paper over and make a big design, covering the whole paper, that has all the pathways combined. Use your three different colors to create three different pathways connected and overlapping. Put your pens away and pick up your paper. Look at your curved design. Dance that design through space. When the music ends,

freeze in a shape from your design. We will dance each pathway design separately and then we will dance the combined pathway design. Remember to use your whole body and different body parts and to use the elements of dance. If your design goes from high to low so should you. If your design has little and big lines so should you move little and big." Music that has straight, curvy and zigzag qualities will help support the dancers.

5. **STRING:** "I am going to give each of you a piece of string four feet long. Take your string and make a straight pathway on the floor. Can you jump in a straight pathway along the string? Can you move backwards in a straight pathway ... move slowly and quickly ... take big steps and little steps ... do strong movements and light movements ... do high movements and low movements ... tiptoe ... float ... slash ... roll along the string in a straight pathway? Now, create a curved pathway with your string. (Some very young dancers may need a little assistance.) Your pathway does not have to look like your neighbor's pathway. You could make a circle, spiral, the letter C or S -- anything with curves. Let's try some dancing on this pathway. Can you skip ... hop ... turn ... glide backwards ... move sharply and smoothly? (Continue with many different challenges.) Can you make a zigzag pathway with your string? Make the letter Z, or mountains, sharp teeth, a crown -- anything with angles. How can you dance in a zigzag pathway? Can you poke ... punch ... float ... slide ... gallop ... leap ... stretch high and low ... swing forward and backward ... advance and retreat? Try creating two pathways with your string -- half curved and half straight or half zigzag and half curved." You may need a longer string. You can use yarn, rope, draw with chalk on the floor or sidewalk or put tape on the floor. If you dance in a gymnasium with lines on the floor you can use those but an individual prop is more fun!

6. **PAINTERS:** "Find a partner. One of you will be a painter and the other the paint. If you are the painter use your arm as a huge brush. Paint pathways in the space in front of you. In the beginning make the pathways simple. Choose curved, straight or zigzag -- don't mix them up. I will put a few examples on the board but you can make up your own. As you paint your pathway in space your partner, the paint, will follow your pathway using his or her whole body to create your pathway. After each design has been 'painted,' change roles. As you become better at painting the pathways, create more complex designs. Mix the pathways up so that you use two or three different pathways in a design." Instead of following the painter simultaneously, the "paint" can watch the design, try to remember it and then recreate the design when the painter is finished. This is for more experienced dancers or as a follow-up exploration.

7. **NAMES:** "Think of your whole body being a huge pen or crayon. Write your name through space. Think of the pathways you use for the letters in your name. You can use printed or cursive writing. Some letters are made up of only curves, some only straight lines and some only zigzag lines. Many letters are made up of two types of lines. Your name dance will probably use several different pathways. It will probably change levels because letters are different sizes and levels. It may change qualities because some letters are smooth and some sharp. You may choose to write just your first name or your whole name. Remember to try to use your whole body, not just your feet or arms." A variation would be to use different body parts to write the name. Spelling words, phone numbers and vocabulary words can be used instead of names.

8. **SHADOWING:** "Find a partner. (This can also be done in trios.) If you are the leader choose a pathway and dance through general space in that pathway. Your partner will follow your movements and pathway. When the music stops, freeze together in a connected shape describing the pathway you were using. If you were dancing in a curved pathway, freeze in a curved shape. When the music begins again the follower becomes the leader and dances in a different pathway."

9. **SOUNDS:** "I am going to make three different sounds. Each sound represents a different pathway. 'SSSHHHHHHH' is a straight pathway. 'ZIP! ZIP! ZIP!'" is a zigzag pathway. 'WHOOOOO, WHOOOO, WHOOOO' is a curved pathway. When you hear a sound, dance any way you want to in that pathway. When you hear that same sound again, try dancing in a different way in that pathway." Ask for other sound ideas and choose dancers to be the sound makers.

10. **INSTRUMENT SOUNDS:** Choose three instruments to represent the three pathways -- for example: gong or cymbal -- straight, shaker or slide whistle -- curved, rhythm sticks or castanet -- zigzag. "When you hear the cymbal move in a straight pathway. Keep moving until you hear the shaker, then change to a curved pathway. When you hear the rhythm sticks, move in a zigzag pathway. Try to change your movement while moving in the designated pathways."

11. **BACK TO BACK:** "Find a partner. Stand back to back. I will call out three shapes. Make those shapes with your partner, facing any direction. Hold the last shape. When I give the signal to dance away you must dance in the pathway suggested by your last shape. It might go like this -- 'Curved (you make a curved shape with your partner), straight (straight shape), zigzag (zigzag shape), dance away (dance in a zigzag pathway), back to back (find your partner or a new one and stand back to back).' We will continue in this way until the music ends. Remember to change levels, directions, size, speed and force as you dance in the different pathways."

12. **BODY HALF:** "Can you make a curved pathway on the floor with your feet while you make a straight pathway in the air with your arms? The top and bottom halves of your body will be moving differently. Try to be very clear with your pathways. Can you make a straight pathway on the floor while making a zigzag pathway in the air? Try a zigzag pathway on the floor and a curved pathway in the air." Try other combinations. Holding up line designs can be helpful and fun. Right and left body halves can be challenging. Turn the designs vertically for left and right halves.

Top body half

Bottom body half

140

13. **CONES AND SPOTS:** Set up either traffic cones or spots in a scattered formation in the room. Of course, you can always use both at the same time. "I know you have all done dot-to-dot pictures. I want you to draw lines from one cone or spot to another. Think of different ways of dancing in straight pathways from one 'dot' to the next. Use different directions and levels. Use different body parts in ways that will reinforce the idea of straight pathways. Now, try zigzag pathways between the dots. Think of what kind of picture you are creating. It should be different from the straight pathway picture. The lines should zigzag back and forth. Use your body to reinforce the concept of zigzag pathways. Now think of a maze. Draw curved lines around the cones or spots, never touching them. Use your body to reinforce the concept of curved pathways."

14. **MAGICIAN AND ZOMBIE:** "Find a partner. One of you will come forward and pick a piece of plastic (streamer or scarf). You will be the magician. Your partner will be the zombie (robot). The magician will move the plastic in many different ways. Move it in straight pathways up and down and side to side. Shake it in zigzag pathways. Swirl it in curved pathways. The zombie will react to the plastic and move the way the plastic makes him or her feel like moving. The magician may move in self or general space but must always face the zombie. Try to make the zombie change levels, size and speed as she/he moves in different pathways. When I give the signal, change roles." This is a wonderful exercise in focus and concentration and works well with inexperienced or older dancers who may be inhibited. They are able to focus on an object instead of a person.

15. **OBSTACLE COURSE:** Create an obstacle course using anything you have at hand -- cones, spots, benches, chairs, desks, ropes, milk cartons, stretchybands between cones, etc. "Dance any way you want to through the obstacle course. Use different pathways and different movements. Go over, under, around, through and between the obstacles. Change your way of dancing around the obstacles each time you meet them. In other words, don't always go under the bench, try over and around. Change your pathways. Use the elements of dance to make your pathway obstacle dance interesting."

16. **PROPS:** Use them in the activities above or try:
STREAMERS/SCARVES/PLASTIC -- Trace the pathways on the floor. Use them for paint brushes in "Painters." Move them in the air in different pathways.
STRETCHYBANDS -- Form curved, straight and angular shapes. Travel in different pathways with them.
BALLOONS -- Hold them and move in curved pathways. Bat them in zigzag pathways. Roll or kick them in straight pathways.

17. **CIRCLES:** "Dance around the room in different pathways. When I give the signal, form a small circle with two or three other dancers and move together in the circle -- in and out, around, swaying side to side, etc. Then dance away again by yourself. Next time come together in a circle of five or six. Move together in a circular pathway. Dance away." Continue until the whole class forms a circle and moves together. This is great for parent/toddler classes and a good way for any class to get to know each other.

18. **ACTIVITY SONGS:** Check the "Activity Music List" for songs to use with 2-7 year olds. Although the songs may not mention pathways directly, they focus on traveling through space. You can direct the dancers to move in different pathways as the songs play.

SHAPING

1. **THREE SHAPES:** "Can you make a curved shape? Can you move that curved shape in a curved pathway? Try moving a straight shape in a straight pathway. Can you make a zigzag shape and move it in a zigzag pathway? Let's try those three types of shapes again but make them different and change your way of dancing them in their pathways. Now let's try dancing a straight shape in a curved pathway. How does that feel? How does that look? Try a zigzag shape in a straight pathway? Does that feel and look different from a zigzag shape in a zigzag pathway? Try dancing a curved shape in a zigzag pathway." Continue on in this way trying different combinations of shape and pathway and discussing the results.

2. **BODY PARTS:** "Take your arm and draw a curved pathway in the air. Let your body follow your arm. Freeze when I give the signal. Did you end in a curved shape? Take your elbow and draw a zigzag pathway in the air. Freeze. Are you in a zigzag shape? Take your leg and draw a straight pathway in the air. Freeze. Are you in a straight shape? Let's use other body parts to help us create different shapes that are curved, straight and zigzag."

3. **PICTURES:** "Look at this design. It is curved. Can you make a curved shape like this design? It does not have to look like the design exactly but try to capture the feeling. Try making a shape based on this zigzag design ... this straight design." Continue in this way. You can make designs on paper or on the blackboard. The dancers can create designs for each other or you can bring in reproductions of famous works of art.

4. **STRING:** "Take a piece of string (4 feet long) and throw it up in the air. Look at the shape the string landed in on the floor. Can you make a shape with your body like the shape of the string on the floor? Now, make your own design with the string and copy it with a body shape. Is it curved, straight or zigzag? Alternate tossing the string up and copying it and designing your own shape and copying it." Ask dancers to move around and copy other dancers' string shapes.

5. **BODY HALF:** "Can you make a curvy shape with the lower half of your body and a straight shape with the top half? Can you make a straight shape with the lower half and a zigzag shape with the top half ... curved shape with the top half and zigzag shape with the lower half?" Try many combinations.

6. **LEVELS:** "Can you make a curved shape on a high level ... move in a curved pathway to a medium level where you make a zigzag shape ... move in a zigzag pathway to a low level where you make a straight shape ... move in a straight pathway to a high level where you make a zigzag shape ... move in a zigzag pathway to a low level where you make a curved shape ... move in a curvy pathway to a medium level where you make a straight shape?" Continue on mixing up levels, pathways and shapes.

7. **SPOTS:** "Make a curved shape on your spot. Dance in a curved pathway to a new spot. Shake out your shape and make a straight shape. Dance in that shape in a straight pathway to a new spot. Shake out your shape and make a zigzag shape. Dance in a zigzag pathway to a new spot and make a curved shape on a different level." Continue in this way encouraging use of size, level, direction, speed and force.

8. **GROUP SCULPTOR AND CLAY:** "Half of the room will stand in empty spaces. The other half will dance around the statues in curved pathways while sculpting the statues into curved shapes. Sculpt one body part and then move on to another statue. Curve around the statues as you do the sculpting. When the music stops, stand back and view the curved statues you created. Remember to mold your statues gently. Now, move back and forth between the statues in straight or zigzag pathways molding the statues into straight or zigzag shapes. Stand back and view your artistry. Did you feel differently when you were moving and molding curved and straight/zigzag? How did the sculptors feel and how did the statues feel? What were some differences? What feelings did the different statues convey when you viewed them?" Be sure to change roles.

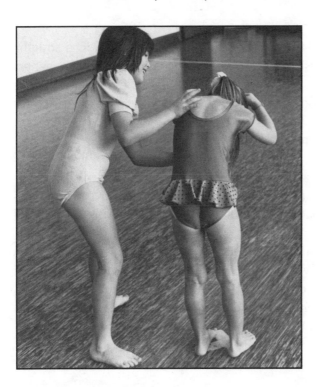

9. **SHAPE CHAIN:** "Connect to one another in straight shapes forming a straight line across the space. Connect to one another in curved shapes forming a circle in the space. Connect to one another in zigzag shapes forming a zigzag line through the space." If you have a large class they can combine pathways forming a line that is straight, zigzagged and then curved.

10. **SHAPE MUSEUM:** Half the class will form statues. Choose a curved, zigzagged or straight shape. Choose different levels. The other half will dance around the statues. If you are a curved statue and you are copied by a dancer, then you will become free and dance in curved pathways until you copy a statue. The type of shape that you copy will determine the kind of pathway you will dance in when you become free. Remember to hold your shape until someone copies you. Dance in curved pathways around the statues and in straight and zigzag pathways between the statues."

11. **MACHINES:** This activity can be done in small or large groups. "Connect on to another shape, forming a curved, zigzag or straight shape. Move one body part drawing curved, zigzag or straight pathways in the air. When I turn on the sound, make a sound that reinforces your pathway -- a curved, straight or zigzag sound. If you are in the audience look for the different pathways and listen to the different sounds."

12. **PAIRS:** "Stand a little bit apart. Now reach toward each other and join your shapes together with a straight line body position. Perhaps a straight leg stretches to touch a straight arm. Freeze so that the two of you create a straight statue. Connect together with a curved line. Then try a zigzag line. Now find new ways of connecting with those three lines or combine lines."

13. **PROPS:** Add streamers, stretchybands or Chinese jump ropes to the activities above to create even more visual pathway shapes.

INSTRUMENTS

1. **MUSIC:** "When you hear the marching (4/4 meter) music, play and move in a straight pathway. When you hear the waltz (3/4 meter) music, play and move in a curved pathway. When you hear polka (2/4 meter) music, play and move in a zigzag pathway." "Lead the Band" from *Play Your Instruments and Make a Pretty Sound* is a good selection for this.

2. **CONES:** "Move around or between the cones in different pathways as you play."

3. **FREEZE:** "Play your instrument and move in a curved pathway. When the music stops, freeze in a curved shape. Now play and move in a zigzag pathway. Freeze. Now play and move in a straight pathway." Instead of pausing the music, change pathways on different musical phrases.

4. **TAKE TURNS:** "When I play the cymbals, all the dancers with cymbals play and move in a straight pathway while the others freeze in a shape. When I play the sticks, all the dancers with sticks play and move in a zigzag pathway. When I play the shakers, all the dancers with shakers play and move in a curved pathway. Now all the dancers will play and move together in their pathways." Alternate sounds for short times so the dancers do not have to freeze for too long.

DEVELOPING SKILLS

1. **LOCOMOTOR MOVEMENTS:** Practice the locomotor movements in different pathways. Point out that when moving in a straight pathway the most natural body position is one that is vertical. If you want to move with ease in a curved pathway, your body needs to curve in the direction you are moving. When curving or circling left, your body should curve or lean left. When moving with ease in a zigzag pathway, your body needs to make sudden shifts from left to right, right to left, forward to backward or backward to forward. This is most easily accomplished if you stay grounded, using bent knees, which allows you to shift weight. See the "Locomotor Movement" chapter for more ways to practice movements in different pathways.

2. **NONLOCOMOTOR MOVEMENTS:** Practice doing nonlocomotor movements in self space. Certain movements draw certain pathways in the air. Carving, twisting, turning, swinging create curved pathways in self space. Pushing, pulling, stretching, slashing, gliding, punching create straight pathways. Poking, flicking, dabbing, dodging, bending, shaking create zigzag pathways in self space. Some people may disagree, but this is how I like to view these movements. Discuss with the dancers their impressions. When you take the nonlocomotor movements through general space, the easiest pathway to move in is a straight pathway. Even turning is most easily accomplished in a straight line across the floor. However, you should practice these nonlocomotor movements through general space in all pathways.

3. **SLIDING:** Practice zigzag slides. Slide eight times forward left, then eight times forward right across the floor. Next, try four slides left and four slides right, then two slides left and two slides right. Encourage the dancers to bend their knees in order to shift weight quickly from left to right. Try one slide right and one left repeatedly. This is the Soupy Sales Shuffle.

4. **GALLOPING/POLKA:** Practice four gallops with the right foot leading and then four gallops with the left foot leading repeatedly. Encourage the dancers to lean slightly right and left to help with the weight shift. Next, try two gallops with the right foot and two gallops with the left foot. Practice doing this turning to the right or left. This is the POLKA. Practice holding both hands with a partner. The reason the polka can seem so difficult is because you are doing three pathways simultaneously. You are moving in a zigzag pathway because of the constant shift of weight from left to right. You are turning (curved pathway) while moving in a straight (or curved) pathway down the floor. However, if the polka is explored through pathways instead of steps, the dancers learn it more quickly and easily.

5. **RIVER RUN:** Practice running like a river -- smoothly and in a curved pathway. The arms are by your sides, not stiff, but controlled. I use the image of invisible arms. The body must curve or lean right and left in whatever direction the pathway curves. Keep the knees bent and body relaxed. This will allow you to run very quickly but smoothly in a curved pathway. You may add swirls whenever you feel like it.

6. **MARCHING:** Marching is a good step for straight pathways because the accent is always on the same foot (2/4 or 4/4 beat). Practice marching in different directions, with different sized steps and different speeds in straight pathways.

7. **LUNGING:** Lunges (see "Locomotor Movement" chapter) can be practiced in straight pathways by keeping the steps and body surface forward. Lunges can be done in zigzag pathways by rotating the legs and body outward on the diagonal, alternating right and left facings.

8. **WALTZ RUN:** The waltz run (three quick steps -- down, up, up) can be done in any pathway, but lends itself to zigzags because the accent changes from the right foot to the left foot with every three steps (3/4 meter). You would move three steps to the forward right (down, up, up), then three steps to the forward left (down, up, up), then to the right, etc. Rotation of the hip joint outward helps the dancer perform this step in a zigzag pathway.

9. **JUMPS AND HOPS:** Practice these two movements in straight and curved pathways, then try some zigzag combinations -- forward, backward, forward, backward; left, right, left, right; forward, backward, left, right.

10. **STEP HOP:** Practice step hops in straight, curved and zigzagged pathways. A step hop is similar to a skip except that it is even in rhythm (2/4 meter). A skip has uneven rhythm (6/8). A nice step hop combination is: step hop, hop, hop; step hop, hop, hop; step hop, step hop, step hop, step hop. The step hop, hop, hops could be done in a straight pathway while the step hops are done in a zigzag or circular pathway.

11. **SCHOTTISCHE:** The schottische (shotish) is a common folk dance step. It is: step, step, step hop; step, step, step hop; step hop, step hop, step hop, step hop (4/4 time). This step can be done in all pathways, with or without partners.

12. **GALLOP WITH ARMS:** Practice galloping or skipping with the arms swinging forward and backward. The legs/knees move in a zigzag pathway (up and down) while the arms swing in a curved pathway.

13. **FANCY SKIP:** Practice the fancy skip described in "Direction: Developing Skills." Focus on the idea of pathways -- arms trace curved pathways in the air, front leg traces a zigzag pathway and the back leg traces a straight pathway.

TURNING

1. **CHAÎNÉS:** Practice chaînés (she nay) turns in a straight pathway across the floor, in a circular pathway, and a zigzag pathway by shifting weight and changing directions every four turns or so.

2. **COPY CAT:** Let dancers create different turns. Choose several turns to copy and decide in which pathways to do the turns.

3. **LEVELS:** Practice turning across the floor sinking and rising to give the impression of a zigzag pathway in the air.

4. **BARREL TURNS:** Practice barrel turns and leap turns in a circular pathway.

COMBINING MOVEMENTS

1. **WORD CARDS:** Choose six word cards using a combination of locomotor and nonlocomotor movements. Put the words into a logical sequence such as sway, turn, skip, slash, gallop, stretch. Perform the sequence in a straight pathway, a curved pathway and a zigzag pathway. Then divide the sequence in half and choose two pathways to use, perhaps you will do the first half in a curved pathway and the second half in a zigzag pathway. Then divide the sequence into thirds and use all three pathways.

2. **PARTNERS:** Create a simple combination such as slide, run, jump, shape. Have the dancers do the combination in a straight pathway to their partners then do it away from their partners in a curved pathway. Try different combinations of pathways.

3. **ABC:** Create a combination using all three pathways: March 4 counts in a straight pathway, slide right, left, right, left 8 counts in a zigzag pathway, river run 4 counts in a curved pathway. Repeat. Add arm movements. Use the waltz run, polka, schottische and other steps for more complex combinations.

4. **FOLK DANCE:** Many folk dances make use of different pathways. Gustav's Skoal -- straight and curvy; Virginia Reel -- straight, curvy and zigzag; Mayim -- straight and curvy; Greek and Native American dances -- curvy; Ve David -- straight and curvy; Tea and Rice -- straight, curvy and zigzag. There are many others. You can create your own repeating patterns to many folk dances such as zigzag slide 8 counts, turn 8 counts, move any way in a straight pathway 8 counts, run backward to your partner 8 counts, create four shapes with your partner 16 counts, turn away from your partner 8 counts.

5. **PICTURES:** Choose three pathway designs and put them in an order. Create movement for them and perform.

6. **CINQUAIN:** Create a pathway cinquain. Read the words as the dancers perform. Let the dancers create parts of the cinquain for variation.

Pathways
Curved, straight
Swirling, dodging, pushing
Bodies connecting through space
Lines

7. **LINE DESIGN:** Have each dancer draw a line connecting to the previous one on a long piece of paper or the blackboard. Each line should represent a specific pathway. When the line is completed, choose a movement to represent each line sequence. The shape, level, size and pathway of the line should give you an idea for movement. Put the movements together into a combination that follows the order of the line and perform as a group study. If the class is large put dancers into pairs. One can draw the line and the other can choose the movement.

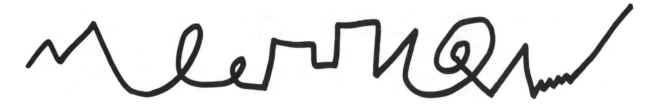

LEAPING

1. **CARTONS:** Create different pathways with the cartons. Remind the dancers about the mechanics of moving in different pathways. Straight bodies for straight pathways, curved bodies for circular pathways and shifting weight for zigzag pathways. Create specific pathways with the cartons.

2. **COMBINATIONS:** Using cartons or spots create a course that combines pathways in different ways.

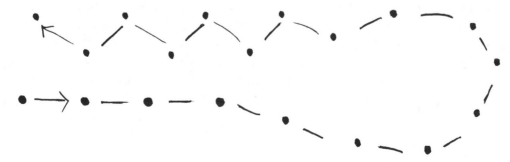

3. **ARMS/LEGS:** Do straight, curved or zigzag arm shapes and movements while leaping through empty space. Try leg shapes that use a bent front leg and straight back leg, straight front leg and bent back leg or both legs bent.

4. **GROUPS:** Divide the class into groups and have them create their own leaping course with cartons and cones and spots. Each group should have the opportunity to try all the courses.

5. **LINES:** Create a circular course with cartons or spots and add a straight section using benches or a line on the floor. Leap in a circular pathway to the line then travel on the line or bench in a straight pathway. End in a curved, straight or zigzag shape on a spot. Instead of a straight pathway, create a zigzag path with the benches or lines.

FREE DANCING/IMPROVISATION

Choose an activity under "Exploring the Concept." There are also several activities under "Combining Movements" and "Choreographing" that would make good improvs for dancers ages 8-adult.

CHOREOGRAPHING

1. **NAMES:** Individual dancers or groups of dancers can create dances based on the pathways created by their names, addresses, phone numbers, names of famous people or places.

2. **ART WORKS:** Bring in reproductions of famous art works. Have groups choose a picture, find the pathways (lines) in the picture and create a dance using the picture as a point of reference.

3. **PICTURES:** Have dancers draw designs or use designs created earlier in class. They can create a dance drawing the designs through space with body parts and the whole body.

4. **LINE TRIOS:** Each trio of dancers creates a design by drawing one type of line on a piece of paper. Each design should have a curved line, a zigzag line and a straight line. The trio creates a dance from that design. All the dancers could do every line. Each dancer could do his or her own line. The lines could be danced simultaneously or one after the other. There are many choices to be made. You could direct the choices or it could be up to the dancers. Remember to encourage the dancers to begin and end in a shape.

5. **GROUP LINES:** Groups of dancers can create line designs and create a dance based on their design.

6. **MOVEMENT MAPS:** Create a movement map. Draw a circle, a square and a triangle in different places on your paper. Connect each shape with a different line -- curved, straight and zigzag. Choose a movement for each shape and a movement for each line. Choose a starting place (one of the shapes) and perform the dance. You will begin and end at the same place. The maps can be more complex by adding more shapes and pathways. You do not have to begin and end at the same place. Several dancers can perform their maps at the same time. You can teach map skills by adding compass directions.

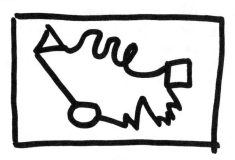 

7. **ABA or ABC:** Create a dance based on two different pathways -- curved/straight/curved or zigzag/curved/zigzag, etc. Or create a dance based on any variation of curved/straight/zigzag.

8. **DIAGRAMS:** Have each dancer draw a diagram using two or three pathways. Let them think of movement to portray their diagram. Sometimes it is fun to trade diagrams with a partner. Your partner may create a dance very different from your dance.

9. **FEELINGS:** Put these three words in an order and create a dance based on them: CONFUSED, DIRECT, MEANDERING. Discuss which pathways were used to portray which words. Could the audience guess the order? Were the movements clear? What pathways should choreographers use to portray certain feelings? Think of other words such as: FRANTIC, WONDERING, CONFIDENT or BASHFUL, AGGRESSIVE, HATEFUL or ECSTATIC, LOVING, BORED.

10. **SOUNDS:** Create movement and your own sounds with mouth, body parts or instruments to accompany your movement. This can be started as an individual improvisation where a dancer chooses one pathway and one sound, then dancers find two other people who have different pathway phrases and sounds and they put together a dance. Or individuals can create three sounds and pathway phrases and they can form groups by chance and set a piece which contains multiple pathways and sounds.

11. **WORDS:** Improvise movements to the words below. Then match pathways to words and create a dance in ABA, ABC or broken form. Some word ideas: giggle, slink, ooze, wiggle, soar, pace, totter, bounce, swirl, wander, shuffle, reel, meander, snatch.

LESSON ON PATHWAY

Ages 5, 6, 7, or 8   *Length: 30 minutes**

WARMING-UP

Dance Exercises/Technique: Do three rhyming exercises sitting and three standing focusing on PATHWAY.

Introducing the Concept: PATHWAY: curved, straight, zigzag. See, say and do the words.

EXPLORING THE CONCEPT

Exploring the Concept: "Drawing" #4
Draw different pathway designs and then dance them. Music: "Enter Sunlight" for curved pathways, "Midnight Moon" for straight pathways, "Tipsy" for zigzag pathways and "Far East Blues" for combined pathways - *Movin'*.

DEVELOPING SKILLS

Developing Skills: "Sliding" #3
Practice sliding in a zigzag pathway.

Turning: "Chaînés" #1
Practice chaînés turns in straight and curved pathways.

Combining Movements: "Folk Dance" #4
Do a simple combination to "Te Ve Orez" (Israeli folk dance): river run for 8 counts, zigzag slide for 8 counts, your own movement in a straight pathway for 8 counts, chainee turn in a curved pathway for 8 counts. Music: "Te Ve Orez" - *Rhythmically Moving 1*.

CREATING

Free Dancing/Improvisation: "Pictures" #3
Hold up designs for the dancers to "draw" through space using different pathways. Music: repeat music from Exploring the Concept.

COOLING DOWN

Visualization: Visualize moving in different pathways as you say the pathway words.

*For a 60 minute lesson: Do 20 minutes of exercises and add Leaping "Cartons" #1.

LESSON ON PATHWAY

Ages: 9-Adult   *Length: 30-60 minutes*

WARMING UP

Dance Exercises/Technique: For a 60 minute lesson do 20 minutes of exercises focusing on PATH-WAY.

Introducing the Concept: PATHWAY: curved, straight, zigzag. See, say and do the words.

EXPLORING THE CONCEPT

Exploring the Concept: "Body Half" #12
Draw straight pathways on the floor with feet while drawing curved pathways in the air with arms. Try other combinations. Music: "Far East Blues" - *Movin'.*

Shaping: "Shape Chain" #9
Form curved shapes in a curved line, straight shapes in a straight line, etc. Music: selections from *Movin'* or *The Essential Jarre.*

DEVELOPING SKILLS

Developing Skills: "Step Hop" #10
Practice step hops in different pathways. Music: "Belfast Hornpipe" - *James Galway's Greatest Hits.*

CREATING

Free Dancing/Improvising: For a 30 minute lesson do Exploring the Concept "Names" #7. Write your name in space using different pathways. Music: "Fisherman's Dream" - *Emerald.*

Choreographing: For a 60 minute lesson do "Line Trios" #4.
Trios draw line designs and choreograph studies based on designs. Music: dancers create sounds to accompany dance or New Age selections.

COOLING DOWN

Sharing/Evaluating Choreography: For a 30 minute lesson have half the class at a time show name improvs. Briefly discuss. For a 60 minute lesson have trios show studies as you hold up designs. Discuss and evaluate.

CHAPTER 14

FOCUS
Single Focus, Multi-focus

INTRODUCING THE CONCEPT

"FOCUS is the concept we are learning today. Focus can mean several things in dance. Focus can be where the dancer is looking. If a dancer is using SINGLE FOCUS, he or she is looking at a single object, person or body part or in a single direction. If a dancer is using MULTI-FOCUS he or she is looking at several objects or people simultaneously or moving his or her focus around the space.

"FOCUS can also be where the audience's attention is directed. A dancer can make the audience focus on a particular body part by accentuating that part or isolating that part. A choreographer can make the audience focus on a certain area of the stage by staging the dancing in that area. In these two cases the audience would have a SINGLE FOCUS. In another instance, the choreographer may stage action in several areas on stage simultaneously or a group of dancers might dance filling the stage with movement. The audience would have multi-focus. FOCUS is a very important concept in dance. How a dancer or choreographer uses FOCUS can support the movement themes or detract from the meaning of the piece."

EXPLORING THE CONCEPT

1. **HOCUS POCUS:** "Hocus Pocus put your elbow on a high level and FOCUS! Now, let your elbow move you through space as you focus on it. Hocus Pocus put your wrist on your stomach and FOCUS! Can you move through space this way? Hocus Pocus put your hand behind your back and FOCUS! Continue to focus on your hand while you move through space." Continue with other challenges.

2. **MAGIC SPOT:** "I am going to give you an invisible magic spot. Throw the spot toward the wall farthest from you. Focus on it, now gallop to the spot. Throw it toward a corner, focus. Dance with big movements to the spot. Throw your spot on the ceiling, focus. Now turn under your spot as you look at it. Throw your spot on to another dancer and focus on your spot. Now dance around as you focus on your spot, which will be moving around the room!" Continue with other challenges by naming places, people and body parts on which to throw the magic spot and different ways of moving to the magic spot.

3. **FIND THE OBJECT:** "I will call out an object in the room. Focus on the object and then dance to it. Make a shape near the object and maintain your focus. Focus on the clock -- gallop to the clock and make a shape. Focus on the window -- move at a low level to the window and make a low shape. Focus on the ceiling -- stretch toward the ceiling." Continue with many objects and even people.

4. **FIND THE COLOR:** Put pieces of colored paper around the room or use the colors already in the room. "Focus on something yellow. Dance to the yellow color and make a special shape showing how you feel about yellow. Find the color blue and focus on it. Move at a low level to the blue color." Continue in this way. Color limited students may have a problem with this activity.

5. **LISTEN AND LOOK:** "Dance around the room (be more structured if necessary). When you hear a drum beat (or some other signal) stop and focus somewhere, focus on a new place for the second drum beat and focus on the drummer for the third beat. Then continue dancing until you hear the drum beat again." Play three sets of drum beats in between the dancing. It is fun for the drummer to move around so that the dancers must find him or her on the third beat.

6. **SHADOWING:** "Stand behind a partner. Focus on your partner and copy his/her movements as you travel behind your partner through space. When the music stops, freeze and focus on each other as you make a connected shape, then change leaders." Give inexperienced dancers lots of suggestions on how to move through space using the elements of dance.

7. **CHANGE LEADERS:** "I will call out a name. Focus on that person and copy his or her movements until I call a new name, then quickly focus on that person and copy his or her movements. Leaders will have to think quickly as will the followers." Change leaders every 15 seconds or so.

8. **BODY PARTS:** "Focus on your hand and let it pull you through space. Focus on your toes ... stomach ... hip ... back ... knees ... wrist. Let the body part you are focusing on pull you through space. Watch where you're going. Try to maintain your focus on the body part I name and use your side vision to avoid collisions."

154

9. **ZOMBIE AND THE MAGICIAN:** "Find a partner. One of you will be a magician and one will be a zombie. You will then change roles. The magician moves a prop (plastic, scarf, streamer) in many different ways in self and/or general space. Zombie, you focus on the prop and move the way the prop directs you. You do not have to look just like the prop, rather let the prop 'tell' you how to move." Change roles. Changing from slow to fast music helps the magician think of new ways of moving the prop.

10. **16 COUNTS:** "Dance away from your partner and back to your partner in 16 counts. Your partner dances in self space for 16 counts while you are dancing in general space. You must both keep your focus on each other the whole 16 counts. Watch out for other dancers. After each set of counts you will change places, so that you alternate moving in self and general space." Try different counts and direct the ways of moving, if necessary.

11. **SHADOW/MIRROR:** "Follow a leader's movements through general space. Focus on your leader's back. When the music changes, face each other and mirror your leader's movements in self space, focusing on your leader's front." Change leaders.

12. **TOGETHER AND APART:** "Dance away from your partner focusing anywhere. On the signal, focus directly at your partner and move toward each other, mirroring your partner's movements. Feel like magnets being drawn together. On the signal, dance away focusing anywhere. On the next signal, focus on each other (you're the leader now) and mirror each other's movements as you move together." Continue, alternating single and multi-focus and leadership.

13. **FOLK DANCE:** Choose a folk dance that has clear musical changes. "Every time the music changes, change your focus and keep that focus, as you dance, until the music changes again. Try focusing on another dancer, an object, in a direction and/or on one of your body parts."

14. **IMAGERY:** "Show me with your body and your focus: someone's chasing you ... a bird high in the sky is showing you how to fly ... you're deep sea diving amongst hundreds of beautiful fish ... a large gorilla is about to sit on you and your legs won't move ... you see your best friend far away ... you're in a haunted house ... you're trying to catch up with your friend ... you're falling down a tunnel ... you're reaching for an apple high in a tree." Let the dancers think of other situations. Remind them to use the elements of dance to make their movement interesting.

15. **PROPS:** Alternate single and multi-focus with props. Bat the balloon as you focus on it, then carry the balloon and move your focus around. Focus on the plastic or scarf as you move it, then move your focus around.

16. **ACTIVITY SONGS:** Choose a song from the "Activity Music List" for ages 2-7. Change focus on the pauses or when the music changes. The songs listed under "Relationships" are also good for focusing on a partner or prop as you dance.

17. **MORE IDEAS:** There are activities from other chapters that can be used for FOCUS such as "Shape Museum" and "Level Boogie." Any activity that requires working with a partner, in a group or using a prop can be used to explore and practice focus.

SHAPING

1. **HOCUS POCUS:** See #1 above. Make focused shapes but don't travel through general space.

2. **MAGIC SPOT:** See #2 above. Make shapes over, under, around, beside, far from, near to, on, off the magic spot.

3. **LISTEN AND LOOK:** "For every drum beat make a shape focusing in a new direction. Your sharp change of focus should create a new shape."

4. **INTERNAL FOCUS:** "Try making shapes with your eyes closed. Is this easier or harder than with your eyes open? Do you know why?"

5. **QUICK SHAPES:** "Change focus and shape very quickly. Try to maintain balance. A strong focus should help. Try big and small shapes, curved and angular, strong and light shapes."

6. **DUETS:** "Find a partner. Focus on each other's knees and make a shape. Focus on elbows and change shape. Try changing focus and shapes slowly and quickly." Continue naming other body parts or focal points.

7. **PROPS:** "Put your prop behind you and focus on it. Put it above you and focus. Put it beside you and focus. How does your shape change?"

8. **MIRROR:** "Find a partner. Make shapes slowly and let your partner copy your shapes. Make shapes quickly and let your partner try to copy the shapes. Now change leadership. Focusing directly on your partner will help you copy his or her shapes."

9. **OTHER IDEAS:** Shaping activities from other chapters that require working with a partner or group can be used to explore FOCUS. For example a "Machine" could be made in which each dancer must focus on another dancer's moving body part. The addition of focus could be added to "Shape Chain," so that each dancer must focus on the connection made to another dancer or all dancers in the line of shapes decide on a similar focus.

INSTRUMENTS

1. **FOLLOW THE LEADER:** "In pairs or short lines, follow a leader dancing and playing the instruments. Focus on the person in front of you." Change leaders often.

2. **PAUSE:** "Play and dance. When the music stops, pause in a shape and focus on your instrument."

3. **FREEZE:** "Play and dance using multi-focus. When the music stops, freeze and focus on the window." Continue naming objects, people, colors or spots on which the dancers can focus.

4. **RHYTHMS:** Play music with different rhythms, sounds or tempos. Change the focus and the way the instrument is played on each change of music.

5. **INTERNAL FOCUS:** "Focus on your instrument as you play and dance. When the music pauses, close your eyes and freeze in a silent shape." Try to vary the length of the pauses.

DEVELOPING SKILLS

1. **LOCOMOTOR MOVEMENTS:** Practice locomotor movements with changes in focus. Discuss what is difficult, strange or easy. "Run and look forward, backward, sideways, up, down, at someone else, at your hand, etc."

2. **NONLOCOMOTOR MOVEMENTS:** Explore focus with nonlocomotor movements. Some movements make you have multi-focus while others cause single focus. Punch, press, glide and dab are direct or single-focused movements. Float, slash, flick and wring are indirect or multi-focused movements. Try these movements and be aware of focus. Try other movements and decide what kind of focus they create.

3. **SINGLE/MULTI-FOCUS:** Alternate focusing directly at something as you move and moving your focus around as you dance. Discuss the difference in how the movement looks and feels.

4. **OBJECTS:** Practice doing locomotor skills to different objects as you focus on them. "Focus on the mirror and gallop to it. Focus on the wall and skip to it."

5. **PARTNERS:** Practice locomotor skills to and from a partner as you focus on him or her.

6. **ECHO:** The leader does four counts of movement, then the partner echos the movement. The dancers are facing and focusing on each other as they alternate moving and watching. Continue on. Try other counts -- 8 counts, 2 counts, etc. Young dancers could echo the teacher.

7. **CANON:** Partners stand one behind the other. The leader does four counts of movement, the partner then copies the four counts while the leader is doing four new counts. The follower is always four counts behind the leader. Remember to do simple movements -- march, jump, punch, clap, walk, etc. Change leaders.

8. **COUNTS:** Practice walking, jumping, hopping, crawling or leaping while changing focus every four counts in 4/4 meter, every two counts in 2/4 meter and every three counts in 3/4 meter.

TURNING

1. **SPOTTING:** Focus on a spot on the wall (a piece of paper or a big face helps younger students). Turn through space toward the spot while trying to keep your eyes on the spot. You can also practice spotting in self space. You look at the spot for as long as you can then whip the head around to focus on the spot again. This is how ballet dancers keep from getting dizzy as they turn.

2. **INTERNAL SPOTTING:** Do not look at a spot and try turning in your self space as quickly as you can. Think about focusing inward as a skater does. A skater spins so quickly he or she cannot focus on a spot, so they focus on nothing.

3. **BODY PARTS:** Practice turning both in self space and general space while focusing on different body parts.

4. **PARTNERS:** Turn toward a partner. Use your partner as your focal point.

COMBINING MOVEMENTS

1. **LOCOMOTOR/NONLOCOMOTOR:** Alternate locomotor movements and single focus with nonlocomotor movements and multi-focus. Walk forward/focus forward, float/focus anywhere, walk backward/focus backward , punch/focus anywhere, etc. The locomotor skill could always be the same and the nonlocomotor skill always different or each movement could be different (run, punch, skip, poke) or you could choose one locomotor and one nonlocomotor skill (skip, swing, skip, swing). Whatever you try, remember to alternate single and multi-focus.

2. **WORD CARDS:** Select 5 word cards and put them together into a combination. Add different focuses to each movement or section of movements. "Turn, float, skip, swirl, fall." Turn/focus on a spot, float/focus all over, skip/focus forward, swirl/focus inward, fall/focus down. The dancers can choose the focus or draw ideas from a hat.

3. **CINQUAIN:** Create a cinquain about focus. Read the poem as the students perform the dance.

Focus
Single, multi
Seeking, hiding, searching
We find, then run
Eyes

4. **FOLK DANCE:** Create a combination to folk dance music. Change the focus on each new section of music. Do a partner folk dance and concentrate on focusing on your partner.

5. **PARTNERS:** Create a combination dancing to and from a partner or switching partners. Concentrate on focusing on your partner or finding a new one quickly.

6. **HAUNTED HOUSE:** Create a combination based on the idea of dancing in a haunted house: creep into the house looking everywhere (multi-focus), hear a noise in the attic (focus up), hear a noise

in the basement (focus down), hear a noise in the next room (focus side), run forward (focus forward), run backward (focus backward), a ghost says "boo" (jump up and fall down in a faint with eyes closed), wake up and begin again! This is but one idea.

7. **ACTIVITY SONGS:** Choose songs from the "Activity Music List" for ages 2-7 that explore focus through working with a partner or a prop or finding objects or changes in the music.

LEAPING

1. **CARTONS:** Leap over cartons and focus out at a wall, not down at the cartons.   Use spots on the wall for a focal point.

2. **PAIRS:** Leap toward a partner, focusing on each other and as you pass each other.

3. **CHANGE:** Change your focus each time you leap -- down, out, up, side, etc.

4. **BODY PARTS:** Focus on a body part as you leap so that you create a special shape in the air.

5. **ARMS:** Practice making special arm shapes or movements as you leap so that your arms become the focal point.

6. **LEGS:** Practice making special leg shapes and movements as you leap so that your legs become the focal point.

FREE DANCING/IMPROVISING

Choose an idea from "Exploring the Concept" that is not too structured. Some ideas from "Combining Movements" and "Choreography" can be used as structured improvisations with older or experienced dancers.

CHOREOGRAPHING

1. **FLOCKING:** See the chapter on "LEVELS." The dancers have to focus on the leader and copy his or her movement.

2. **HAUNTED HOUSE:** Have dancers create a Haunted House dance as described in "Combining Movements" #6. Let them create their own sequence.

3. **PARTNERS:** Pairs or trios create a dance focusing on each other.

4. **PROPS:** Create dances using props. Alternate single and multi-focus.

5. **ABA:** Create a dance based on single focus/multi- focus/single focus or the reverse. Or focus on your hand/a partner/your hand. Or focus on a partner/a prop/a partner, etc.

6. **ABC:** Create a dance with three different focal points -- looking up, looking backward, looking everywhere or looking down, looking side to side, looking at another dancer, etc. Discuss how the different focuses make one feel. Do they connote a certain mood or idea? One idea could bring you on "stage," the next move you around stage and the third pull you off stage.

7. **CINQUAIN:** Have individuals or groups create their own cinquain about focus.

8. **IMPROVISATION:** Let pairs or trios of dancers pull cards out of a hat. Each pair improvises a dance following the directions on the card. The audience tries to guess what the card said and discusses how each dance made them feel. Cards might say: "Dance always focusing down or up." "Dance focusing on each other." "Dance never looking at each other." "Dance focusing on an audience member." "Dance focusing everywhere." "Dance focusing on a body part of your partner." "Dance focusing on one of your body parts." "Dance changing your focus sharply." "Dance making your back the focus of the dance." "Dance making the corner of the room the focal point." These cards could also be given to students to create set pieces instead of improvisation.

9. **OTHER:** Have dancers set pieces using an idea from "Exploring the Concept." Imagery (# 14) is a fun idea on which to build a dance. The audience could guess the situation the dancers chose to describe through dance. Also, any dances using partners such as mirroring, shadowing, back to back, etc. are good for focus.

LESSON ON FOCUS

Ages: 9-Adult   *Length: 30-60 minutes*

WARMING UP

Dance Exercises/Technique: Do 20 minutes of exercises for a 60 minute lesson. Do 5-10 minutes of exercises or a Quick Warm-up Activity for a 30 minute lesson.

Introducing the Concept: FOCUS: single focus, multi-focus. See, say and do the words.

EXPLORING THE CONCEPT

Exploring the Concept: "Shadow/Mirror" #11
Partners focus on each other as they shadow and mirror movements through space. Music: "Inima" - *Solitude.*

Shaping: "Internal Focus" #4
Make shapes with eyes closed. Music: "Pause" - *Movin'.*

DEVELOPING SKILLS

Developing Skills: "Echo" #6
Echo partner's movements. Music: "Echo" - *Rhythmically Moving 1.*

CREATING

Choreographing: For 30 minute class do "Improvisation" #8.
Dancers improvise different focus situations. Music: *Essential Jarre.* For 60 minute class do "ABC" #6. Create dances with three different focal points. Can be done in solos and performed simultaneously or in small groups and performed separately.

COOLING DOWN

Sharing/Evaluating Choreography: Dancers discuss how different focal points make them feel.

LESSON ON FOCUS

Ages: 4, 5, 6, 7, or 8   *Length: 30 minutes**

WARMING UP

Dance Exercises/Technique: Do 5-10 minutes of rhyming exercises emphasizing FOCUS.

Introducing the Concept: FOCUS: single focus and multi-focus. See, say and do the words.

EXPLORING THE CONCEPT

Exploring the Concept: "Magic Spot" #2
Dancers focus on a magic spot as they move around the room. Music: "Children's Dance" - *Windham Hill Sampler 81.*

Shaping: "Hocus Pocus" #1
Make shapes while focusing on different body parts.

DEVELOPING SKILLS

Developing Skills: "Locomotor" #1 and "Nonlocomotor" #2
Practice different skills while changing focus. Music: "Jamaican Holiday" - *Movin'.*

CREATING

Free Dancing/Improvising: Exploring the Concept "Zombie and Magician" #9
Partners make each other move by moving a prop in many different ways. Music: "Slow and Fast" - *Feel of Music.*

COOLING DOWN

Visualizing: Dancers close eyes and use internal focus to visualize a restful spot as they relax muscles.

*For a 60 minute lesson: Do 15 minutes of exercises, add Instrument or Turning activity and Leaping.

CHAPTER 15

SPEED
Slow, Medium, Fast

INTRODUCING THE CONCEPT

"Today we are going to study time. How do you tell time? Yes, a clock or a watch helps you tell time. A clock measures time into seconds, minutes and hours. Time is an important part of dance, also. Every movement you do takes time. We can measure movement just as a clock does. We can move different SPEEDS just as the hands on a clock move different speeds to measure time. We can move fast as the second hand does, medium speed as the minute hand does and slowly as the hour hand does. We can move many different speeds all the way from very fast to very slow."

EXPLORING THE CONCEPT

1. **SLOW MOTION:** "Move in slow motion, very, very slowly ... now fast! fast! fast! sloooooooooooow ... fast fast fast fast fast ... hurry up there is no time to waste ... now slowly, you have all the time in the world ... now fast, hurry, hurry ... and now move at a normal speed any way you want to." Continue alternating fast and slow in this manner.

2. **SLOW/FAST:** "Listen carefully to the music. When it is slow, dance slowly. Try moving in different directions, on different levels, with different size, in self space and general space. When the music changes speed, you change speed. How can you move quickly in new and different ways?"
   After this exploration try the following. "Now we are going to try to move opposite to the music. This may feel odd or difficult, but try it. When the music is fast, move slowly. When the music is slow, move quickly." Discuss the dancers' reactions. As dancers we do not always want to mimic the music. It is as important to learn to move against the speed or rhythm of the music as it is to learn to move with the beat.

3. **BODY PARTS:** "Try moving your hand -- just your hand -- very slowly. Now, move it quickly. Move an arm slowly then quickly. Try moving a leg very slowly, then very quickly." Continue with other body parts at different speeds.

4. **COUNTS:** "Grow bigger and bigger for 16 counts then shrink slowly for 16 counts. Now 8 counts ... 4 counts ... 2 counts ... 1 count! Let's try rising for 16 counts and sinking for 16 counts ... 8 counts ... 4 counts ... 2 counts ... 1 count! Now make up your own simple movement for 16 counts like twisting or stretching or bending or turning. Do that movement in 8 counts, 4 counts, 2 counts and 1 count. Be careful on the 1 count not to move too sharply. Let's try a new movement to counts. Does your movement speed up? Why?" (You have less TIME in which to do your movement.)

5. **16 COUNTS:** "Find a perfect spot. I will count to 16 at a medium speed. Take a step for every count. You can walk, jump, hop, run, float, glide, turn or whatever but you can only move on the count. You must move away from your spot and be back on your spot on count 16. Try to use your arms in an interesting way. Here we go. Remember to take a step for every count. Listen to the speed of my voice." Change the counts and change the speed each time. With large numbers you can count quickly and with small numbers you can count slowly. With large classes, dancers can work in pairs -- one moving in self space while the other moves through general space.

6. **MIRRORING:** "Find a partner (or follow the teacher/leader). When the music is slow, the leader will move slowly in self space and the partner will mirror the leader's movements. When the music is fast, the leader will move quickly and the partner will try to mirror the leader's movements. This will be harder. When the music is slow again, the other dancer will be the leader. When the music is fast, the new leader will move quickly. When the music is slow for the third time both dancers will dance away from each other any way and at any speed they choose." If all the dancers are mirroring one leader they can follow the leader in self space for slow/fast, then general space for slow/fast, then each dance their own way for the third slow section.

7. **SHADOWING:** "Find a partner. Shadow, or follow, your partner's movements through general space slowly. When the music stops make a shape together. When the music begins you will

be the leader for slow dancing. When the music stops, make a shape with your partner. Now follow your partner through general space quickly. Make a shape and then you are the leader for fast dancing. Keep changing leadership and speeds."

8. **SLOWLAND/FASTLAND:** "I am going to divide the room in half. (Use cones, a bench, milk cartons, a line or tape.) This half is Fastland, that half is Slowland. When you are in Fastland you must dance different ways quickly. When you are in Slowland, of course you must dance slowly. You can travel from land to land at any time. If you want to dance medium speed, dance on the border between the two lands!" Play background music without a strong tempo. With young dancers, you might be more directed -- moving together from one land to another.

9. **SELF AND GENERAL:** "Move very slowly through general space. Now freeze in a shape and move that shape in self space as quickly as you can by shaking it or wiggling it. Now move slowly through general space in a different way. Make a new shape and move it quickly in self space. " Do this four to five times then change. "Now move quickly through general space. Make a new shape and move that shape slowly by swaying or twisting it." Continue in this way.

10. **THIRDS:** "I am going to divide the room into three sections or thirds. The first section is for fast dancing, the second for medium speed dancing and the third for slow dancing. Let's all start in the first section ... now move to the medium section. Try many different ways of moving. Let's dance to the third section and explore slow motion dancing. Now, move freely from one section to another changing your speed appropriately for each section. Try to watch other dancers in other sections. Sense how their speed is different from yours. Is it faster or slower?"

11. **FEET:** Cut two big feet out of paper (12 inches), four medium sized feet (6 inches) and eight little feet (3 inches). "I have brought some feet with me today. These two big feet are big slow steps. The four medium sized feet are regular medium steps and the eight little feet are small fast steps. Let's arrange these in an order from big to little. Now, take two big slow steps, four medium sized steps

and eight little fast steps. (Think in terms of half notes, quarter notes and eighth notes.) What can we do besides walking? (Lunge, lunge, jump, jump, jump, jump, run run run run run run run run.) Let's try making up a song. Jump, jump, jump, jump, run a lit-tle, run a lit-tle, slooow dooown." Try new steps and different songs. The dancers will help you!

12. **NOTES:** Prepare pieces of paper before the lesson. You will need four pieces of 9x12 construction paper. Leave one whole. Cut one in half, one in quarters and one in eighths. You may want to write note values on the paper but it is not imperative. "Look at this big piece of paper. This represents a whole note. If we cut this piece of paper in half, what do we have? (2 halves) These two pieces represent two half notes. Two half notes equal one whole note. If we should cut each half note in half, how many pieces will we have? (4) These four pieces are quarter notes. Four quarter notes equal a whole note. If we should cut each quarter note in half, how many pieces would we have? (8) These eight pieces represent eighth notes. There are eight eighth notes to a whole note. (Arrange the pieces in a pyramid with the whole note at the top.) Let's clap these notes starting from the whole note and finishing with the eighth notes. Stretch your clap out for the duration of the whole and half notes. Now let's think of a different movement for each note. What is a slow movement that can take four beats to do? (Stretch, twist, bend, swing, push, lunge, etc.) Now think of a movement for half notes, quarter notes and eighth notes. Instead of clapping let's put these movements together. Stretch 2, 3, 4, push 2, push 2, poke, poke, poke, poke, shake 2, 3, 4, 5, 6, 7, 8." Try other movements and other combinations by rearranging the pieces of paper.

13. **MOVING BEATS:** "Listen to my drum beat (or claps). I am going to beat very slowly. Now I will beat out a medium tempo. Listen to the fast drum beats. Try to move on each beat. I will keep changing speed and you try to follow. When you hear silence, freeze in a shape. Try to change your movement as you follow the tempo. Try to use your arms as well as your feet to keep the beat. Now, I am going to divide the class into thirds. One group will move only on the slow beats, one on the medium beats and one on the fast beats. Each group will need to listen carefully to their tempo or speed. When you hear another group's tempo, freeze in a shape until you hear your tempo again. You may move anywhere in the room but try to stay with your group." The groups may create a special movement for their tempo or they may do any movement. You may give the groups a special pathway or they may move anywhere. With more advanced students, you could play sixteenth notes, eighth notes, quarter notes, half notes and whole notes using five groups instead of three. Instead of beats you could use the sounds: TA (quarter notes), TAKA (eighth notes), TAKADIMI (sixteenth notes) and TAKITA (triplets).

14. **KEEP THE BEAT:** "Everybody will move around the room stepping on each beat of the drum. Try different ways of stepping besides just walking or walk in different directions and with different arm movements. I will beat a medium tempo and say a number like 30. I will start counting, but after I get to ten I will stop counting and drumming. You need to keep moving at the same speed and count silently, then stop when you reach 30. Ready, go! Did you all stop at the same time? Each of us moves at a different rate because our heart beats at different rates. When you play an instrument or dance together, it is important to keep the same beat as your fellow musicians and dancers.
"Let's try again. This time we will count to 40. Did you speed up or slow down? Let's try 20. Is it easier to keep the beat for a longer or shorter time? (shorter) Now we will move around to the beat of my drum and while we are moving I will call out a number. As soon as I say the number, freeze and start counting the number to yourself silently as you stay in your place. When you finish counting begin moving again. Did you begin as my drum started beating? (It is important that the teacher be

able to keep a steady beat!) I will play different speeds and call out different numbers. See if you can keep the beat."

15. **TEMPO TAG:** "We are going to play tag but in this tag all players are equal. Everyone must move to the beat of my drum (or claps). You must take a step on each beat and no more. When you are tagged, raise your hand and call out your name so everyone knows who is 'it.' When I change the speed, change with me -- a step for every beat. If you go faster than the beat you are automatically 'it.'" This is a great tag game because the fast and slow people have an equal chance. After the dancers understand the game, encourage a variety of steps, directions, levels and arm movements.

16. **NOTES AND MOVEMENTS:** "What different movements can you think of for whole notes? I will play (or hum/sing) whole notes and you explore different movements. (Using 4/4 time works best for now. Other rhythms can be explored in the rhythm lesson. The dancers can also make sounds for the notes.) I will play one whole note then rest for a whole note and continue that way. When I rest you freeze." Continue in this way exploring movements for half notes, quarter notes and eighth notes. It helps to put a four beat rest between measures. This gives the dancer a sense of duration and a chance to think of a new idea. Share ideas or choose some that work best to put into a combination. Try using the whole body and isolating body parts.

17. **ACCELERATION:** "Try doing a simple movement very slowly. Now start to speed up or accelerate that movement until you are moving very quickly. Then begin to decelerate until you are moving slowly again. Did the movement change as you accelerated? (It usually does.) Start with a simple movement with one body part. Then try more body parts, then your whole body. Try to keep the movement clear. Try not to change the movement."

18. **MACHINES:** "Choose a tempo. (Slow, medium, fast for young dancers; whole, half, quarter and eighth notes for intermediate dancers.) One at a time make a shape which connects to another shape and move one body part at the tempo you chose. Try not to get mixed up by the other dancers' tempos around you. Maintain YOUR speed. Choose a sound to accompany your movement. When the machine is finished we should hear and see many different tempos. This creates a rhythm." More advanced dancers might try two different speeds in their bodies simultaneously. One movement could be accompanied by a mouth sound, the other by a body sound (stamp, clap, snap).

19. **PROPS:** INSTRUMENTS -- use rhythm instruments with any of the previous explorations. They can be played while dancing or groups can play while others dance.
STREAMERS, PLASTIC, SCARVES, BALLOONS and STRETCHYBANDS can be used in many of the previous explorations to add more variety as the dancers move quickly and slowly.

20. **ACTIVITY SONGS:** Check the "Activity Music List" for songs to use with 2-7 year olds that help explore the concept of speed.

SHAPING

1. **STRETCH/POP:** "Stretch slowly into a shape. Yawn into another shape. Push slowly into a third shape. Curl slowly into a fourth shape. Now, pop into a shape. Burst into a shape. Slash into a shape. Collapse into a shape. Rise slowly into a shape. Melt into a shape. Spin quickly into a shape. Jump into a shape." Repeat, changing levels, size and direction.

169

2. **BEATS:** "Change your shape everytime you hear the drum beat. Sometimes there will be pauses between shapes and sometimes the shape will change quickly." Beat whole, half, quarter and eighth notes.

3. **ECHO:** "I am going to make a shape for four beats, then you copy the shape for four beats. Then I will make a new shape and you will echo the shape. We do not move at the same time. You are my echo. After awhile I will make a new shape every two beats. You echo my shape after two beats. Can you echo my shape after 1 beat? Me, you, me, you, me you?!" Make sure the music is not too fast and has a strong beat. This can also be done in partners.

4. **TRAVELING SHAPES:** "Make a shape. Can you move that shape slowly through space? Now move that shape quickly through space. Shake the shape out and try a new shape. What shapes are easier to move quickly? (High or medium level, two legged shapes.) What shapes are more easily moved slowly?"

5. **PAIRS:** "Find a partner. One of you make a shape. The other dancer will slowly move over, under or around that shape and connect his or her shape onto your shape. Now, you move slowly over, under or around that shape and make a new connected shape. Keep moving and connecting shapes so that you travel in a line through space. Going back the other way, move quickly -- shape shape shape!" This can also be done in groups.

170

6. **NEGATIVE/POSITIVE SPACE:** "Find a partner. The leader will take 8 slow counts to form a shape with negative space (empty space). The follower will make three different shapes quickly in the negative space(s). I will count '1 2 3 4 5 6 7 8' (the leader is making a shape slowly), then I will say 'shape 1! shape 2! shape 3!' (the follower is making three shapes quickly, filling up the negative spaces in the leader's shape). Hold the third shape and look around at each pair of statues. Change leaders after each turn."

7. **SHAPE MUSEUM:** "Half of the class will form shapes on different levels in empty spaces. The other half will dance around the statues. When you come to a statue you like, copy it exactly and hold your shape until someone copies you. When you are copied, come alive and dance to another statue. Listen carefully to the music. When the music is fast, dance quickly and copy the statue as quickly as possible. When the music is slow, dance slowly and copy the statue slowly. Feel as though you are dancing in slow motion or fast forward."

8. **GROUP SCULPTOR AND CLAY:** "Half the class will stand in empty spaces. The other half will dance around the statues and move different body parts to create ever-changing sculptures. If the music is fast, dance quickly around the statues and shape the statues quickly but carefully. If the music is slow, dance slowly and shape the statues slowly." Change roles and then discuss how the statues felt being moved slowly and quickly.

9. **MOVE AND REST:** "Take eight counts to make a shape. Hold that shape for eight counts. Take four counts to make a new shape. Hold the shape for four counts. Take two counts to make another shape. Hold that shape for two counts. Take one count to make a shape. Hold that shape for one count." Play around with the counts and rests. You might end the combination with a sixteen count shape, for instance. Encourage the dancers to change levels during the slow shapes and directions during the fast shapes. Ask the dancers to look at each other's shapes during the rests.

INSTRUMENTS

1. **TEMPO:** Instruments can be used in any of the tempo games described in "Exploring the Concept."

2. **CONDUCTOR:** Choose someone to conduct the orchestra. They can signal fast and slow tempos. The dancers can sit and play or move and play.

3. **SKIP AROUND THE CIRCLE:** Dancers take turns dancing around the circle of musicians. The orchestra follows the speed of the dancer and accompanies his or her movement.

4. **SONGS:** Check the "Activity Music List" for many songs relating to tempo. The dancers can move and play to these songs.

DEVELOPING SKILLS

1. **LOCOMOTOR MOVEMENTS:** Practice different locomotor movements at different speeds: fast walk, slow run, slow and fast jumps, hops, skips, gallops and slides. See the "Locomotor Movement" chapter for more ideas.

2. **NONLOCOMOTOR MOVEMENTS:** Do nonlocomotor movements normally and have the dancers decide which ones are naturally done at fast, slow or medium tempos -- flick (fast), stretch (slow), bend (medium), swing (medium), twist (medium or slow), slash (fast), float (slow), push/press (slow), dab (fast), punch (fast), shake (fast), turn (any tempo). Now try to change the speed of these movements and discuss the outcome. Some of the movements will turn into other movements. See the "Nonlocomotor Movement" chapter for more ideas.

3. **TEMPO TAG:** Tempo tag (explained under "Exploring the Concept") can be used to practice locomotor skills. Call out different movements as you play different tempos. The players must use the designated movement such as jumping, lunging, running, etc.

4. **FEET/NOTES:** Use the feet or notes described under "Exploring the Concept" to practice different locomotor skills. Arrange the feet or notes in patterns and have the dancers decide what locomotor movements should be used for which tempos.

5. **KEEP THE BEAT:** Practice locomotor movements to specific beats. Encourage the dancers to move on the designated beat (whether half notes, quarter notes or eighth notes). You can help them by counting and giving cues. Then have them try keeping the beat without your help.

6. **BODY HALF:** Practice slow nonlocomotor movements in the upper body half (arms) and fast locomotor movements in the lower body half (legs) such as floating/run, stretching/ jump, pushing/ gallop. Then try the reverse such as shaking/lunge and flicking/walk.

TURNING

1. **FAST/SLOW:** "When the music is fast turn quickly, when the music is slow turn slowly. Turn in self and general space."

2. **COPY CAT:** "Make up two slow and two fast turns. Share them with the class (or teach then to a friend). We will copy them."

3. **LEVELS:** "Try slow low turns and fast high turns. Now try slow high turns and fast low turns. Try medium speed turns at a middle level."

4. **ARMS:** "Try turning your feet quickly and your arms slowly. Now, try turning your feet slowly and your arms quickly."

5. **ACCELERATE:** "Start turning very slowly. Accelerate until you are turning very quickly. Then decelerate until you are turning slowly again."

COMBINING MOVEMENTS

1. **FOLK MUSIC:** Make up combinations to folk dance music. Some songs that change speed: Savila Se Bela Loza, Fjaškern, Seven Jumps, La Raspa, Gustav's Skoal.

2. **SLOW/FAST:** Combine slow and fast movements such as: walk, run, spin, stretch, melt (accelerating/decelerating) or crawl, roll fast, stretch, flick, float. (Slow/fast/slow/fast/slow.)

3. **ACCELERATING:** Create a simple combination and try to do it faster and faster: walk, turn, move backwards, freeze, jump. Then try to do it slower and slower.

4. **HALF TIME/DOUBLE TIME:** Try a familiar combination twice as fast and twice as slow.

5. **CINQUAIN:** Create a cinquain about speed. Read the poem as the dancers move. Sometimes let the dancers create parts of the cinquain.

Speed
Fast, slow
Spinning, stretching, slashing
We can change time
Tempo

6. **FEET/NOTES:** Combine the feet and notes (from "Exploring the Concept") into a combination of tempos and movements: "walk, walk, run a lit-tle, slow down."

LEAPING

1. **CARTONS:** Place four to five cartons close together on one side and two cartons far apart on the other side. The dancers should do four to five leaps in a row (no extra steps in between) and then two big leaps with several steps in between. This gives the feeling of fast feet and slow feet -- leap leap leap leap, run, run, run, leap, run, run, run, leap. Make sure the four cartons are the right length apart for the length of the dancers' legs.

2. **SCATTERED:** Scatter the cartons around the room. When the music is fast, all the dancers leap quickly over the cartons. When the music is slow all the dancers leap "slowly" over the cartons. To me, a slow leap is a big, suspended leap. A fast leap is a quick, bursting leap. Remember to tell the dancers to look out, not down so they can see other dancers. Two dancers approaching the same carton should both move away.

3. **ARMS:** Arms can float for slow leaps and burst for fast leaps.

4. **BENCH:** Leap over objects or empty space quickly. When you reach the bench (or line), walk slowly across it as you would on a tightrope, then continue on with quick leaps.

5. **CONES:** Leap quickly, then move slowly between or around cones. Alternate.

6. **RUN LEAP:** Try different combinations of leaping and running: run, leap, run, leap; run, run, leap; run, run, run, leap; leap, leap, leap, leap.

FREE DANCING/IMPROVISATION

For free dancing, choose an activity under "Exploring the Concept" that is not too structured. For improvisation look for activities under "Combining Movements" or "Choreographing."

CHOREOGRAPHING

1. **WORD CARDS:** Give groups five to six word cards. Have them create a dance that accelerates and decelerates arranging the cards in a logical order and adding "fast" and "slow" where necessary. For example: crawl, walk, skip, run, dash; spin, run, hop, float, melt; walk, turn, run, skip, crawl.

2. **FEET/NOTES:** Give groups the feet or notes and have them arrange them in a pattern. Then have each group create a dance to a different group's pattern, not their own.

3. **ABA or ABC:** Individuals, pairs or groups create dances that are slow/fast/slow, fast/slow/fast or slow/medium/fast. Have the audience guess the pattern.

4. **TRIOS:** Each dancer creates a short phrase of fast movement, medium movement, slow movement and a freeze. The phrase can be in any order: slow, medium, freeze, fast; fast, slow, freeze, medium; medium, freeze, fast, slow, etc. Each dancer in the trio enters the "stage," does a movement and then exits. For example: enter with fast movement, freeze, dance with medium speed movements and exit with a slow movement phrase. The dancers in the trio can perform together. This may also be done as a chance dance, letting solo dancers enter and exit the space at will. Watch for varying tempo and magical moments as rhythms are created by dancers moving together with different speeds.

5. **VARIATIONS ON A THEME:** Have small groups create a simple phrase or use one from the combining movement section of the lesson. When they know their phrase ask them to vary the speed. Then have them create a dance based only on this phrase which changes tempo. Dancers can move simultaneously, in opposition, in canon, echo, whatever!

6. **GROUPS:** Divide the class into groups. Each group creates a dance which has them rise together, move in a special way as a group to a new spot and then sink in a group shape. Give each group a certain speed or have groups try different speeds. Encourage the groups to practice so that the dancers in the group move as one.

7. **SUITE:** Individuals, pairs or groups create a suite. Each group could choose an element as a focus for their choreography and create a dance in three sections that begins with medium speed, moves to slow speed and ends with fast movement. For example: The dance element is body parts. The first section focuses on head movements that move with medium speed, the second section focuses on slow arm movements and the last section focuses on fast feet movements. The element could be pathways -- curved pathways in medium speed, slow straight pathways and fast zigzag pathways.

LESSON ON SPEED

Ages: 3, 4, 5, 6, or 7   *Length: 30 minutes**

WARMING UP

Dance Exercises/Technique: Rhyming exercises emphasizing SPEED.

Introducing the Concept: SPEED: slow, medium, fast. See, say and do the words.

EXPLORING THE CONCEPT

Exploring the Concept: "Slowland/Fastland" #8
Dancers dance quickly in one half the room and slowly in the other half. Music: "Baroque and Blues" - *Suite for Flute and Jazz Piano.*

Instruments: "Songs" #4
"Walking Notes" - *Feel of Music.* Play and move medium, slow and fast.

DEVELOPING SKILLS

Turning: "Fast/Slow" #1
Turn quickly and slowly. Music: "Slow and Fast" - *Feel of Music.*

Combining Movements: "Cinquain" #5
Practice and perform the cinquain.

CREATING

Free Dancing/Improvising: Exploring the Concept "Slow/Fast" #2. Respond to the tempo of the music. Add scarves or streamers if available. Music: "Inima" - *Solitude.*

*For a 60 minute lesson: Do 15-20 minutes of exercises, Leaping #1 and a Goodbye Dance.

LESSON ON SPEED

Ages: 8-Adult   Length: 30-60 minutes

WARMING UP

Warm-up Activity: For a 30 minute lesson do "Aerobic Shape Museum" described under "Quick Warm-ups."

Dance Exercises/Technique: For a 60 minute lesson do 20 minutes of technique.

Introducing the Concept: SPEED: slow, medium, fast. See, say and do the words.

EXPLORING THE CONCEPT

Exploring the Concept: "Feet" #11
Create rhythm combinations with paper feet cut in different sizes to represent different note values.
Music: voice.

DEVELOPING SKILLS

Developing Skills: "Body Half" #6
Practice moving arms slowly and legs quickly, then try the reverse.

Combining Movements: "Accelerating" #3
Create a simple combination and perform it faster and faster.

CREATING

Free Dancing/Improvising: For a 30 minute lesson do Exploring the Concept "Thirds" #10.
The room is divided into three sections and dancers change speed in each section.

Choreographing: For a 60 minute lesson do "Word Cards #1
Dancers create combinations that accelerate or decelerate.

COOLING DOWN

Sharing/Evaluating Choreography: Dancers show studies and audience discusses whether dance accelerated or decelerated and other concepts used.

CHAPTER 16

RHYTHM
Pulse, Breath, Pattern, Accent

INTRODUCING THE CONCEPT

In dance, we think of RHYTHM as being the pattern of flow or movement. Run in place for a few seconds. Now, put your fingers on your wrist, neck or heart. Find your PULSE. It is an even rhythm. This even rhythm can change speeds but it maintains a steady beat, like a machine. Pay attention to your BREATHING. Sometimes you take long breaths, sometimes short breaths. Your breathing produces an uneven rhythm. Sometimes we like to follow the rhythm of our PULSE and move in an even rhythm. Other times we like to follow the rhythm of our BREATH and move in an uneven rhythm.

We can also create PATTERNS by mixing up different speeds and by ACCENTING different beats or movements. Count 1-2-3-4, 1-2-3-4 and move on each beat. Now, count 1-2-3-4, 1-2-3-4 and do one movement for counts 1 and 2 (half note) and a movement for count 3 and a movement for count 4. You have created a RHYTHMIC PATTERN by doing a slow movement and two faster movements. Count to 16 and move on every beat. Now let's group the notes together in different ways by ACCENTING different beats. Group the beats into sets of four: 1-2-3-4, 1-2-3-4, 1-2-3-4, 1-2-3-4. Make a strong movement on the first beat of each set. This creates a rhythmic pattern that is like marching. Group the beats into sets of three: 1-2-3, 1-2-3, 1-2-3, 1-2-3. This creates a rhythmic pattern that is like waltzing or swinging. Group the beats into sets of two: 1-2, 1-2, 1-2, 1-2. This creates a rhythmic pattern that works well for jumping and hopping. Group the beats into sets of five: 1-2-3-4-5, 1-2-3-4-5, 1-2-3-4-5. This creates an unusual rhythmic pattern.

EXPLORING THE CONCEPT

1. **NAMES:** "Find the rhythm in your name. How many syllables does your name have? First create an even rhythm with your name. Say each syllable the same speed: George Wash-ing-ton: 1-2-3-4. Ab-ra-ham Lin-coln: 1-2-3-4-5. Repeat your name over and over and find a simple movement to do such as walking, jumping, punching, dabbing, etc. Now, create an uneven rhythm with your name. Use your breath and breathe each syllable in and out. G e o r g e Wash ing ton (long, short, short, medium). Instead of doing specific movements for each syllable, let your body follow the flow of your breath as though a wind was making you move. Now, create a rhythmic pattern with your name. Create a specific pattern that you can repeat over and over: George Wash-ing ton."

Create different movements for each syllable: push, run, run, jump or stretch, jump, jump, slash, etc. Discuss the different feelings between even and uneven rhythms. You might want to divide this into three different explorations or extend it through other parts of the lesson such as choreography. Use spelling and vocabulary words instead of personal names for variety.

2. **MUSIC:** "I am going to play musical selections that have different rhythms. Listen to the rhythm and explore movements that express the rhythm. Each time I change the music, change your rhythm and movement." Play 4/4 marches, 3/4 waltzes and ragtime, 2/4 polkas, 3/8 mazurkas, 6/8 gallops. Also try different styles such as blues, folk, jazz, electronic and classical.

3. **FEET:** Cut big feet out of paper (12 inches long), medium feet (8 inches) and small feet (4 inches). Laminate them for longer use. "The big feet represent half notes, the medium feet are quarter notes and the small feet are eighth notes. Who would like to create a rhythmic pattern with the feet? Remember, the small feet are too little to travel alone so they must stay in pairs. (It is difficult to have solitary eighth notes mixed in, so I make this rule with my students. Advanced students may not need this rule.) Let's try this rhythm moving through space." You might use different words to represent the different notes such as daaa for half notes, di for quarter notes, and dada for two eighth notes. You can "say" the rhythm as you move: "daaa, daaa, di, di, di, di, dada, dada, dada, dada." Try different rhythms, ones that repeat and ones that do not. For example a repeating rhythm might be: di, dada, di, dada. A nonrepeating rhythm: di, dada, daaa. Have your students create different movements for the different sized paper feet. Translate the feet into notes if desired and write the music on the blackboard. Add sounds using the body, mouth or rhythm instruments.

4. **COLORS:** Assign movements to different colors: Blue = giant step or lunge, yellow = walk, green = run, purple = gallop, slide or skip and red = freeze in a shape. "Create a rhythmic pattern with your colored paper. Two yellows, four greens, two blues and a red = walk, walk, run, run, run, run, lunge, lunge, freeze. Clap your pattern and then try moving it. (Experienced dancers can make the pattern more complex by moving different body parts and changing levels or directions.) Leave your pattern on the floor and take eight counts to move to someone else's pattern. Clap the new pattern and then try dancing this pattern." For variation ask your students to create longer patterns or repeating patterns.

5. **CORNERS:** Assign a different movement to each corner such as gallop, run, walk, float. Divide the dancers into four groups and send each group to a corner. "When I play a gallop rhythm, the dancers in the gallop corner should gallop through space. When I play a walking rhythm, the

walking corner dancers should move. When I play the running rhythm, the running corner moves and when I play a floating rhythm (or create a breathy noise) the floaters move. When I am not playing your rhythm, freeze in a special shape. When I say 'change corners', rotate to the next corner and you will try a new movement and rhythm." Experienced dancers can work with more complex rhythms and movements.

6. **BODY PARTS:** "Say this rhythm along with me: ta-ta-taka-ta, ta-ta-taaaa (use any sound with which you feel comfortable). Put this rhythm in your head, your shoulders, arms, ribs, hips, knees, feet, whole body! We will say the rhythm all together as we move different body parts. Try this rhythm: taka-taka-taka-ta, taaaa-taaaa." Try many different rhythms in all body parts.

7. **ECHO:** "I will move for 4 counts, then you echo my movement for 4 counts. When I move you are still, when I am still you move. We do not move at the same time. You are my echo!" Use a variety of movements. Movements that are even and repeat are simplest such as four punches, four jumps, etc. Then try some patterns such as two punches and a slow stretch, four quick flicks and two twists, etc. Try an eight count echo, also. Try this activity in pairs.

8. **CANON:** "I will move continuously and you will copy my movements but you will start four counts after I start! We will not look the same because you will be doing my movements after I do them. You will always be four counts behind so you will have to watch my new movements and remember them while you are doing my old movements!" This exploration is for intermediate grades and up or experienced dancers. As with the echo game it is best to start with simple repeated patterns. Some teachers like to put four counts of rest or clapping between four counts of movement but I find this to be more confusing. Try this also in pairs, trios or quartets (dancers form a line) moving through general space. Leaders change at your signal.

9. **SIMPLE SONGS:** Find the rhythmic patterns in simple songs such as "Row Your Boat." Create movement patterns to fit the rhythm patterns.

10. **FUNNY PHRASES:** "Say funny rhythmical phrases such as 'boom a chick a boom' in many different ways and explore movement that expresses the phrase. Say it loudly and do strong or big movement. Say it softly and do light or small movement. Say it with joy and do joyous movement. Say it sadly and do sorrowful movement. Say it quickly, say it slowly, say it cool, say it silly."

11. **RHYTHM CIRCLE:** "Make a big circle (or several smaller circles) by the time I count to eight. A leader will move around the inside of the circle doing a simple movement and sound (jumping and clapping, pushing/pulling and whooshing, etc.). As the leader passes in front of you, copy the movement and sound. When the leader gets back to his/her beginning spot, the next person will start a new movement and sound. Keep doing the previous movement/sound until the new leader passes in front of you. Be aware of the changing movements and rhythms and the different rhythms happening simultaneously." For variation, have new leaders begin after the previous leader has passed four or five people. This will create many simultaneous rhythms and the students will not have to repeat the same movement for such a long time period.

12. **COPY THE RHYTHM:** "I will clap a rhythm, then you copy my rhythm in movement. Then I will do a rhythm with movement and you copy my rhythm by clapping." Try this activity with partners.

13. **MACHINES:** "Create a simple rhythmic pattern (or use one from a previous exploration). One at a time come to the center of the room and do your pattern through movement, adding sound to it. As you come to the center connect on to another dancer so that we have a musical machine. Keep repeating your pattern until the machine is complete. Try to listen to the 'music' and feel the many different rhythms created by the dancers as you do your own pattern!" This can also be done in small groups.

14. **ACCENT ECHO:** "I will do a movement on the first beat of the first measure. You copy my movement on the first beat of the second measure." Continue to echo accents. For accompaniment play music with different rhythms - 3/4, 2/4, 6/8, 5/4 or try beating the drum as you move or use an accompanist or a metronome. If you do this in partners you can more easily be the accompanist.

15. **BODY ACCENTS:** "Move a different body part on the first beat of every measure and freeze on the other beats. Now move a body part on the accent and do a locomotor movement on the unaccented beats. Now try freezing on the first beat and moving a body part on the remaining beats." Clap the beats or beat a drum, sticks or triangle. Explore different meters.

16. **ACCENTS IN DIRECTIONS:** "As you move through general space, change directions on the first beat of every measure. Try different locomotor movements. Do you notice a difference between 4/4 and 3/4 time? With 4/4 time you always change directions with the same foot. If you start stepping on the accent with the right foot you will continue to use the right foot. With 3/4 time you change feet each time you change direction. Why?"

17. **MOVING ACCENTS:** "We are going to move the accent one beat over in each measure: <u>1</u>-2-3-4, 1-<u>2</u>-3-4, 1-2-<u>3</u>-4, 1-2-3-<u>4</u>, <u>1</u>-2-3-4. Clap the moving accent. Move a body part on each

accent. Move through general space creating a special movement on the moving accents. How does this make you feel?" The movement is syncopated because of the changing accents.

18. **HEART AND LUNGS:** "Find your pulse. Explore steady, even movements to accompany your heart beat. Now, listen to your breathing. Let your body move and flow to the natural rhythm of your lungs moving in and out. Alternate even movements to a pulse and uneven breath movements. Respond to your heart then respond to your lungs. Feel the difference."

19. **WORLD MUSIC:** "I am going to play many different styles of music from all over the world. You will hear many different rhythms. Respond to each rhythm with movement and when the music stops, freeze in a shape." Play short selections. Dancers of all ages enjoy moving to these unusual sounds and rhythms. Discuss the music and the feelings and rhythms they evoked when the exploration is over.

20. **OPPOSITES:** "Try moving with breath rhythms to this music that has a very strong beat. Now, try keeping a steady beat in your movement as you move to this environmental music. Why is this hard to do?" Try other opposites such as moving slowly to fast music and vice versa or moving in 4/4 time to waltz music.

21. **PROPS:** Use different props with the activities above. Scarves support breath rhythms. Plastic film and balloons can be kicked, batted and tossed in even or breath rhythms. Stretchybands can be used to create the pulsing heart rhythms as well as the flowing breath rhythms. Rhythm instruments can be used with all the activities.

22. **ACTIVITY SONGS:** Check the "Activity Music List" for songs to use with 2-7 year olds that help explore the concept of rhythm.

SHAPING

1. **SURPRISE SHAPES:** "Find a partner. If you are the leader make slow motion shapes for your partner to copy. Every so often surprise your partner with an accented shape -- change levels, direction, speed or force. See if your partner can copy your surprise shape. Then continue making slow motion shapes. When I give the signal, change leaders."

2. **ECHO SHAPES:** "Find a partner and face each other. The leader will make a shape on the first beat of the first measure. The follower will copy the shape on the first beat of the second measure. The leader makes a new shape on the first beat of the third measure and the follower copies the shape on the first beat of the fourth measure, etc." Explore different meters and/or have the leader take two or three beats to create a shape, for variation. You could do this in trios and quartets, having each person copy the shape on successive beats. Remember to change leaders.

3. **SHADOW SHAPES:** "Find a partner and stand one in front of the other. The leader will do a simple rhythmic pattern that travels through space such as jump, jump, turn and then freeze in a shape. The shadow will then copy the pattern and shape. Then the shadow will be the leader and do a new rhythmic pattern such as run, run, jump, punch and freeze in a shape and the partner will copy when the leader is frozen. Remember to change levels, force, pathways and movements and to use different body parts."

4. **SHAPE CHAIN:** "Using breath rhythms, one at a time move into a shape that connects to another dancer until we have a chain or line of shapes stretching across the floor. Feel like a wind is blowing you into the line. At my signal let your breath blow you away from the line into a new shape in your own self space. At my new signal let your breath blow all of you at the same time into a new group shape."

5. **CHANGING RHYTHMS:** "Change your shape on every beat of the drum. (Beat steady beats.) Now create a new shape every time I hit the triangle. Let your breath move you into the shape and use the length of the sound to make your shape. (Beat a simple repeating rhythm pattern.) Try to change your shape on every beat. Listen to the changing rhythms -- pulse, breath and pattern. Change the way you make shapes when I change my rhythms." If you do not have instruments, use mouth or body sounds to create the three types of rhythm.

6. **RHYTHMIC PATTERNS:** "Make shapes following the rhythmic pattern I've written on the blackboard (or feet patterns or color patterns from "Explorations"). If the pattern is half note, quarter note, quarter note then you make one shape for two counts and then two quick shapes. We will repeat the pattern several times. You can repeat the same shapes or try new shapes each time." You can count or use words like sha-ape, shape, shape. Try several different patterns.

7. **STRETCH/POP:** "Stretch into a shape slowly then pop three times into three different shapes --ssstretchhh, pop, pop, pop! Try this pattern: pop, pop, ssstretchhh, pop, ssstretchhh. Remember to try different slow and quick shapes each time." Explore a variety of rhythmic patterns.

8. **ACCENTS:** "Think of a number between one and ten. I will count to ten and when I come to your number jump into a shape as you yell out your number." Practice several times and then beat the drum or clap without counting so that the dancers have to keep count themselves. This is a fun

and exciting shape game because several dancers will be making shapes on the same count and some counts will have no shapes. Interesting rhythms occur. Try different numbers of counts. Make the game more complex by asking dancers to choose two or three numbers.

9. **STILLNESS:** "Stillness is an important part of rhythm. Explore different ways of freezing in shapes. Move and freeze in a shape letting the movement die or droop. Move and freeze in a shape but feel as though you are still moving. Which feels better or more exciting? Which looks better? Stillness should create a sense of expectation -- what is going to happen next? Stillness should not be boring. How can dancers make stillness feel alive? Watch and help each other."

INSTRUMENTS

1. **RHYTHM:** Instruments can be used in any of the activities described previously. The dancers could play and move or half the class could be the orchestra and half the dancers. Reverse roles.

2. **ACCENT:** Play instruments on the first beat of every measure and dance on the unaccented beats or be still on the accent and play and dance on the unaccented beats.

3. **CIRCLE:** Dancers sit in a circle with instruments. Each dancer moves around the circle in his/her own way and the orchestra picks up the rhythm and accompanies the dancer.

4. **MUSICIAN:** Each dancer plays a special rhythmic pattern with an instrument while the other dancers respond to the rhythm through movement.

5. **SONGS:** There are many good songs in the "Activity Music List" for rhythm instruments.

DEVELOPING SKILLS

1. **BASIC LOCOMOTOR SKILLS:** Discuss the rhythm of different locomotor skills and practice them with emphasis on rhythm, accent and counts. Walking is done to a moderate tempo usually in 4/4 meter but try also a 5/4 meter. Running is a quick tempo usually in 4/4 meter but try it also in 3/4 meter. Jumping and hopping can be any tempo and are usually done to 2/4 or 4/4 meter, but can be done in 3/4 or 5/4 meter. Step-hopping is done in 2/4 meter. Skipping, galloping and sliding are usually done in 6/8 meter. See the "Locomotor Movement" chapter for more ideas.

2. **WALTZ RUN:** The waltz run is sometimes called a triplet by dancers, but it really is not a musical triplet. You take three steps, creating an accent on the first beat by bending the stepping leg in plié and doing the other two steps in relevé (down, up, up). The accenting leg changes from right to left with each measure because of the 3/4 meter. Practice the waltz run slowly, increasing the tempo with practice. With young children I use the image of falling off the curb to create the downward accent and stepping back up on the curb for the other two steps. Add different arm movements.

3. **SCHOTTISCHE:** The schottische (shotish) is a folk dance step with a very nice rhythm: step, step, step hop; step, step, step hop; step hop, step hop, step hop, step hop. It is done in 4/4 meter. Practice many different variations: in different directions, with different leg shapes, with different arm shapes, different sized steps and hops, different speeds, turning on the four step hops, rocking back and forth on the four step hops, with a partner, etc.

4. **POLKA:** The polka is a most exhilarating dance step. It is done in 2/4 meter. The easiest way to teach it is to start with galloping. Practice four gallops with the right foot, then four with the left foot, then the right, left, etc. Then practice two gallops with the right, two left, two right, two left, etc. Then practice doing this as you turn to the right traveling through space. Practice turning to the left. You are ready to practice with a partner. One person hold the other's waist, the other person hold your partner's shoulders. Practice the polka together. You should be mirroring each other's leg movements.

5. **NONLOCOMOTOR MOVEMENTS:** Practice nonlocomotor movements to different rhythms. Try swinging, twisting and bending to 3/4 meter and 4/4 meter. Does the movement feel different done in different meter? Try sharp movements on accented beats such as punch, slash, poke, kick, dab, flick. Try smooth movements for four to eight counts such as float, glide, press, twist.

6. **THREES AND FOURS:** Practice changing from 3/4 meter to 4/4 meter as you do walking and running movements across the floor: Walk 2-3-4, walk 2-3-4, walk 2-3, walk 2-3, walk 2-3-4, walk 2-3-4, walk 2-3, walk 2-3. This is difficult because the accented foot changes: right 2-3-4, right 2-3-4, right 2-3, left 2-3, right 2-3-4, right 2-3-4, right 2-3, left 2-3, etc. Try adding arms that move on the accented beats.

7. **COUNTS:** Practice skills to counts: four counts jumping, four counts punching, four counts jumping, etc. or eight counts running, four counts resting, eight counts running. Young or inexperienced dancers have a difficult time keeping the beat. Help them by counting initially, then play a drum beat or clap, then see if they can count to music, then have them move to beats, then to silence, then to beats. Can they keep the beat without accompaniment?

8. **BREATH:** Practice breath rhythms: give the students 16 counts to complete a phrase such as run, twirl, jump three times and freeze. Let the students perform the phrase using their breath -- no beats or music -- any way they want to within the allotted time (16 counts). Let them practice several variations and then show them to the class. Some may choose to freeze for five counts while others may freeze for one count. The pattern will be performed in different ways because each student will base the pattern on their own breathing instead of a dictated rhythm.

TURNING

1. **ACCENTS:** Initiate your turn on the first beat of the measure and follow through or continue it on the unaccented beats. Try 4/4, 3/4, 5/4, 6/8 and 2/4 meters. Try a variety of turns and ways to initiate the turns.

2. **COMBINATIONS:** Include different turns in the rhythmic patterns that the students and you create.

3. **PATTERNS:** Create a rhythmic pattern of turns: slow, slow, quick, quick, slow or quick, quick, slow, quick, quick, slow, etc. Discover what turns work best in slow motion and what turns can be done quickly.

4. **BREATH:** Let your breath swirl and spin you through space. Explore different turns that are initiated by breath rhythms rather than by mechanical rhythms. With young children, try "blowing" them through space with your own breath, reminding them to turn. They enjoy this and soon pick up the concept themselves.

COMBINING MOVEMENTS

1. **FEET:** Choose a combination that you or your students created using the feet patterns from "Exploring the Concept." Practice the combination with drum beats or clapping, then with music.

2. **COLORS:** Choose a combination created earlier in the lesson using the colored paper. Practice this combination, perhaps adding another element of dance (size, level, direction, etc.) to make it more complex.

3. **PHONE NUMBERS:** Choose a phone number and create a combination based on the counts: 515-2093 - five jumps, one punch, five jumps, two flicks, rest or freeze, nine walks backward and three hip movements. The dancers can practice the combination while counting aloud as accompaniment.

4. **MATH RHYTHMS:** Create a combination from math problems: 6 + 6 = 12. Six runs, make a plus sign with your body, six runs, make an equal sign, twelve runs. Try it with a partner: #1 jumps six times toward #2, #2 then jumps six times toward #1, together they jump twelve times!

5. **ACCENTS:** Create a combination to a sentence like "I love dancing!" Do a different movement for each word I = shape, love = run, run leap, dancing = turn. Now do the combination three different times accenting a different word each time with your voice AND your movement. I love dancing! I LOVE dancing! I love DANCING!

6. **CONVERSATIONS:** In pairs, dancers ask and answer questions through movement and words.

"What do you like to eat?" "I like piz-za!"

"Where are you go-ing?" "To the cin-e-ma."

Try conversations without words, just movement.

7. **POETRY:** Create combinations to short poems or lines of poetry that have interesting rhythms.

8. **ART:** Draw a line design (see PATHWAYS) and create a rhythmic pattern and movement inspired by the design. Add sound.

9. **CINQUAIN:** Create a cinquain about rhythm and read the words as the dancers perform.

Rhythm
Pulse, breath
Swinging, swirling, skipping
Movement creates rhythmic patterns
Music

10. **WORDS:** Create combinations using dance words --

jump, jump, run-a-lit-tle, stretch wide (4/4 meter).

Turn a-round, turn a-round, fall dooown (3/4 meter).

LEAPING

1. **CARTONS:** Place milk cartons in a line or horseshoe design with different spacings between them. For example: four cartons two to three feet apart, a wide space and then two cartons stacked up, another wide space and two cartons stacked up, and then two cartons two to three feet apart. Do not play music. Listen to the rhythms of the feet as they travel over the cartons -- leap, leap, leap, leap, run, run, run, leap, run, run, run, leap, run, run, run, leap, leap.

2. **RUN/LEAP:** Create different rhythmic patterns with runs and leaps. Run, run, leap. Run, run, run, leap. Run, leap, run, leap, etc. Repeat the same pattern a number of times before teaching a new pattern.

3. **BREATH:** Using breath rhythms move through space and leap whenever you breathe in and run when you breathe out. Try the reverse. Which feels more natural to you?

FREE DANCING/IMPROVISATION

Choose an activity under "Exploring the Concept" that is not too structured for free dancing. Activities under "Combining Movements" and "Choreographing" could become structured improvisations for older students.

CHOREOGRAPHING

1. **FEET:** Give groups sets of different sized feet cut out of paper. Have them create their own rhythmic pattern, set movement to it and perform for the other students.

2. **COLORS:** Give pairs or groups of students colored paper. Ask them to assign specific movements to specific colors. Have them arrange the colors in a pattern and perform the dance. The other groups can guess what movement each color represents.

3. **PHONE NUMBERS:** Ask each student to create their own phone number dance as described in "Combining Movements." Have three or four dancers show their dances simultaneously and enjoy the many different rhythms. Besides phone numbers try addresses, math problems, social security numbers, I.D. numbers, etc.

4. **POETRY:** Ask students to select a poem and choreograph a dance based on the rhythm and feeling of the poem. Shel Silverstein, e.e. cummings, Mother Goose (for young dancers) and Haiku poetry are good places to start. The students' own poetry can also be used. It is fun to give the same poem to each group and watch the different interpretations.

5. **ART WORKS:** Bring in different art works and discuss the rhythm in the work. Is the rhythm mechanical or does it have breath? Cubism represents a more mechanical rhythm while some impressionist paintings have more of a free flow quality. Are there patterns that repeat that could be portrayed through movement? Choreograph a dance based on a work of art.

6. **CONVERSATIONS:** Ask partners to choreograph a dance based on a conversation. Start with real words, add movement and then perhaps sounds in place of the words or do the dance in silence. Does the mood of the conversation change? Are feelings portrayed? Can the audience guess what the conversation is about?

7. **ABA:** In pairs or groups choreograph a dance based on pulse and breath rhythms -- pulse/breath/pulse or breath/pulse/breath. Try dances based on alternating pulse and pattern or alternating meters: 4/4 - 3/4 - 4/4 or 3/4 - 2/4 - 3/4.

8. **ABC:** Choreograph a suite using different meters 4/4 - 3/4 - 6/8 or different rhythmic styles such as electronic/classical/jazz or country/blues/rock.

9. **SONGS:** Choose a simple song such as "Are You Sleeping, Brother John." Divide into four groups. Let each group choreograph one verse of the song, doing a movement for each syllable. Have each group teach the others so that everyone knows the whole song and dance. Perform the dance in a round.

10. **ENTER AND EXIT:** Ask each student to choreograph a short dance that is made up of eight counts of quick movement, eight counts of slow movement, eight counts of stillness and an eight count rhythmic pattern. Each dancer should choose their own order, but during the course of the dance they must enter and exit the stage space. You may give them the option to repeat any eight count phrase or require that they enter and exit by thirty-two counts. Choose three to five dancers to enter at the same time from different sides of the space. Watch the resulting rhythms and magical moments that happen by chance. Accompaniment could be a steady drum beat or music with a steady beat.

11. **DRAW A RHYTHM:** Have individuals, pairs or groups draw a design or series of simple pictures. Ask them to create a sound for each picture and then a movement or do the movement first and add the sounds. Share the dances and designs.

A.   B.

12. **ORCHESTRA:** Divide into four groups and ask each group to choreograph an eight count phrase that moves in self or general space. Have them add body, mouth or instrument accompaniment. You are the conductor and lead the moving orchestra by pointing and gesturing with your arms: all groups play/dance together for eight counts, then each group plays/dances alone, half the group plays/dances and then the other half plays/dances, finally all play/dance loudly with big movements, then all are still for eight counts and they repeat the whole pattern again. Have the groups stand or sit in a semi-circle so that they can watch each other.

13. **PROPS:** Choreograph dances using props in different ways to enhance different rhythms. Try ABA dances: prop/no prop/prop and vice versa.

LESSON ON RHYTHM

Ages: 5, 6, 7, or 8   *Length: 30 minutes*

WARMING UP

Dance Exercises/Technique: Do rhyming exercises emphasizing the rhythm and rhyme of each exercise.

Introducing the Concept: RHYTHM: pulse, breath, pattern, accent. See, say and do the words.

EXPLORING THE CONCEPT

Exploring the Concept: "Corners" #5
Each corner represents a different rhythm. Dancers divide into corners and respond to their rhythm. Music: drum beat and vocal sounds.

DEVELOPING SKILLS

Developing Skills: "Counts" #7
Practice skills you are currently working on and do them to a specified number of counts. Music: any music with a clear beat.

CREATING

Free Dancing/Improvising: Exploring the Concept "World Music" #19. Dancers respond to rhythms from around the world. Remind dancers to use many elements of dance such as level, direction, etc. Music: selections from *Music from Distant Corners of the World.*

COOLING DOWN

Goodbye Dance or slow breathing.

LESSON ON RHYTHM

Ages: 9-Adult   Length: 45-60 minutes

WARMING-UP

Warm-up Activity: Do marching or mechanical movements to a 4/4 meter, swinging movements to a 3/4 meter and jumpy, jazzy movements to a 2/4 meter.

Dance Exercises/Technique: Do 15-20 minutes of technique emphasizing the rhythm of each exercise. (For a 90 minute class do 30 minutes of technique.)

EXPLORING THE CONCEPT

Exploring the Concept: "Body Parts" #6
After putting the rhythm in body parts, move the rhythm through general space.

DEVELOPING SKILLS

Developing Skills: "Waltz Run" #2
Practice the waltz run, changing speeds and adding arm movements.

Combining Movements: "Words" #10
Create a combination waltz run, waltz run, stretch, curl, turn, turn balance. "Down-up-up, down-up-up, stretch, curl, turn-a-round, turn-a-round, bal-ance."

CREATING

Choreographing: "Enter and Exit" #10
Dancers create a phrase of 8 counts slow movement, 8 counts fast, 8 counts stillness and 8 counts rhythmic pattern. Perform in any order. For a 45 minute class let half the class perform at a time. For a 60 minute class let 5-7 dancers perform at a time.

COOLING DOWN

Sharing/Evaluating Choreography: Discuss the magic moments that happen by chance as dancers enter and exit the stage space. Discuss the rhythms created by the dancers.

CHAPTER 17

ENERGY
Smooth (Sustained), Sharp (Sudden)

INTRODUCING THE CONCEPT

"Today we are going to explore two different kinds of ENERGY. We might ask ourselves 'How can we move our muscles? What kind of ENERGY can we create?' How does it feel to put your hands in fingerpaint and move them across the paper? Yes, it feels SMOOTH. You can keep moving your hands around the paper without stopping. How do you think it feels to touch a cactus or a porcupine? Yes, SHARP! Your hand touches and pulls away and stops. Our muscles can move SMOOTHLY or SHARPLY. Another image that might help us understand sharp and smooth is to think of musical instruments. To play a violin you use smooth, continuous motions to create a sustained sound. Another name for SMOOTH is sustained. On a drum you use sharp movements to create a percussive sound. Another name for SHARP is sudden or percussive. Imagine you are fingerpainting in your self space. Use your arm muscles, leg muscles and back muscles to create smooth movements. Now, imagine you are stuck in between two big cactuses. Use muscles in different body parts to create sharp, sudden movements as you try to escape from the thorns."

EXPLORING THE CONCEPT

1. **WORDS:** "I am going to call out a word. If you think the word is a smooth movement, move that way in self space. If you think the word is a sharp movement, move that way through general space. (You could use spots -- moving on them for smooth and around them for sharp.) Float (smooth) ... Punch (sharp) ... Glide (smooth) ... Poke (sharp) ... Stretch (smooth) ... Press (smooth) ... Flick (sharp) ... Melt (smooth) ... Kick (sharp) ... Slash (sharp) ... Pull (smooth) ... Dab (sharp) ... Dodge (sharp) ... twist (smooth) ... Sway (smooth). Can you think of other ways to move smoothly and sharply?"

2. **SELF/GENERAL:** "Move smoothly any way you can think of through general space. When the music stops and you hear my drum (or claps) move sharply in your self space. When the smooth music begins again, move smoothly through space in a different way. You could change your level, your direction, your speed or your size of movements. When I beat the drum move sharply in a new way in self space." Continue for several times then change to sharp dancing through general space and smooth dancing in self space. You and the dancers might say "smooooooooth" and "sharp! sharp! sharp!" as they are moving to reinforce the vocabulary.

3. **CORNER-MIDDLE-SIDE:** "Start in a shape in the middle of the room. I will call out a place and a movement. Do that movement to the place I named. When you reach the place keep doing the movement in self space until I call out a new place. Any corner - poking ... any side - floating ... middle - stretching ... any side - rolling smoothly ... opposite side - rolling sharply ... any corner - jumping and punching ... opposite corner - jumping and floating ... middle - dancing backward smoothly ... end in a sharp group shape in the middle." You can be as simple or as complex in your directions as is warranted for the experience of your students. You can continue for as long as the students are involved or keep the challenges to a minimum. This is a very flexible exploration.

4. **MIRRORING:** "Find a partner (or mirror a group leader). The leader will move smoothly in self space while the music is smooth. When the music becomes sharp, the leader will move sharply. The follower will mirror the leader's movements. Then we will change roles. Remember you can change levels, the size of your movements, your speed and the direction in which your body parts move." You can vary this exploration by asking the dancers to dance in self space for one quality and general space for the other.

5. **SHADOWING:** "Find a partner. If you are the leader, move smoothly through general space while your partner follows you, until the music stops. When the music stops freeze in a smooth shape with your partner. When the music begins the other person is the leader for smooth dancing. When you are the leader again, move sharply and freeze in a sharp shape with your partner. Keep switching leaders and types of energy."

6. **MACHINES:** "One at a time move smoothly into the center of the room and make a smooth shape connected to another person. Move just one of your body parts smoothly and think of a smooth sound to accompany the movement. When everyone is connected and moving I will turn on the machine's sound. Make your sound and we will think of a name for your smooth machine." Do the same thing with sharp movements and sounds. Talk about the different energies and how different the machines look and sound. Try a mixed up machine -- some sharp and some smooth movements. Do this in small or large groups.

7. **ENVIRONMENTS:** "I am going to change our environment. I will call out a new place. Visualize this place and then begin to move smoothly or sharply, depending on what is in the new environment. Cactusville ... Cloud Mountain ... Mosquito Junction ... Foggy End ... Milkshake River ... Thorny Town ... Windy City ... Briar Patch ... Cottonwood ... Broken Glass Hill ... Silkydale ... Whipping Cream Springs ... Stoneyburg." Elicit environments and names from the dancers.

8. **COPY CAT:** "Dance smoothly any way that you want to. I will call someone's name and we will copy that person's movement until I give the signal to dance sharply. In 20 seconds, I will call a new name, we will copy that person's sharp movements and then I will give the signal to dance smoothly again." Continue on. With small classes everyone will have a turn at leader. With large classes, you can call out two or three names and dancers can choose whom to copy or you can repeat this activity later on with other concepts.

9. **GROUPS:** "Half the class will move through space smoothly and slowly. The other half will move sharply and quickly around, between, under and over the smooth dancers. Then we will change roles. Be aware of the spaces between dancers. Look for the empty spaces to move in and through. Change levels, directions and size."

10. **CLAP HANDS:** Sing "Clap Your Hands" substituting smooth and sharp. "Clap, clap, clap your hands, clap your hands so sharply. Wave, wave, wave your hands, wave your hands so smoothly." Bend knees sharply ... poke fingers sharply ... float arms smoothly ... turn head smoothly ... punch elbows sharply ... slide feet smoothly, etc.

11. **SMOOTHLAND AND SHARPLAND:** "This half of the room is Smoothland and the other half is Sharpland. Only ghosts live in Smoothland. They float, glide and swirl smoothly through space. In Sharpland, only karate masters live. They chop, slash, flick and punch through space. Remember, to slash and punch the EMPTY space. You may travel from one land to the other changing your energy." It is fun to add props -- scarves, streamers or plastic in Smoothland and rhythm sticks, Chuk'ems or balloons in Sharpland.

12. **VERBS:** "I am going to call out many different verbs or action words. These verbs will help you change the energy of the space around you. Dance these verbs and feel how the energy of the room changes with each word. Shake the space ... squeeze the space ... poke the space ... mold the space ... shatter the space ... tickle the space ... slash the space ... paint the space ... caress the space ... swat the space." Ask the dancers for more verbs.

13. **SLOW AND FAST:** "Move through space smoothly and slowly. Change your level, direction and pathway. Now, move smoothly but quickly. Try moving sharply and quickly. Now move sharply and slowly. You have to do the sharp movement quickly but you can slow down the spaces between movements so that there is a sense of slowness."

14. **PARTNERS:** "Find a partner. Make a sharp shape. Your partner will copy that shape. You are now free to dance around sharply. When you leave, your partner will change to a smooth or different sharp shape. Dance back to your partner and copy the new shape. Now your partner is free to dance around while you make a new shape. Whatever type of shape you make -- sharp or smooth -- is the type of dancing you do through general space. You and your partner will take turns making shapes and dancing through space."

15. **WORD CARDS:** " I am going to hold up (or say) different words. Dance the word on the card and decide which energy -- sharp or smooth -- the word best describes. We will make a list of sharp and smooth actions. Some words can be either sharp or smooth." Slash, flick, punch, dab, dodge, kick, poke, shake are some sharp actions. Float, press, wring, glide, swirl, stretch, melt are some smooth actions. Turn, twist, walk, run, leap can be either sharp or smooth.

16. **EXCHANGE:** "Find a partner. Choose opposite energies. Dance toward your partner using your energy. As you pass each other, exchange energies and dance to your partner's spot with his/her energy. For example, you may be floating and your partner may be slashing. As you meet and pass each other you start doing slashing movements and your partner will do floating movements. Try several different opposite energies. Try to exchange at exactly the same moment."

17. **CIRCLE COPY CAT:** "Form a big circle. I will call a name. That person will go to the center of the circle and dance with a certain energy. All the dancers in the circle will try to copy that movement energy as they move around in a circle. Every time a new person moves to the center of the circle, the energy will change and the people in the circle will copy that energy. Dancers in the middle, keep your movement simple and your quality clear. Dancers in the circle, do your best to keep moving around the circle and try to copy the energy even if you may not be able to copy the movement exactly. We will change the direction of the circle from time to time." This may also be done in a circular formation but moving only in self space.

18. **FORCE FIELD:** See chapter on "Weight." Use sharp and smooth movements and shapes.

19. **WORLD MUSIC:** "Listen to the music from all over the world. I will play short sections of many different kinds of music. If the music sounds sustained, move smoothly. If the music sounds sudden or percussive, move sharply. Change the way you move sharply and smoothly by changing direction, level, size, and speed. When the music pauses, freeze in a sharp or smooth shape."

20. **PROPS:** STRETCHYBANDS -- Stretch smoothly then pop sharply. Do individually or with partners.

PLASTIC -- Punch, kick, slash plastic sharply. Float, glide, twirl with plastic smoothly. You could use the imagery of anger and tenderness.

BALLOONS -- Bat them sharply with different body parts, then hold them with different body parts and dance smoothly.

STREAMERS -- Shake them sharply, then twirl them smoothly, using different body parts.

21. **ACTIVITY SONGS:** Check the "Activity Music List" for songs to use with 2-7 year olds. Although the songs may not mention the words "sharp" and "smooth," they use sharp and smooth movements like flick and float.

SHAPING

1. **3 SHAPES:** "Stretch into a smooth, rounded shape. Now pop into 3 sharp shapes. I will say 'smooooth -- sharp! sharp! sharp!' Remember to change the level, direction and size of your shapes each time."

2. **4 SHAPES:** "Make a smooth, curved shape. Now try a sharp, angular shape. Try to make a sharp, straight shape and a smooth, twisted shape. Change your level and make four different shapes again. Can you change the size of your shapes and make four small or big curved, angular, straight and twisted shapes? Let's try to make these four types of shapes slowly and quickly. Let's try to make these shapes moving smoothly from one type to another. Now, try moving sharply from one type to another."

3. **COPY CAT:** "Dance smoothly around the room. When I stop the music, freeze. I will call someone's name. Copy their shape. Is it a sharp or smooth shape? Now dance sharply around the room. I will call a new name. Is their shape sharp or smooth? Dance any way around the room. I will call another name. Copy their shape. Is it sharp or smooth?" Continue in this way.

4. **BODY HALF:** "Can you make a smooth shape with the top half of your body and a sharp shape with the bottom half? Now reverse that. Try a sharp shape on the right side and a smooth shape with the left side of your body. Now reverse that. Can you make a smooth shape with your right arm and left leg and a sharp shape with your left arm and right leg!? Now reverse that!" Try many different shapes on different levels with different energy and different body halves.

5. **SCULPTOR AND CLAY:** "Find a partner. Shape your partner into a smooth, rounded shape on any level. Let your partner shape you into a smooth shape. Now sculpt a sharp, angular shape. Let your partner sculpt you. Remember to move each other gently and carefully. Use all your dance words to create an interesting statue. Can your statues come alive and move through space with the energy in which they were sculpted?"

6. **GROUP SCULPTOR AND CLAY:** "Half of the class (or group) will be clay and half will be sculptors. Sculptors, you will move smoothly around the clay sculpting different body parts into smooth shapes. Remember to move from one statue to another so that the statues are continually changing. When the music stops, the sculptors will stand back and view the museum of smooth shapes. Then I will change the music and the sculptors will dance sharply around the statues and

sculpt sharp shapes. Remember to still be gentle. When the music stops we will view the sharp museum." Change roles and then discuss the different feelings the statues had being molded sharply and smoothly and the feelings the sculptors had.

7. **SHAPE MUSEUM:** Divide the class into statues and dancers. "If you are a statue please make a sharp or smooth shape in an empty spot. Let's make sure we have shapes on different levels. When the music begins the museum will open and the dancers will enter. Move smoothly or sharply to a statue. Copy that statue exactly. Now the statue will come alive and become a dancer. If you were making a sharp shape, dance sharply. If you were making a smooth shape, dance smoothly to a new statue. Copy that statue and hold your shape until someone copies you. We will continue until the music ends. If you are dancing when the music ends find a statue to copy. If you are a statue when the music ends, hold your shape. We should see pairs of statues in smooth and sharp shapes."

8. **POSITIVE AND NEGATIVE SPACE:** "Find a partner. One of you will make a smooth shape with a lot of negative space (empty space). The other dancer will make three sharp shapes in the negative space and hold the last shape. You can fill the space with sharp body parts or your whole body. Then change roles. Now, the sharp dancer makes a smooth shape and the smooth dancer makes the three sharp shapes. Keep changing roles." This can also be done in groups.

9. **FILL THE SPACE:** "Find a partner. One of you will make a shape that moves slightly with a certain kind of energy. Perhaps your shape will shake slightly or sway slightly or twitch. The shape needs to have a big empty space in it. Your partner will fill the empty space with movement based on the energy the shape evokes. A swaying shape would be filled with smooth movements. A shaking shape would be filled with sharp movements. Change roles and energies." This can also be done in groups.

10. **LEVELS:** "Think of three different shapes on three different levels. Move suddenly to your medium level shape, move smoothly to your high level shape and ease into your low level shape." Try other shapes and another order. Partners could work together, playing off each other's energies and levels.

11. **PROPS:** Use props in the activities above to add new dimensions to the shapes.

INSTRUMENTS

1. **SLOW AND FAST:** Play instruments quickly and move sharply. Play instruments slowly and move smoothly. Reverse.

2. **REACTIONS:** Have a dancer move sharply or smoothly. Let the musicians react with their instruments. Take turns or work in pairs.

3. **SECTIONS:** Divide the room into four sections. Put percussive instruments in one section, shakers in another, triangles or gongs in the third section and nothing in the fourth. Dancers travel in pairs from section to section. One plays the instrument while the other dances. In the fourth section the musician has to make body or mouth sounds. Change roles.

4. **SHADOW:** Follow your partner's smooth or sharp rhythms and movements as you move and play.

5. **SMOOTHLAND AND SHARPLAND:** Divide the room in half. Put percussive instruments in Sharpland and sustained instruments in Smoothland. Dancers move from one half to the other, playing and moving sharply or smoothly. Older dancers can do this activity. Do not call the divisions Smoothland and Sharpland.

DEVELOPING SKILLS

1. **LOCOMOTOR:** Practice different locomotor movements smoothly and sharply. Try a smooth, sustained walk and run. Then try a sharp walk and run. Use of the arms sharply will help reinforce the energy. Try sharp and smooth jumps and hops; slides and gallops and skips. Encourage smooth gliding and floating movements or sharp punching and slashing movements. For something

different try doing locomotor movements with arms and hands instead of legs and feet. See the "Movement" chapter for more ideas.

2. **NONLOCOMOTOR:** Practice different nonlocomotor movements smoothly and sharply. Slash, punch, poke, flick, dab, kick, dodge and shake are some sharp movements. Can these be done smoothly? (No, they change quality.) Float, glide, press, wring, melt, stretch and carve are some smooth movements. Can these be done sharply? (They will change quality and character.) Turn, twist, push, and bend can be done smoothly or sharply. Swing, sway and rock begin with sudden energy and follow through with smooth energy. Practice all the nonlocomotor movements with the whole body and with different body parts.

3. **BODY HALF:** Practice doing sharp movements with the lower body while moving the upper body smoothly. Reverse. Skip with punching knees while floating the arms. Skate smoothly with the legs while slashing the arms, etc.

4. **RIVER RUN:** Practice running as smoothly as possible. Keep the arms close to your sides, not stiff but not moving. Keep the knees bent. Try running in straight and curvy pathways.

5. **ZIGZAGS:** Practice sliding back and forth to the right and the left. Try four slides each direction, then two slides each direction. This should give a sharp energy to the slides. Add zigzag arms for fun.

6. **JUMPS:** Practice jumping forward and backward, then side to side. Now jump forward, backward, side, side. Add sharp arm movements. Try this with hops!

7. **ISOLATED PARTS:** Practice moving your whole body smoothly while one body part moves sharply. Change the part that is isolated. Try moving your whole body sharply while one part moves smoothly. Try this skill on different levels.

8. **RHYTHMS:** Practice marching to marches (sharp), swaying, swinging, turning or floating to waltzes (smooth) and kicking, jumping, slashing or poking to jazz music.

TURNING

1. **SHARP AND SMOOTH:** Practice turning sharply and smoothly. Add arm movements to reinforce the energies.

2. **SELF AND GENERAL:** Alternate smooth turns through general space with sharp turns in self space. Reverse.

3. **LEVELS:** Practice smooth turns on a low level and sharp turns on a high level. Reverse.

4. **PATHWAYS:** Practice turning smoothly in a curved pathway or in a circle. Then practice turning sharply to the right then back to the left, to the right, to the left in a zigzag pathway.

5. **SPEEDS:** Practice fast smooth turns and slow sharp turns. Then try fast sharp turns and smooth slow turns.

COMBINING MOVEMENTS

1. **ALTERNATE:** Create a combination that alternates smooth and sharp movements -- slash, float, jump, glide, punch.

2. **ABA:** Create a combination that moves sharply/smoothly/sharply or the reverse. Poke, punch/press, swirl/skip, slash. Float, glide/kick, dodge/ sway, melt.

3. **WORD CARDS:** Have the dancers categorize the word cards into sharp and smooth movements. Pick five to six words and put them into an order and perform.

4. **7 JUMPS:** Using the folkdance music "Seven Jumps", do sharp movements for the sixteen count phrase. Do smooth movements on the sustained notes. If you do not have the music, alternate percussive sounds and smooth sounds made with instruments, mouth or body.

5. **PARTNERS:** Dance smoothly to your partner (directed or free), make three sharp shapes with your partner and dance away sharply. Dance sharply to your partner. Make one smooth, sustained shape. Dance away smoothly. Repeat several times.

6. **OPPOSITES:** Dance to your partner with the opposite energy. When you reach your partner exchange energies and dance away with your partner's energy.

7. **RHYTHMS:** Create a combination to march, waltz and jazz music. Perhaps four measures of marches (4/4 meter), two measures of smooth turning (3/4 meter) and four measures of poking jumps (2/4 meter). If counting you would go: 1-2-3-4, 2-2-3-4, 3-2-3-4, 4-2-3-4, 1-2-3, 2-2-3, 1-2, 2-2, 3-2, 4-2.

8. **FLOCKING:** See the section on "LEVEL." Concentrate on sharp and smooth movements and shapes.

LEAPING

1. **CARTONS:** Float and burst over the cartons.

2. **STREAMERS:** Hold streamers in each hand. Float the arms and streamers as you leap smoothly, shake the streamers as you leap sharply. This can also be done with plastic instead of streamers.

3. **SCATTERED:** Scatter the cartons around the room. Float or burst over the cartons. When the music stops, find a carton and make a smooth or sharp shape over the carton.

4. **SPOTS:** Float or burst over the cartons, when you come to a spot, stop and make a sharp or smooth shape then continue leaping.

5. **TRAVELING:** Do bursting leaps from one corner to the other moving on a diagonal path. Do smooth movements traveling to the adjacent corner, then smooth leaps to the opposite corner and sharp movements traveling to the beginning corner. You should be traveling in a figure eight. Leap on the diagonal from corner to corner and travel smoothly and sharply across the ends of the room.

6. **ARMS:** Add slashing, punching, poking arm movements or floating, gliding, still arm movements to your leaps.

FREE DANCING/IMPROVISATION

Choose an activity under "Exploring the Concept" that is not too structured. There are also several activities under "Combining Movements" and "Choreographing" that would make good improvisations for dancers ages 8 - adult.

CHOREOGRAPHING

1. **ABA:** Create a dance that is sharp/smooth/sharp or smooth/sharp/smooth. This can be done individually, in duets, trios or groups.

2. **WORD CARDS:** Pick five word cards out of a hat. Put the cards in an order and create a dance such as jump, turn, punch, freeze. Add different energies to the combination, perhaps: jump sharply, turn smoothly, punch sharply and freeze in a sharp shape.

3. **CINQUAIN:** Create a cinquain with the help of the dancers and read it as they perform.

Force

Sharp, smooth

Slashing, swirling, swaying

We can shake the space

Energy

4. **IMAGES:** Think of words that evoke different energies. Let the dancers choose three words and create an energy suite. Wiggle, swirl, sneeze. Squeeze, tickle, caress. Chop, rub, cough.

5. **ENVIRONMENTS:** Let the dancers choose two opposite environments and ask them to create a dance describing these environments. Let the audience guess them. Brier patch and skating pond. Outer space and a volcano, etc.

6. **SOUNDS:** Have each dancer think of a movement and sound that is either sharp or smooth. Put dancers in groups and have them create a dance based on each other's sounds and movements.

7. **CHANCE DANCE:** Pick four actions and assign numbers to them. Have dancers pick four cards with numbers on them. They must perform their combination according to the order they picked their cards. The actions might be: 1. Float 2. Slash 3. Flick 4. Melt. Your four cards may be: 1, 1, 3, 2. Your dance would be: Float, float, flick, slash. Dancers might form trios and perform their combinations together.

8. **PROPS:** Choose two different props. Create a dance with two different energies and the two props. Try one, three or four props. Discuss how the props helped or hindered the dancers as they created different energies.

LESSON ON ENERGY

Ages: 4, 5, 6, 7, or 8   Length: 30-45 minutes

WARMING UP

Dance Exercises/Technique: Do 5-15 minutes of rhyming exercises emphasizing ENERGY.

Introducing the Concept: ENERGY: sharp (sudden), smooth (sustained). See, say and do the words.

EXPLORING THE CONCEPT

Exploring the Concept: "Corner-Middle-Side" #3
Call out places and movements: corner poking sharply, middle floating smoothly. Make a sharp or smooth shape when you get to the corner, middle or side. Music: "Haunted House" - *Movin'*.

DEVELOPING SKILLS

Developing Skills: "River Run" #4
Practice running smoothly. Music: "Enter Sunlight" - *Movin'*.

Turning: "Sharp and Smooth" #1
Practice turning while moving the arms sharply. Music: "Tipsy" - *Movin'*.

Combining Movements: "Activity Song"
"Flick a Fly" - *Walter the Waltzing Worm*. River run, gallop and turn smoothly then flick sharply on "flick a fly".

CREATING

Free Dancing/Improvising: Exploring the Concept "Smoothland and Sharpland" #11
Half the class has scarves and half has plastic film, Chuk-'ems or no prop. When the music is slow, half the class dances smoothly and slowly with scarves and half dances sharply and slowly with another prop or nothing. When the music is fast, change props and the one half will dance smoothly and quickly with scarves, the other half will dance sharply and quickly with the other prop. Music: "Inima" - *Solitude*.

COOLING DOWN

Relaxing: Close your eyes and breathe smoothly.

LESSON ON ENERGY

Ages: 9-Adult   *Length: 45-60 minutes*

WARMING UP

Warm-up Activity: Mirror smooth and sharp movements.

Dance Exercises/Technique: Do 10-20 minutes of technique (depending on length of class) emphasizing smooth and sharp movements.

Introducing the Concept: ENERGY: sharp (sudden), smooth (sustained). See, say and do the words.

EXPLORING THE CONCEPT

Exploring the Concept: "Words #1
Choose word cards and move through space smoothly and sharply.

Shaping: "Sculptor and Clay" #5
Sculpt each other into shapes describing verbs that are sharp and smooth such as punching, floating, swirling, flicking.

DEVELOPING SKILLS

Combining Movements: "Word Cards" #3
The class works together to create a combination from 5 word cards such as float, flick, slash, swirl, melt. Practice and perform.

CREATING

Choreographing: For a 45 minute lesson do "Images" #4. Call out expressive verbs and let dancers improvise. For a 60 minute class do "Sounds" #6. The dancers create sharp and smooth sounds and then movement to accompany these sounds.

COOLING DOWN

Sharing/Evaluating Choreography: For a 45 minute lesson divide the class in half. Each half shares improvs. For a 60 minute class let small groups share studies individually. Discuss the energies and other elements used.

CHAPTER 18

WEIGHT
Strong, Light

INTRODUCING THE CONCEPT

"Today our words are STRONG and LIGHT. How strong can you be? What makes you strong? Yes, your muscles. Can you touch the muscle in your arm and make that muscle bulge? Does your muscle feel hard? Is it squeezing together? Now, relax your muscle. Pretend you are picking up a feather. Touch your arm muscle. Is it hard or soft? By controlling the amount of muscles we use we can control the amount of force we make. If we need a STRONG degree of FORCE to do an action we make our muscles STRONG by squeezing (contracting) them. If we need a LIGHT degree of FORCE we relax our muscles. The more muscles we use the stronger the force, the less muscles the lighter the force. The more we use our muscles the stronger they will become. We can also see the use of WEIGHT in our movement. The weight can be strong, firm, gripped or light, fine, delicate, airborne. We can combine WEIGHT and ENERGY. Can you do a strong, smooth movement (press) ... a strong, sharp movement (slash) ... a light, smooth movement (float) ...a light, sharp movement (flick)?"

EXPLORING THE CONCEPT

1. **MUSCLES AND BONES:** "Feel as though you are all muscle. You are strong and powerful. Nothing can harm you. Move through the space with strength and power. Make your muscles bulge. What are some ways you can move strongly ... push ... pull ... run ... leap ... jump ... stretch ... punch ... twist? Now, relax your muscles. Feel as though you had no muscles, you are only a skeleton, you have only bones. You are light as a feather. You might float through the ceiling you are so light. What are some ways you can move lightly ... glide ... float ... flick ... twirl ... tip-toe ... melt?" Alternate strong and light movements focusing on the image of muscles and bones.

2. **STRONGLAND/LIGHTLAND:** "This half of the room is Strongland. The people who live in this land are powerful. They use their muscles all the time to create a lot of force. But their muscles get tired so they take a vacation in Lightland, which is the other half of the room. In Lightland their muscles relax. They don't have to create very much force to move. They can float and fly lightly through space, giving their muscles a rest. Let's start in Strongland. When you need to give your muscles a vacation go visit Lightland. When you are ready to be strong and powerful again, dance back to Strongland." Dancers may move back and forth at will. Encourage dancers to use different directions and change their speed, level and size of movement.

3. **LOUD AND SOFT:** "When the music is loud dance strongly, using your muscles to create a lot of force. When the music is soft dance lightly, hardly using your muscles at all. Remember to change levels and directions as you move. Try to vary your speed and size of movement. Now dance lightly when the music is loud and dance strongly when the music is soft." Discuss the dancers' feelings about the different music. Did one type of music seem to fit best with strong or light movements? Did the way they moved strongly or lightly change when the music changed?

4. **BODY HALF:** "Make the muscles in your legs hard by pushing down into the ground. Try to keep the upper body -- chest, arms, neck -- loose and light. Can you move through space with strong, powerful legs and light, floaty arms and neck? Can you move at a low level? Let's try the opposite. Can you make your arm and chest muscles hard and strong? Now, let your leg muscles relax and feel like seaweed. Can you move through space like this? Can you move on a low level? Try right and left body halves. Squeeze the muscles on your left side and relax the muscles on your right side. Can you move through space? Try hopping on your left side. Try other ways of moving keeping the left side strong and the right side light. Now reverse."

5. **ISOLATED PARTS:** "Make just your arm strong and all your other body parts light and loose. Now try one leg strong and all other parts light. Can you make just your stomach strong and all other parts light? Breathe slowly and that will help relax your muscles. Try making your arm light and all other parts strong ... leg light and all other parts strong." Continue with different body parts strong or light. The ability to isolate body parts comes in handy when you are in pain. When you have a broken bone, are giving birth or in the dentist's chair, if you can relax as many muscles as possible, the pain decreases. Dancers could work in pairs, testing to see if the isolated parts are opposite in weight to the rest of the parts.

6. **WORD CARDS:** "Look at the word I hold up (or call out) and try that word through movement. Now tell me whether that word makes you move strongly or lightly -- are you using a lot of muscle or just a little? Press (strong) ... float (light) ... slash (strong) ... flick (light) ... dab (light) ... punch (strong)

... glide (light). Now let's try those words again and try to do them with as many different body parts as possible. Now try to involve the whole body."

7. **SHARE THE WEIGHT:** "Find a partner. Stand apart and press your palms together at shoulder level. (Young dancers can press against the walls to begin with and then find a partner.) PRESS your partner so that your weight is behind your arms, but don't push your partner down. Share the weight between you. Your elbows and knees should be slightly bent and you should feel balanced. You do not have to be the same size to share your weight. You should feel comfortable but strong in this position. Now, hold onto each other's wrists and pull back. Your arms should be straight and your knees bent so that you feel as though you are sitting in a chair. Share the weight again. You should feel comfortable but strong. Pull yourselves to standing and press together. Press apart to standing and then pull together." Keep changing partners so the dancers can work with many different sizes and weights of people. When the dancers feel comfortable with this, try sharing weight standing side to side and pulling with one arm, then sharing weight on different levels and on opposite levels. Remind the dancers to use their center of gravity (pelvis) to stay grounded and in control of their bodies. Remind them to "sit down in a chair" before sharing weight. This will key them into using the pelvis and bending the knees.

8. **FRONT TO FRONT:** "When I say 'PRESS' find a partner, stand front to front and press palms together sharing the weight. When I say 'DANCE' move away and dance lightly. If I say 'PULL' find a new partner, stand front to front and pull away from each other sharing the weight until I say 'DANCE' again. Remember to dance lightly when you are away from your partner and to press or pull strongly with your partner." Encourage different ways of dancing lightly and pressing or pulling strongly.

9. **MIRRORING:** "Find a partner (or follow a common leader). The leader will make strong muscle shapes, moving forcefully in self space. The follower will mirror those movements. When I give a signal the leader will move lightly in self space. Then we will change leaders and do it again. Remember, you can change levels and use a few or many body parts. You can also change speeds." Using loud and soft music or strong and light music helps the dancers. Images such as super heroes and floating astronauts may also provide the dancer with new ideas.

10. **SHADOWING:** "Find a partner. The leader will move strongly through general space. The follower will copy the leader's movements. When the music stops form a connected shape that is light, airy and buoyant. When the music begins again the follower becomes the leader moving strongly through space. When the first leader becomes leader again, move lightly through space then form a strong, powerful, earthbound shape with your partner." Continue to alternate leaders and strong and light movement and shapes.

11. **16 COUNTS:** "Find a partner. One of you will dance in self space, the other in general space, then you will change. I will say '16 counts slashing.' The self space dancer moves in self space slashing for 16 counts. The general space dancer slashes away and back to her partner by 16 counts. End in a strong connected shape if the movement was strong or a light connected shape if the movement was light. Now change places -- self space dancer dances in general space and vice versa. 16 counts floating ... 20 counts punching ... 10 counts pressing ... 8 counts flicking ... 25 counts stomping ... 15 counts gliding."

12. **MAGIC HANDS:** "Find a partner. Touch fingertips together very lightly. Move around the room sharing leadership and keeping the fingertips just touching. Try dancing different ways and even on different levels. This takes a lot of cooperation, sensitivity and sharing. When I give the signal press your hands together and move strongly and powerfully through space. Do not let your hands come apart. How did you feel when you were moving together lightly? (Delicate, caring, friendly, soft might be some answers.) How did you feel when you were moving strongly? (Powerful, mean, aggressive, in control could be some answers.)

13. **SOUNDS:** "I am going to play different sounds on different instruments. Listen to the sound for a few beats then move the way the sound makes you feel -- strongly or lightly. When I stop, freeze in a shape and listen to the new sound." With large classes, half the class can be the orchestra, taking turns playing instruments. Instead of instruments, sounds can be made with the body or mouth. Discuss why different sounds make you feel like moving in different ways.

14. **FORCE FIELD:** "Form a circle. I will do a simple movement that is very strong. The next person will do the same movement but with less force. We will continue around the circle until we get to the end. By that time the movement should be light. Then we will start with a light movement and add force until the movement is strong. The movement will have to change a little, but try to keep your movement as similar to the leader's as possible. After you have done your movement freeze in the ending shape." Try alternating strong and light movements around the circle. Try doing the movement before yours and then adding your own opposite movement so that each person does two movements -- a strong one and a light one or a light one and a strong one.

15. **IMAGES:** "I am going to say a word, you dance the word. Bricks ... feathers ... Superman ... helium balloons ... snow ... bulls ... dried leaves ... boulders ... parachutes ... rocket ships ... thunder

... seaweed." Ask the dancers for ideas for other strong and light images and let them dance the different words.

16. **PROPS:** STRETCHYBANDS -- With a partner or by yourself, stretch the stretchybands strongly, then toss, float or twirl them lightly.

PLASTIC -- Punch the plastic, then float with the plastic.

BALLOONS -- Bat the balloons strongly then lightly or carry them as you dance lightly, then bat them strongly with different body parts.

STREAMERS -- Dance lightly with them, then make strong shapes holding each end.

17. **ACTIVITY SONGS:** Check the "Activity Music List" for songs to use with 2-7 year olds. Although the words "strong" and "light" may not appear in the song, the movements directed by the song may be strong and light. You may also reinforce the concept by asking for strong and light movements throughout the song.

SHAPING

1. **BONES AND MUSCLES:** "Make a strong muscle person shape. Now, let your muscles relax and make a light shape. Imagine moving a skeleton into a shape and make that shape. Try a new strong muscle shape. Let your muscles melt and make a skeleton shape without muscles. Try a strong shape on a different level. Try a light shape on a different level. Try a strong backward shape, a light backward shape." Continue in this way.

2. **ISOLATED BODY PARTS:** "Make a strong shape with your whole body. Let the muscles in one arm collapse and look at that shape. Make another strong shape. Let the muscles in one leg relax. Make a light shape. Contract all the muscles in one arm. How did your shape change?" Continue in this way.

3. **SCULPTOR AND CLAY:** "Mold your partner into a strong looking shape. Let your partner mold you into a strong shape. Now mold each other into light shapes. Remember to mold each other gently and to create a strong base for the statue. Try different levels and sizes." This can be done in trios. The sculptor molds two shapes, one strong and one light.

4. **SHAPE MUSEUM:** "Half the class will make strong shapes in self space. The other half will dance lightly around the shapes. If you are dancing, copy a strong shape and hold it until someone copies you. Then you are free to dance lightly and copy a different strong shape." Try the reverse. Dancers dance strongly and copy light shapes.

5. **WEIGHT SHARING:** "Find a partner. Make strong shapes together sharing your weight. Make them interesting by changing your leg shape, level or the body parts sharing the weight. Remember to keep your knees bent." Try this in groups of three and four. Young dancers can make shapes pressing against a wall or the floor or each other.

6. **WEIGHT BEARING:** "Make a strong shape, bearing all your weight on three body parts. Let your muscles melt and create a light shape on three body parts. Try a strong shape on two parts, melt to a light shape on two parts. Try a light shape on one part. Squeeze your muscles together until you have a strong shape on one body part." Continue in this way.

7. **CONNECTIONS:** "Make a strong shape with your partner. Without breaking the connection, let your muscles relax into a different light shape. Smoothly make a new connection as you create another strong shape. Keep the connection as you make a new light shape." Continue in this way, encouraging the dancers to move smoothly from one shape and connection to another.

8. **SHAPE CHAIN:** "One at a time make a strong shape connected to the previous shape. The line of shapes should extend across the room like a chain. You should all be sharing weight, pulling or pressing on each other and helping to hold the line of shapes together. When the last shape is in place, melt carefully to the ground. Starting with the last shape, make a light shape with a delicate connection back across the room." Discuss how the different shapes felt and the problems inherent with each type of connection.

9. **SPOTS:** "Make a strong, grounded shape on your spot. Move your shape to a different spot. Relax your muscles and create a light airy shape on the spot. Move that shape to a new spot. Keep the light quality as you move." Continue in this manner, encouraging the dancers to use levels, direction, speed and size.

10. **STRETCHYBANDS:** "Make a strong shape with your stretchyband by stretching it. Now let your stretchyband go so that it 'snaps' into a loose shape and make a light shape with your body. Stretch into a new strong shape, relax into a light shape." Continue. It is fun to say "boing" when the stretchyband snaps.

11. **POSITIVE AND NEGATIVE:** "Find a partner. One of you will make a strong shape with negative (empty) space. The other dancer will make a light shape filling the negative space. Now the light dancer will make a strong shape and the strong dancer will fill the space with a light shape." Continue. Stretchybands add a new dimension as they help define the negative space.

12. **MACHINES:** "One at a time make a strong shape connecting to another dancer. Connect to the other dancer in an interesting way, using a different body part or another level. Move one body part strongly. When I 'turn on' the sound, make a strong noise to accompany your movement. Let's look at the 'machine' and think of what it might be used for." Also create a "light" machine and a machine combining strong and light movement and sound. Try small groups, large groups or the whole class.

INSTRUMENTS

1. **LOUD and SOFT:** Play loudly and dance strongly, play softly and dance lightly.

2. **REACTIONS:** Dancers take turns playing their instrument while all the other dancers react to the sound with strong and light movements.

3. **SHADOW/MIRROR:** Use instruments with mirroring and shadowing described in "Exploring the Concept."

3. **STRONGLAND:** Use instruments with this exploration described in "Exploring the Concept."

4. **MACHINES:** Use instruments in this "Shaping" activity.

DEVELOPING SKILLS

1. **LOCOMOTOR MOVEMENT:** Practice locomotor movements using strong and light force. See the "Locomotor Movement" chapter for more ideas. Try a strong, forceful walk and a light, airy walk. Try a fast, powerful run and a light, lifted run. Images such as a football player and a gazelle may help. Practice a strong jump (kangaroo) and a light jump (ping pong balls), a strong gallop (stallion) and a light gallop (pony), a strong leap (lion) and a light leap (deer). Images only help if the dancers are familiar with the objects and creatures you mention.

2. **NONLOCOMOTOR MOVEMENTS:** Practice different nonlocomotor movements. See the "Nonlocomotor Movement" chapter for more ideas. Discuss which are strong, which are light and which can be either. Slash, punch, press, wring (strong); float, glide, dab, flick (light); turn, stretch, bend, twist (either).

3. **LUNGE/TIPTOE:** Practice lunges (see "Movement" section) pressing with arms as you move through space. Practice tiptoe steps with light arm movements.

4. **CONTACT:** Practice moving with a partner sharing weight, always staying in contact with each other.

5. **BODY HALF:** Practice strong locomotor movements in the lower half of the body while doing light movements in the upper half. Reverse. (Powerful walk/floating arms, punching arms/tiptoe walk, etc.)

6. **LIFTS:** Practice different lifts. The lifter must think strong. The lifted must think light. See *On the Count of One* for lifts.

7. **FALLS:** Practice falling lightly by sinking to the ground. Watching a feather or leaf fall helps the dancers to find ways of falling lightly. Practice falling strongly to the ground. Watching a rock or book fall helps show the dancers ways to fall with weight. Remember to discuss safety. Never fall on knees. Try to cushion falls by rolling on shoulder or buttocks.

Start by doing low falls from a kneeling or sitting position. If possible, first practice standing falls on mats or padded material. Try falls that sink lightly to the ground and rebound strongly or falls that press to the ground and rebound lightly or falls that sink and rebound lightly or press and rebound strongly.

TURNING

1. **FEATHERS AND BRICKS:** Imagine holding bricks in your hands as you turn strongly. Then imagine holding feathers in your hands as you turn lightly. Try self space and general space turns.

2. **DROP TURN:** Hold hands with a partner. Pull back but share the weight. As you turn together, one dancer squats down while the other is up, then jumps up as the other goes down. You are going up and down as you turn around.

3. **COPY CAT:** Think of three ways to turn strongly or in strong shapes. Think of three ways to turn lightly or in light shapes. Share your favorite turn with the class. (Or dancers in large classes can teach a friend.)

4. **STRONG LAND/LIGHT LAND:** Turn strongly in different ways in one half of the room, then turn through space to Light Land and turn lightly.

5. **PARTNERS:** Turn lightly to a partner. Press palms together and push off strongly, turning strongly away from your partner. Try the opposite - turning forcefully to a partner, connecting lightly and turning away lightly.

COMBINING MOVEMENTS

1. **WORD CARDS:** Create a combination alternating strong and light movements - punch, float, stomp, twirl, muscle shape. Or moving from strong to light -- slash, kick, run, glide, float, balance. Or light to strong -- dab, flick, twist, press, lunge, squeeze.

2. **PARTNERS:** Create a combination in which partners move toward each other and away -- lunge/press four times, then tiptoe/float eight times toward your partner, make a pressing or pulling shape with your partner for eight counts, then dance away lightly or strongly. Repeat.

3. **FOLK DANCE:** Create a combination of strong and light movements to folk dance music that has clear changes in phrasing: Mayim, Seven Jumps, Doudlebska Polka, Gustav's Skoal, etc.

4. **SOUNDS:** Create a combination to a variety of sounds that complement strong and light movements.

5. **CINQUAIN:** Create a cinquain about weight with or without the help of the dancers. Read the words as the dancers perform.

Weight

Strong, Light

Pressing, floating, pulling

Our muscles make shapes

Force

6. **FALLS:** Create a combination of falls and rebounds as described in "Developing Skills."

7. **IMAGES:** Create a combination as in "Word Cards" but use image words such as "bricks, feathers, smoke, falling trees, balloons" or "crashing, dashing, swirling, twirling, smoting, floating."

8. **ACTIVITY SONGS:** Choose a song from the "Activity Music List" that relates to weight.

LEAPING

1. **CARTONS:** Burst over cartons. Float over cartons.

2. **ARMS:** As you leap make strong, powerful arm shapes or movements and light, airy arm shapes or movements.

3. **SPOTS:** Leap strongly and make a light shape on the spot. Leap lightly and make a strong shape on the spot.

4. **BENCH:** Burst over cartons, move lightly across a bench, then leap lightly over cartons.

5. **RUN/LEAP:** Run lightly between strong leaps. Run powerfully between light, airy leaps.

6. **SCATTERED:** Scatter cartons or spots (or just move in a scattered fashion) around the room. Leap powerfully over the cartons (or empty space). When the music stops, make a light balancing shape over a carton or spot. Now, leap lightly over the cartons and when the music stops make a strong, grounded shape over the carton. Keep alternating light and strong leaps and shapes.

7. **PARTNERS:** Leap toward a partner, then make a strong or light shape with your partner and leap past them.

FREE DANCING/IMPROVISATION

Choose an activity under "Exploring the Concept" that is not too structured. Also, ideas under "Combining Movements" make nice improvisations.

CHOREOGRAPHING

1. **IMAGES:** Give small groups three images from "Exploring the Concept" #15. Have them create a dance using these images. Other groups can guess the images.

2. **ABA:** Individuals, pairs or small groups create a strong/light/strong dance or a light/strong/light dance.

3. **WORD CARDS:** Groups put five to six word cards into a logical sequence and perform. They might alternate strong and light movements, move from light to strong, move from strong to light or do an ABA form.

4. **SPECIAL PLACES:** Each group chooses two to three special places in the room that are strong spots. As they dance lightly through space they do strong movements whenever they move into or through the special places. Groups could also do the reverse (light spots).

5. **PARTNERS:** Create a dance with a partner in which you are always in contact with each other. Or create a dance in which you dance strongly together and lightly apart or lightly together and strongly apart. It is fun to give different pairs different problems. The audience can discuss the results.

6. **PROPS:** Create a dance using a prop during the strong or light section or throughout the dance. Good props are stretchybands, plastic, balloons, scarves, elastic bands or Chinese jump ropes.

7. **SOUNDS:** Form the class into small groups. Have each dancer in the group think of a sound and movement. Dancers teach their movement/sound to each other and then they decide on a logical sequence or form for the movements. Movements could be done simultaneously, in canon or in a defined order or sequence. A dance is created and performed for the other groups. This can also be done in pairs or trios.

8. **EMOTIONS:** Give individuals, pairs, trios or groups a card with an emotion written on it. They create a dance focusing on this emotion. Let the audience guess the emotion and define the force used to portray the emotion. This could also be done this way: give the dancers a card on which strong or light is written. Have the dancers create a short study. Ask the audience to come up with an emotion that fits the study or a way the study makes them feel.

LESSON ON WEIGHT

Ages: 4, 5, 6, 7, or 8   *Length: 30 minutes*

WARMING UP

Dance Exercises/Technique: Do rhyming exercises emphasizing strong and light movements.

Introducing the Concept: WEIGHT: strong, light. See, say and do the words.

EXPLORING THE CONCEPT

Exploring the Concept: "Loud and Soft" #3
Do strong movements when the music is loud and light movements when the music is soft. Music: "Soft and Loud" - *The Feel of Music.*

Shaping: "Stretchybands" #10
Make strong shapes with the stretchybands and pop into loose, light shapes. Music: selections from *The Essential Jarre.*

DEVELOPING SKILLS

Developing Skills: "Locomotor Movements" #1
Practice different movements strongly and lightly. Music: "Walk Around The Circle" - *Learning Basic Skills Through Music Vocabulary* or strong and light drum beats.

Combining Movements: "Cinquain" #4
Create a cinquain and add sounds to accompany the movement.

CREATING
Free Dancing/Improvising: Exploring the Concept "Front to Front" #8
Press against a partner and then dance away lightly, leaping over cartons or spots. Repeat until music ends. Music: "Arkansas Traveler" - *Rhythmically Moving 1.*

COOLING DOWN

Visualizing: Close eyes and visualize your body floating lightly through space.

LESSON ON WEIGHT

Ages: 9-Adult   *Length: 45-60 minutes*

WARMING UP

Warm-up Activity: For a 60 minute class start with Exploring the Concept "Loud and Soft" #3.

Dance Exercises/Technique: Do 15-20 minutes of technique emphasizing smooth and sharp movements.

Introducing the Concept: WEIGHT: strong, light. See, say and do the words.

EXPLORING THE CONCEPT

Exploring the Concept: " Magic Hands" #12
Touch partner lightly and dance through space. Press against partner strongly and dance through space. Music: "Far East Blues" - *Movin'*.

Shaping: "Shape Chain" #8
Connect strong shapes together in a chain, then connect light shapes together.

DEVELOPING SKILLS

Developing Skills: "Contact" #4
Practice moving always in contact with a partner. Music: "Another Country" - *Dreams of Children.*

CREATING

Choreographing: "Emotions" #8
Individuals choose cards with emotions written on them. Each dancer choreographs a solo. Choose 5-7 dancers (more for a 45 minute class) to perform their solos simultaneously.

COOLING DOWN

Sharing/Evaluating Choreography: Guess the emotions portrayed and the weight used to portray them. Also discuss the magic moments created by chance and remember them for future dances.

CHAPTER 19

FLOW
Free, Bound

INTRODUCING THE CONCEPT

"When you turn on a faucet in the bathtub, the water flows freely out of the faucet and keeps flowing until you turn the faucet off. We can dance like this -- continually moving, swirling, flying, rolling -- our movement always flowing freely. Let's try this. (Come together again.) We call this FREE FLOW movement. When we turn the faucet off, the water stops, it is controlled. We can stop our movement, also. We can control our movement. If we turn the faucet on and off, the water flows, then stops, flows, then stops. We can move like this -- running and stopping, jumping and freezing, turning and making a shape. Now, try this type of movement. (Come together again.) We call this BOUND FLOW movement. FREE FLOW movement allows us to continually move. Free flow movement often gives you the feeling of being off-balance and a little out of control. BOUND FLOW movement allows us to stop or change direction at any moment. Bound flow movement gives you the feeling of being on-balance or in control."

We also use the word flow when talking about movement IN the body. Simultaneous flow is when the body parts and joints move at the same time, like a marionette. Successive flow is when the movement travels from one body part to another, like a wave or snake. A third kind of flow is the flow BETWEEN movements. When putting movements together, the dancers should flow freely from one movement to another, instead of doing steps then pausing to do different steps. Dancers need to create TRANSITIONS between movements so that the movements flow easily together. These two aspects of flow -- flow in the body and flow between movements -- are touched upon in this chapter.

EXPLORING THE CONCEPT

1. **NONLOCOMOTOR AND LOCOMOTOR MOVEMENTS:** "Try swinging your whole body. Swing freely, keeping the movements free and continuous. Now swing and stop the swing. Stop it low, stop it high, stop it anywhere. Swing and stop, swing and stop, swing and stop. Did the free flow swing feel different from the bound flow swing? How? Try gliding through space freely, swooping and swirling. Now glide and stop, glide and stop, glide and stop. How quickly can you stop? Can you stop and balance? Are you in complete control of your body? What helps you stop and be on-balance?" (Keeping knees bent, contracting stomach muscles and bringing body parts closer together.) Continue with other movements, alternating free and bound flow.

2. **LEAVES:** "Find a perfect spot. Think of being leaves. I will be the wind and blow you all around the room. Try to keep moving and never stop. Try swirling, leaping, falling, rolling, swinging. Think of that leaf being caught by a big wind and having to move wherever the wind blows. Remember, free movement does not mean out of control. As dancers, you need to always be aware of your space and other's. When the wind stops blowing, sink to the ground. I will call on someone else to be the wind and you can try different free flowing movements." Choose as many dancers to be the wind as time allows. Free flow movement can be tiring so do not continue too long.

3: **WATER AND ICE:** "Feel like a river flowing through the room. Move in a curved pathway, swirling around boulders, leaping over old logs, cascading over waterfalls. Remember to be aware of the other rivers in the room! When I give the signal ("freeze," drum beat, music off, etc.), the river will turn to ice. Freeze in a shape wherever you are, until I give the signal for the ice to melt and the water to flow. Sometimes the rivers will flow for awhile until they turn to ice. Other times the rivers will flow and freeze, flow and freeze, flow and freeze. You will have to use bound flow in order to freeze quickly on the signal." Another image is astronauts in outer space (free flow) and robots (bound flow).

4. **SHADOWING:** "Find a partner. Follow your partner through general space. Your partner will be moving freely. Try to stay with your partner and to follow his or her movements. When the music stops, freeze together in a shape and change leaders. Next time the music stops, freeze, change leaders again and move with bound flow." After each person has been the leader for both free and bound flow discuss which type of movement was easiest to follow. It is much easier to follow bound flow movement because it is controlled and usually more restricted. This can be done in self space with the partners MIRRORING each other's free and bound movements.

5. **16 COUNTS:** "Find a partner. One of you will move in self space first and the other in general space. Then you will change roles. If I say '16 counts free flow,' the self space person will dance in self space with free flow and the general space person will dance around the room and return to his/ her partner by count 16. Make a connected shape together. Then, change roles and dance for 16 counts in bound flow." Continue with different counts and free and bound flow movements. During free flow movement encourage your students to let the head tip off the spine allowing for more off-

balance and free movement. During bound flow movement encourage your students to be aware of how vertical the spine and head are which helps them to stay balanced and in control.

6. **MOVE AND STOP:** "Dance with free flow through general space. When you hear the drum beats, change to bound flow. Continue moving to the drum beats until you hear the free flow music. How quickly and smoothly can you change your flow of movement?"

7. **BODY HALF:** "Can you move the top of your body with free flow while keeping the lower half controlled? Now, try moving the top of your body with bound flow and moving your legs freely." This is difficult.

8. **MOVE AND BALANCE:** "Move freely through space. When I give a signal, stop and balance in a shape. Can you hold your shape? Are you on-balance? It is hard to stop free flow movement. What can you do to help? (Bend your knees, contract stomach muscles, pull body parts in.) Now move through space with bound flow. When you hear the signal. Stop and balance. Is it easier to balance after moving in bound flow? (Yes.)" Alternate free and bound flow and balancing so that the dancers will have a chance to practice stopping their free flow movement.

9. **PROPS:** Use different props with free and bound flow. Scarves are good for encouraging free flow movement. Balloons are good for encouraging bound flow movement. Stretchybands can be used for both - swirl with the stretchyband then stretch and make shapes with it. Use props in many of the above activities.

10. **WORLD MUSIC:** Create a tape of music from many cultures or use selections from *Music From Distant Corners of the World*. Have your students respond to the music using free and bound flow movements.

11. **ACTIVITY SONGS:** Check the "Activity Music List" for "Pause," "Balance," and "Flow" songs to use with young dancers.

SHAPING

1. **3 SHAPES:** "Make three shapes, stopping between each shape. Now make three shapes but move freely from one shape to another. Try three new bound flow shapes. Try three new free flow shapes. "

2. **FREEZE/MELT:** "Freeze in a shape. Melt into a new shape. Freeze in a different shape. Melt into a contrasting shape." Encourage change of levels, direction, size.

3. **SHAPE CHAIN:** "One dancer will make a shape in the corner of the room. When I call your name, dance with free flow movements around the room and connect onto the next dancer in the line, making a bound shape. When all the dancers are connected together, can the chain move a little with bound flow movements? When I give the signal, break apart with free flow."

4. **NEGATIVE/POSITIVE SPACE:** "Find a partner. One dancer makes a shape. The other dancer flows through, over or around the shape and forms his/her own shape. Now the first dancer flows through the negative or empty space created by his/her partner's new shape. Keep flowing through each other's shapes and creating new shapes."

5. **SUCCESSIVE SHAPES:** "Freeze in a shape. Now change the shape by letting movement start in your head and flow from one body part to another until it reaches your feet and you have a new shape. Try letting the flow move from finger tip to finger tip. This is called successive body flow. Now, change your shape by moving all your body parts and joints at once. This is called simultaneous body flow." Continue practicing making shapes using successive and simultaneous flow. Simultaneous flow is easier.

7. **SHAPE MUSEUM:** "Half of the class will make shapes. The other half will flow freely around the shapes and then copy a shape. When a shape is copied, the shape will come alive and move with free flow and copy another shape. Hold your shape until someone copies you. Now try moving around the statues with bound flow. Which feels better? (Answers will vary.) With what flow is it easier to stop and copy a shape?" (Bound flow.)

INSTRUMENTS

1. **ABA:** March and play with bound flow, dance freely without playing your instrument, march and play with bound flow, again. Try dancing with free flow as you play, then moving with bound flow and being silent, then moving and playing with free flow again.

2. **FREELAND/BOUNDLAND:** Play and move freely in one half the room, change to bound flow in the other half.

3. **PAUSE:** Play and dance freely, then freeze in a quiet shape on the pauses. Encourage the students to freeze in many different shapes.

4. **REACTIONS:** Let half the class play percussively while the other half dances with bound flow. Then let the musicians create smooth sounds and let the dancers move with free flow. Reverse roles. Another idea is to let the dancers move first and have the musicians react.

DEVELOPING SKILLS

1. **LOCOMOTOR AND NONLOCOMOTOR:** Practice different skills with free and bound flow. Some movements are naturally free -- swirling, running, flying, swinging. Some are naturally bound -- walking, hopping, punching, jumping. Try many movements free and bound and discuss the ease or difficulty of the movement related to the flow.

2. **RIVER RUN:** Practice running freely in a curved pathway, but with arms down at your sides quiet and controlled.

3. **DODGE:** Dodging takes a lot of control. It is a bound flow movement. Practice dodging around objects or people, staying centered and shifting weight quickly from one leg to the other.

4. **HEAD TO SPINE:** With bound flow movement, the head stays in vertical line with the spine. This helps balance and control. With free flow movement the head and spine can tilt off the vertical. This gives a feeling of freedom and less restraint. It is scary to tilt your head (in any direction) because you have less control and balance. Practice this concept so that the dancers become used to the feeling. Dancers should practice moving freely through space, allowing their neck and back muscles to relax and soften so that the head and spine can move freely.

5. **SUCCESSIVE/SIMULTANEOUS:** Practice successive movement that flows from joint to joint and body part to body part (like a snake) and simultaneous movement that moves in the joints and body parts at the same time (more like a puppet).

6. **FREE/BOUND:** Analyze the skill you are currently practicing in terms of free and bound flow. If the skill is skipping, how can your students use free flow to move with ease through space while also using bound flow to give the movement itself clarity and definition? Most of dance skills use a combination of free and bound flow. Practice free flow so that your dancers move with ease and grace. Practice bound flow so that your dancers are aware of the shape of the body parts and the connection of one part to another.

7. **TRANSITIONS:** Practice the movement between movements. Encourage your students to focus on what they do between steps. How do they get from one movement to another? How can they do it with economy and clarity? Take time to focus on transitional movement rather than on particular steps.

TURNING

1. **SWIRLING:** Practice swirling through space using free flow. Let all the body parts move freely.

2. **CHAÎNÉS TURNS:** Practice chaînés turns -- turns that move through space usually stepping on the balls of the feet with straight legs. Chaînés turns require using bound flow within the body and free flow through space.

3. **CREATIVE:** Have dancers create their own turns -- using both free and bound flow.

4. **ARMS:** Practice turns with arms controlled and arms that move freely. Is one easier than the other? Usually a controlled arm movement helps the dancer maintain balance. However, free flowing arm movements are wonderful to watch.

COMBINING MOVEMENTS

1. **WORD CARDS:** Choose free and bound flow words and create a phrase: swirl, run, jump, punch, float, freeze. Encourage the dancers to flow from one movement to another.

2. **CINQUAIN:** Create a cinquain and read the words as the dancers perform the movements:

    Flow
    Free, Bound
    Swirling, dodging, floating
    Dancers fly through space
    Flow

3. **MOVE AND BALANCE:** Create a combination that alternates movements with balancing shapes -- run, balance, twirl, balance, float, balance.

4. **FREE/BOUND:** Do free flow movement to one end of the room and return with bound flow.

5. **PARTNERS:** Move with free flow to your partner, move with bound flow with your partner, move with free flow away from your partner. Reverse.

6. **SEQUENCES:** Create a simple combination and practice moving from one movement to the other with free flow. Create transitions between movements -- glue movements together to create a combination that flows smoothly. Do the combination without flow between movements and discuss the difference in how the combination feels and looks.

8. **FOLK DANCE:** Perform folk dances that have free and bound flow such as Pljeskavac, Zemer Atik, Doudlebska Polka, Seven Jumps, Shoemaker, Ve David. Accentuate the different sections.

LEAPING

1. **CARTONS AND SPOTS:** Alternate cartons and spots. Leap over cartons and spots with free flow. Next, leap over cartons and freeze in a shape on the spots.

2. **FREE AND BOUND:** Do leap patterns to the end of the room with bound flow. Travel along the end of the room with free flow. Do leap patterns back to the other end. Leap patterns: run, run, leap; run, leap, run, leap; run, run, run, leap; etc.

3: **SCARVES:** Leap with scarves. Try to move scarves freely to encourage loose light arm movements above strong controlled leg movements.

4. **SCATTERED:** Scatter cartons or spots around the room. Dancers leap freely over the spots/ cartons. When the music stops the dancers move with bound flow between the spots or freeze in shapes over the spots.

FREE DANCING/IMPROVISATION

Choose an activity from "Exploring the Concept" that is not too structured. Some ideas from "Combining Movements" make good improvs for older students.

CHOREOGRAPHING

1. **ABA:** Create a dance with flow that is free/bound/free or bound/free/bound.

2. **AAB:** Create a dance with flow that is free/free/bound or bound/bound/free. The second section could be varied slightly by changing level, speed, size, using a prop, etc.

3. **ENTER/EXIT:** Pairs or groups enter the "stage" with bound flow movement and exit with free flow movement or exchange flow with a partner in the center as they exit and enter.

4. **MOLECULES:** Create a molecule dance: use free flow movement to designate gas, bound flow movement for solids and a combination of free and bound for liquids. Portray something solid, such as ice, changing to a liquid and then to a gas. Dances can be created about volcanoes, glaciers, popsicles, etc.

5. **PROPS:** Use props that encourage free or bound flow such as scarves and balloons. Then try scarves for bound flow and balloons for free flow. Alternate props, share props, etc.

6. **CHANCE DANCE:** Create a chance dance as described in the chapter on "Place." Use free and bound movements for the choices. For example: 1 = swirl, 2 = run, 3 = dodge, 4 = freeze.

7. **ASTRONAUTS AND ROBOTS:** Create a dance with some dancers as astronauts floating in outer space and some as robots. Or use the images of leaves and trees or rivers and logs.

8. **CINQUAIN AND HAIKU:** Create cinquains about free flow movement, choreograph movement and perform the piece. Create or find Haiku, choreograph movement using bound flow and perform the piece. Discuss the differences.

9. **SIMULTANEOUS/SUCCESSIVE:** Create a dance which uses simultaneous body flow, then successive flow, then simultaneous flow or the reverse. Or divide into simultaneous flow groups and successive flow groups and discuss and compare the different dances.

10. **TRANSITIONS:** Create dances with a focus on smooth transitions and dances without smooth transitions. This can be done quickly by using four or five movement words put into a sequence. Dancers work on transitions between the movements and then perform without the transitions. Discuss the difference.

LESSON ON FLOW

*Ages: 4, 5, 6, 7, or 8   Length: 30 minutes**

WARMING UP

Dance Exercises/Technique: Rhyming exercises emphasizing flow between movements.

Introducing the Concept: FLOW: free, bound. See, say and do the words.

EXPLORING THE CONCEPT

Exploring the Concept: "Leaves" #2
Dancers are blown through space like leaves and then freeze and move with bound flow. Music: selections from *Oxygene.*

Instruments: "ABA" #1
Alternate moving with free and bound flow and playing and not playing your instrument.

DEVELOPING SKILLS

Developing Skills: "River Run" #2 and Zigzag slide
Practice running with free flow and sliding back and forth with bound flow. Alternate skills. Music: "Enter Sunlight" for running and "Funky Penguin" for sliding - *Movin'.*

Combining Movements: "Move and Balance" #3
Do a combination of movement and balancing shapes. Music: voice or drum.

CREATING

Free Dancing/Improvisation: "World Music" #10
React to music from different countries moving with free and bound flow. Move with a prop if desired. Music: selections from *Music from Distant Corners of the World.*

*For a 60 minute lesson: Do 15 minutes of exercises, Shaping #2, Leaping #4 and a Goodbye Dance.

LESSON ON FLOW

Ages: 9-Adult   *Length: 45-60 minutes*

WARMING UP

Warm-up Activity: Exploring the Concept "Move and Balance" #8

Dance Exercises/Technique: Do 10 -20 minutes of technique emphasizing the flow between movements.

Introducing the Concept: FLOW: free, bound. See, say and do the words.

EXPLORING THE CONCEPT

Exploring the Concept: "Shadowing" #4
Shadow partner's free and bound flow movements through and in space. Music: selections from *Emerald.*

Shaping: "Negative/Positive Space" #4
Partners create shapes in each other's negative space and then move with free flow. Music: "Irlandaise" - *Suite for Flute and Jazz Piano.*

DEVELOPING SKILLS

Developing Skills: "Transitions" #7
Dancers do a simple combination of movements, stopping between each one, and then repeat the combination flowing from one movement to another. Music: no music the first time, voice or music with flow the second time.

CREATING

Free Dance/ Improvising: For a 45 minute class do Combining Movements "Cinquain" #2. Dancers help create a cinquain and make choices on how it should be performed.

Choreographing: For a 60 minute class do "Chance Dance" #6
Dancers create a solo based on four actions - swirl, run, dodge, freeze. 5-7 dancers perform their solos simultaneously.

COOLING DOWN

Sharing/Evaluating Choreography: For 45 minute class, divide the class in half and watch the cinquain and briefly discuss the use of flow. For a 60 minute class, watch the chance dance and discuss the use of flow and the magical moments created by chance.

CHAPTER 20

BODY PARTS

INTRODUCING THE CONCEPT

"What does a musician use to make music? Yes, an instrument. What does a painter use to create a painting? Yes, paint and usually a brush. What does a writer use to write a story? Yes, a pen, typewriter or computer. What does a dancer use to create a dance? Yes, his or her body! Dancers don't need anything but themselves -- their bodies and minds. Sometimes we like to dance with the whole body and sometimes we like to dance with just one or two body parts. How many body parts do you think make up your whole body? Let's name as many as we can think of and move them somehow as we name them." Refer to your dance elements chart.

EXPLORING THE CONCEPT

1. **ISOLATED PARTS:** "We're going to do a body part dance. I will call out a body part every time the music stops. Try to isolate that part and dance with just that part, keeping your other body parts still. Think of all the different ways of moving that one body part. We will be dancing mostly in our self space." Call out "legs," "feet," "knees" several times so that dancers can move through

227

general space if they wish. Suggest some ways of moving different parts if they are having difficulty coming up with their own ideas, such as moving them in different directions, levels, speeds, and pathways.

2. **SPECIAL PARTS:** "I will call out a body part as you are moving. Visualize that part being very special and all your other parts being invisible. You can move other parts, but the part I name should be dancing the most. Someone entering the room should say, 'Oh, look at all the heads dancing!' instead of 'look at all the people dancing.' Every time I call out a new part, make that part very special." You can call out two or three parts at a time for variation.

3. **MIXED UP PARTS:** "Try using your hands and arms like feet and legs. Can you jump your hands, gallop your hands ... run ... hop ... slide ... leap your hands? Now use your feet and legs like hands and arms. Can you slash your feet, punch your feet ... float ... shake ... poke ... push ... pull ... twist ... swing your feet? Try doing these movements on different levels."

4. **ADD-A-PART:** "Shake your arm. Keep shaking it while you nod your head. Now add jumping legs. Can you add wiggling hips? Freeze and relax your muscles. Twist your neck gently, add a poking arm, wiggling fingers, bending spine and sliding legs!" Continue with other challenges. Make them simple or complex, depending on the dancers' ability level.

5. **SIMON SAYS:** "Simon says shake your hips, Simon says slash your arms, Simon says wiggle your toes, Simon says gallop your feet, poke your fingers. Whoops, if you were poking your fingers, freeze for 10 seconds." Continue with many different movement commands that move in self and general space. Dancers should freeze for a short time only. The purpose is to move different body parts, not to remain still.

6. **HEAD TO TOE:** "Let's take a movement and have it travel from your head to your toes and back again. Start with shaking. Shake your head, now your shoulders, your arms, your hands, your torso, your hips, your knees, your legs, your feet, back to your legs, knees, hips, torso, hands, arms, shoulders, head! Can you do that with floating ... poking ... stretching ... twisting ... bending?" Ask the dancers for movement ideas.

7. **LEADING PARTS:** "When I call out a body part, let that part pull or lead you through space. How quickly can you change leading parts when I call out a new part? The part I call out should be the part farthest out from your body as you dance through space." Name many different parts including ear, tongue, wrist, heel, knuckles, chin, etc.

8. **FINGER-BODY-FINGER:** "Make a shape focusing on your little finger. When the music starts begin dancing with just your little finger. Now add your other fingers ... your arm ... your head ... your other arm ... your torso ... your hips ... a leg ... the other leg. Now, your whole body is dancing through space. Take away a leg ... your other leg ... your hips ... your torso ... an arm ... your head. Now just an arm is dancing ... now just a hand ... now just your little finger."

9. **NUMBERED PARTS:** "Move around the room on three parts ... on three different parts ... on two parts ... on one part ... on a different one part ... on five parts ... on four parts ... four different parts ... ten parts." Continue with different numbers. Encourage several different solutions for the same number of parts.

10. **BODY HALVES:** "Dance with half your body, keeping the other half still. Try a different half ... try a different half. What is the one half you haven't danced with. Try that half. Can you dance with a quarter of your body parts ... three quarters?" Explore the different quarter and three-quarter possibilities.

11. **GLUE:** "Glue your feet and one hand to the floor. What other parts can you move? Glue your back to the floor. What parts can you move? Glue your elbows and knees to the floor. What parts can you move? Glue your bottom to the floor. What can you move? Glue one foot and one hand to the floor. What can you move?" Explore other challenges.

12. **BACK TO BACK:** "Stand back to back with a partner. Turn around and connect your elbows together. Connect your shoulders ... connect your heads. Now dance away doing a head dance. Come back to back with a new partner. Connect wrists ... ankles ... hips. Dance away doing a hip dance." Continue in this fashion always dancing through space with the last body part named.

13. **CONNECTED PARTS:** "Find a partner. Connect legs together and find a way of moving through space together. Relax and connect wrists. Find a new way of moving through space together. Relax and connect backs. How can you move through space with this connection? Connect with

another pair of dancers. Can the four of you connect elbows and move ... ankles ... shoulders ... heads? Can the whole class connect together and move!"

14. **MIRRORING:** Partners mirror each other's movements. The teacher calls out specific body parts or the leader moves parts from head to toes. The next leader moves from toes to head. This can be done in pairs facing each other or in trios in the shape of a triangle. In a triangle, the two followers stand side by side behind the leader. The leader faces forward. Leadership changes when the leader turns toward another person in the triangle. As that person follows the leader turning, he or she will be facing a new forward direction and will no longer see his or her partners so becomes the new leader.

15. **SHADOWING:** Partners shadow (follow) each other's movements through space. The leader accentuates one body part. When the music pauses, the pair connects that body part together. When the music resumes, the leadership changes and so does the body part. Dancers continue to change leadership and body part movements until the music ends.

16. **SPACE BETWEEN:** "Find a partner. Choose a body part such as hands or knees. Keep the empty space between your body parts equal as you move around the room together sharing the leadership. When I say change, choose a new body part as your invisible connection and keep moving, keeping the space between you equal." With inexperienced dancers, choose a specific leader and alternate leadership when the body part connection changes.

17. **BODY PART STORY:** Tell a story with a body part. "Two feet are walking down the street...." "Two hands go for a walk in the jungle...." "A head goes for a trip in outer space...." The body part does all the action. The other parts are still. Refer to your dance elements chart for locomotor and nonlocomotor actions that the body part can do.

18. **EMOTIONS:** "Can you do a sad hand dance? How would hands move if they were very sad? Would they move quickly or slowly? Would they be sharp or smooth ... strong or light ... high or low? Now try a happy hand dance. What is different? How did the elements change? Can you do an angry hand dance? What elements did you use to show anger? What about a shy hand dance? Let's try using our feet to show our emotions." Try different body parts and different emotions. Refer to the dance elements so that the body parts really dance instead of doing pantomime.

19: **SONGS:** There are many songs that focus on body parts. "Clap Your Hands" and "Looby Loo" or "Hokey Pokey" have been discussed in previous chapters. Try "Old McDonald had an arm, e i e i o, with a poke poke here and a poke poke there, here a poke, there a poke, everywhere a poke poke," etc. "If you're happy and you know it, stamp your feet ...." "This is the way we float our arms, float our arms, float our arms ...." Children's song books are filled with rhymes that you can adapt for exploring body parts.

20. **PROPS:** We usually hold props in our hands. Explore holding different props with different body parts and dance. Put props on different parts and dance. Dance around and touch different body parts to props such as cones, spots, benches, chairs.

21. **ACTIVITY SONGS:** Check the songs on the "Activity Music List" for songs about body parts for ages 2-7.

SHAPING

1. **CONNECT:** "Connect your wrist to your ankle and freeze in a shape. Connect your head to your toes and make a shape. Connect your shoulder to your knee ... your toes to your nose ... your elbows to your stomach ... your heel to your other heel." Continue on with other challenges. Solicit ideas from the dancers.

2. **ADD-A-PART:** "Put your arm somewhere, add your leg in a shape, put your head somewhere, put your other hand somewhere, put your knee somewhere and freeze in that shape. Shake out the shape." Continue with other shapes adding parts one at a time.

3. **GLUE:** "Create a shape by gluing three body parts to the ground. Glue five parts to a wall. Glue four parts to the ground. Glue two parts from your upper body and two from your lower body to a wall." Continue on.

4. **SPECIAL PART:** "Choose a body part. Make a shape which emphasizes your special body part. We will try to guess everyone's special part. Choose a new part, change your level and create a new shape."

5. **HIGH-LOW:** "Can you make a shape in which high parts are on a low level? Can you make a shape in which low parts are on a high level? Can you make a shape in which a low body part is on a high level and a high body part is on a low level? (Head down and feet up.) Can you try that a different way?" Explore many high/low shapes.

6. **MACHINES:** "One at a time, make a shape connecting on to someone else in the 'machine' (group statues). You may connect on to anyone. Fill up the empty spaces to make an

interesting machine shape. Move one body part. Everyone must move a DIFFERENT body part. Think of a sound for your movement. When I turn on the 'volume' make your sound. How many different body parts can we see moving?"

7. **TRIOS :** "Find two friends and create a shape in which you each connect a different part together. For example, knees are connected or elbows or backs. Try several different shapes. Now create a shape in which you each connect a different part together. Try several of these shapes. Show your favorite shape to the class." Of course, this may be done in pairs or small groups.

8. **SHAPE CHAIN:** "Someone will make a shape to begin the chain. Now, each dancer will connect, one at a time, to the previous shape, forming a chain of shapes across the room. You must connect on to a different body part. If the person before you used an arm to connect on to the previous shape, you cannot use your arm. When the chain is completed we will make note of all the different body part connections."

9. **SCULPTOR AND CLAY:** "Choose a body part. Sculpt your partner into a shape that emphasizes your body part. Make it so clear that we would title your statue 'Legs' or 'Hips.' Mold other parts to emphasize your special part. Do not just mold your special part. Choose a level (high, medium or low) on which to mold your clay that will help you. We will look at the statues and give them titles."

10. **UNDER THE BLANKET:** Make a shape under the blanket (large piece of material). Choose a body part and stick that part up or out from your body underneath the blanket. We will try to guess which part is poking out."

11. **PROPS:** Create shapes with scarves, stretchybands, plastic or streamers on different body parts. Make shapes on spots or near cones, touching different body parts to the prop.

INSTRUMENTS

1. **SOUNDS:** "When the 'orchestra' (half or part of the class) plays the triangles, move your head. When they play the sticks, move your legs. When you hear the cymbals, dance with your arms." You can assign other body parts to other instruments. You can be the orchestra and all the students can dance or half the class can play and half dance. This can also be less structured. Students can move any body part on any instrument. Change body parts when the instrument changes.

2. **BODY PARTS:** "Try to play the instruments with different body parts. Can you hold the instrument in your feet and play!"

3. **MUSIC:** "Move different parts when you hear different sections of the music. When you hear the fast part, play in a quick tempo and move your arms. When you hear the slow part, play slowly and dance your legs." For variation, use folk music and assign body parts to different rhythmic sections or use classical music and assign body parts to different instruments or sections.

4. **MOVE AND PLAY:** "Move different parts as you play. Play your instrument and stomp your feet. Play and nod your head. Play and shrug your shoulders. Play and bend your knees."

DEVELOPING SKILLS

1. **LOCOMOTOR/NONLOCOMOTOR:** Practice doing locomotor movements with a special arm, head, shoulder or torso movement. See the "Movement" chapters for more ideas. For example: skip and swing the arms, run and gently nod the head, jump and gently twist the torso, hop and shrug the shoulders, etc.

2. **BODY HALF:** Practice doing locomotor movements with the legs, keeping the other body parts still or controlled. Practice doing nonlocomotor movements with the upper body and keep the lower body still. Practice locomotor skills with the lower half of the body and nonlocomotor skills with the upper half simultaneously. Running legs/floating arms, jumping legs/punching arms, skipping legs/swinging arms.

3. **ARMS:** Practice special arm movements while doing simple leg movements -- arms up, down, right, left while walking; arms circle slowly while running; arms out, in, up, down while jumping, etc.

4. **JAZZ WALKS:** In jazz dance, isolated body parts are used quite often. Practice walking with the pelvis rocking forward and backward or side to side. Knees must be bent to free up the pelvis. Practice walks with sharp arm movements in and out and up and down. Practice walks with head movements left, forward, right forward or up, forward, down, forward. Combine these actions.

5. **NUMBERS:** Practice moving around the room on different numbers of body parts. Try moving on three parts. Try three other parts. Try four parts ... another way of moving on four parts. (This is good for arm and shoulder strength.) Try moving on one part (hopping) ... two parts (jumping, running, leaping, etc.) ... five parts ... all your parts (slithering or rolling).

6. **ACCENTUATE:** Practice different locomotor movements while accentuating a special body part. Jump and accentuate the elbows. Leap and accentuate the knees. Skip and accentuate the shoulders.

7. **ACTIVITY SONGS:** Choose a locomotor activity song from the "Activity Music List" and emphasize body parts as you move through the song.

TURNING

1. **SEPARATE PARTS:** Turn, or revolve different body parts separately -- head turning, arms circling, legs circling, etc. Try turning in and through space while circling one or more body parts.

2. **SPECIAL PART:** Create turns focusing on one body part -- leg emphasized, head emphasized, hands emphasized, hips emphasized, etc. Have dancers create their own and then share with the class.

3. **ARMS:** Practice turning while doing different arm movements. They could open and close, shake, slash, poke, float or be held in different shapes.

4. **CONNECTIONS:** Practice turns with body parts connected to one another -- hands on shoulders or hips, one hand and one foot connected, one hand on one knee, one foot on one knee, hand connected to opposite elbow, etc.

COMBINING MOVEMENTS

1. **WORD CARDS:** Pair up locomotor words and body parts and put together into a combination -- skip/head, turn/arms, swing/legs, stretch/torso, melt/all parts. Emphasize the designated part when doing the steps.

2. **SPECIAL PART:** Have the class pick one body part as the special part. Create a combination alternating the special part with other parts -- HEAD dance, feet dance, HEAD dance, arms dance, HEAD dance, hips dance.

3. **FOLK DANCE:** Do folk dances that emphasize body parts -- Looby Loo, Hokey Pokey, Seven Jumps, Virginia Reel, Tanko Bushi, and Shoemaker are a few body part folk dances.

4. **CINQUAIN:** Create a body part cinquain. Read the poem as the dancers perform.

Body parts	Arms
Moving, still	Curved, angular
Running, swinging, nodding	Extending, curling, grasping
Connecting with another	We hug with them
Dancers	Body Parts

5. **OTHER IDEAS:** Choose combinations from other chapters and emphasize the use of different body parts while doing the combination.

LEAPING

1. **LEGS:** Practice special leaps. Stag leap -- front leg bent, back leg straight. Butterfly leap - both legs kicking back. Double stag -- front leg bends then back leg bends. Knee leap - knees come up to chest as you leap. Split leap -- both legs straight.

2. **SPECIAL PART:** As you leap do a movement with a selected body part -- shake hands, nod head, shrug shoulders, etc.

3. **SPOTS:** Leap with special legs or arms then make a shape touching special body parts to a spot or cone.

4. **BENCH:** Leap, emphasizing special body parts. When you come to the bench move across it emphasizing a body part -- wriggle on stomach, tiptoe, dance hands across, scoot on your bottom, etc.

FREE DANCING/IMPROVISATION

Choose an activity from "Exploring the Concept" that is not too structured or create an improvisation based on an idea from "Combining Movements" or "Choreographing."

CHOREOGRAPHING

1. **ABA:** Choose two different body parts and create a dance -- head/arms/head, arms/feet/arms, shoulders/legs/shoulders.

2. **3 PARTS:** Choose three different body parts. Create a suite of dances emphasizing each body part - head dances at medium speed, legs dance at slow speed, arms dance at fast speed. This can be done in solos, pairs, trios or groups.

Photo by P. Petroff

3. **PART AND WHOLE:** Create a dance isolating different parts and then using the parts together as an integrated whole -- head/whole body/foot/whole body/elbows. Discuss the feelings one has watching isolation versus integration.

4. **GESTURES:** Take an everyday gesture and using the elements, expand it to create a dance. Wave hello - - try the gesture with different body parts, on different levels, with different speed, energy, weight. Other gestures might include brushing your teeth, mixing a cake, ironing a shirt, tossing a ball, shutting a door. Each group could take one gesture and create a dance or duets and solos could be created and then performed simultaneously.

5. **EXIT AND ENTER:** In trios, each dancer chooses a body part and creates a short dance emphasizing his/her part. They choose an order to enter and exit the stage area. For variation, the dancers could exchange body parts or integrate all the parts for a finale.

6. **BODY HALF:** Pairs -- each person chooses a body half (someone is upper body and someone lower or right and left). They create a dance of separate body halves which together equals a whole person. They could exchange body halves. They could move closely together to form one body or move apart giving the impression of two halves dancing through space.

7. **PROPS:** Create a dance moving a prop from body part to body part or emphasizing one body part.

LESSON ON BODY PARTS

Ages: 4-10   Length: 30 minutes*

WARMING UP

Warm-up Activity: "This Is the Way We Shake a Leg" (Tune: Mulberry Bush). Move many body parts different ways. Solicit additional ideas from dancers.

Introducing the Concept: BODY PARTS: head, hips, knees, etc. See, say and do the words.

EXPLORING THE CONCEPT

Exploring the Concept: "Special Parts" #2
Dance different body parts through and in space. Music: "Surprise Song" - *Walter the Waltzing Worm.*

Shaping: "Under the Blanket" #10
Dancers make shapes under a piece of material, emphasizing a body part.

DEVELOPING SKILLS

Turning: "Arms" #3
Create different turns with different arm movements. Have the dancers name the movements to build vocabulary - poking, shaking, slashing, etc. Music: "Turning" - *Turning: Turning Back.*

Combining Movements: "Folk Dance" #3
Do the "Shoemaker's Dance" but use different body parts when making the shoes: "wind the thread, break the thread, pound the nails." Wind with head, elbows, hips, etc. Practice different locomotor skills on the polka section. Music: "Shoemaker's Dance" - *Rhythmically Moving Series.*

CREATING

Free Dancing/Improvising: Exploring the Concept "Activity Song" #21 or "Isolated Parts" #1
Dance to "Body Rock" - *Kids in Motion* or use any music and call out body parts for dancers to emphasize.

*For a 60 minute class: Do 15 minutes of technique, Leaping #2 and a Goodbye Dance.

LESSON ON BODY PARTS

Age: 11-Adult   Length: 45-60 minutes

WARMING UP

Warm-up Activity: Echo leader's movements.   Music: popular or jazz music.

Dance Exercises/Technique: For a 60 minute class do 15-20 minutes of technique emphasizing different body parts.

Introducing the Concept: BODY PARTS: pelvis, feet, spine, etc. See, say and do the words.

EXPLORING THE CONCEPT

Exploring the Concept: "Space Between" #16
Choose a body part and move with a partner through space maintaining an invisible connection between each other's specified body part. Try several different body parts. Music: "Javanaise" - *Suite for Flute and Jazz Piano.*

DEVELOPING SKILLS

Developing Skills: "Accentuate" #6
Practice locomotor skills while accentuating different body parts.

Combining Movements: "Special Parts" #2
Create a combination alternating different body parts with one specified body part: feet dance, head dance, elbows dance, head dance, etc. Music: "Baroque and Blues" - *Suite for Flute and Jazz Piano.*

CREATING

Choreographing: "Body Half" #6
Pairs create a dance of separate body halves which together equal a whole person. Music: selections from *Emerald* or *Windham Hill Samplers.*

COOLING DOWN

Sharing/Evaluating Choreography: Share the duets and discuss the use of body halves and the relationship between the two dancers. If time is limited, show several duets simultaneously.

CHAPTER 21

BODY SHAPES
Curved, Straight, Angular, Twisted
Symmetrical, Asymmetrical

INTRODUCING THE CONCEPT

"Your body can make many interesting shapes. Try making a CURVED shape. Think about hugging a huge beach ball with your arms, legs and back. Now, try a STRAIGHT shape. Let your body parts stretch out into space so that nothing bends. Move into an ANGULAR shape by bending all your joints, even your fingers and toes! Stretch into a different straight shape. Now, feel as though someone were twisting both ends of your body the way you would twist up a taffy wrapper and form a TWISTED shape. Today we are going to explore many different ways of creating these shapes and moving them through space."

Experienced dancers might want to explore SYMMETRICAL and ASYMMETRICAL SHAPES: "Look at my shape. (Make a simple symmetrical shape.) Imagine a line down the center of my body from my head to the floor, does each half of my body look exactly the same? Yes, they are SYMMETRICAL or even. Now, I will move just one body part. Does each half of my body look the same? No, now my shape is ASYMMETRICAL or uneven -- each half is a little bit different. Copy my symmetrical shape. Does each half of your body feel the same? On your own, move one body part. Does each half feel symmetrical now or does your body shape feel asymmetrical?"

EXPLORING THE CONCEPT

1. **CREATING SHAPES:** "I want you to try moving from one shape to another without stopping. Use all your body parts, even the parts inside your body, to help create wonderful shapes. Try changing directions, levels and size as you move from one shape to another. Curve ... stretch ... bend ... twist ... stretch ... bend ... twist ... curve ... stretch ... twist ... bend ... curve ... stretch." Pause between words so that your students can feel the curved, straight, angular and twisted shapes. The point of this exploration is to move into and out of shapes instead of creating shapes in a vacuum. To me, dance is moving in and out of shapes, not just a series of shapes. The movement between shapes is as important as the shapes themselves.

2. **TRAVELING SHAPES:** "Create a curved shape. Find a natural way to move that shape to a new place. Stretch into a straight shape. Move that shape a different way to a new spot. Bend into an angular shape and move that shape to a new spot, perhaps changing levels or directions. Twist into a twisted shape and move to a new spot changing speeds or force." Repeat several times, encouraging your students to use the dance elements to create new shapes and ways of traveling the shapes through space.

3. **FLOWING SHAPES:** "I want you to dance with free flow through space. Feel as though you are being blown by wind. When I give the signal, freeze. What is your shape? Are you twisted, curved, angular or straight? This time when you move through space make shapes as you move. Freeze and notice your shape. Is it different? When the music plays, create moving, flowing shapes through space. When the music freezes, freeze in a shape and think about what kind of shape it is."

4. **MOVING SHAPES:** "Curve your body parts to create a curved shape. Now stretch out your shape as you move through general space and end in a straight shape. Bend your joints and let that action propel you through space, ending in an angular shape. Twist your body, letting the twisting motion move you to a new place in space." Continue this exploration, suggesting level, direction, size and speed changes. This is not as easy as it sounds. Encourage your students to use natural motions, not forced movement. If they use all their body parts inside and out and do the shapes and movements fully, feeling the shapes, their movement should have great clarity and beauty.

5. **KALEIDOSCOPE SHAPES:** "Think about the shapes inside a kaleidoscope. The shapes and patterns move from one to another. I will name four shapes. Move smoothly from one shape to another thinking about the kaleidoscope. Let's try moving in self space first. Twisted ... straight ... angular ... curved. Now let's try moving through general space creating transitions between the shapes. Straight ... curved ... twisted ... angular.

6. **COPY A SHAPE:** "Everyone make twisted shapes. When the music freezes, I will call out someone's name and everyone will copy his/her twisted shape. Then we will make curved shapes until the music stops and I call a new name. We will all copy that person's curved shape." Continue, choosing as many students as possible. Copying other people's shapes gives the students new ideas and expands their movement vocabulary.

7. **SHAPE MUSEUM:** "Half of the class will make statues throughout the room. Make your shapes clear -- curved, straight, angular or twisted. The other half will dance around the statues. The dancers will copy the statues but not exactly. If you copy a straight statue, make a different straight

statue in front or beside it. Copy the idea of straight, but do not copy the exact shape. When a statue is copied, it becomes free to dance around the other statues and then copy one. Dancers change to statues when they copy one and statues become dancers when they are copied. Remember to copy the type of shape, not the exact shape." You can have the dancers move in a directed way, such as in the shape of the statue they were just forming, or move freely.

8. **JUNIOR SHAPE MUSEUM:** "Half the class will make interesting statues. The other half will dance around the statues. When I say 'copy a statue,' the dancers will each find a statue to copy exactly. Then I will say 'old statues dance away' and the old statues will dance any way they want to until I say 'copy a statue.' " Continue on. A demonstration helps young children. Very young children could hold streamers. The teacher would say "Blue streamers make a special statue shape. Green streamers dance around. Green streamers copy a statue. Now blue streamers dance around. Blue streamers copy a statue. Green streamers dance around."

9. **BACK TO BACK:** "Stand back to back with someone. Now make a curved shape together, a straight shape and a twisted shape. Dance away with twisting movements. Back to back! Make an angular shape together, a straight shape and a curved shape. Dance away with curving motions. Back to back! One make a straight and the other make a curved shape, change, now both make an angular shape and dance away with bending motions." Continue on with similar challenges.

10. **GROUP SCULPTOR AND CLAY:** "Half the class are lumps of clay and half are sculptors. Then we will change roles. The sculptors will move with curving movements around the clay and mold a body part into a curve as they dance by. The clay will be forever changing shape as different dancers shape them. When the music stops, the sculptors will stand back and look at their curvy creations. Then we will change roles." Try other shapes and movements. Try all the shapes simultaneously.

11. **PICTURES:** "I am going to hold up two shape pictures. I want you to copy one shape with your body, then move into the next shape and then move back to the first shape." You could show very simple geometric shape pictures, more interesting designs created by your students or sophisticated art works by Calder, Mondrian, Klee and Picasso.

12. **NEGATIVE SPACE:** "Find a partner. One of you will make a shape with lots of empty space. The other will fill the negative space with a different type of shape. As soon as the space has been filled, the first dancer will create another shape with negative space. The partner will move into the negative space and fill it with a new shape. The transitions between the shapes are as important as the shapes. Try to keep the flow of movement continuous." After three or four shapes, let the dancers change roles. Remind the dancers of the four types of shapes so that they might fill a curved shape with a straight shape or fill a straight shape with an angular shape. This can be done in trios or quartets.

13. **SHAPES THROUGH SPACE:** "Find a partner. One of you will make a shape. The other dancer will use that shape to initiate a way of moving through space. If your partner is in an angular shape with legs crossed you might move through space with angular movements in a criss cross pathway. Dance away and back to your partner, then make a different shape in front of your partner. Now your partner has to use your shape to initiate a way of moving through space. Maybe you made a twisted shape. Your partner might move in a zig zag pathway with twisting movements." You could let the partners move at their own pace or be more directed by giving a certain number of counts during which the dancers can move. It is fun to see how dancers relate to each other's shapes.

14. **SYMMETRICAL AND ASYMMETRICAL:** "Make some symmetrical shapes. Look at your friend's shapes. How do symmetrical shapes make you feel? Yes, symmetry connotes peace, comfort, harmony and stability. Try some uneven or asymmetrical shapes. How does asymmetry make you feel? Asymmetry often connotes adventure, excitement or opposition."

242

15. **PARTNERS:** "Make a symmetrical shape by yourself. Now dance your shape to a partner and make a symmetrical shape together using your first shapes. How can you do that? You cannot stand side by side but you can make your shapes one in front of the other! Now make an asymmetrical shape together with those two shapes. Now make a symmetrical shape together by making the same shape as each other. How can you take these shapes and create an asymmetrical shape together? This time create an asymmetrical shape by yourself and make a symmetrical shape together and then an asymmetrical shape together." Explore these problems in trios and groups.

16. **TOGETHER/APART:** "Form a symmetrical shape alone. Now dance through general space to a partner, keeping your movement as symmetrical as possible. Make a symmetrical shape with your partner, then an asymmetrical shape. Now dance away from your partner with asymmetrical movement. Form a trio and an asymmetrical shape, then symmetrical shape. Dance away with symmetrical movement. Form a quartet and create a symmetrical shape, then an asymmetrical shape and dance away with asymmetrical movement." Continue on ending with the whole class or stop at quartets.

17. **WORDS:** "I will say a word and you form a shape that describes that word. Is it symmetrical or asymmetrical? Now describe the word through movement. What kind of movement are you doing?" Try words such as anger, peace, fear, love, comfort, hate, etc. OR have the dancers create symmetrical and asymmetrical shapes and then think of words to match the shapes.

18. **PROPS:** STRETCHYBANDS -- create different shapes inside and outside the stretchybands.
STRING - toss long pieces of string in the air and copy the shape of the string as it lands on the floor.
STREAMERS -- decorate shapes with streamers or use streamers as lines to create geometric shapes between dancers.
SCARVES/PLASTIC -- let the prop become a special part of the shape or make shapes around the prop.
SHEET or PARACHUTE - - make secret shapes under the material, let others guess the shape.

19. **ACTIVITY SONGS:** Choose a song from the "Activity Music List" that focuses on shapes for children ages 2-7.

SHAPING

Choose explorations from any of the other element chapters under this heading. Focus on the shape words (curved, angular, straight and twisted) instead of another dance element. Below are a few examples:

1. **ADD-A-PART:** "Make a curved shape with your arm. Add a twisted leg. Add a bent elbow. Add a straight knee. Freeze and look at everyone's shape!" Continue on. Ask your students for ideas.

2. **BODY HALVES:** "Make a twisted shape with your top half and a bent shape with your lower half. Make a curved shape with your right half and a straight shape with your left half. Let your left half curve into your center and your right half stretch away into a straight shape. Let you lower half bend while your upper half twists." Continue on in this way asking for static and moving shapes.

3. **SCULPTOR AND CLAY:** "Mold your partner into a twisted, curved, angular, straight, symmetrical or asymmetrical shape. Change roles. Try sculptures that combine different shapes. Try sculptures on different levels."

4. **MIRRORING:** "Face your partner and move slowly from curved to twisted to straight to angular shapes. Your partner must copy your movement. Also try moving from symmetrical shapes to asymmetrical shapes." Young children can mirror you. Older students might need to be given ideas as they mirror each other.

5. **XEROXED SHAPES:** "Make a curved shape, close your eyes and remember that shape. Move in a curvy pathway and make the same curved shape. Now try a twisted shape. Twist through space and form the same twisted shape." Continue with the other shapes.

INSTRUMENTS

1. **PAUSE:** "When the music plays, dance through space and play your instrument. Think about making shapes as you move. When the music pauses, freeze in a special shape." You could give specific suggestions during the pauses such as freeze in a twisted, curved, angular, straight, symmetrical or asymmetrical shape.

2. **HALF NOTES:** "Play your instrument and make a shape on the first and third beat of every measure. You will have two counts (half note) to make your shape -- ONE two, THREE four."

3. **ACCENT:** "Play your instrument and make a shape on the first beat of every measure. Hold your shape for the other three beats but keep playing your instrument. Remember to change types of shapes and levels, direction, size and force."

4: **ECHO:** "Stand face to face with a partner. Take turns being the leader. The leader will play and make a shape on the first beat and the follower will echo the sound and shape on the third beat. Continue until I give the signal to change leaders." Dancers can echo on any designated beat depending on their experience. Leave it open for young children and explore different meters with experienced dancers.

5. **COUNTS:** "Play your instrument and make a shape for eight counts. Move that shape through general space while you play for another eight counts. Freeze in that shape and play for eight counts more. Start again with a new shape." Play around with the counts. For example, dancers could make a shape for four counts, move for eight counts and freeze for four counts.

6. **TWISTING TRIANGLES:** "Everyone play and dance. When I give the signal, freeze in a special shape. I will call out an instrument and a shaping movement such as 'triangles twisting.' Those playing triangles make twisting shapes until I give the signal for all to play and dance." Alternate everyone dancing with designated instruments and shapes.

DEVELOPING SKILLS

1. **LOCOMOTOR MOVEMENTS:** Practice different locomotor movements in different shapes. See the "Locomotor Movement" chapter for more ideas. Try jumping in a twisted shape, galloping in a curved shape, hopping in a straight shape, skipping in an angular shape, etc. You could also practice doing all the shapes while doing one locomotor movement -- run in twisted, curved, angular and straight shapes. Discuss what is easiest, what is hardest and why?

2. **NONLOCOMOTOR MOVEMENT:** Practice different nonlocomotor movements in different shapes. See the "Nonlocomotor Movement" chapter for more ideas. Try floating in curved shapes, straight shapes, angular shapes and twisted shapes. Which shapes feel most natural for floating movements? Try many other nonlocomotor movements in different shapes.

3. **BODY HALVES:** Practice moving through space with your upper body in a curved shape and your lower body in a straight shape. Try moving with your lower body in a bent shape and your upper body in a twisted shape ... upper body bent and lower body twisted ... lower body curved and upper body straight! Besides moving in frozen shapes, try moving in moving shapes -- twisting the upper body while bending the lower body ... carving the upper body while stretching the lower body, etc. Also try moving right and left body halves instead of upper and lower body halves.

4. **SYMMETRY AND ASYMMETRY:** Practice moving through space with symmetrical movement. The only locomotor movement you can do that is symmetrical is jumping. However, you can create symmetrical shapes with your arms and torso while doing different locomotor movements so that the movement looks fairly symmetrical. Walking, running and skipping might be considered symmetrical because the legs alternate, while galloping and hopping might be considered asymmetrical because one leg is always the leader. Sliding can look symmetrical because the legs open and close together. Practice movement that looks asymmetrical. Experienced students enjoy discussing and dissecting these movements. Younger students enjoy just doing them.

5. **PARTNERS:** Partners face each other across the room. One dancer makes a shape and does a movement toward the center. The other dancer copies the shape and movement. When they reach each other they do the movement away and back to their places. The follower then becomes the leader. They keep taking turns. This can also be done shadowing, with the leader in front of the follower. This activity helps dancers to expand their movement vocabulary by practicing unfamiliar movements.

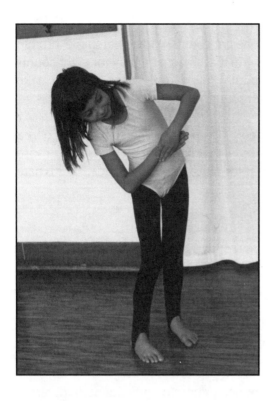

6. **MOVE AND STOP:** Practice moving and then stopping suddenly in a shape. Practice making different shapes when you freeze, instead of the same familiar shape. You could call out different types of shapes before the freeze to help your students be more creative.

7. **SHAPING:** Practice moving into shapes. Run and stretch until you cannot stretch anymore and you pause in a straight shape. Twist through space and end in a twisted shape. Curve the space and end in a curved shape. Bend through the space until you end in an angular shape.

TURNING

1. **SHAPES:** Practice turning in different shapes. Try chaînés turns in angular, curved, straight and twisted shapes. Try turning in a straight shape while pivoting on one foot. Practice pivot turns in other shapes. Practice jumping and hopping turns in different shapes. Practice turns on different levels in different shapes.

2. **TURN AND STOP:** Practice turning and then ending in a special shape. Practice holding the shape maintaining your balance. Direct the shapes or let them be free.

3. **CURVED/STRAIGHT:** Practice turning in a curved shape then a straight shape. Keep alternating curved and straight shapes as you turn. This might be a good way to introduce barrel turns or leap turns.

4. **TWISTS:** Turn to the right in four counts, moving through a straight shape to a curved shape ending in a twisted shape. Do the same to the left. Alternate right and left turns. These shapes should be natural, formed in the course of turning. However, if you think in terms of shapes, the movement will be bigger and clearer. The turns will be more exciting. You can also practice an eight count turn.

5. **SYMMETRY AND ASYMMETRY:** I think it is very helpful to do chaînées turns (walking turns that travel in a continuous direction through space) in symmetrical shapes. If you think of keeping your body symmetrical as you turn, you will be able to turn faster. When performing other turns such as pirouettes, piqué turns or off balance turns, it is helpful to concentrate on turning in asymmetrical shapes. When creating exciting new turns, focus on strong asymmetrical shapes. Concentrating on holding a shape as you turn will help you maintain your balance and make the shape of the turn clear.

COMBINING MOVEMENTS

1. **FOLK DANCES:** Seven Jumps is a popular folk dance that alternates skipping with making different shapes. Do the authentic version and/or have your students create their own shapes. When performing Looby Loo put shapes into the circle instead of body parts. "Put a twisted shape in, put a twisted shape out, give your shape a shake, shake, shake and turn your shape about." Also, use folk dance music for your own combinations.

2. **WORD CARDS:** Choose four locomotor/nonlocomotor words and put them into a sequence. Add four shape words to the movement words and create a dance -- curved walk, straight jump, twisted turn, angular float.

3. **COUNTS:** Create a combination to counts -- make a twisted shape for eight counts, turn in the shape for eight counts, move eight counts changing the shape into a straight shape OR turn into a curved shape for four counts, melt into a straight shape for four counts, roll in the straight shape for four counts and rise into a twisted shape.

4. **MOVE AND STOP:** Create a combination of movement and shapes -- skip, shape, shape, shape, turn; run, shape, turn, shape, float, shape; jump, symmetrical shape, slide, asymmetrical shape, stretch, symmetrical shape.

5. **CINQUAIN:** You and/or your students create a cinquain about shapes. Read the poem as the dancers perform it.

Shapes
Curved, straight
Twisting, bending, stretching
Dancers sculpting the space
Bodies

6. **CANON:** Create a combination that alternates movement and shaping such as fancy skip eight counts, make a twisted shape for eight counts. The second line or group of dancers should start moving when the first group starts shaping. Each group begins eight counts after the preceding group. This is nice to watch because locomotor movement is juxtaposed with nonlocomotor movement.

7. **SHAPE STORY:** Create a story about a shape that has many adventures. "Twisted shape went skipping down the road toward the dark forest. A witch came along and turned twisted shape into a little angular shape. This shape crept out of the dark forest into a big wind. The wind spun angular shape around and around until it turned into a big curvy shape. Big curvy shape rolled down a hill and bumped into a magician. The magician changed big curvy shape back into twisted shape and twisted shape ran home and fell asleep."

247

8. **SYMMETRY/ASYMMETRY:** Create a combination that alternates symmetrical and asymmetrical movement and shapes.

9. **ACTIVITY SONGS:** Choose a song for ages 2-7 from the "Activity Music List" that focuses on shapes.

LEAPING

1. **PHOTOS:** Encourage the dancers to make shapes as they leap that are so clear that you could take a photograph of the shape. Show photos or pictures of dancers leaping to give your students ideas. Encourage the dancers to also think about their shape between leaps.

2. **LEAP AND STOP:** Leap and then stop in a shape. Alternate leaps and shapes. It is difficult to stop the momentum of leaping. Encourage your students to bend the knees to help stop and make the shape strong and clear.

3. **GROUP SHAPES:** Leap over cartons or through empty space and then stop and freeze in a shape. Each dancer will join the group shape at the end of their leaps to form a large statue.

4. **LEG SHAPES:** Practice leaps with the front leg bent (stag leap), with the back leg bent, with both legs bent, with legs kicking backward (butterfly leap), with both legs straight (split leap), with both knees punching upward.

5. **PARTNERS:** Leap down opposite sides of the room. Come together and make a special shape, then leap together down the center of the room. Think also about the shapes you make as you are leaping.

6. **ARMS:** Focus on arm shapes. Call out shapes as the dancers leap. Use shape words (curved, twisted, symmetrical and asymmetrical, etc.) or letter shapes (Y, T, P, O, L).

FREE DANCING/IMPROVISATION

Choose an activity under "Exploring the Concept" that is not too structured. Some activities under "Combining Movements" might also make good improvisations for older students.

CHOREOGRAPHING

1. **WORD CARDS:** Have groups put shape words into a sequence and create a dance. It is fun to give each group or pair the same sequence and see all the different solutions.

2. **ABA:** Choose two shape words and create a dance - curved/twisted/curved, straight/angular/ straight, etc. Instead of just making three static shapes, the dancers need to make moving shapes. Add a prop to one of the sections for variety.

3. **SUITE:** Choose three shape words and create a suite. Perhaps, twisting medium speed, curving slow speed and bending fast speed. Add a prop to one or more sections for variety.

4. **DANCE BY CHANCE:** See the section on PLACE, "Choreographing" #5. If you want to, use two movements and two specific shapes such as 1 = walk, 2 = twisted shape, 3 = roll, 4 = curved shape or 1 = jump, 2 = turn, 3 = low symmetrical shape, 4 = high asymmetrical shape. This exercise helps dancers see the importance of stillness in choreography. Dancers do not always have to be moving.

5. **CINQUAIN:** Have groups write and perform their own cinquains or choreograph their own movement to a common cinquain.

6. **ART WORKS:** Choose a famous work of art by Klee, Mondrian, Picasso, Calder or some other artist who uses strong shapes. Let each group choose three shapes from the picture and create transitions based on shapes and lines in the picture to connect the three shapes. Discuss the results.

7. **FEELINGS:** Assign different groups or pairs a type of shape. Have each group design a study around the shape. Discuss the feelings the shapes evoke. Twisted shapes and movement -- anguish, fear ? Angular shapes and movement -- confusion, humor? Curved shapes -- love, comfort? Straight shapes -- dogmatic, aggressive?

8. **KALEIDOSCOPE:** Divide into groups. Have half the group choose three shapes and create transitions between the shapes. Have the other half relate to the shapes moving in, around and through the changing shapes. Dancers could change roles if they want to. Young dancers can work in pairs. One dancer makes continuous shapes in self space, the other dancer moves around the shaper.

9. **SYMMETRY AND ASYMMETRY:** Create tableaux based on symmetrical and asymmetrical shapes. Create transitions between the tableaux. Use words to help motivate movement - love/hate/reconciliation; coming/meeting/parting; work/play/sleep; birth/life/death; youth/middle age/old age, etc.

10. **MOVEMENT MAPS:** Draw three geometric shapes on paper. Connect the shapes with curved, straight or zig zag lines. Choose a type of shape to make for each geometric shape and choose a type of movement to do on the lines. Transpose the map to the room space and perform your dance. For example: straight shapes where the square is, carving through space on the curvy line, angular shapes where the triangle is, lunging on the straight line, curved shapes where the circle is, twisting on the zig zag line. This may be done in trios and groups, also.

LESSON ON BODY SHAPES

Ages: 4, 5, 6, 7, or 8   Length: 30 minutes*

WARMING UP

Dance Exercises/Technique: Do rhyming exercises that emphasize body part and whole body shapes.

Introducing the Concept: BODY SHAPES: curved, angular, straight, twisted. See, say and do the words.

EXPLORING THE CONCEPT

Exploring the Concept: "Copy a Shape" #6
Dancers form shapes and then copy somebody's shape. Music: African music or something lively.

DEVELOPING SKILLS

Developing Skills: "Move and Stop" #6
Dance through space then freeze in special shapes. Music: "Pause" - *Movin'.*

Combining Movements: "Shape Story" #7
Create a story about a shape and the adventures it has.

CREATING

Free Dancing/Improvising: Exploring the Concept "Back to Back" #9
Dancers form shapes back to back and then dance through space in different shapes and ways.

COOLING DOWN

Relaxation: Stretch and curl into shapes.

*For a 60 minute class: Do 15 minutes of technique, Shaping #1, Leaping #2 and a Goodbye Dance.

LESSON ON BODY SHAPES

Ages: 9-Adult   *Length: 45-60 minutes*

WARMING UP

Warm-up Activity: "Shape Museum" from "Quick Warm-ups"

Dance Exercises/Technique: For a 60 minute class do 15-20 minutes of technique emphasizing the shape of body parts and the whole body.

Introducing the Concept: BODY SHAPES: curved, angular, twisted, straight, symmetrical, asymmetrical. See, say and do the words.

EXPLORING THE CONCEPT

Exploring the Concept: "Partners" #15
Form symmetrical and asymmetrical shapes with a partner. Music: selections from *Simple Pleasures* by Bobby McFerrin.

DEVELOPING SKILLS

Turning: "Symmetry and Asymmetry" #5
Practice turning in symmetrical and asymmetrical shapes.

Combining Movements: "Move and Stop" #4
Create a combination of locomotor movement, including turning and shapes: Turn, shape, run, shape, turn, shape, run, shape. Add arm movements. Music: selection from *Simple Pleasures.*

CREATING

Choreographing: "Movement Maps" #10
Draw maps on paper. Choreograph dances using different shapes and different movements based on your map.

COOLING DOWN

Sharing/Evaluating Choreography: Show dances and discuss the use of shapes and symmetrical and asymmetrical movement.

CHAPTER 22

RELATIONSHIPS

INTRODUCING THE CONCEPT

"A RELATIONSHIP is a connection between two or more people or things. In dance we can explore the relationship that our body parts have to one another; the relationship that we have to another dancer or to a group of dancers; the relationship that we have to another object or prop. Certain words can help us explore different ways of relating or connecting. As we say each word, form a relationship with your body parts (or prop) that describes the meaning of the word: OVER (stretch your hand over your head, foot over your hand, etc.) ... UNDER (place your hand under your foot, head under your hand, etc.) ... AROUND (hands around your ankle) ... THROUGH (arm through a circle created by your other arm) ... ON (hands on your knees) ... OFF (hands off your knees) ... ABOVE ... BELOW ... NEAR ... FAR ... BESIDE ... BETWEEN ... IN ...OUT.

"When we work with partners and in groups, we will be using these words and other words such as MIRROR, SHADOW, MEET, PART, ALONE, TOGETHER, CONNECT, UNISON, and CONTRAST to create different RELATIONSHIPS with other dancers.

"When we choreograph and perform our choreography, we might also explore the relationship of the dancers to the audience; the relationship of the choreography to the music or musicians; the relationship of movement to the performance space. The use of different relationships makes dance very exciting to perform and to watch."

Note: When introducing the concept of RELATIONSHIPS for the first time, you may choose to focus on only one or two aspects such as relationships between dancers and relationships between dancers and props. As your students become more experienced you will want to explore the other forms of relationships.

EXPLORING THE CONCEPT

Relationships Between Body Parts

1. **DANCING SHAPES:** "Make a shape with your hand OVER your head. When the music begins, dance through space keeping the relationship of your hand over your head. You may move in many different ways but your hand should stay over your head until the music pauses. When there is a pause I will name a new body part relationship. Make a shape describing the new relationship, then dance through space when the music resumes." Explore some unusual relationships such as feet OVER head, hand UNDER foot, elbow ON hip, hands BETWEEN legs, head FAR from shoulders, toes NEAR nose, ear BESIDE knee, hands AROUND ankle.

2. **FOLLOW THE PART:** "Let different body parts lead you through space. One body part is the leader and all the other body parts have to follow. When the music changes (or give a signal), I will name a new body part. That part becomes the leader and leads you through space. Head ... knees ... bottom ... toes ... elbows ... nose ... heels ... stomach ... tongue ... spine ... hips ... shoulders." Variation: add different dance elements -- head backwards, sideways; elbows up, down; hips fast, slow; arms smooth, sharp; legs strong, light, etc. The body part still leads, but leads the other parts in a specified way.

3. **SPACE BETWEEN:** "Make a shape with your body parts as far from each other as possible (a big shape). Try moving through space keeping the space between your body parts always the same. Make a shape with your body parts close together (a small shape). Move this shape through space, trying to keep the space between body parts the same. Make a medium sized shape with your body parts not too far or too near and move that shape through space. Which shape was easiest to move? (Probably the last shape.) Now try constantly changing the space between your body parts as you move through space. How does that make you feel?"

4. **SIMON SAYS:** "Simon says put your hand ON your foot, Simon says put your heel OVER your knee, Simon says put your elbows BETWEEN your feet, put your toes TOGETHER! Whoops, Simon didn't say to do that. Let's try again." Continue naming body parts and relationship words (prepositions). I do not like penalizing students who miss, so we just continue on and students can keep track of their misses themselves and try to improve the next time we play. Of course, you can do this activity without playing Simon Says.

5. **BODY HALVES:** "Try creating different relationships in opposite halves of your body. Make a shape with upper body parts near each other and lower body parts far away and move that shape through space. Try a shape in which body parts on the right side are near and body parts on the left side are far and move through space. Try the opposite of these shapes. Try moving your upper body parts together and apart as you dance through space. Try this with your lower body and right and left halves of the body." (This activity is for dancers with some experience.)

OTHER IDEAS: Look in the "Body Part" section for more ways to explore relationships between body parts. Check the "Activity Music List" for songs for ages 2-7 that focus on body parts and relationships.

Relationships Between Dancers

6. **FIND A FRIEND:** "We are going to do a dance in which you will be continually forming new relationships. When I say, 'Find a friend', make a shape with another dancer as quickly as possible. Now dance away. 'Find a friend!' Choose a new friend with which to make a shape. Now, dance away. 'Find a friend!' Dance away."

7. **MIRROR/SHADOW:** "Find a partner. (This can also be done in trios and quartets.) Face each other and choose a leader. When the music starts, the leader will dance in self space and the follower will mirror (copy) the leader's movements. Your relationship is near and face to face. When I give the signal, the leader will turn around and dance through general space. The follower will shadow (copy) the leader's movements. Your relationship is still near but now it is back to face. When I give another signal, freeze, face each other and change leaders. Repeat the dance with the new leader."

8. **PARTNER PREPOSITIONS:** "Find a partner. Shadow your partner's movements through general space. When the music stops I will say two prepositions such as 'under and over.' Make a statue together describing the prepositions. Try to make the statue without talking. Create a cooperative relationship, sensing each other's movements. When the music resumes, dance through general space and your partner will follow until the music pauses and I call out two new prepositions such as 'around and through.'" Some other prepositional pairs are: on/off, above/below, and in/out. Try single prepositions such as beside, far, near, apart, together, between, alone, connected.

9. **FIND THE LEADER:** "I will call out a name. Find that dancer and move the way the leader is moving. When the music pauses, I will call out the name of a new leader. Find that dancer and copy his/her movement." This is an excellent activity because your students will be expanding their movement vocabulary by trying other dancers' movements. Leaders may move in self or general space. Change leaders fairly quickly.

10. **BACK TO BACK:** "When I call out 'back to back,' stand back to back with another dancer as quickly as possible, then I will state two relationships. Demonstrate those relationships together, then dance away when the music plays. 'Back to back' ... high/low (one dancer high, one low) ... inside/outside (one dancer inside the other's shape) ... now dance far away from your partner. 'Back to back' ... together/apart (connecting together with some body parts, stretching away with other body parts) ... side by side ... dance away." Think of many relationships. You could use prepositions but you could also use the dance elements -- strong/light, sharp/smooth, big/little, etc.

11. **HUMAN OBSTACLE COURSE:** "I would like half the class to create interesting shapes and forms such as tunnels, bridges, lumps, a forest of statues, geometric shapes, etc. The other half will move through the obstacle course. As you move through, think of many different ways of relating to the obstacles, always being gentle and careful." Be sure to change roles. You may need to be more directed with young children, asking simply for "logs and lumps" for dancers to go over and under. Older students can work together to create wonderful "playgrounds."

12. **16 COUNTS:** "Find a partner. One will move in self space first and the other in general space. I will count to 16. The general space dancer will travel away from and back to his/her partner by the time I count to 16. The self space dancer will dance in his/her space for 16 counts. Each pair must

maintain eye contact with each other at all times. When I reach 16 you should be connected in a shape. Then you will change roles as I count another number." You can be as directed or free as is necessary. Your students can dance any way they wish or you can give them ideas such as 16 counts backward, 12 counts high and low, 20 counts slashing, etc. Discuss how maintaining eye contact makes one feel and how it looks as one watches others.

13. **ADD A FRIEND:** "Dance through space (direct their movement or let them move freely). Find a friend by the time I count to five and dance together in self space. You may dance connected somehow or just near each other. Dance away. Find two friends and dance together. Dance away. Find three or four friends and dance together. Dance away. Find five or six friends and dance together. Dance away. Everybody dance together. Now dance away." Music that has a verse and chorus or two distinct sections works well with this exploration. You may need to be more directed by asking your students to hold hands while dancing together (good for parents and toddlers) or by giving them ideas of how to dance together.

14. **OVER AND UNDER, AROUND AND THROUGH:** "Find a partner. Moving smoothly and slowly, without discussion, dance under, over, around and through each other. Think about snakes slithering, twisting and gliding around one another. Sense each other so that your movements can be continuous. Create transitions between shapes and movements. Relate to each other without words." Change partners. Discuss how it feels to work with different people. What adjustments need to be made? Do you relate more easily to some dancers than to others? It is usually easier to dance with someone who has a similar movement style.

15. **MAGIC HANDS:** "Find a partner. Place one of your hands twelve inches from one of your partner's hands. Dance through space in many different ways. Your partner must follow you, always keeping the same relationship -- twelve inches between hands. Change leaders. Now change body parts. Try magic elbows, knees, hips, heads, spines." Try this activity in trios or small groups with experienced students.

16. **ECHO:** "I am going to move for four counts, then I will freeze for four counts while you echo my movement for four counts. I will move, you will move, I will move, you will move. You will need to focus on me, remember my movements and then copy them." This can also be done in partners. More advanced students can try this in canon: there are no freezes; the leader is always moving 4 counts ahead of the follower.

17. **CONVERSATIONS:** "Find a partner. Say something through movement. Let your partner relate to what you 'said' through movement. Relate and react to what he/she said. Continue taking turns, moving in self and general space, using body language instead of voices. Notice the relationships you create with your body depending on what you are 'saying' and how you are feeling. Are you over your partner ... near ... far ... under ... beside?"

18. **TRIANGLE MIRRORING:** "Form a triangle without holding hands, with two friends. You should all be facing the same way, about three to five feet apart, with one person in front and two side by side behind the leader. The person who cannot see the other two dancers is the leader. The leader will move in self space when the music begins and the other two will copy the leader's movements. When the leader wants to stop he/she will turn to the right or left to face a new leader. The other two dancers turn also because they are following the leader. The new leader is the person who cannot see the other two dancers because he/she is now in front! Continue moving and changing leadership at will. Maintain the triangular relationship." This can also be done in a diamond formation. The value of this exploration is that the leaders have control of how long they want to be leaders and the followers expand their movement vocabulary by trying others' movements.

19. **MOUNTAINS AND TUNNELS:** "Half of you will be mountains and tunnels and the other half will be dancers. The tunnels should form a shape that someone can go under or through. When a dancer has gone under you, carefully change into a mountain that someone could go over. The mountains cannot be too high. The tunnels cannot be too low. The dancers will move carefully under, over, around and through the tunnels and mountains. Remember to change shapes each time a dancer has related to you. When I give the signal we will change roles."

OTHER IDEAS: Whenever you work with partners or groups, relationships are formed. Check the other concept chapters for many explorations using relationships. Instead of focusing on the specified concept, focus on the idea of relationships. Check the "Activity Record List" for songs for ages 2-7 that focus on relationships.

Relationships Between Body Parts or Dancers and Objects

20. **MAGICIAN AND ZOMBIE:** "Find a partner (very young children can follow you). One of you will have a piece of plastic film (scarf, string, or ribbon). That person is the magician. The dancer without the plastic is the zombie. We will change roles so each person gets to be the magician. The magician moves the plastic in many different ways, always facing the zombie. The zombie follows the plastic, moving any way the plastic makes the zombie feel like moving. Magicians, remember to move the plastic high and low, fast and slow, smooth and sharp. Turn it, shake it, squeeze it. Be magical!" Change roles several times. 30 - 45 seconds is long enough for each turn. Everyone loves this exploration. It is excellent for increasing concentration and movement vocabulary.

21. **OBSTACLE COURSE:** Set up a course using many objects such as cones, stretchybands stretched between cones to produce bridges or tunnels, material over benches for tunnels or caves, spots for jumping on, benches or chairs to go over and under, etc. Have the dancers explore many different ways of relating to all the different objects. Let them move through the course in a random or directed fashion.

22. **SCARVES OR PLASTIC:** "Choose a scarf (or plastic film). Form a relationship with your scarf by making a shape that relates to your scarf and makes your scarf the focus of attention. Dance through general space in many different ways, changing your relationship to the scarf. (Toss the scarf, kick the scarf, shake the scarf, dance under the scarf, etc.) When the music pauses I will name a special relationship. Make a shape demonstrating that relationship. (Over, under, beside, above, around, etc.)" Alternate free dancing and directed relationships.

23. **STRETCHYBANDS:** "Find a partner. Holding one stretchyband between you, dance through space. Change directions, levels, size and pathways. Instead of choosing a leader, try relating to each other without words. Share the stretchyband and the leadership. Instead of holding the stretchyband with your hands, try relating to it by holding it with other body parts."

24. **BALLOONS:** "When the music is fast hold your balloon and dance through general space. Try holding your balloon with different body parts. When the music is slow, bat the balloon with different body parts in self space. Try changing levels, directions, speed and qualities."

OTHER IDEAS: In each concept chapter, at the end of "Exploring the Concept" are more ways to explore props. When using these ideas, focus on the concept of relationships. Check the "Activity Music List" for songs for ages 2-7 that focus on props and relationships.

SHAPING

1. **BODY PARTS:** "Put your hand over your head, put you head below your knees, put one foot on the other foot and freeze in that shape! Put a foot over your head, put your chin on your knee, put your elbows beside your hips and freeze in that shape!" Try many other body part relationship shapes. Ask your students for ideas. Try moving in those shapes!

2. **MORE BODY PARTS:** "Create a shape in which one body part is through another. Try a shape in which one body part is around another. Can you put two parts around another? Make a shape with one body part between two other body parts. Create a shape with one body part over another. Try that on another level. Can you do it in a different direction? Create a shape with two body parts together and two body parts apart." Think of other shape problems. This can also be done with partners.

3. **WORDS:** "Make a shape using different body parts that describes over/under ... around/ through ... together/apart ... above/below ... on/off ... near/far ... in/out ... beside/between." You might ask the dancers to create transitions from one statue to another or to think of two or three different statues for the same words and create transitions between those statues. This would be a good problem for choreography.

4. **STATUES:** "Who would like to begin building a giant statue by making a shape in the middle of the room? Now, when I call your name, make a shape that relates to another shape in the statue. You might connect to another shape, be over, under, around, beside, between another shape. When everyone is connected let's think of a name for the statue." This can be done in small or large groups and even trios and quartets. You can be very directed and ask for an "Over" statue. Everyone must make a shape that is somehow over another shape. Try an "Under" statue, an "Around" statue, a "Between" statue. These statues are challenging and fun. They make strong statements. Do this in groups so that the dancers can view the statues and discuss the feelings that these statues evoke.

5. **MACHINES:** "Someone make a shape in the middle of the room and move a body part like a machine part. Now, one at a time, connect to a person in the machine and move a different body part. Think of how you will relate to the moving parts. Will you move faster or slower? Will you move under, over, around, between the moving parts? Let's look at the machine and think about what it might be used for." Add sounds for more fun. Talk about the relationships of people and body parts. Add props for a fancy machine. Give groups the name of a machine first and have them design the machine. The type of machine could be real or fanciful.

6. **PHOTOS:** "Find a partner and make a shape together that states a specific relationship such as friends/enemies, king/subject, master/slave, mother/daughter, father/son, teacher/pupil, etc. Think about the relationship words and use them to help you create a 'photograph' that the other dancers could title." You can also work the other way. Start with the words (under/over, around/through, together/apart, etc.), have the students design "photos" and then think of what the photos suggest. These photos could come alive and dance, maintaining the relationships and using appropriate movement. Photos can also be done in groups. Historical scenes make excellent photos as do current events or controversies. Use the other dance elements or antonyms such as strong/light, high/low, big/ little, sharp/smooth, forward/backward to help define the relationships even more.

7. **SECRET SHAPES:** "I am going to ask two people at a time to make a shape together under this big sheet. Think about your relationship. Will you be together or apart, over and under, around and through, beside? When your shape is frozen under the sheet we will try to guess your relationship. I will remove the sheet and we will look at the shape, name the relationship and then try to make the same shape." Pairs outside the sheet could make a guess about the shape and try to make the secret shape before seeing it.

8. **SCULPTOR AND CLAY:** "Find a partner. One of you will be the sculptor and one the clay. The sculptor will gently mold the clay into a shape. Think about your relationship. The sculptor is the artist, gently creating a statue. The clay is an inanimate object, relying on the sculptor for animation. Change roles." This activity can be directed or free. You may ask for specific kinds of sculptures based on relationship words, the elements of dance, verbs, emotions, etc. or leave it wide open. Structure is easier for inexperienced dancers to deal with. The statues could come alive and/ or other dancers could guess or name the sculptures. This can also be done in trios and small groups.

9. **WEIGHT SHARING:** "Find a partner. Stand face to face with your partner, hold on to each other's wrists and pull away from each other. You must pull equally, sharing the weight between you. Feel as though you are sitting in a chair, knees bent and moving from your center. Now, press your palms together, still keeping the knees bent and moving from the center, step away from each other until you are pushing against each other but sharing your weight between you. Your relationship must be equal. One cannot be stronger or weaker than the other. You must find the balance. Find another partner and press and pull equally." Change partners a number of times so that your students learn to adjust to different people and learn to form new and trusting relationships. Try other weight sharing shapes such as back to back, side to side and on different levels. Let your students explore carefully and share their ideas with each other.

260

10. **NEGATIVE SPACE:** "Find a partner. One dancer will make a shape with lots of negative space (empty space). When I give the signal, the other dancer will make a shape that fills up some or all of the negative space. Think of the words around, through, between, under, over, in, out to help you think of ways to fill the negative space. When I give a new signal, change roles." Adding other dance elements creates even more interesting relationship shapes. Try filling a smooth shape with a sharp shape...a big shape with a little shape...a high shape with a low shape...a strong shape with a light shape...a twisting shape with a shaking shape. Try moving in and out of the shapes, adding transitional movement between shapes. This can be done in groups or in "Shape Museum."

11. **COMPARATIVES:** "Form a trio by the time I count to five. (A remaining student can join a trio to form a quartet.) Choose an adjective or adverb. Now, through shapes, show me the positive, comparative and superlative degree of the word you chose. Each shape will have a special relationship to the following shape. We might see a big shape, a bigger shape and then the biggest shape. You must work closely together because the big shape cannot be too big. A trio might choose twisted, more twisted, most twisted. The first dancer would make a shape that is a little bit twisted while the third dancer makes a very twisted shape." You can give trios words, brainstorm words or have groups choose their own words. Guess the words as each group shows their shapes.

12. **LINE-OF-SHAPES:** "Create a line of shapes across the room by forming a relationship with the dancer preceding you. You might connect to that dancer, fill the dancer's negative space, make a shape beside, around or over the dancer. You have many choices. When our line is complete we can look at all the different relationships and what they say to us." You might try several directed lines such as "everyone connect" or "everyone fill the negative space" then try a free line. You might also do directed lines in groups and then a free line with the whole class. You could add movement by having the dancers travel down the line before adding their own shape. They could react through movement to the various shapes in the line or choose to move any way they wish.

13. **PROPS:** Props can be used in any of the previous explorations to add variety and dimension. Focus on the relationship of body parts to props and props to dancers.

INSTRUMENTS

1. **HALF AN INSTRUMENT:** "Choose one rhythm stick or one cymbal. In order to make music you will have to find a friend. Sticks can play together, cymbals can play together and sticks can play with cymbals. When the music begins, dance through space. When you dance by someone, pause and play your instruments together. Remember to cooperate and play together gently so that you hit instruments together, not each other! Try to play with everyone in the room before the song ends."

2. **SOUND DANCE:** "Find a friend. One dancer will play music while the other dancer reacts to that music through movement. Stay close togther. Change roles on my signal." This can also be done in groups with half the class being the orchestra and half reacting to the music. The orchestra can all play together or each musician can take a short turn to play a solo.

3. **DANCERS LEAD:** "When I call your name, put down your instrument and do a short dance solo. The rest of us will follow your movement with our instruments and accompany your dance." If the dancers are shy ask for duets or trios. The solos should be very quick. Give the orchestra a chance

to react and play and then move on so that everyone has a chance and the orchestra has to concentrate, listen and think.

4. **CONDUCTOR:** "I will choose someone to conduct the orchestra. You must watch the conductor carefully and follow his/her lead." You should give the conductors specific movements for loud/soft, fast/slow, etc. The orchestra can play and dance in self space or general space. Obviously, it is a greater challenge to dance and play in general space and watch the conductor than to do this in self space. Change conductors frequently.

5. **WORDS:** "Play your instrument and dance through space using the elements of dance. When the music pauses, stop and listen for the relationship word. Show me what that word means using your instrument. When the music resumes, find a new way to dance and play." During the pauses call out: under, over, around, through, beside, far, near, on, off, etc. Dancers should put their instruments over, under, on their bodies or a body part.

6. **MIRROR/SHADOW:** Partners or groups can follow the leader's movements and music mirroring or shadowing.

DEVELOPING SKILLS

1. **LOCOMOTOR:** Practice the basic locomotor skills in partners. Practice moving together side by side in different directions, maintaining a close relationship with one another. Practice moving one in front of the other, changing directions. Practice locomotor skills in trios and small groups. Practice changing speeds. This practice will have an excellent carryover into group choreography, where the dancers need to sense each other in space.

2. **NONLOCOMOTOR:** Practice nonlocomotor movements in partners. Try floating, punching, gliding, shaking, twisting around, over, under and through each other. Maintain relationships using focus or touch. After practicing in pairs move to trios and small groups. This practice will create a sense of cooperation and group bonding.

3. **HAND IN HAND:** Practice the basic locomotor movements holding hands with a partner. This is more difficult than moving side by side. Practice changing speed, directions and levels. Try trios and quartets holding hands in a line, then try circles. Discuss the different relationships in lines and circles and the different feelings evoked. Practicing circle movement is great for young children. Besides moving clockwise and counterclockwise, it is fun to move forward into the circle, coming close together and moving back out, stretching far apart. The idea of a "magic ring" that never breaks because everyone cooperates and shares space is a helpful idea to introduce.

4. **FOOT TO FOOT:** Practice locomotor and nonlocomotor movements with a partner connected together with body parts other than hands. This can become quite humorous and challenging.

5. **SLIDING:** Practice sliding with a partner front to front, back to back, side to side, front to back. Practice holding hands and without touching. Practice the hinge slide: holding outside hands, slide together front to front then back to back, front to front and back to back. You turn away and toward your partner like a door on a hinge.

262

6. **BODY PARTS:** Practice the skills you are currently developing but discuss them in terms of body part relationships. What is the relationship of the arms to the legs ... to the back ... to each other? What is the relationship of the legs to each other ... to the arms ... to the hips ... to the back? What is the relationship of the head to the back ... to the shoulders ... to the arms? What is the relationship of the eyes to the floor ... ceiling ... other dancers? This discussion and subsequent practice will help clarify body shape and movement. You will notice the movement becoming clearer and more defined. Extensions will be greater, movement will be stronger and skills will be better developed.

7. **CONTACT IMPROV:** Practice working with a partner, always maintaining contact in some way. Begin with the "Weight Sharing" described under "Shaping" and develop that idea creating transitions between shapes. Combine the weight sharing with #2 above. Contact can be maintained with many different body parts. A very trusting relationship must develop between dancers. This should be done with experienced dancers, not very young children.

8. **MEETING AND PARTING:** Practice locomotor and nonlocomotor skills coming toward and away from a partner or group of dancers, passing between each other, moving through and around others, etc. This develops the skill of relating to people and space.

9. **LIFTS:** Simple lifts can be introduced and practiced in a controlled environment where safety and injury prevention are of uppermost concern. All the dancers must work to make a lift successful. Timing is important, sensing each other is essential. The dancers must prepare and lift together. There must be trust. Each must do their part. Explore different ways of lifting, making different connections, using different body parts. Try different groupings -- two lifting one, one lifting one, three lifting one or two, etc. Check the bibliography for modern dance books that describe specific lifting and partnering techniques.

TURNING

1. **ARMS:** Practice turns focusing on the use of the arms. Arm movements can help or hinder turns. Explore different ways of using the arms. Try wrapping the arms around the body as you twist to prepare for a turn then opening them out as you turn then wrapping them around as you end the turn. Is this helpful or not? Does it help to have the arms above the head...one arm above and one below? Does it help to have the arms reaching far out to the side or near to the body? Does it help to move the arm in and out or to keep the arms still? Only through exploration and discussion can each student find the way that feels best to him/her. The arms may be used to advantage differently for different turns.

2. **BODY PARTS:** Try creating unusual relationships of your body parts to each other as you turn. Try turning with your head below a leg...feet above your stomach...arms behind your back...hips reaching to the right or left...pelvis reaching backward...feet far from each other...feet near to hands. Some beautiful and unusual turns may be created.

3. **PARTNERS:** Try different turns connected to a partner. Change levels and speed. Try doing different locomotor movements as you turn such as the polka, jumping, sliding, hopping, schottische. Cooperate and share the weight and space. Try turning in trios.

4. **MEETING/PARTING:** Practice turns that move toward and away from each other or that pass through or around other dancers. Maintaining spatial relationships is difficult while you are turning. Focus will help.

5. **PROPS:** Practice turns using props. Turn with the prop on different body parts. Move the prop in different ways as you turn. Think about the relationship of the prop to the body as you move. How can the prop enhance the turn? When might the use of a prop hinder turning? Try turning with a partner, using the prop to connect the two of you.

COMBINING MOVEMENTS

1. **FOLK DANCES:** Do folk dances that use a variety of relationships. Troika and the Crested Hen are done in trios. Gustav's Skoal is performed in squares of eight and partners are changed during the dance. Ve'David moves from partners to a circle to groups. In Mayim the dancers come close together and move far apart. La Raspa is done with partners. Greek and American Indian dances have line leaders. Greensleeves is performed in quartets. Adapt these dances to fit your dancers' experience or have your students create their own dances using different relationships to folk music.

2. **WORD CARDS:** Choose four or five relationship word cards and put them into a sequence to practice. One such sequence might be "over, around, together, connect." Dancers might move over then around real or imaginary objects or people, come together and end in a connected shape.

3. **CINQUAIN:** Create a cinquain about relationships such as the one below. Read the poem as class performs it.

Relationships
Alone, together
Mirroring, shadowing, parting
Creating connections with eyes
Friends

4. **PARTNERS:** Create combinations in which partners can dance toward each other, dance together and then dance away. Young dancers might skip to a partner, do a special turn with a partner and float way. More experienced dancers might turn to a partner, move over and under each other, then waltz run away. Experienced dancers might do a series of movements to a partner, perform lifts or share weight, then repeat the first combination backwards or in retrograde (backwards in sequence, not direction). I work with eight year olds who can do this -- experienced is not the same as old.

5. **TRIOS:** Practice familiar combinations in trios. Try different relationships -- side by side, in a circle, meeting and parting, one in front of the others.

6. **BODY PARTS:** Practice combinations in which a certain body part changes relationships to the other body parts. Hands might move above the head, behind the back, below the knees and on the floor.

7. **CANON:** Practice combinations in canon or round so that each dancer or group starts four to eight counts after the group preceding them.

8. **FLOCKING:** In small groups, the leader improvises a simple combination of movements then freezes in a shape. The followers, like a flock of birds, copy the combination. A new leader then takes off in a different direction and the flock follows again. Two relationships are set up here -- one with the leader and one with members of the flock. The flock should move after the leader as one entity, all at the same time and with the same rhythm. This is difficult. The combinations should be clear and simple.

With young children or inexperienced dancers it works well to call out a simple combination such as jump, turn, float, freeze. The leaders can perform it in their own special way.

9. **PROPS:** Props may be added to combinations. Focus on the relationship of the prop to the movement and to the dancers.

10. **ACTIVITY SONGS:** Songs from The "Activity Music List" which focus on relationships can be used with dancers ages 2-7.

LEAPING

1. **OBJECTS:** Practice leaps over spots, cartons, shoes.

2. **BODY PARTS:** Discuss the relationship of different body parts to each other in leaps. Try different leg and arm shapes. Encourage the focus to be forward, not down.

3. **PARTNERS:** Have partners leap side by side down the middle of the room to the other end of the room and then move apart and dance alone down the sides of the room. A variation would be to have partners leap alone, meet in a shape and then leap together.

4. **LUMPS AND LEAPS:** "Half of you will be lumps and half will be leapers. Then we will change roles. The lumps should make small shapes on the ground. The leapers will leap over the shapes being very careful not to touch a lump. When I give the signal leapers and lumps will change places." Encourage a variety of different lump shapes but be sure that they are low to the ground. Obviously, there are risks involved and this should not be done with an undisciplined class. A relationship of trusting and caring needs to be present. Change roles frequently.

5. **TOGETHER:** Try leaping in quartets. Try leaping toward a partner or group and away. Try two groups leaping through each other. Try leaping toward a partner, around the partner and away from the partner.

6. **PROPS:** Add props to leaps. How can props enhance leaps, how might they detract?

266

FREE DANCING/IMPROVISATION

Choose an activity under "Exploring the Concept" that is not too structured. Many activities under "Combining Movements" could be used for structured improvisation with older or experienced students.

CHOREOGRAPHING

1. **ABA:** Dancers choose two relationship words and create a dance based on ABA form such as under/over/under, around/through/around, beside/between/beside, on/off/on. Solos can be created focusing on body part relationships or prop relationships. Duets, trios and small groups can choreograph dances focusing on relationships between dancers and/or props.

2. **SUITE:** Dances can be created in suite form, choosing three relationship words. Section one might be "around" (medium speed), section two could be "between" (slow speed) and section three might be "far" (fast speed). Discuss the feelings or meanings the different words evoke. Another way to use the suite form would be to demonstrate the different kinds of relationships: section one - body part relationships, section two - relationships between dancers, section three - relationships between objects.

3. **COMPARATIVES:** See #11 under "Shaping." Trios could create dances describing comparatives. This might be done in suite form, canon or theme in variation.

4. **CONVERSATIONS:** See #17 under "Exploring the Concept." Develop the idea of conversations into a relationship dance that might begin with an argument and move to a resolution.

5. **CONTACT IMPROV:** See #7 under "Developing Skills." Ask the dancers to create a dance using contact improvisation. Let them improvise and then begin to set some of the movements so that the final piece is a combination of improvisation and choreographed movements.

6. **EMOTIONS:** Let the dancers choose emotion words to use as the foundation for their choreography. Have other dancers guess the words and discuss what kind of relationships evoked what emotions. In solos, the relationship of body parts to body parts will help define the emotion. In portraying anger, the body parts may be close together or they may move apart and together. When performing duets or group dances the relationship of the dancers to each other will be important. In describing loneliness, the dancers may move by themselves in their own self spaces. You may approach emotions in the opposite way by starting with relationship words and discussing what emotions are evoked by certain relationships.

7. **MUSIC:** The relationship of the dance to the music or lack of music is very important. Explore moving to different kinds of music and then have different groups create dances to different musical forms. Try moving against the music and discuss how this feels and looks. Discuss the use of silence or unusual sound or moving to the spoken word. Have groups choreograph studies without music and then set them the task of finding appropriate music for their studies. In contrast, have groups start with a piece of music and create dances based on their choices.

8. **UNISON AND CONTRAST:** Have some groups create pieces in which all the movement is done in unison. Have other groups choreograph dances in which all the movement is done in contrast to one another. Ask a third set to choreograph a dance where unison and contrast are combined. Discuss the results.

9. **NARRATIVE:** In narrative dances relationships are very important because the choreographer is telling a story. Have the dancers create simple scenarios on which to base dances. After the pieces have been shown discuss the relationships. Was the story clear? Could the relationships be made stronger? How? Were the relationship words used by the choreographer to make the relationships clear? Were different dance elements used to help clarify relationships? Some very simple scenarios might include: meeting/parting, searching/ finding, anger/resolution, danger/safety, anticipation/ pleasure.

10. **CINQUAIN:** Ask dancers to create their own cinquains to perform for others. See #3 under "Combining Movements."

11. **AUDIENCE:** When dancers perform their compositions discuss the role of the audience. How can dancers relate to the audience? (By focusing out to them, projecting their feelings, being aware that they are out there.) How do dancers shut out the audience? (By looking down or within, by not projecting their feelings, by dancing just for themselves.) Demonstrate both ways. As an audience member which do you prefer?

12. **SPACE:** How a dancer uses the stage space is important in choreography. Explore several ways through improvisation and discuss the results. Use only the front of the stage ... dance only in the upstage area ... dance only stage right or left .. .divide the stage and dance far right and far left ... focus all the movement stage center ... dance in the corners of the stage ... fill the whole space with movement ... choose three special areas and dance in those ... move from area to area. The ideas are endless, especially when you deal with numbers of dancers - three versus five versus twelve, etc. The important thing to remember is that the dancers' relationship to the stage space is very important. How a choreographer uses the space can help or hinder his/her message.

13. **PROPS:** Explore the use of props in the choreographic problems described above. When using props it is important to remind the choreographers to USE the prop. Is the prop vital to the dance or just another idea thrown in? If the dance has meaning without the prop, reevaluate its need. The audience is often frustrated to see a large statue or hangings on stage that have no relevance to the piece. Even a small prop that is not used very much is distracting. However, a prop that is cleverly manipulated or used with meaning is a delight!

LESSON ON RELATIONSHIPS

Ages: 5, 6, 7, or 8   Length: 30 minutes*

WARMING UP

Warm-up Activity: Exploring the Concept "Scarves" #22
Dance with scarves, then make a directed relationship shape on the pauses. Music: "Seven Jumps" - *Rhythmically Moving 2.*

Introducing the Concept: RELATIONSHIPS: over, under, around, through, etc. See, say and do the words.

EXPLORING THE CONCEPT

Exploring the Concept: "Space Between" #3
Move through space with a partner keeping the distance between you (far, near or medium) the same.
Music: selection from *The Essential Jarre.*

DEVELOPING SKILLS

Developing Skills: "Sliding" #5
Practice the hinge slide with a partner, sliding together front to front and back to back. Music: "Funky Penguin" - *Movin'.*

Combining Movements: "Partners" #4
Practice the following combination: hinge slide with a partner 16 counts, form three balancing shapes connecting with your partner, do mirroring movements away from each other (one is the leader), do mirroring movements toward each other (the other is the leader). Repeat from the beginning. Music: "Funky Penguin" - *Movin'.*

CREATING

Free Dancing/Improvising: "Mountains and Tunnels" #19
Half the class forms mountain or tunnel shapes while the other half dances over and under the shapes. Reverse roles. Music: "Rhythm in the Pews" - *Deep Breakfast.*

COOLING DOWN

Goodbye Dance: With a partner.

*For a 60 minute class: Do 15 minutes of rhyming exercises, Instruments #1 and Leaping #3.

LESSON ON RELATIONSHIPS

Ages: 9-Adult   Length: 45-60 minutes

WARMING UP

Warm-up Activity: Exploring the Concept "Scarves" #22
Variation: dancers move through space with any prop, if prop is not available relate to body parts instead of a prop. When the music pauses, dancers form a directed relationship shape with their prop or body part. Music: anything lively, pause the music yourself.

Dance Exercises/Technique: Do 10-20 minutes of technique emphasizing body part relationships.

Introducing the Concept: RELATIONSHIPS: over, under, around, through, etc. See, say and do the words.

EXPLORING THE CONCEPT

Exploring the Concept: "Magic Hands" #15
Dance your hands in relationship to your partner's hands, keeping them 12 inches apart at all times. Try other body parts. Music: selection from *Annie's Song*.

DEVELOPING SKILLS

Turning: "Partners" #3
Practice different turns with a partner. Music: "Veloce" - *Suite for Flute and Jazz Piano.*

CREATING

Choreographing: "Suite" #2
Choose three relationship words and put them into an order. Decide whether relationship will be with person, prop or body parts. Do in duets or small groups.

COOLING DOWN

Sharing/Evaluating Choreography: Discuss the dances and what relationships were chosen and how they were created.

CHAPTER 23

BALANCE
On-Balance, Off-Balance

INTRODUCING THE CONCEPT

"Today our special word is BALANCE. When we stand on two legs we are ON-BALANCE. What does it mean to be on-balance? (Your muscles hold you up and you don't fall down.) What does it mean to be OFF-BALANCE? (You feel wobbly and/or fall.) Why can't we float around in any shape the way an astronaut can in space? (Gravity keeps us grounded.) We know that we can balance on two feet. Your two feet are your base of support -- that is what is supporting your weight now. Can you be on-balance with just one foot touching the floor? Why is this harder? (Your base of support is smaller.) Can you balance on your back ... two feet and a hand ... two hands and a foot? Try balancing on four body parts. Now make that base smaller by bringing those parts together. Is it harder to balance in this shape? (Yes.) Balance in a shape. Now tip that shape until you go off-balance. What makes you fall or change your base of support? (The body weight is no longer over your base of support, so gravity pulls you down.)

"In dance we like to make exciting movements and shapes. To help us keep our balance when our base of support is small, we use our stomach muscles. Besides using stomach muscles, we can imagine strings pulling us equally in all directions: strings pull us equally forwards and backwards, left side and right side and up and down. If one of our strings pulls too much in any direction, we lose our balance. Feel as though you are suspended in space by the directional pull of your strings as you balance on only one body part."

EXPLORING THE CONCEPT

1. **MOVE AND BALANCE:** "Gallop around the room. When the music stops (or you give a signal) freeze in a one legged balanced shape. Remember to contract your stomach muscles and feel the equal pull of your imaginary strings." Alternate directed movement (run backward, skip, float, etc.) with balanced shapes.

2. **SPOT BALANCING:** "Dance any way you like around the spots. When you hear the signal, find the spot nearest you and make a special balancing shape. Try to hold it until I give the signal to move again." Encourage balancing shapes on different levels, in different directions, with different size, etc.

3. **BODY PARTS:** "In your self space try balancing on five parts, three parts, two parts, one part, twenty parts (fingers and toes)! Try balancing on four parts. Now can you find four parts to balance on that are different or create a different shape? Try two different shapes while balancing on three body parts. Can you make a smooth transition between the two shapes?" Continue on with similar challenges.

4. **BODY PARTS IN PAIRS:** "Try moving through space on three body parts, four body parts, one body part. Find a friend and try to move together balancing on four parts between you. Try three parts, two parts, one part (for older children)!" This takes a great deal of cooperation and often ends in giggles and wonderful creativity!

5. **MOVING BALANCES:** "Can you move in your self space while balancing on one leg? Feel like an astronaut floating in space. Your standing leg is the rope holding you to the space ship. Your body parts are floating freely in space. Remember to use your stomach muscles to help you. Try floating at a low level. Balancing on your buttocks, back, shoulders or stomach, feel like seaweed floating up to reach the light. Keep moving in different ways while maintaining your balance."

6. **SHADOW BALANCES:** "Follow your partner around the room. When the music stops make a connected shape with your partner while balancing on one leg. Don't expect your partner to hold you up. Share the weight and use your stomach muscles. Create a good base of support between you. When the music begins again you will be the leader and your partner will follow your movements until the music stops, then make a new balanced but connected shape." Encourage different movements through space, giving ideas if necessary. Remind the dancers of the movement elements when making balanced shapes so that they try different levels, size, directions, etc.

7. **PARTNER BALANCES:** "Find a partner. One of you will stay in self space and move in place while balancing on one body part. The other dancer will travel through general space. The general space dancer will travel away and back to your partner to form a connected balanced shape. Then

272

the self space dancer will take a turn through general space while the general space dancer stays balancing in self space." You may have them move for a specified number of counts, or give signals, or pause the music as cues for returning to the connected shape before reversing roles. Encourage movement on different levels and in different directions, speed and energy.

8. **BALANCE AND FALL:** "Make a balanced shape. Tip that shape until you go off-balance, fall, roll and return to a balanced shape. When you fall, be careful. Fall on soft body parts such as buttocks and back of shoulder. Try balancing, tipping, curling, falling, rolling, recovering. Keep elbows and knees curled in and protected. Feel as though all the wind has been knocked out of you as you fall and roll." Encourage daring but safety, also.

9. **SHAPE MUSEUM:** "Balance in a shape. When a dancer copies your shape you are free to dance around until you copy someone else's balancing shape." Half of the class forms shapes while half are moving around the shapes. Encourage dancers to balance until copied, but allow them to change legs if they are getting tired or to remake the shape if they lose their balance.

10. **PROPS:** "Try balancing your prop (streamer, plastic, scarf, balloon) on different body parts as you travel through space. OR move with your prop any way you like (try tossing, kicking, catching, holding, wrapping, floating, etc.) Then, when the music stops (or changes) try balancing the prop on a body part while you make a balanced shape in self space." Alternate self and general space movement.

11. **ACTIVITY SONGS:** Choose a balance song from the "Activity Music List" for ages 2-7.

SHAPING

1. **YOGA SHAPES:** Choose yoga shapes that require balance (stork, tree, bird, bee, "v"). Have dancers practice these shapes in self space. Discuss the different bases of support.

2. **COPY CAT:** "Think of a shape you haven't tried before that requires balancing on different body parts, perhaps two feet and one hand or two elbows and one knee. Try to make your non-balancing body parts an interesting part of your shape. Now, each one of you will show your shape and we will try it." Discuss the various bases of support, what makes the shape interesting and what other movement elements are used in the shape (level, direction, size, etc.).

3. **PARTNER BALANCES:** "Find a partner. Make a connected balancing shape so that together three body parts are touching the ground. You could do this with one leg from each of you and one person's hand touching the ground. Find another solution. Try a connected shape with four parts touching the ground, try five parts, two parts. Remember you need to share the weight. Do not expect your partner to hold you up. Use your stomach muscles and imaginary strings."

4. **CONNECTED BALANCES:** "Find a partner. Try balancing one of your legs on your partner while your partner does the same. Can you make other balancing shapes connecting a body part to your partner, without holding hands with your partner? Try connecting elbows while balancing on one leg. Try connecting hips, finger tips, knees." This results in a shape that has a sense of lightness compared with the grounded quality of the shapes in #3. It also requires greater balance.

5. **BALANCES IN A LINE:** "One at a time, you will connect to each other across the room in a balanced shape. Try to hold your shape until everyone has connected onto the line. If you lose your balance, remake your shape. As you connect to a shape you can help out by supporting that shape, if possible, while you make your own shape. As you make your shape you can dance through the empty space created by the balancing shapes until you reach your spot to connect." Sometimes the line will crumble and fall if one dancer loses balance. This can be fun but can also be dangerous if people are tightly connected. Therefore, suggest light connections and responsibility for your own shape. Large classes can be divided into groups with lots of reinforcement going to the lines that maintain their balance.

6. **MACHINES:** "We are going to create a balancing machine. One at a time connect yourself to anyone in the machine. You must connect in a balancing shape and you must move at least one other body part to keep the machine going. Try to connect at different levels and in empty spaces so the machine is interesting." You can have the dancers add sounds and try to give a name to the machine. This can be done in small or large groups.

7. **MIRRORING:** "Find a partner. Leaders will do a slow motion dance while balancing on one leg. Followers will try to mirror the dance. If you lose your balance, regain it and continue. Try to change levels and try to dance very smoothly. You may change legs whenever you want to and you may try other bases of support. When the music stops, change leaders."

8. **TRIO BALANCES:** "Find two friends. Each of you create three different balancing shapes. Now, starting apart, do shape number one, tip, roll together and rebound into your number two shape connected; tip, roll away and rebound into your number three shape apart." This can be very exciting to watch. You may wish to have the dancers perfect this combination during the choreography section of class and perform it for their peers.

9. **PROPS:** Try adding props to any of the shape explorations. Try balancing on props in directed or free shapes. Try balancing props on different body parts while making shapes. Try to change shapes while balancing props on body parts. Use the stretchybands or Chinese jump ropes to help keep your balance in a shape by stretching the stretchyband with your leg and arms.

INSTRUMENTS

1. **PAUSE:** Move and play, then balance on the sustained notes or pauses in the music.

2. **BODY PARTS:** Balance your instrument on a body part during the pauses or certain sections of the music.

3. **SHAPES:** Play and move, then balance in a shape over your instrument during the pauses.

4. **PHRASES:** Play and balance during one phrase of music and play and move during the other phrase. As accompaniment a two part folk dance works well or a song with verse and chorus.

DEVELOPING SKILLS

1. **MOVE AND STOP:** "Run smoothly and quickly through general space. When I give the signal, stop as quickly as possible and balance in a shape. Hold it until I give the signal to move." The skill of moving quickly and stopping quickly is further developed by having dancers balance after stopping. You may try other locomotor movements to add variety and to practice those actions. See the "Movement" chapter for more ideas.

2. **HOPPING:** Hopping is the locomotor movement that requires the most balance. When practicing hopping, remember to have the dancers change hopping legs often to build up muscles equally in both legs. Very young children will have trouble hopping on their non-dominant leg. Encourage practice and give lots of reinforcement. Young dancers might hold on to a bar, a hand or a wall to give them some support initially. Try hopping holding on to a bar with both hands, then one hand, then no hands. Practice hopping in self space first then through general space, then add direction, different leg shapes, size and quality.

3. **JOP:** Jop is a combination of a jump and a hop. It is known in ballet as a sissone. You take off from two feet and land on one foot. It requires some balance. Practice the jop in self space always landing on the same foot. Then try landing on the other foot, then alternate feet, then move through general space. Try the jop traveling side to side instead of forward. Encourage the use of arms in directed or free shapes. Explore small and big jops, strong and light jops, low and high jops.

4. **SLOW WALK:** Explore long, smooth, slow walks trying to keep the legs continually moving as they pass from back to front. This requires the use of stomach muscles and good alignment in order to maintain balance. Try forward, sideways and backward walks. This exploration could develop the walk into a lunge, bending the front landing leg deeply before bringing the back leg through.

5. **TIPPING:** Practice tipping, rolling and rising. Talk about safe ways to fall and land (rolling on shoulder, curling knees and elbows in to protect them). Do it slowly then try to speed up.

6. **FALLING:** Practice different falls - front, side, back, split (see *On the Count of One* for details). Try stretching, falling and recovering in a balanced shape at a low, medium or high level.

TURNING

1. **SLOW:** "Try turning slowly on one leg by lifting the heel of the supporting foot and turning in place on the ball of the foot. Try different free leg shapes -- low, straight and back; high, bent and back; medium, bent and sideways; similar shapes forward; holding the free leg; a partner holding the free leg. Try turning with the free leg in the air and one foot and two hands as your base of support. Make up other shapes."

2. **FAST:** "Try spinning on one leg. Twist one way and untwist quickly to create a spinning action. Try many different shapes while spinning. Remember to spin right and left. Add interesting arm movements and shapes. Try spinning while balancing on your seat and hands, tummy and hands, back and feet."

3. **TURN AND STOP:** "Turn quickly through general space, stop at the signal and balance in a shape. Turn back the other way and stop and balance. If you get too dizzy, stop and jump up and down. This will bring some of the blood from your head back to your toes." Balancing after turning is difficult.

4. **PIQUÉ (pee-kay) TURN:** "Step on the ball of one foot, bringing the other foot up to your knee (your legs make the shape of a number 4) and turn, then step down with the free leg. Step up and turn, step down. You are balancing on the ball of your foot (half pointe) as you turn. Try making a different shape with the free leg as you turn. Use your arms to help. They come together as you step up and turn and open out as you step down." The turn can be done in a series across the floor or around the room.

276

COMBINING MOVEMENTS

1. **YOGA:** Use yoga shapes in a story. Each time a shape is named the dancers form that shape: "Once upon a time there was a BIRD. The BIRD lived in a tall TREE. The BIRD had a friend FROG and another friend COBRA. One day the WOODCHOPPER came into the forest and started to chop down the TREES. BIRD was very frightened and flew to friend FROG and asked for help. But FROG said he was too little to help. BIRD flew to COBRA and COBRA said yessssssssssss, I will help you. So COBRA wound around the TREE that BIRD lived in. The next day WOODCHOPPER came to the forest and started to chop down BIRD'S TREE but then he saw COBRA and was very frightened and he ran out of the forest. BIRD lived for a long time in the forest with friend FROG and COBRA." You can create many other stories. See *Be a Frog, or a Bird, or a Tree* by Rachel Carr for yoga shapes.

2. **SENTENCE:** Create a movement sentence which focuses on balance such as: Balance, spin, hop, stretch, tip, roll, balance. Create sounds for each word or use new age music as a background. Perform several times.

3. **SEVEN JUMPS:** Using the folk dance music Seven Jumps, move in a directed or free way until the "hum," then balance until the music begins again. As the hums get longer the balancing will get harder. Also, try performing the authentic version which requires seven specific balance shapes or create seven new shapes.

4. **FIND A FRIEND:** Dance in a directed or free way until the teacher says "choose a friend and balance." Find a partner and balance together in different shapes until the teacher says "dance away."

5. **WORD CARDS:** Choose movements from word cards that could require balancing (float, hop, spin, stretch, melt, fall, etc.) and put them together to create a phrase. You could also alternate off-balance movements with on-balance movements - tip, walk, float, jump. You might also take on-balance actions and try to make them go off-balance.

6. **PARTNER:** Perform a combination of movements to a partner, balance with your partner and dance away.

7. **CINQUAIN:** Create a cinquain about balance. Read the poem as the dancers perform.

Balance
On, Off
Floating, Tipping, Falling
Moving like an astronaut
Gravity

LEAPING

1. **SPOTS:** "Leap over the cartons. When you reach a spot, stop and make a balancing shape on the spot. Try a new shape or new base of support each time."

2. **BEAM:** "Leap over the cartons. When your reach the bench (beam) move across it as though it were a balance beam. Jump off and continue leaping." Be prepared to help young children across. Encourage older children to create interesting movements on the bench that require some balancing.

3. **PROPS:** "Can you balance spots on your hands while you leap? You will have to leap very smoothly. Try balancing streamers over your arms." This will help dancers extend their arms while leaping. Young children could balance props from one spot to another between leaps.

4. **COMBINATIONS:** Practice different leaping combinations such as run, run, run, leap; run, leap, run, leap; run, run, leap, etc. Do a balanced shape at the end of the combination if desired.

5. **LEGS:** Practice leaps using different leg shapes -- both straight, one bent/one straight, etc.

FREE DANCING/IMPROVISATION

Choose an activity from "Exploring the Concept" that is not too structured. Some of the ideas from "Choreographing" can be used as structured improvs with older students.

CHOREOGRAPHING

1. **YOGA:** Have dancers choose several yoga balance shapes and create their own story.

2. **ABA:** Partners, trios or small groups create a dance that is on-balance/off-balance/on-balance or the opposite. Props may be added.

3. **CANON:** Partners, trios or small groups create a phrase that moves on-balance to off-balance. Then have the group perform the dance in canon so that there are dancers always moving off-balance. This has a very dizzying effect on the audience. Discuss the results.

4. **MONTAGE:** Have groups create a dance in which some dancers create a montage of off-balance shapes while other dancers move around and through these shapes. More advanced dancers can let their shapes fall while the general space dancers try to catch them. This requires trust and the ability to fall safely.

5. **DANCE BY CHANCE:** See #5 in "Choreographing" in the chapter on PLACE. One of the four actions would be "balancing shape."

6. **PROPS:** Create a suite in which you dance without a prop, dance while balancing a prop on different body parts and dance balancing on or around the prop.

LESSON ON BALANCE

Ages: 3, 4, 5, 6, 7, or 8   *Length: 30 minutes*

WARMING UP

Dance Exercises/Technique: Do rhyming exercises that emphasize balance.

Introducing the Concept: BALANCE: on balance, off balance. See, say and do the words.

EXPLORING THE CONCEPT

Shaping: "Yoga Shapes" #1
Practice yoga balancing shapes, move through general space between shapes.

DEVELOPING SKILLS

Combining Movements: "Yoga Story" #1
Use the yoga shapes to create a story. The dancers form the shapes as you tell the story.

Developing Skills: "Hopping" #2
Practice hopping on different legs. Older dancers can practice hopping with different leg and arm shapes. Music: "Jamaican Holiday" - *Movin'.*

CREATING

Free Dancing/Improvising: "Spot Balancing" #2
Variation: dance around spots, then balance on the spots. Have fewer spots than dancers for ages 5-8 so that the dancers must balance on a spot with a friend. Music: "Children's Dance" - *Windham Hill Sampler 81.*

COOLING DOWN

Balance the spot on a body part and move slowly to a designated place to return the spots.

LESSON ON BALANCE

Ages: 9-Adult   *Length: 45-60 minutes*

WARMING UP

Warm-up Activity: Exploring the Concept "Shadow Balances" #6
Partners shadow each other's movements and balance together in a shape.
Music: "Pause" - *Movin'.*

Dance Exercises/Technique: Do 10-20 minutes of technique emphasizing balance.

Introducing the Concept: BALANCE: on balance, off balance. See, say and do the words.

EXPLORING THE CONCEPT

Exploring the Concept: "Balance and Fall" #8
Do balancing shapes, then tip off balance and fall, roll and recover. Repeat. Music: "Celestial Soda Pop" - *Deep Breakfast.*

Shaping: "Machine" #6
Groups create machines balancing on each other. Music: dancers create own machine noises.

DEVELOPING SKILLS

Developing Skills: "Jop" #3
Practice the jop (jump to a hop) in different directions and with different arm movements. Music: "Belfast Hornpipe" - *James Galway's Greatest Hits.*

CREATING

Choreographing: For a 45 minute lesson do "Props" #7. Have dancers create a simple solo using a prop. Show many solos simultaneously. For a 60 minute lesson do "ABA" #2. Groups of dancers create an off-balance/on-balance/off-balance dance. Props are optional.

COOLING DOWN

Sharing/Evaluating Choreography: Discuss the studies and how the dancers created off-balance movement and shapes.

CHAPTER 24

LOCOMOTOR MOVEMENT

Locomotor movement is movement that travels through space. It is like a locomotive engine; it takes you from one place to another. The "Developing Skills" part of the lesson is when you focus on introducing and practicing specific locomotor skills. However, the dancers are using locomotor movements throughout the class and it is important to name these movements and encourage your students to use many different movements as they explore the dance concepts, play rhythm instruments, improvise and choreograph. In this way, your students will be practicing familiar movements even as they learn new ones. The concept chapters contain many more ideas for using locomotor movements in creative ways.

Basic Locomotor Movements

WALK

WALK: You walk by transferring weight from one foot to the other, keeping continual contact with the floor. In a natural walk the heel makes contact with the floor first, then you move through the ball and toes to step with the other foot. The tempo is moderate, the stance erect, the leg swings freely from the hip and the arms swing in opposition to the leg.

AGES: Ages 1-2 should practice walking in different directions and pathways, on different levels and with changes in speed. Ages 3 - adult should practice all variations of walking.

Variations and Mechanics of Walking

PLACE: When walking in self space you place the whole foot on the floor and flex the knee more as in marching.

LEVEL: When walking on tiptoe you walk on the balls of the feet with legs almost straight. At a medium level you bend the knees and at a low level you bend the knees fully and walk on the balls of the feet.

SIZE: When taking long strides you generally step on the balls of the feet first and bend the landing leg rather fully. Reaching forward with the opposite arm helps maintain balance. When taking very short steps you tend to step with the whole foot, bend the knee slightly and have little hip flexion. Arms barely move.

DIRECTION: When walking backward the body tends to lean slightly forward and the toes touch first rather than the heel. When walking sideways the following foot can step next to the leading foot (step together), it can cross always in front or back, or it can alternate front and back as in the grapevine step. When walking sideways and crossing feet, the legs are usually rotated outward. When turning right it is easiest to step with the right foot, when turning left it is easiest to use the left foot.

PATHWAY: When walking in a curved pathway the torso should curve in the direction you are going. When walking in a straight pathway the torso is straight. When walking in a zigzag pathway the torso is straight but twists sharply to change direction. A sharp change of focus helps direct the body in the new direction, also.

FOCUS: When walking in a certain direction it is helpful to focus in that direction. When focusing up or down while walking it is slightly harder to maintain your balance. Maintaining your spatial pulls will help maintain balance.

SPEED: When walking quickly the steps are shorter; when walking slowly the steps are longer but this can be reversed.

RHYTHM: Rhythmic patterns can be created by changing the length of the walks -- short, long, long, short, etc.

ENERGY: When walking smoothly you step on the ball of the foot first; when walking sharply the heel lands first and the knee and hip action is decreased.

WEIGHT: When walking lightly you step primarily on the ball of the foot; when walking strongly, the whole foot may be placed on the floor at once, as in stamping.

BODY PARTS/SHAPES: Arms may be moved in many ways or held in different shapes. The torso can be bent, straight, twisted or curved. Varying the arm and torso movements and shapes away from the natural form will require practice but leads to exciting new ways of walking.

RELATIONSHIPS: Try matching your steps to that of a partner's. Walk toward and away from someone. Walk over or under someone or thing. Walk around, between and through people or objects. Your focus and/or body shape may have to change.

RUN

RUN: You run by transferring your weight from the ball and toes of one foot to the ball and toes of the other foot. For a second you have no contact with the floor and are suspended in air. Your hips, knees and ankles are flexed. Your body leans slightly forward, your arms are slightly bent at the elbow and swing in opposition to the leg.

AGES: Ages 1-2 should practice running in place and through space forward and backward. Ages 3-4 should practice running in different pathways and qualities. Ages 5-adult should practice all variations.

Variations and Mechanics of Running

PLACE: When running in place, the knees have more flexion and the arms stay bent at the sides of the body, instead of swinging in opposition.

LEVEL: When springing high in the air the ankle and knee flexion is increased as you take off and land; swinging the arms strongly upward helps to lift the body up. The tempo of the run slows down. When trying to run at a low level, the body is bent forward and you take off and land on the whole foot.

SIZE: When running with long strides, the leg stretches almost straight in the air and then flexes deeply on landing. The arms swing forward and backward in opposition to the legs. When running with short strides, the knee flexes in the air and then straightens as the foot lands. The arms stay bent by the sides of the body.

DIRECTION: When running backward the body leans forward. When running in any direction the pelvis should lead. When running sideways the following foot can step next to the leading foot, cross always in front or back or alternate crossing front and back.

PATHWAY: When running in different pathways the same principles apply as with walking except that the body positions are exaggerated.

FOCUS: See Walking.

SPEED: When running slowly you stay suspended longer. When running quickly through general space the knee flexion is increased. When running quickly in place the knee flexion is decreased.

ENERGY: When running smoothly, elbow flexion and knee flexion are decreased; when running sharply, elbow flexion and knee flexion are increased.

WEIGHT: When running strongly, knee flexion and ankle flexion are increased. When running lightly, knee flexion and ankle flexion are decreased

BODY PARTS/SHAPES: The arms can move in many different ways and be held in different shapes. The torso can make curved, straight, angular and twisted shapes. Running in unusual ways requires coordination and balance. Through exploration and practice this can be achieved.

RELATIONSHIPS: Try running beside a partner. Try running around, beside, between, over, under and through objects or people. You will have to change the speed, shape, level and size of your steps and body.

LEAP

LEAP: A leap is an exaggerated run. The upward and forward direction is increased, the suspension in the air is longer, the knee and ankle action is increased on take-off and landing. The legs in the air can be extended forward and backward, side to side (in side leaps) or bent in various shapes. The leap is usually done in combination with running. Keep leaping to a minimum if you are dancing on a floor laid on cement.

AGES: Ages 1-2 should practice leaps moving forward by stepping over objects such as milk or egg cartons. Ages 3-4 can leap over objects placed in different pathways, stacked low and medium, narrow and wide, by moving quickly and slowly, strongly and lightly, sharply and smoothly. Ages 5-7 should focus on arm shapes as they explore different leaps over objects. Ages 8-adult can learn specific leaps such as the side leap, stag and butterfly leap. They can leap without the aid of objects. This age group should explore all variations.

Variations and Mechanics of Leaping

Specific variations are listed in each concept chapter under "Leaping." When leaping, it is important to remember to focus forward, not downward. The more momentum you have, the higher the leap. To gain momentum you must run, push off the floor using proper knee flexion, pull in the gut and lift the arms, but not the shoulders. When landing, always flex the knee and roll through the toes, ball and heel of the foot that lands first.

JUMP

JUMP: When you jump, you take off on both feet, lift into the air and land on both feet. When taking off and landing you flex your knees and ankles. When landing, you quickly roll through the toes, balls then heels of your feet. On take-off the process is reversed. Lift into the air can be better achieved if you pull in your gut and lift your arms, not shoulders, to a medium or high level. Keep jumping to a minimum if you are dancing on a floor laid on cement.

AGES: Ages 1-2 can jump with the help of parents. Hold the child with one hand under the buttocks and one arm around the waist. Lift the child in a gentle bouncing motion up and down from under the buttocks (like a "Johnny Jump-up"). Never lift a young child off the ground by pulling up on his or her arms. Ages 2 1/2-3 can do simple jumps in place and moving forward. Ages 4-5 can jump in different directions, with different size and speed and add arm variations. Ages 6-adult can do all variations.

Variations and Mechanics of Jumping

PLACE: Jumps can be done in self space or travelling through space. Travelling jumps are slightly harder to perform.

LEVEL: High jumps require more ankle and knee flexion than do low jumps. In the air, the legs can extend downward toward the floor or the knees can be pulled up so that the feet are farther off the ground.

SIZE: Travelling jumps can be close together or far apart. Doing broad jumps require greater knee and ankle flexion. A forward swing of the arm helps propel the body forward.

DIRECTION: Jumps can be performed in all directions. When jumping backward, lean slightly forward. Think of leading with the pelvis, not the torso, when changing directions and jumping.

PATHWAY: When jumping in curved pathways, curve the torso in the direction you are jumping; for straight pathways, keep the torso straight; for zigzag pathways, lead with the pelvis and keep the torso straight.

FOCUS: Your direction of gaze should be forward. However, once the jump is mastered, explore different points of focus. Changing your focus will make balancing more difficult.

SPEED: Quick jumps will be smaller and lower than jumps done at moderate speed. Less ankle and knee flexion will be required. Slow jumps will be bigger and/or higher. More ankle and knee flexion will be required.

RHYTHM: Slow and fast jumps can be combined to create rhythmic patterns. The size and height of the jumps will also be affected.

ENERGY: A normal jump has a sharp, percussive quality. It is difficult to make a jump look smooth. Try using smooth arm movemnts and slower jumps to create a feeling of sustained movement or try fast, small bounces to give a sense of gliding through space.

WEIGHT: A normal jump has a feeling of strength and moderately heavy weight. Light jumps may be smaller and lower than strong jumps. Explore different ways to make contact with the floor that create strong and light jumps.

BODY PARTS/SHAPES: Changing your body shape while jumping will make it more difficult to jump but creates exciting movement. Try many different arm movements and shapes - some will help you jump and some will hinder your jumping. Experiment with different leg shapes while in the air. Try jumping body parts other than legs (arms jumping, elbows and head jumping). Try a "jop" -- a jump that lands in a hop: take off on both feet and land on one foot. This is like a sissone in ballet.

RELATIONSHIPS: Try jumping beside a friend. Can you jump the same distance or height? Try jumping while holding hands or connecting another body part. Try jumping on and off objects. Try jumping over objects. Try jumping between and around objects or people. You will have to change the size of your body and steps.

HOP

HOP: When you hop, you take off on one foot and land on the same foot. The knee and ankle of the hopping foot are flexed, then extend in the air and are flexed again on landing. When landing, roll through the toes, ball and heel of the hopping foot as with jumping. The free leg is bent so that it makes no contact with the floor. The arms may swing upward as you hop in the air. Be sure to practice hopping with each leg. Keep hopping to a minumum if you are dancing on a floor laid on cement.

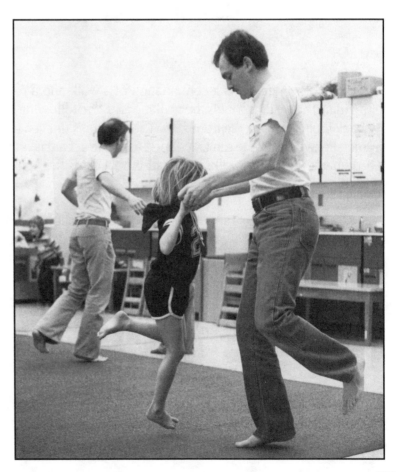

AGES: Ages 1-2 should concentrate on jumping, rather than hopping, as they do not yet have the strength or balance to lift off of one leg. However, in parent/toddler classes you can experiment with hopping in the following way: hold on to the child with one hand under the buttocks, as in jumping, and one arm around the waist while also holding one leg off the floor. Bounce the child gently up and down on one foot. Change legs.

Ages 2 1/2 - 3 should practice hopping holding on to a barre, ledge, chair or hand. A great way for parents and children to practice hopping: face each other holding hands, then the parent places one of his/her feet beneath the child's foot, gently holding it off the ground while the child hops on the other foot. Do not pull on the child's arms, simply support the child, helping him/her to balance. Hopping along with the child gives a better sense of the movement but is not absolutely necessary.

Ages 4 - 5 can practice hopping holding on to a person or object with one hand then trying it on their own.

Ages 6 - adult can try all variations. Hopping is an excellent way to strengthen BOTH legs if you remind your students to change legs.

Variations and Mechanics of Hopping

The same principles apply to hopping as to jumping except that hopping is more difficult because you must lift your whole body with one leg instead of two. Also, your base of support is smaller so maintaining your balance is much more difficult.

Combined Locomotor Movements

GALLOP

GALLOP: A gallop is a combination of a walk and a run. One foot leads with the other foot following. The leading foot is the walking foot, the following foot is the running foot. It is as though the back foot is chasing the front foot. The rhythm is uneven - long, short, long, short. The walk and lift-off take two beats, the run takes one beat. The accent is on the walk. In a series of gallops the run is a preparation for the walk, which further accents the walk. Music in 6/8 meter works well for galloping.

AGES: Ages 2 1/2 - 3 should be introduced to galloping. Holding a hand and galloping with the child or using the image of one leg chasing or following the other works well. Be sure to practice with each leg leading. Ages 4 - 6 should explore gallops in pathways, with changes in size and height, and with simple arm movements such as swinging or shaking after mastering the natural gallop. Ages 7 - adult should explore all the variations.

Variations and Mechanics of Galloping

PLACE: The gallop naturally travels through space. However, it is possible to gallop in place.

LEVEL: By increasing the flexion in the knee and ankle on the walking foot you can increase the level of the gallop. When you are in the air, your legs extend downward. To gallop at a lower level, you must keep the knees and ankles flexed, stay close to the ground and lean slightly forward.

288

SIZE: The gallop can be done with long or short strides. There is less knee and ankle flexion on the short strides and more on the long strides.

DIRECTION: The gallop is usually done in a forward direction but can be done backward. When moving backward the toe makes contact with the floor before the heel does. A gallop to the side is generally known as a slide. A gallop which turns while the leading foot pivots in place is known as a "buzz" turn. In this turn, the running foot pushes you around the pivoting, walking foot.

PATHWAY: When galloping in a curved pathway, the body leans toward the direction of the leading leg. When changing directions, it is easiest to change leading legs. When galloping in a straight pathway, the torso remains straight. When galloping in a zigzag pathway, it is easiest to change leading legs quickly when changing direction. Changing focus and twisting the torso also help change direction quickly.

FOCUS: The direction of gaze is usually in the direction of movement. When you explore different focuses your balance will be affected.

SPEED: When you gallop faster your steps will be shorter. When you gallop slowly, your steps will be longer.

RHYTHM: You can change the rhythm of the gallop by making the running step higher and moving into the walking step more quickly.

ENERGY: To make a gallop percussive, flex the knees and elbows sharply in the air. Smooth out your gallop by taking, long loping strides and keep the arms still or floating.

WEIGHT: A strong gallop can be accomplished by greater flexion in the knees and ankles causing a more forceful take-off and landing. A light gallop is created by less flexion while stepping on the toes and ball of the feet first, rather than the heels.

BODY PARTS/SHAPES: Adding arm movements and body shapes while galloping is more difficult and should be introduced after the natural gallop is mastered.

RELATIONSHIPS: Try galloping with a partner side by side. Try galloping like a team of horses, one in back of the other, holding hands. Try a team of three horses side by side or in the shape of a triangle moving forward or around in a circle. Try a team of four horses in the shape of a square moving forward and then around in a circle. Try galloping over, around and between objects or people.

SLIDE

SLIDE: The slide is a gallop moving sideways. All the principles for the gallop apply to the slide, except that the slide is always done in a sideward direction.

AGES: Slides can be introduced to students ages 1 1/2 - 3. Face the child and hold hands. Move sideways, first stepping sideways with one foot and then bringing the other foot next to the first foot. Move sideways in a step-together fashion with the right foot leading and then the left foot leading. Slowly increase the speed of your movement, add the lift in the air and change to the uneven rhythm of a slide. Ages 3 - 4 can learn the slide through imitation. The commonest error is to move in a forward direction with the feet while twisting the head to face the teacher. The students think they are sliding but they are really galloping. I ask them to connect their belly buttons to mine with an invisible string, to paint the sides of their bodies and lead with that side, to stretch the right arm out when sliding right and stretch the left arm out when sliding left. All these images help. This age group can practice sliding with a partner. Ages 5 - 7 can explore different arm movements, levels, sizes and relationships. Ages 8 - adult can do all variations.

Variations and Mechanics of Sliding

The variations and mechanics of galloping can be applied to sliding except the slide is done sideways.

Sliding is a very important movement to introduce to young children. It is the one locomotor movement that very young children can perform that forces them to use each side of their bodies. We all have a dominant leg, just as we have a dominant hand. A child will find it easiest to slide with the dominant leg leading. With practice a child should be able to slide right and left with ease. If a child keeps crossing the dominant leg over the other leg while going sideways this may be an indication of a problem with laterality. It is helpful to pick up on such a problem early so that corrective measures can be taken. Practicing sliding with this child one-on-one is helpful, as well as doing other cross-lateral and bi-lateral movements such as hopping and swinging.

Remember, when you practice sliding back and forth across the room, face the same wall as you travel back and forth. If you change facings you will not be changing leading legs.

SKIP

SKIP: A skip is a combination of a hop and a walk. It is more difficult to do than a gallop or slide because the leading leg alternates. The walk is taken on one foot, which provides the take-off for the hop which lifts you in the air. The landing is made on the same foot. Then the other foot steps, hops and lands. The rhythm of the skip is opposite to the rhythm of the gallop. The walk takes one beat, the hop takes two beats. The rhythm is short, long, short, long. The accent is on the hop.

AGES: Children usually skip naturally by the age of 5. Skipping can be taught to 3 - 4 year olds but there is so much else to teach them that I usually wait. I often ask for galloping OR skipping movements when teaching young children. This way, children who are able to skip can do that movement but children who are not ready to skip feel comfortable galloping.

Young children learning to skip often do a movement that is a combination of a skip and a walk because they find it difficult to switch legs. This is fine. Keep encouraging them to bring the other knee up and forward and soon they will.

If you want to help a particular child, face the child and hold hands. Ask the child to imitate your movements. As you skip backwards the child will skip forwards mirroring your leg movements. Provide lift and support through the arms. Playing music with a strong skipping rhythm provides additional support.

Ages 5 - 7 can practice different arm movements, skip in different pathways, experiment with size, level and speed and skip with a partner or with a group around in a circle. Ages 8 - adult can explore all variations.

Mechanics and Variations of Skipping

PLACE: Skips are usually done travelling through space but can be done in place.

LEVEL: A high level can be achieived by taking a short walking step and a high hop. A low level is achieved by taking a long step and a low hop.

SIZE: Skipping may be done with long or short steps and wide or narrow arm shapes or movements.

DIRECTION: Skipping is usually done in a forward direction, but can be done backward, sideward and turning.

PATHWAY: The same principles apply when skipping in pathways as they do for the other locomotor movements.

FOCUS: The focus is forward. Changing the focus makes balance more difficult.

SPEED: The skip is usually done at a moderate tempo. By taking smaller steps and hops you can skip faster. By increasing the length of the walk and height of the hop you can skip more slowly.

RHYTHM: By taking a long step and a short hop you can reverse the rhythm of the skip.   Try putting runs and skips into patterns: run, run, skip; run, run, run, skip; run, skip, run, skip.

ENERGY: A skip is naturally percussive. By using less ankle and knee flexion and gently swinging the arms you might produce a smoother quality.

WEIGHT: Stomping, instead of walking, will produce more power and lift in the hop and give the skip a strong feeling. Walking lightly with the balls of the feet touching the floor first will produce a light hop.

BODY PARTS/SHAPES: Try different arm movements and body shapes. Explore different leg shapes with the free leg. Allow your students to master the natural skip before changing its shape and form.

RELATIONSHIPS: Practice skipping with a partner. Try different ways of holding hands and making connections. Skip around in a circle in small groups and large groups. Skip next to, behind and in front of others while holding hands.

CRAWL

CRAWL: A crawl is a movement in which the hands and knees, the hands and feet or the hands alone are used to move a person through space. The crawl can be explored at any age, although children who have just learned to walk are not very interested in crawling. Crawling is very good for arm and shoulder strength and should be encouraged at all age levels.

Variations of the Crawl

PLACE: Crawl in place moving in a circular pathway. Crawl through space.

LEVEL: Try crawling on hands and feet with your buttocks high in the air so that you are at a medium level. Crawl on hands, stomach and legs so that you are as low as possible. This is slithering.

SIZE: Try taking long strides and short strides.

DIRECTION: Try crawling forward, backward and sideways in different shapes.

PATHWAY: Crawl in zigzag, curved and straight pathways.

FOCUS: Focus up, down and sideways when you crawl.

SPEED: Try crawling quickly, but if on hands and knees be careful. Try crawling slowly.

RHYTHM: The crawl is usually done in a walking rhythm but can be explored using rhythmic patterns such as slow-slow-quick-quick-slow.

ENERGY: Crawling is naturally more sharp than smooth but explore both ways of moving.

WEIGHT: Try crawling strongly like a powerful animal or lightly like an insect.

BODY PARTS/SHAPES: Try crawling with the right hand and foot (or knee) and then the left side.

Try crawling with opposite hands and feet - right hand and left foot move together then left hand and right foot move together. Try moving the hands first and then the feet. Try these three variations on hands and knees. Try crawling on your hands and feet with your stomach facing upward instead of downward.

RELATIONSHIPS: Try having someone hold your legs and walk on your hands forward or backward. Crawl over, under and around others.

ROLL

ROLL: A roll is a movement done low to the ground where the prone or curled body is used to move you through space. Rolling can be introduced to infants and toddlers with the parent's help. Children age 3 can begin to experiment with rolling. Children age 5 and up can explore variations of rolling.

Variations of the Roll

Rolling can be explored using all the elements of dance. The greatest variation comes in the shape and direction of the roll. Try rolls that are done with the body lying long against the floor like a log. Try the log roll with arms above the head and by the sides. Try a knee roll where you roll from your knees to your bottom to your knees, etc. using the hands to help propel you through space. Your body should be in a round shape. Try opening and closing your legs as you roll. Try a sideways roll curled into a ball in which you roll on your back, over to your knees and hands and on to your back again. Try forward and backward rolls on mats. These are the most hazardous rolls and should not be done without supervision.

Dance Steps

WALTZ

WALTZ RUN: The waltz run is a combination of three runs done in 3/4 time. Traditionally, the first run is accented more than the other two by bending the landing leg more and then straightening on the other two runs. The legs move in a down, up, up pattern. The body can lean somewhat in the direction of the accented foot. Because the accent of the waltz run changes from left foot to right foot, this step has a pleasant swaying quality.

AGES: The waltz run can be introduced to children who are able to skip. Exaggerating the down, up, up through discussion of levels or images (falling off a curb and getting back on or stepping in and out of a hole) will be helpful. You might also practice the 3/4 meter and accent by clapping or stamping. Practice moving in a zigzag pathway to accentuate the change of feet on each accent. Older students can practice many variations of the waltz run.

Variations of the Waltz Run

PLACE: The waltz run can be done in self space exaggerating the side to side swaying motion. Through general space, practice moving smoothly with a slight swaying motion of the upper body.

LEVEL: Exaggerate the down, up, up by running in a deep plié and then in relevé.

SIZE: Practice long strides and short strides.

DIRECTION: Try moving side-to-side right and left and then sideways right, crossing the left foot over the right and sideways left, crossing the right foot over the left. Practice moving backward. This is challenging but fun!

PATHWAY: Try moving in straight, curved and zigzag pathways using the same principles discussed for other locomotor movements.

FOCUS: Try changing the focus by looking down as you step down and then looking up as you step down. This is a challenge in coordination and balance.

SPEED: Practice increasing the speed of the waltz run until you are skimming the floor.

RHYTHM: The rhythm of the waltz run is even. By changing the rhythm you alter the step. Review and accentuate the even rhythm.

ENERGY: The natural energy of the waltz run is smooth. Try doing sharp movements contrasted with smooth movements.

WEIGHT: The waltz run is usually done with light movements. However, strong movements are enjoyable to perform and watch.

BODY PARTS/SHAPES: The body can be erect or sway slightly from side to side. Explore a variety of arm movements and shapes that complement or contrast the leg movements.

RELATIONSHIPS: Practice the waltz run with a partner side by side exploring different hand holds or without holding hands. Practice in a trio, side by side, one in front of the others or holding hands in a triangle and in a circle. Practice in groups in circles, moving forward and backward or around the circle. Practice in lines, moving side by side or front to back and through each other.

STEP-HOP

STEP-HOP: The step-hop is a combination of a walk and a hop. It is sometimes confused with skipping but the step-hop is even in rhythm and done in 2/4 meter. The walk is forward and strongly accented. The walk provides the take-off for the hop which is done in place. The free foot in the hop is usually bent under the body. When the step is repeated it is done with the other foot. The step and hop are equal in timing with the accent on the step.

AGES: The step-hop can be introduced around the age of six but should follow mastery of the preceding locomotor steps. Some teachers find it helpful to teach the step-hop before the skip. I find that my young students find the step-hop a little boring and prefer the rhythm of the skip. The fun in step-hopping comes with the many variations that can be introduced after the age of six.

Variations of the Step-Hop

PLACE: The step-hop can be done in self space and this is a good way to introduce this step. When the students can step-hop in place have them travel forward through general space.

LEVEL: Try bending deeply on the step to rise high on the hop. Bend slightly on the step and you will rise low on the hop.

SIZE: Practice long steps and short steps. You can do fast small step-hops and slow big step-hops.

DIRECTION: The step-hop is normally done forward but can be performed in any direction. Explore changing the direction of the free leg as well as the stepping leg. When moving backward put the free leg forward and backward. When moving sideways right, let the left leg cross in front of the hopping leg. Reverse when moving left.

PATHWAY: Try moving in a zigzag pathway, changing direction on each step. Then try taking three step-hops in one direction and three step-hops in the other direction. The latter is much easier. Try moving in curved pathways, curving the upper body as you move.

FOCUS: Try changing the focus sharply on the hops, then try changing focus on the steps.

SPEED: The speed can be changed by increasing and decreasing the size of the steps. The bigger the step-hop, the slower the speed.

RHYTHM: The step-hop can be done in 3/4 meter by pausing after the step and before the hop: step-pause-hop, step-pause-hop. You can also add an action with the free foot between the step and hop. You could tap the toe front or back, brush the ball of the foot front or back, stamp or kick the free foot. You could also add an arm movement such as step-slash-hop, step-flick-hop, step-swing-hop. Try 4/4 meter by doing step-hop-hop-hop, step-hop-hop-hop.

ENERGY: The step-hop has a sharp quality. Try moving smoothly across the floor with gliding movements.

WEIGHT: The step-hop can be done forcefully with strong weight or gently with light weight.

BODY PARTS/SHAPES: Try moving the arms in many different ways such as hands on hips, arms folded across the chest, reaching to the sides, swinging forward and backward or across and side. Try changing the shape of the leg and foot from bent to straight, flexed to pointed. Try doing the step-hop in different body shapes with back arched or stomach contracted.

RELATIONSHIPS: Practice the step-hop with a partner side by side, face to face, front to back. Practice connecting in different ways and moving forward, sideways or in a circle. Practice in trios and groups coming forward and backward into a circle or moving around the circle. Practice in lines moving side-to-side with leg variations or facing forward.

SCHOTTISCHE

SCHOTTISCHE: The schottische (shotish) is a combination of three short running steps and a hop. The three running steps move forward with an accent on the first run. The hop is done on the foot which takes the third running step, the next set of steps begins on the other foot (right-left-right-hop, left-right-left-hop). The schottische is done in 4/4 meter. A step is taken on each beat The accent is on the first run with a secondary accent on the third run.

AGES: Like the step-hop, the schottische can be introduced around the age of six but should not be introduced until your students have mastered the preceding locomotor movements. Students with some experience enjoy exploring many variations of the schottische.

Variations of the Schottische

PLACE: The schottische should be practiced in place first. Try clapping the rhythm by clapping on the first three beats (running steps) and holding on the fourth beat (hop). Run in place and lift the leg on the fourth beat. Run in place and hop on the fourth beat. Move forward through general space on the runs and hop in place.

LEVEL: Try hopping high and hopping low. Bending the leg and pushing off the floor will help gain height. Remember to land on a bent leg, moving through the toe, ball and heel of the foot.

SIZE: Try long running strides and short running strides. Notice how the hop is affected by the size of your stride.

DIRECTION: Try moving backward, around and sideways. The sideward schottische is common in folk dancing. When moving sideways try a side-together-side running pattern with the free leg swinging across the hopping leg or try a step-cross-step pattern with the second step crossing in front or back of the other leg.

PATHWAY: Try a zigzag pathway, changing direction every four or twelve beats. Try moving in a curved pathway, letting the body curve in the direction you are traveling.

FOCUS: Change the focus sharply on the first or fourth beat or keep the focus in the direction of movement.

SPEED: Try fast and slow runs. How does this affect the size of steps and height of the hop?

RHYTHM: You could change to a 3/4 meter by doing only two runs (run-run-hop). In this variation the accented leg does not alternate. Therefore you always hop on the same foot (right-left-hop, right-left-hop). Try combining the step-hop and schottische to form rhythmic patterns: step-step-step-hop, step-step-step-hop, step-hop, step-hop, step-hop, step-hop (4/4 meter and 2/4 meter).

ENERGY: The runs move in a smooth gliding manner while the hop makes a sharp accent. Practice making the runs sharp also or try moving the arms sharply as the legs move smoothly. Change the movement to step-hop-hop-hop for a sharper quality. This would not be a true schottische but is still a fun step to do.

WEIGHT: The schottische can be performed with a strong, forceful quality or a light, delicate quality. Try both ways and discuss the different feelings evoked by the change of weight.

BODY PARTS/SHAPES: Try different variations in the shape of the free leg. It can be straight or bent. It can be placed forward, back or side. It can swing, kick or be held. Explore different arm movements as described in the step-hop. Try arching and bending the back in different directions. Try a rocking horse movement where you move in place swinging the free leg forward on the first hop and backward on the second hop. Lean your body forward as the leg swings back and backward as the leg swings forward.

RELATIONSHIPS: Practice connecting with a partner in different ways: hands on shoulders facing side by side or face to face; around waists; side by side with hands linked across stomachs. Practice moving around in a circle or one going forward while the other goes back in the same line of direction. Try one person kneeling and the other doing the schottische around the partner. Practice variations in groups.

TWO-STEP

TWO-STEP: The two-step is a combination of three walking steps. It is used often in folk, jazz and social dancing. Done to the right side, the right foot steps side, the left foot steps next to the right foot and the right foot steps side again (step-together-step). Done forward, the right foot steps forward, the left foot steps forward to close beside the right foot and the right foot steps forward again. The step is done backward in the same way. The two-step is done in 2/4 meter. The first two steps are equally divided on the first beat and the third step is taken on the second beat and lasts twice as long as the first two (step-together, step or eighth note-eighth note, quarter note). You might count 1 and 2 or quick-quick slow.

AGES: The two-step is more difficult than the other steps because of the rhythm and the closing step. Introduce the two-step to ages 8 and up after they have mastered the other steps. Experienced students can explore different variations.

Variations of the Two-Step

PLACE: Master the two-step in place before moving through general space. Clap three times and hold. Walk in place, accenting the first step and pausing after the third step. Repeat the step in place from side to side saying "step-together-step-hold" over and over. Try moving through general space.

LEVEL: Try leaping sideways on the first step and doing small, low steps side by side on the other two steps (often done in English country dances). The rhythm changes to a quarter note followed by two eight notes.

SIZE: Try taking short steps on the first two steps and a long step on the third step.

DIRECTION: The two-step is naturally performed in a sideways direction usually while turning. Try turning to the right on the first set and left on the second. Keep turning back and forth. Then try doing the two-step with quarter turns right or left. Then try doing the step with half turns right or left like a top turn. Practice the two-step forward and backward.

PATHWAY: Try a zigzag pathway moving forward or back on the diagonal. Try a curved pathway as you do the two-step turning.

SPEED: Try slow and fast two-steps.

RHYTHM: Change the rhythm from two eighth notes and a quarter note to a quarter note followed by two eighth notes. Do not attempt this until the dancers are quite comfortable with the original rhythm.

ENERGY: The two-step should have a smooth, gliding quality when doing social and folk dancing but can have a sharp quality when used in jazz or country dances.

WEIGHT: The two-step used in social and folk has a light quality while the two-step used in jazz and country dance often has a stronger quality.

BODY PARTS/SHAPES: Explore different arm shapes while doing the two-step.

RELATIONSHIPS: Do the two-step with a partner side by side and holding hands. Try the hinge turn, moving forward in a series of face-to-face and back-to-back turns. Try turning together around the room in waist-shoulder or closed social dance position.

GRAPEVINE

GRAPEVINE: The grapevine step is commonly used in folk dances. It is a series of side steps in which one foot crosses alternately in front of, and behind, the other foot. "Step left side, cross right foot in front, step left side, cross right foot behind." A simple and successful way to teach the grapevine is described in the chapter on "Directions" under "Developing Skills."

JOP

JOP: The jop (known in ballet terms as sissonne) is a step which combines a jump with a hop (jop). Take off from both feet (jump) but land on one foot. Practice doing this step in self space and traveling through general space. Practice landing always on the same foot and then alternate landing feet. Explore different arm movements and different elements of dance with the jop.

OTHER LOCOMOTOR MOVEMENTS

OTHER LOCOMOTOR MOVEMENTS might include slither, dash, dart, creep, flee, stamp, tip-toe, prance, soar, fly, bounce, polka, wobble, totter, skate, shuffle, sneak, waddle.

CHAPTER 25

NONLOCOMOTOR MOVEMENT

Nonlocomotor movement, sometimes called axial movement, is movement that moves around the axis of the body (the spine) rather than movement which takes the body through space. Many of the nonlocomotor movements are done with the torso, arms and head. The feet and legs may be involved but serve primarily as a base of support, helping the dancer maintain balance or give a greater dimension to the movement. The top half of the body (the half concerned with nonlocomotor movements) is often considered to be the expressive half, while the lower half serves as the supportive half.

Nonlocomotor movements when combined with locomotor movements form many of the dance movements used in different dance styles and techniques. Nonlocomotor movements should be explored alone and then in conjunction with the locomotor movements. Unfamiliar nonlocomotor movements can be introduced in the "Developing Skills" section of your lesson. The use of familiar nonlocomotor movements should be encouraged throughout the entire lesson.

All age groups should explore the many nonlocomotor movements described below. As your students become more experienced, they can practice these nonlocomotor movements in conjunction with different elements of dance.

Basic Nonlocomotor Movement

STRETCH

STRETCH: A stretch is a full extension of any body part.

Variations of Stretching

PLACE: Stretch in self space. Stretch through general space while walking, running, jumping, hopping, etc.

LEVEL: Stretch on different levels.

SIZE: Stretch is naturally a movement that reaches far from the center of the body. Stretch slightly, then stretch as far as possible.

DIRECTION: Stretch in all possible directions and on all planes.

PATHWAY: Stretches naturally move in a straight pathway away from center. Try stretching in curved pathways (twisting) and zigzag pathways (bending and stretching). Try moving in different pathways as you stretch.

SPEED: Vary the speed of your stretches from very fast (a thrust) to very slow.

ENERGY: Stretch smoothly (slowly) and sharply (quickly).

WEIGHT: Stretch strongly and lightly.

BODY PARTS: Stretch every body part.

RELATIONSHIPS: Stretch toward and away from other dancers. Stretch body parts toward and away from each other. Stretch your whole body or body parts through the empty spaces in shapes created by other dancers.

IMAGES: Yawning, reaching for something, growing, opening.

BEND

BEND: A bend is a movement that brings two body parts closer together. It could be considered the opposite of the stretch and occurs at the joints of the body.

Variations of Bending

PLACE: Bend at all the joints in self space. Bend while walking, running, leaping, etc.

LEVEL: Practice bending body parts while on different levels.

SIZE: The bend naturally brings body parts closer to center. The bend can be as big or as little as the joint allows.

DIRECTION: Different body parts bend in different directions -- trunk can bend forward, sideward and slightly backward. Arms (at elbows) can bend down/side and up/side, forward/up and forward/down. Legs (at knees) can bend forward/up and side/up (lifting the leg) or backward (lower leg going back). What directions can neck, fingers, toes, wrists and ankles bend?

PATHWAY: The bend moves in a zigzag pathway. Practice bending while moving through space in different pathways.

SPEED: Bend slowly and quickly.

ENERGY: Bend smoothly (slowly) and sharply (quickly).

WEIGHT: Bend strongly and lightly.

BODY PARTS: Find all the joints that allow body parts to bend.

RELATIONSHIPS: Bend body parts toward each other. Connect bent body parts with another dancer -- connect at elbows, knees, ankles, wrists.

IMAGES: Machines, robots, marionettes, door or lid closing, fan folding.

TWIST

TWIST: When twisting, you rotate a part of your body around an axis. You can twist your arm at the shoulder, your leg at the hip and your trunk and head around the spinal column. Other body parts can twist but with less dimension. You can twist body parts clockwise or counterclockwise.

Variations of Twisting

PLACE: Twist body parts in self space. Practice twisting as you move through general space while doing different locomotor movements.

LEVEL: Twist different body parts while on different levels.

SIZE: Twist large body parts such as arms, legs, trunk and small body parts such as wrists, ankles and fingers. Practice twisting as great or as small as the joint allows.

DIRECTION: Practice rotating arms and legs inward and outward. Rotate trunk and head around to the left and to the right. Practice twisting arms and legs in front of you, in back of you, to the side, stretching up and down.

PATHWAY: The natural shape of a twist is curved. Accentuate the curve as you twist arms and trunk around the spinal column. Practice twisting in general space in different pathways.

SPEED: Try twisting quickly and slowly.

ENERGY: Twist smoothly and sharply.

WEIGHT: Twist with strength and with lightness.

BODY PARTS: Twist as many different body parts as possible.

RELATIONSHIPS: Twist around a partner clockwise then counter clockwise. Twist body parts around other body parts.

IMAGES: Stripe around a candy cane, pretzel, tying knots, tightening a screw, twisting on or off a bottle cap.

SWING

SWING: A swing is movement of a body part in an arc or circle. The swing begins with the release of the swinging part into gravity, then the lift and suspension on the other side of the arc and the drop back into the gravity pull again. The swing is distinguished from the sway by the weight of the drop and the moment of suspension before the drop again. The arms can swing from the shoulders, the head from the neck, the trunk from the hips and the legs (one at a time) from the hips.

Variations of Swinging

PLACE: Swing body parts in self space. Practice swinging body parts while traveling through general space. Try letting the swinging motion be the impetus that moves you through space.

LEVEL: Practice swinging body parts on different levels and practice letting your swing move through different levels (high-low-high).

SIZE: Small swings are created by using less force, large swings are created by increasing the force that begins the swing. The arc can go from very small to large to a full circle.

DIRECTION: Try arm, leg and torso swings that move forward and backward, then side to side. All swings involve the up/down direction. Practice swinging arms together in the same direction, in opposition, in a figure eight shape, in half circles and full circles. When swinging the leg in different directions, pull in the gut and stand tall on the stationary leg to maintain balance.

PATHWAY: The swing draws a curved pathway in the air. Practice swinging while moving through space in different pathways. Zigzag pathways can be created by sliding right and left while swinging the arms in a full circle to the right and then to the left.

SPEED: Swings cannot be done too slowly or too quickly or they lose their swinging quality. The swing starts slowly, drops with speed and the slows down at the height of suspension. Explore swinging with different speed and discuss the results.

ENERGY: The swing is a smooth movement. A sharp movement can be used to initiate a swing but it gives a different quality to the movement. Try doing sharp swings and discuss the results.

WEIGHT: Weight is the most important part of a swing. Without weight the swing becomes a sway. The swing moves from light (suspension) to strong (drop) to light (suspension) weight.

BODY PARTS: Practice swinging different body parts. Which parts can swing most easily? (Arms, legs, torso, head.) Hands and feet can swing slightly.

RELATIONSHIPS: Practice swinging different body parts simultaneously - arm and leg, two arms and leg, head and leg, head and arms, etc. Practice swinging while mirroring a partner and then in opposition to a partner. Try this in a side-to-side direction and then forward and backward.

IMAGES: Roller coaster, playground swing, trapeze, elephant trunk, hammock, big wave.

Combined Nonlocomotor Movements

PUSH: A movement away from the center of the body, starting with a bend and extending to a stretch. Explore pushing many different body parts in different directions, with different dimensions, on different levels, with changes in speed, energy and weight.

IMAGES: pushing a piano, swing, grocery cart, balloon, against another person.

PULL: A movement toward the center of the body, starting with a stretch and moving to a bend. Explore the pull as you did the push.

IMAGES: pulling a rope, a kite, a car, another person.

FALL: A fall is a change of body position from standing, kneeling or sitting to a prone position on the floor. A fall is generally a sudden movement but can be done gradually. When falling, the weight should rest on the thigh, buttocks, side of the leg or back of the shoulder rather than on the knees, elbows and base of the spine. Practice falling in different directions, from different levels, with changes in speed, energy and weight.

IMAGES: falling leaves, snow, boulders, bowling pins, trees, feathers, waterfalls, eggs.

MELT: Melting is similar to falling except that it is done more gradually and in a more liquid fashion than a fall.

IMAGES: melting wax, ice, popsicles, lava.

ROCK: A rock is a transfer of weight from one body part to another side to side or front to back. Tension is maintained in the body parts. It can be done standing, sitting or lying down. Explore rocking on different body parts, in different directions, on different levels, with changes in speed, size, energy and weight. Try rocking with a partner.

IMAGES: rocking chair or horse, cradle, windshield wipers, ringing bells.

SWAY: Sway is similar to a rock except that less force is used so that it has a slower, softer quality. The body is more relaxed so that the movement has less suspension than when rocking. Explore swaying in different directions, on different body parts and levels, with changes in size, speed, energy and weight.

IMAGES: trees in a gentle breeze, swings, grasses in the wind.

SHAKE: Shake is a sharp, quick action done by moving body parts quickly back and forth or side to side. The speed of shaking can be changed slightly but if done too slowly the vibratory quality is lost. Body parts can shake separately or simultaneously. Explore shaking in different directions, on different levels, while moving through space, with changes in size and weight.

IMAGES: rattlesnake, shivering with cold or fear, baby rattles, earthquake, blender, maracas.

LUNGE: A lunge is a combination of a stretch and a bend. The leg is stretched away from the body in any direction and then bends as the weight is transferred from the standing leg to the stretched leg. The body leans in the direction of the lunge. Explore lunging in different directions and on different levels (standing and kneeling), and with changes in speed, size, energy and weight. Try moving through space with a series of lunges. Explore different arm movements while lunging. Lunge toward and away from a partner.

IMAGES: falling and being caught, leaning, fencing, sword thrust.

CONTRACT: Contracting movement is strong movement which pulls into the center of the body. The opposite of contracting is expanding or stretching. Contracting is different from bending because the movement is not initiated in the joints but rather in the gut or stomach muscles. The contraction has a hollow feeling to it. Contract on different levels, with changes in size, speed and energy.

IMAGES: balloon bursting or deflating, being punched in the stomach, being a hollow pumpkin, having your insides scooped out.

CURL: Curling is like contracting but is done with less force and brings body parts closer together. Rather than a hollow feeling, curling has a more closed in feeling to it. Curl on different levels, using different body parts, with changes in size, speed, energy and weight.

IMAGES: rug rolling up, hair curling, leaves curling up, snail, spiral, party blowers you blow into that stretch out and curl back up.

TURN: A turn is a movement which allows the body to face a new direction. There must be a shift of weight from one foot to another or from one part of the foot to another part. A turn often begins with a twist but is a fuller movement because of the weight shift and the fact that the whole body must face a new direction, not just part of the body. The body can make a quarter, half, three-quarter or whole turn. Whole turns can be repeated and performed in self space and through general space. Turning can be combined with locomotor movements to create a wide variety of exciting turns. See the "Turning" section in each element chapter to discover ways of turning while exploring all the elements of dance.

IMAGES: spinning tops, merry-go-round, whirlpool, tornado, propellers.

FLOAT: Floating is smooth, light movement that moves in an indirect fashion. (Indirect means that the movement does not move in a specific line of direction or with a specific focus but moves through several directions and planes and has a scattered quality.) You can float on different levels, in different directions with changes in size and rhythm but if you change the energy or weight of the float you alter its quality completely.

IMAGES: helium balloons, astronauts in outer space, feathers falling, clouds, fish, seaweed.

GLIDE: Gliding is smooth, light, direct movement. (Direct means that the movement has a specific line of direction or focus. Rather than having a scattered focus, the movement has a quality of directness and purpose.) Gliding can be done with different body parts (arms are easiest), moving through different levels, with changes in dimension, length and speed. Changing the energy and weight of the glide will result in a different movement.

IMAGES: paper airplanes, hang gliders, ice skating.

FLICK: Flicking is sharp, light, indirect movement. Try flicking with different body parts, in different directions and on different levels, with changes in rhythm and size. You cannot change the weight, speed or energy of the flick.

IMAGES: flicking away insects, flicking hair off your face, horses flicking tails or manes.

DAB: Dabbing is sharp, light, direct movement. Dab with different body parts, on different levels, in different directions, with changes in rhythm and size. Changing the energy and weight will alter the movement.

IMAGES: finger painting polka dots, putting on make-up or lotion, bird pecking, playing a note on the piano.

SLASH: Slashing is sharp, strong, indirect movement. Explore slashing using the elements of dance as described above.

IMAGES: cutting the air, sword fighting, slicing something, moving through tall, thick grass.

PUNCH: Punching is sharp, strong, direct movement. Explore punching using the elements of dance as described above.

IMAGES: boxing, punching bag, making a hole in the air, rocket ships.

WRING: Wringing is smooth, strong and indirect movement. Explore wringing using the elements of dance as described above.

IMAGES: wring out a wet towel, twist the top off a jar, squeeze (wring) the water out of a sponge.

PRESS: Pressing is smooth, strong, direct movement. Explore pressing using the elements of dance as described above.

IMAGES: cider press, pressing clothes down to shut the drawer, pressing earth down around plants, pushing a heavy object, pressing against another person, pushing a revolving door.

OTHER NONLOCOMOTOR MOVEMENTS might include, spin, swirl, dodge, lift, kick, poke, wiggle, shiver, shrink, rise, sink, whirl, burst, grow, jab, explode, twitch, chop.

CHAPTER 26

COOLING DOWN

Cooling down is the closure part of class. It is an important part of each lesson and should always be included, if possible. There are several ways to cool-down, some more appropriate for certain ages than others. These are described below.

GOOD-BYE DANCE

The good-bye dance is an excellent way to end one hour classes with ages 2 - 7. One, two or three at a time, the dancers dance across the room to where you (or their parents in parent/ toddler classes) are seated. They can dance any way they choose as long as they use the lesson's concept. For instance, if the lesson is on LEVELS, they must change level as they dance in their own special way. Be sure to reinforce the elements of dance and interesting movements they are using by verbally naming them. Encourage the other dancers, who are waiting their turn, to watch the special dances. This activity should move quickly, never taking too long. It is a good way for you to evaluate how well the students are understanding the dance concepts you introduce each week. If the students are just running down to the end of the room, gently send them back and remind them to use the lesson's concept in their dance.

This age group loves to be stamped on hands and feet with interesting ink stamps. I always give one stamp for excellent listening and one stamp for wonderful dancing. At times I give extra stamps to everyone for extraordinary work. I never send a child home without at least one stamp, as I want every child to feel that they can succeed on some level in the class. If a child has been very disruptive, I give him or her a stamp for dancing and tell the child that I know he or she will be an excellent listener next class and will go home with two stamps. If a child doesn't participate, I give a stamp for listening. These children usually modify their behavior fairly quickly because I let them know that I have faith in their ability to do so.

ALIGNMENT

When teaching 3-5 year olds in a one hour class, I do alignment after thirty minutes because the children are tired and need to rest and catch their breath. When teaching thirty minute classes, you may end your class with alignment. Sometimes it is nice to begin class with alignment as a centering activity. This activity should be done in open space and is not very appropriate for classroom settings.

Have the dancers, ages 3 through adult, lie on the floor in an empty space with their legs and arms flat on the floor. Ask them to take three large breaths in and out to relax their muscles and joints. You might also ask them to squeeze all their muscles tightly and then relax into a loose, floppy shape. Move from dancer to dancer, gently bending each leg with the knee stretching toward the chest and the heel bone stretching toward the buttocks. Then lay the leg down. Holding the feet gently but firmly, pull the legs and feet parallel and straight for two seconds. Release. Gently cirle the arms making sure the shoulder joint is loose. Holding the wrists gently but firmly, pull the arms straight by the sides of the body so that the shoulders stretch downwards. The dancers should be relaxed, with body parts feeling heavy, not light. If a student feels tight and tense, ask them to pretend to be asleep so they are loose and floppy like cooked spaghetti. Soon they will learn to relax their muscles. Playing lullabies or gentle music in the background is very helpful.

This exercise will help the dancers feel the back, legs and arms long and straight. When they stand up, the shoulders should be relaxed downward, the arms hanging long by the sides, the feet pointing straight ahead in parallel position, the back long and straight, the heels in a direct line below the buttocks. Your dancers will have good alignment! With young children, it is a good time to say something personal and special to each child as you work on alignment. If you have a very large class, you could do just the arms one day and the legs another. Dancers ages 8 through adults can pair up and work with each other after you have taught them the correct technique.

VISUALIZATION

Visualization is a good way to calm students down after an active dance class. It is also an excellent way to prepare students for performance. Have the students lie down if space is available. Otherwise, they can rest their heads on their desks or sit quietly in their seats. Through visualization the dancers can feel their bodies floating on warm water, see themselves lying peacefully in a sunny meadow, feel a golden light ease their tired muscles or see themselves dancing beautifully in a performance. There are a number of tapes and books that have guided visualizations you can use. Of course, you and your students can also create your own visualizations. See the Bibliography for resources.

308

MIRRORING

Mirroring is an excellent activity to use in classroom space where the desks do not allow room for the students to lie down on the floor. Partner mirroring is not very relaxing but having the class mirror one leader can be very restful. The leader should move slowly and smoothly. Stretching, yawning, twisting, swinging, shaking and bending movements are good for relaxing muscles. All body parts should be moved at one time or another to relieve tension in all the muscles. Peaceful music makes a wonderful background.

Sometimes it is fun to divide the class in half, having each group turn to face each other. The leader stands behind one group, facing the group opposite. The group facing the leader stands up and mirrors the leader's movements. The other group sits down with their back to the leader and watches the group facing them. The leader then changes sides to face the other group and leads the movement again. The leader can add some surprises to the movement such as making faces, jumping up or doing other sharp movements. The two groups enjoy watching each other "perform" as each group follows the leader's movements.

STRETCHING

Stretching muscles after dance class will help lengthen muscles, increase flexibility and prevent muscle cramps. This is a good cool-down after a sixty to ninety minute dance class for ages eight through adults. While the dancers are stretching their muscles, have them review the lesson's concepts, asking them to verbalize the concepts and the elements of dance used throughout the class. Judy Alter's book *Stretch and Strengthen* is an excellent resource for safe and sound stretching exercises.

SHARING AND EVALUATING CHOREOGRAPHY

If your class is working on choreography, you will want to spend the cool-down time having your students watch and evaluate the dances. Before the groups perform their choreography, ask the students in the "audience" to watch for these things:

How did the dancers solve the choreographic problem?
What elements of dance did they use?
What was particularly interesting or different?
What did the dance "say" to you?
What did you see? How were surprises created?
How was this dance different or similar to the other dances shown today?

After each dance, briefly evaluate the pieces, helping your students to increase their ability to see dance and discuss dance intelligently. I feel that this skill is as important as any physical dance skill. You will think of many more discussion questions as the dancers' ability to choreograph improves. The rule in my class is that only positive comments can be made and they should be general, not too personal. If the choreographers do not solve the given problem, help them in a positive way to find a better solution. The dancers in the audience need to be attentive and appreciative, always clapping when the piece is finished.

CHAPTER 27

ADDITIONAL LESSON PLANS FOR INFANTS THROUGH SENIORS

At the end of each chapter on the elements of dance, there are two lesson plans covering the concept discussed in that chapter. These are examples of what can be planned for different age groups and different lengths of time.

In addition to those sample lessons, this chapter presents lesson plans showing what can be done with different age groups, families, junior and senior high school classes, parents and toddlers, and parents and infants -- for a sixty-minute or a thirty-minute class.

Use these examples to build your own lesson plans, making certain to include the five essential elements of warming up, exploring the concept, developing skills, creating, and cooling down.

LESSON FOR 3-4 YEAR OLDS

Length: 60 minutes   *Concept: Body Parts*

WARMING-UP

Dance Exercises/Technique: Rhyming Exercises: choose 5-7 exercises focusing on different body parts. Include a body part song such as "Clap Your Hands."

Introducing the Concept: BODY PARTS: hand, head, hips, etc. Name many parts and move them.

EXPLORING THE CONCEPT

Exploring the Concept: "Body Halves" #10
Dance with top body half while keeping the legs frozen. Then dance with the legs while keeping the top half frozen in a shape. Keep alternating top and bottom half. The last time dance with the whole body. Music: "Pause" - *Movin'*.

Shaping: "Connect" #1
Connect one part to another and make a shape (elbows to knees). Name many pairs. For experienced dancers, occasionally name two pairs to connect into a shape (knees to elbows and shoulder to ear)!

Instruments: "Music" #3
When the music is fast, play fast and move your feet fast. When the music is slow, play slowly and move your head slowly. Name other parts to emphasize when music is slow and fast. Music: "Slow and Fast" - *Feel of Music*.

COOLING DOWN

Relaxation/Alignment: Teacher manipulates body parts as dancers relax muscles while lying on the floor.

DEVELOPING SKILLS

Developing Skills: "Arms" #3
Dancers practice running in curved pathways with arms at their sides (river run). Then they practice jumping with fancy arm movements that they create. Alternate river run with no arms and jumps with fancy arms. Music: 'Celestial Soda Pop"- *Deep Breakfast*.

Combining Movements: "Folk Dance" #3
"Looby Loo" - As you sing: "Here we go Looby Loo, here we go Looby Light, here we go Looby Loo, all on a Saturday night," do simple locomotor movements holding hands in a circle. Then ask a child to name a body part. Use that part as you sing, "I put my (knee) in, I put my (knee) out, I give my (knee) a shake, shake, shake and turn myself about!" Repeat the song until all the children have had a chance to name a body part. Help children to think of many different parts.

Leaping: "Special Part" #2
Focus on arm movements. Show examples of different arm shapes and encourage the dancers to make clear arm shapes as they leap over the cartons. Music: "Rakes of Mallow" - *Rhythmically Moving #2*.

CONTINUED

313

LESSON FOR 3-4 YEAR OLDS -- CONCEPT: BODY PARTS

CREATING

Free Dancing/Improvising: Exploring the Concept "Activity Song" or "Props"
Choose an Activity Song from the Activity Music List that focuses on moving different body parts or have dancers move a prop in many different ways with different body parts. Music: body part or free dance song.

COOLING DOWN

Goodbye Dance: If time allows, have dancers move across the floor while emphasizing a certain body part.

LESSON FOR 3-4 YEAR OLDS

Length: 30 minutes   Concept: Size

WARMING-UP

Dance Exercises/Technique: Rhyming Exercises - select 4-5 exercises and focus on moving big and little, wide and narrow.

Introducing the Concept: SIZE: big, little, near reach, far reach. See, say and do the words.

EXPLORING THE CONCEPT

Exploring the Concept: "Giants and Elves" #5
Dancers move with giant movements when the music is loud and small movements when the music is soft. Add imagery as desired. Music: "Soft and Loud" - *Movin'*.

Shaping: "Balloon Shapes " #6
Blow up into big shapes. Shrink and pop into little shapes. Music: "Celestial Soda Pop" - *Deep Breakfast*.

DEVELOPING SKILLS

Developing Skills: "Objects" #5
Move with giant steps to a spot, jump with little tiny jumps on the spot, run backwards with medium steps away from the spot. Repeat several times. Experienced dancers can jump starting with little jumps and increasing then decreasing the size of the jumps. They can also add arm movements to the locomotor movements.

CREATING

Free Dancing/Improvising: Exploring the Concept "Finger-Body-Finger" #7
Dancers move just their finger then hand, arm, both arms, legs, back until whole body is dancing with large movements. Take body parts away until just the finger is moving. Music: "Brian Boru's March" - *James Galway's Greatest Hits*.

COOLING DOWN

Visualization: Dancers close eyes and breathe deeply as body expands and relaxes. Visualize balloon image.

LESSON FOR 5, 6, OR 7 YEAR OLDS

Length: 60 minutes   Concept: Energy

WARMING-UP

Dance Exercises/Technique: Do 15 minutes of rhyming or regular dance exercises focusing on moving smoothly, rather than sharply.

Introducing the Concept: ENERGY: sharp (sudden), smooth (sustained). See, say and do the words.

EXPLORING THE CONCEPT

Exploring the Concept: "Verbs" #12
Call out verbs and have the dancers describe them through movement: slash, caress, shatter, paint, squeeze, etc. Discuss which are sharp and which are smooth.

Shaping: "Sculptor and Clay" #5
Partners mold each other into sharp and smooth statues.

Instruments: "Reactions" #2
Half the class alternates playing sharp, percussive sounds on their instruments and smooth, sustained sounds while the other half reacts to the sounds with sharp and smooth movements. The teacher can direct when to change energy. Change roles. Variation: musicians react to the dancers' movements.

COOLING DOWN (optional with 6-7 year olds)

Relaxation/Alignment: Teacher manipulates and aligns body parts as dancers relax muscles, lying on the floor.

DEVELOPING SKILLS

Developing Skills: "Jumps" #6
Practice jumping in different directions with sharp and smooth arm movements.

Combining Movements: "Alternate" #1
Practice a combination of smooth and sharp movements such as: swirl, slash, run, flick, stretch. Repeat several times.

CREATING

Choreographing: "Images" #4
Give small groups, duets or trios a card with three sharp and smooth words written on it. The dancers create a simple dance describing the three words. Examples: wiggle, swirl, sneeze; squeeze, tickle, mold; chop, rub, poke. When working with inexperienced dancers, you may wish to create one or two dances together instead of breaking into small groups.

COOLING DOWN

Sharing/Evaluating Choreography: Share the dances and discuss the three words described, the other elements used, the surprises created by the choreographers.

LESSON FOR 5, 6, OR 7 YEAR OLDS

Length: 30 minutes*   *Concept: Speed*

WARMING-UP

Warm-up Activity: Exploring the Concept "16 Counts" #5
Move many different ways to different counts with different speeds. Music: drum or clapping.

Introducing the Concept: SPEED: slow, medium, fast. See, say and do the words.

EXPLORING THE CONCEPT

Exploring the Concept: "Acceleration" #17
Do simple movements and then speed them up: walk, turn, jump, float, swing, melt, punch. Discuss what happens to the movement as you speed it up. Does it change? What is the best tempo for each movement? Music: drum or clapping.

Shaping: Exploring the Concept "Machines" #18
Have groups form machines by connecting body parts to each other while moving one body part with a selected speed. Each body part should move at a different speed in the machine. Sounds can be added to the movement.

DEVELOPING SKILLS

Turning: "Levels" #3
Practice turning with different speeds at different levels. Music: "Slow and Fast" - *Movin'*.

CREATING

Free Dancing/Improvising: Combining Movements "Cinquain" #5
Ask the students to help you write a cinquain about speed as described in the *Speed* chapter. Put the words on the blackboard or large sheet of paper. Have the students think of a slow, medium and fast way of dancing for the movements in the third line. Perform the cinquain together as you read the poem.

COOLING DOWN

Sharing: Have half the class perform the cinquain and discuss the different speeds and what was exciting about the dance. Repeat with the other half.

* For a 60 minute lesson: Do 15 minutes of dance exercises, Leaping #3 and spend a longer time creating, sharing and discussing the cinquains.

LESSON FOR 8, 9, OR 10 YEAR OLDS

Length: 60 minutes   *Concept: Relationships*

WARMING-UP

Introducing the Concept: RELATIONSHIPS: over, under, around, through, above, below, beside, between, on, off, in, out, etc. Say, see and do the words.

Warm-up Activity: Exploring the Concept "Echo" #16
Dancers echo the leader's movements. Music "Echo" - *Rhythmically Moving #1.*

Dance Exercises/Technique: Do 15 minutes of technique focusing on the relationship between body parts.

EXPLORING THE CONCEPT

Exploring the Concept: "Find a Friend" #6
Make shapes with another dancer then dance away. Find new dancers each time with whom to make shapes. For inexperienced dancers, give suggestions for ways of dancing and types of shapes to make. Music: "Another Country" - *Dreams of Children.*

Shaping: "Statues" #4
Make large group statues in which each dancer is OVER another dancer. Try AROUND another dancer, THROUGH another dancer, etc. Music: Japanese bamboo flute music.

DEVELOPING SKILLS

Developing Skills: "Locomotor" #1
Practice running side by side with a partner, not connected physically but connected spatially. In trios, try the two outside people skipping forwards and the middle person skipping backwards. Connect physically and then spatially. Try other movements side by side with two or three people. Music: drum

Combining Movements: "Cinquain" #3 (if time allows)
Have the dancers practice the cinquain suggested in the *Relationships* chapter. As a group, discuss choices for performing the cinquain. Music: "Bricklayer's Daughter" - *Windham Hill Sampler '81.*

CREATING

Choreographing: "ABA" #1
Pairs of dancers choose two relationship words and create an ABA study. For variation, you might give the dancers a choice of using or not using props. Music: selections from *Windham Hill Sampler '81.*

COOLING DOWN

Sharing/Evaluating Choreography: 3-5 duets are performed simultaneously. Dancers discuss the magical moments created by chance, the contrast between duets, the relationships described and the other elements used.

LESSON FOR 8, 9, OR 10 YEAR OLDS

Length: 30 minutes*   *Concept: Weight*

WARMING-UP

Introducing the Concept: WEIGHT: strong, light. See, say and do the words.

Warming-up: Exploring the Concept "Shadowing" #10
Partners shadow each other's strong and light movements and shapes through space. Music: "Far East Blues" - *Movin".*

EXPLORING THE CONCEPT

Exploring the Concept: "Front to Front" #8
Press and pull your partner, sharing weight in self space, then dance away lightly through general space. Music: selection from *The Essential Jarre.*

DEVELOPING SKILLS

Developing Skills: "Nonlocomotor" #2
Practice different nonlocomotor movements and discuss whether they are strong or light. Music: drum, instruments or voice.

Leaping: "Cartons" #1
Burst and float over cartons or empty space. Music: "Blackberry Quadrille" - *Rhythmically Moving #2.*

CREATING

Free Dancing/Improvising: Exploring the Concept "Props" #16
Use stretchybands: move strongly and make strong shapes with the stretchybands, then dance lightly with the bands, using them as you might use scarves (swirling, floating, flying). Alternate strong and light movements. Music: "Seven Jumps" - *Rhythmically Moving #2* or "Inima" - *Solitude.* If you do not have stretchybands or elastic, let dancers react to short selections of world music.

COOLING DOWN

Reviewing Concepts: Stretch muscles strongly, relax muscles lightly as you verbalize the concepts of strong and light.

*For 60 minute lesson: Do 15 minutes of exercises, Shaping #8 and Combining Movements #1.

LESSON FOR ADULTS

Length: 90 minutes   Concept: Flow

WARMING-UP

Introducing the Concept: FLOW: free flow, bound flow. See, say and do the words.

Warm-up Activity: Exploring the Concept "Move and Stop" #6
Alternate moving with free and bound flow. Music: *The Essential Jarre* (some cuts are good for bound flow and some for free flow).

Dance Exercises/Technique: Do 25 minutes of technique emphasizing the free flow of such movements as swings and the bound flow of such movements as tendus. Also emphasize the flow between the movements. Discuss which exercises are best done with free flow and which with bound flow.

EXPLORING THE CONCEPT

Exploring the Concept: "World Music" #10
Dancers respond to short selections of world music with free or bound flow.

Shaping: "Group Sculptor and Clay"
Half the dancers are clay, the others are sculptors. The sculptors flow around the clay, molding the clay into statues. The sculptors use free flow movements and never stop. They simply dance by a statue and change its shape quickly as they flow by. The statues keep changing. Reverse roles.
If time allows, have the sculptors move around the statues with bound flow movement, taking more time to sculpt the statues. Discuss the different feelings evoked by the use of different kinds of flow.
Music: "Fugace" - *Suite for Flute and Jazz Piano*.

DEVELOPING SKILLS

Developing Skills: "Successive/Simultaneous" #5
Practice successive (snake like) movements and simultaneous (marionette like) movements. Discuss the difference. Which has more free flow, which is more bound? Music: rhythms from India (flute/horn for successive, drums for simultaneous).

Combining Movements: "Sequences" #6
Practice a simple combination with and without flow between movements. Discuss the difference. Use a familiar combination or something like: run, turn, shape, shape, shape, turn, run. Try doing movements separately, then put them together with transitions so that the dance has flow.

Leaping: "Free and Bound" #2
Practice different leap patterns using free and bound flow: run-leap, run-leap, run-leap, run-run-run-leap, run-run-run-leap, etc. Music: drum.

CREATING

Choreographing: "Textures"
Dancers feel sandpaper, silk and sponge and then improvise movements that describe these three different textures. Small groups form and create texture studies: put the three textures into an order (ABC); decide which flow fits which textures; create a dance for each texture and add sound that describes the flow and texture. For example: sandpaper - sharp, bound flow movements at a low level; silk - smooth, free flow movements at a high level; sponge - bouncy, bound flow movements that move from high to low. Music: the dancers own sound score.

COOLING DOWN

Sharing/Evaluating Choreography: Show and discuss the dances. What was the order? Did the sound score reinforce the movements/textures? What other dance elements did the dancers use? What created surprises? How were the dances similar? How were they different?

LESSON FOR FAMILIES

Length: 60 minutes   Ages: all ages   Concept: Direction

WARMING-UP

Introducing the Concept: DIRECTION: forward, backward, side, up, down. See, say and do the words.

Warm-up Activity: Exploring the Concept "Back to Back" #11
Couples or families make shapes back to back and then dance away from each other. Dancers may be back to back with the same people every time or with new people. Give suggestions for ways to dance through general space in different directions. Music: "Birdie Fly Down" - *I'm Not Small.*

Dance Exercises/Technique: Do 10 minutes of rhyming exercises.

EXPLORING THE CONCEPT

Exploring the Concept: "16 Counts" #4
Couples move in self and general space in different directions for a specified number of counts. Be flexible about couples: a parent and child could be a couple, siblings could be a couple, family groups could work together - one couple in self space and another couple in general space, trios can be used instead of couples. Music: clapping or counts.

Shaping: "Shape Museum" #7
Dancers move around copying the shapes of other dancers. When a shape is copied that person is free to dance and copy shapes. A parent can make shapes together with a child and/or independently. Music: "Beautiful Day" - *Jump Children.*

Instruments: "Shadow" #4
Follow a partner through space while playing simple instruments. Copy his/her rhythm and movement. Take turns being leader. Families can follow each other. Each takes a turn being the leader. Music: "Homemade Band" - *Homemade Band.*

DEVELOPING SKILLS

Combining Movements: "Folk Dance" #1
Do the Hokey Pokey, Mayim, Looby Loo, Virginia Reel or make up a simple circle dance using directions. For example: slide left in a circle, slide right in a circle, go forward into the circle, go backwards out of the circle, jump up and down and turn around. Repeat 4-5 times. Ask the families for movements to add to the creative folk dance. Music: any simple reel or folk dance from the *Rhythmically Moving* series.

CREATING

Free Dancing/Improvisation: "Props" #12
Choose a prop (streamer, scarf, stretchyband, etc.). Put the prop in different directions and move in those directions. Pull each other forward and backward with the prop. When the music stops make a shape together stretching in different directions. When the music resumes continue moving in different directions. Music: "Seven Jumps" - *Rhythmically Moving #2* or any lively music which you pause manually.

COOLING DOWN

Relaxation: Families rest together. Music: lullaby song.

LESSON FOR HIGH SCHOOL

Length: 50 minutes x 5 days   Concept: Pathway

Monday

WARMING-UP

Introducing the Concept: PATHWAY: curved, straight, zigzag. See, say and do the words.

Dance Exercises/Technique: Do 20 minutes of technique emphasizing the pathways that the arms, back and legs move through and create.

EXPLORING THE CONCEPT

Exploring the Concept: "Names" #7
Write your name in space with body parts and the whole body, emphasizing the different pathways in each letter. Music: "Baroque and Blues" - *Suite for Flute and Jazz Piano.*

DEVELOPING SKILLS

Developing Skills: "Waltz Run" #8
Practice the waltz run in a straight pathway. Music: "Cinderella" - *Emerald* or drum.

Turning: "Chainee" #1
Practice chainee turns with curved arm shapes. "Turning" - *Turning: Turning Back.*

CREATING

Combining Movements: "ABC" #3
Practice a combination in 3/4 meter of 4 measures of waltz runs in a straight pathway, 2 measures of chainee turns and 2 measures of step-hop-hop in a zigzag pathway: "down-up-up, down-up-up, down-up-up, down-up-up, turn-2-3, turn-2-3, step-hop-hop, step-hop-hop." Let dancers create their own arm movements. Music: drum or music with 3/4 meter.

COOLING DOWN

Stretching: Dancers stretch and lengthen muscles as they review the lesson's concepts.

Tuesday

WARMING-UP

Warm-up Activity: Exploring the Concept "Names" #7
Dancers write their phone numbers in space with body parts emphasizing the pathways of the numbers. Music: "Gigue" - *Emerald.*

EXPLORING THE CONCEPT

Shaping: "Group Sculptor and Clay" #8
Dancers sculpt each other into curved, straight and zigzag shapes. Music: "Fisherman's Dream" - *Emerald.*

CONTINUED

LESSON FOR HIGH SCHOOL -- CONCEPT: PATHWAY

DEVELOPING SKILLS

Developing Skills: "River Run" #5
Practice running in a smooth curved pathway without using arms. Music: "Veloce" - *Suite for Flute and Jazz Piano.*

Combining Movements: "ABC" #3
Continue to practice the combination from Monday. Add the river run moving backwards after the step-hops. Emphasize the pathways to make the movement clear.

CREATING

Choreographing: "Arts Works" #2 or "Pictures" #3
Small groups begin creating dances emphasizing pathways based on famous works of art or their own designs.

COOLING DOWN

Relaxation: Breathe deeply and relax muscles.

Wednesday

WARMING-UP

Dance Exercises/Technique: Do 20 minutes of technique, continuing the work started on Monday.

EXPLORING THE CONCEPT

Exploring the Concept: "Painters" #6
In pairs: one "paints" designs in space while the other copies the designs with body movement.
Reverse roles. Music: "Irlandaise" - *Suite for Flute and Jazz Piano.*

DEVELOPING SKILLS

Leaping: "Arms/Legs" #3
Dancers practice leaping with different arm and leg shapes. Try leaping in different pathways. Music: "Fugace" - *Suite for Flute and Jazz Piano.*

Combining Movements: Practice the "ABC" combination with one variation: to and away from a partner; 2 measures of waltz run and 4 measures of step-hop; do a different kind of turn; change the pathways; add some leaps; change the arm movements.

CREATING

Choreographing: Continue developing dance studies begun on Monday.

COOLING DOWN

Relaxation: Deep breathing.

CONTINUED

LESSON FOR HIGH SCHOOL -- CONCEPT: PATHWAY

Thursday

WARMING-UP

Warm-up Activity: Exploring the Concept "Shadowing" #8
Partners shadow each other's movements and make shapes together describing different pathways.
Music: selection from *The Essential Jarre.*

EXPLORING THE CONCEPT

Shaping: "Shape Museum" #10
Copy shapes and move in different pathways around the shapes. Music: African or Latin music.

DEVELOPING SKILLS

Combining Movements: Practice the "ABC" combination from Wednesday or add another variation.

CREATING

Choreographing: Finish studies begun on Tuesday.

COOLING DOWN

Sharing/Evaluating Choreography: Show studies and discuss.

Friday

WARMING-UP

Dance Exercises/Technique: Do 15-20 minutes of technique, continuing work begun on Monday, remembering to emphasize the concept of pathway.

CREATING

Choreographing: Refine the studies based on evaluations from yesterday.

COOLING DOWN

Sharing/Evaluating Choreography: Show the final studies and discuss and evaluate how the dancers used the art works or designs to motivate their movement and use of pathway.

LESSON FOR JUNIOR HIGH SCHOOL

Length: 50 minutes x 5 days   *Concept: Focus*

Monday

WARMING-UP

Introducing the Concept: FOCUS: single focus, multi-focus. See, say and do the words.

Dance Exercises/Technique: Do 20 minutes of technique emphasizing the concept of FOCUS. For example, where do hips focus, feet focus, arms focus, eyes focus, etc. This will help with alignment.

EXPLORING THE CONCEPT

Exploring the Concept: "Shadow/Mirror" #11
Partners mirror and then shadow each other's movements. Music: "Inima" - *Solitude.*

Shaping: Shapes in a Line
Dancers connect to each other forming a line of shapes, focusing on their own point of connection. Music: selection from *Simple Pleasures* (Bobby McFerrin).

DEVELOPING SKILLS

Developing Skills: "Counts" #8
Practice walking, jumping and leaping while changing focus every 8 counts, then 4 counts and 2 counts. Music: drum.

Combining Movements: "Word Cards" #2
Create a combination which changes focus: Turn/focus on a spot, float/focus all over, skip/focus forward, swirl/focus inward, fall/focus down. Music: drum or music with steady beat.

CREATING

Free Dancing/Improvising: Exploring the Concept "Zombie and Magician" #9
Zombie focuses on and follows movement of prop in magician's hand. Music. "Baroque and Blues" - *Suite for Flute and Jazz Piano.*

COOLING DOWN

Stretching: Dancers stretch and relax muscles.

Tuesday

WARMING-UP

Warm-up Activity: Exploring the Concept "Body Parts" #8
Focus on different body parts as they lead you through space. Music: "Word from the Country" - *Dreams of Children.*

CONTINUED

LESSON FOR JUNIOR HIGH SCHOOL -- CONCEPT: FOCUS

DEVELOPING SKILLS

Turning: "Spotting" #1
Practice turning while spotting. Music: "Veloce" - *Suite for Flute and Jazz Piano.*

Combining Movements: "Partners" #5
Practice the combination from Monday but do it toward a partner: Turn and float in self space, skip to a partner, swirl away and fall in a shape. Keep the same focus as Monday but focus on the partner during turning and skipping. Music: "Brian Boru's March" - *James Galway's Greatest Hits.*

CREATING

Choreographing: Combining Movements "Cinquain" #3
Divide class into groups. Have each group create their own third and fourth line for the cinquain written in the *Focus* chapter. Dancers begin work on their study, making choices about relationships, use of other elements, etc.

COOLING DOWN

Visualization: Close eyes, focus inward and breathe deeply, letting muscles relax.

Wednesday

WARMING-UP

Dance Exercises/Technique: Do 20 minutes of technique, continuing with work started on Monday.

EXPLORING THE CONCEPT

Exploring the Concept: "16 Counts" #10
Dance away from and back to your partner by a specified number of counts. Focus continually on partner. Change roles. Music: selection from *The Essential Jarre.*

DEVELOPING SKILLS

Combining Movements: Continue to practice and refine the combination started Monday. Add arm movements to the turn and skip.

CREATING

Free Dancing/Improvising: Choreographing "Improvisation" #9
Dancers are given focus situations to improvise for each other. Music: selections from *The Essential Jarre.*

COOLING DOWN

Sharing: Discuss how different focus situations made you feel.

CONTINUED

LESSON FOR JUNIOR HIGH SCHOOL -- CONCEPT: FOCUS

Thursday

WARMING-UP

Warm-up Activity: Exploring the Concept "Together and Apart" #12
Dance away from partner using multi-focus, dance toward your partner using single focus. Change partners each time. Music: Latin, salsa or marimba music.

DEVELOPING SKILLS

Combining Movements: Practice combination, refining arm movements and focus.

Leaping: "Legs" #6
Practice special leg shapes while leaping such as both bent, both straight, one bent and one straight, etc. Focus out as you leap. Music: "Javanaise" - *Suite for Flute and Jazz Piano*.

CREATING

Choreography: Groups continue to refine cinquain study started on Tuesday.

COOLING DOWN

Stretching: Simple stretches to lengthen and relax muscles.

Friday

WARMING-UP

Dance Exercises/Technique: Do 15 minutes of technique based on exercises developed Monday and Wednesday.

CREATING

Choreography: Finish and practice cinquain studies.

COOLING DOWN

Sharing and evaluating: Groups perform choreography. Dancers discuss the third and fourth lines created by different groups, how focus was used, other elements used, and surprises created.

LESSON FOR PARENTS AND TODDLERS

Ages: walking to 3   Length: 60 minutes   Concept: Balance

WARMING-UP

Introducing the Concept: BALANCE: on-balance, off-balance. See, say and do the words.

Warm-up Activity: Exploring the Concept "Move and Balance" #1
Dance around together, when the music stops make a balancing shape. Parents help children to balance.

Dance Exercises/Technique: "Rhyming Exercises" - *Bounce Like a Ball, Toes to Ceiling, Rowboat* (parent and child face each other and pull back and forth), *Twist in Washing Machine, Mop the Floor, Swing Your Leg* (holding parent's hand), *Jump Around.*

EXPLORING THE CONCEPT

Exploring the Concept: "Body Parts" #3
Try balancing on different body parts. Have parents help children to balance in different shapes, then try moving in different shapes. Music: "Fisherman's Dream" - *Emerald.*

Shaping: "Props" #9
Balance a prop (streamers, scarves, plastic, beanbags) on different body parts, balance on the prop and also move through space while balancing prop on body parts. Music: "Enter Sunlight" - *Movin'.*

DEVELOPING SKILLS

Combining Movements: "Seven Jumps" #3
Dance around together and then make a balance shape on the "hums." As each hum gets longer, make a shape with more people: first balance with your child, then with two couples, then three couples, then four couples, etc. Dance just with your child between the hums. Music: "Seven Jumps" - *Rhythmically Moving #2.*

COOLING DOWN

Relaxation: Parents lie down and take several deep breaths. Children may relax with parents, sit or move around quietly. This is rest time for parents. The teacher keeps an eye on the children. Encourage parents to be aware of tense/tight muscles and breathe deeply to relieve tension in those areas. Music: lullaby

DEVELOPING SKILLS (cont.)

Developing Skills: "Hopping" #2
Practice hopping. See the "Movement" chapter for suggestions of hopping with very young children. Music: "Funky Penguin" - *Movin'.*

EXPLORING THE CONCEPT (cont.)

Instruments: "Shapes" #3
Play one song while parents and children sit and play the instruments. During the second song, move around the room playing instruments until the music pauses. Stop and make a balancing shape. Alternate moving and balancing. Music: "Joy of Music" and "Wildwood" (with stops) - *Feel of Music.*

CONTINUED

LESSON FOR PARENTS AND TODDLERS -- CONCEPT: BALANCE

DEVELOPING SKILLS (cont.)

Leaping: "Beam" #2
Leap or step over cartons, then walk across a bench holding the parent's hand. If a bench is not available, children can stop and balance on a spot.

CREATING

Free Dancing/Improvising: Exploring the Concept "Props" #10
Choose a prop not used earlier and let the parents and children explore freely ways to balance the prop on body parts and to balance on the prop. If you have a parachute, let the whole class play with the chute: children move on top of the chute as parents make little ripples and waves; children go under the chute and make shapes as parents lift it up and down; parents make a big bubble with the chute and children climb up the chute making it go flat; children sit on the chute and parents pull it around like a merry-go-round; everyone lifts the chute and goes under and sits down so that the chute is like a tent and the children dance inside while parents sit and hold the chute down.

LESSON FOR PARENTS AND TODDLERS

Ages: walking - 3   Length: 60 minutes   Concept: Direction

I arrange the Parent/Toddler lesson plan differently from that of other age groups. I have found that the arrangement below and on the following pages helps to keep the very young dancer's interest for a full hour without exhausting the parents or children.

WARMING-UP

Introducing the Concept: DIRECTION: forward, backward, right, left, up, down. See, say and do the words.

Warm-up Activity: Exploring the Concept "Move and Stop" #1
Move in different directions and freeze in a shape pointing in a direction. Parents may hold their children or move independently. Parents should say the direction words as they do them. Parents can manipulate children as they move and make shapes. Music: "Pause" - *Movin'*.

Dance Exercises/Technique: "Rhyming Exercises" - *Bounce Like a Ball, Toes to Ceiling, Rowboat* (parent and child face each other and hold hands while pulling back and forth), *Shake Hands High, Twinkle Little Star, Twist in the Washing Machine, Jump Around* (lift the children who cannot jump independently). Parents manipulate the children who need help.

EXPLORING THE CONCEPT

Exploring the Concept: "Props" #12
Put your prop (streamer, scarf, plastic film, Chuk'em) in front of you and let it pull you forward. Put it behind you and let it pull you backward. Parents can hold onto the other end of the prop and pull and push the children in different directions and/or move independently. Remind parents to use the direction words as they move. Music: "Baroque and Blues" - *Suite for Flute and Jazz Piano*.

Shaping: "Under the Blanket"
Parent and child make a shape together under a large piece of material (old tablecloth or sheet). Remind the couple to make a shape reaching up, down, forward, backward or sideways. The other couples guess the direction used in the shape. Then the teacher pulls the material off the shape and everyone can see the real shape. Variation: Several couples can make shapes together or children can make shapes without parents.

DEVELOPING SKILLS

Turning: "Right and Left" #1
Parents hold children in different ways while turning right and then left in self space and through general space. Parents also try turns holding hands with the children and independently, if possible. Encourage a variety of turns by asking for and giving different suggestions. Music: "Slow and Fast" - *Feel of Music*.

COOLING DOWN

Resting: Parents lie down and take several deep breaths. Children may relax with parents, sit or move around quietly. This is rest time for parents. The teacher keeps an eye on the children. Encourage parents to be aware of tense/tight muscles and breathe deeply to relieve tension in those areas. Visualization can be helpful. Music: lullaby song (helpful in relaxing children also) from the Activity Music List.

CONTINUED

DEVELOPING SKILLS (cont.)

Developing Skills: "Locomotor" #1
Gallop forward to a carpet spot, jump up and down on the spot, slide away from the spot, slide back to the spot, slide around the spot and run backward to your starting place. Spots may be scattered or placed in a line in the middle of the room. Hold one hand while galloping, two hands while jumping and sliding and one hand while running backwards. Very young children may be carried (they will feel the different rhythms of the movements and experience the change of direction). Music: "Funky Penguin" - *Movin'*.

EXPLORING THE CONCEPT (cont.)

Instruments: "Activity Songs"
Choose two songs from the Activity Music List under "Instruments." Have the parents and children play many different instruments to the first song while sitting down. During the second song, encourage everyone to "march" around with their instruments. Call out different directions and movement possibilities (play up high, move down low, play and move backward, etc.) Music: "Beautiful Day" and "Play Your Instruments" - *Homemade Band*.

DEVELOPING SKILLS (cont.)

Leaping: "Cones" #6
Leap over milk cartons, then move backward between the two cones, turn around and continue leaping forward over the milk cartons. Arrange the cartons in two lines on either side of the room with the cones at one end of the room. Parents can help very young dancers by lifting one leg over the carton and also by lifting the whole child over the carton. Say "over" as you help the child. In a matter of weeks everyone will be stepping or leaping over the cartons.

CREATING

Free Dancing/Improvisation: Exploring the Concept "Props" #12
Give each couple a large piece of material and let them explore many ways of using it: pull the children around the room on large pieces of material, make the material into a hammock, with the help of the teacher, and swing a child side to side. Make directional shapes under and on top of the material. Play tug-of-war with the material. Music: any lively music with changes or classical, folk or ethnic music. If you do not have pieces of material, do free dancing to a song selected from the Activity Music List. Let the parents and children dance together in any way they want.

LESSON FOR PARENTS AND INFANTS

Length: 30 minutes   Concept: Body Parts

WARMING-UP

Introducing the Concept: BODY PARTS: head, legs, arms, feet, hands, back, etc. Have the parents say the words as they move the infants' body parts.

Dance Exercises/Technique: Do 10 minutes of simple exercises for infants and parents such as shaking, stretching, bending different body parts.

EXPLORING THE CONCEPT

Exploring the Concept: "Back to Back" #12
Couples connect different body parts together and then dance away, changing levels and directions and speed. Music: "Another Country" - *Dreams of Children.*

DEVELOPING SKILLS

Developing Skills: "Activity Songs" #7
Sing a body part song or choose one from the Activity Music List and move the infant's body parts as you sing.

Instruments: Play instruments in different rhythms. Encourage infants to play shakers and bells in different rhythms. Music: "Homemade Band" - *Homemade Band.*

CREATING

Free Dancing/Improvising: Exploring the Concept "Props" #20
Scarves: put scarves on different body parts, pull infants on scarves, dance under the scarves. Music: "Joy of Music" - *Feel of Music.*

COOLING DOWN

Relaxation: Lie down with infant and breathe deeply, relaxing muscles. Music: lullaby song.

LESSON FOR PARENTS AND INFANTS

Length: 60 minutes   Concept: Place

WARMING-UP

Introducing the Concept: PLACE: self space, general space. See, say and do the words.

Warm-up Activity: "Find a Friend" #4. Parent holds infant and makes a shape with another parent and infant, then the two couples dance away. Couples continue to find new couples to form shapes with and then dance away. Music: "Birdie Fly Down" - *I'm Not Small.*

Dance Exercises/Technique: Do exercises for the infants and the parents. Manipulate the infants as you sing "Clap Your Hands" (shake feet, stretch legs, bend knees, open and close arms, etc.). Bicycle the legs, pull the babies up (sit-ups) and lay them down, roll them over, cross their arms and legs, swing them side to side, hold them under the bottom like a "Johnny Jump-up" and bounce them up and down. Parents can do simple exercises for stomach, legs and back as they hold the infants or let them rest beside them.

EXPLORING THE CONCEPT

Exploring the Concept: "Follow the Leader" #10. Parent holds infant and follows teacher's movements in self space, then dances different ways through general space with infant. Alternate self and general space several times. Music: "Inima" - *Solitude.*

Shaping: "Shape Chain" #11. One couple makes a shape, then another connects on to that shape and another and another, until all couples have connected together to form a line of shapes across the room. Repeat several times. Music: "Irlandaise" - *Suite for Flute and Jazz Piano.*

COOLING DOWN

Relaxation: Infants and mothers lie down and relax together. Encourage deep breathing. This may also be a time to do infant massage. Before resting the parent can gently massage the baby and then they can rest together. Music: a lullaby.

DEVELOPING SKILLS

Turning: "Create-a-Turn" #1. Think of at least five different ways to hold the infant as you turn slowly and quickly in self and general space. Music: "Slow and Fast" - *Feel of Music.*

Instruments: Parent plays different instruments in different rhythms near the infant. Give the infant bells and shakers to hold and help the infant play the instruments in different rhythms. Music: "Play Your Instruments" - *Play Your Instruments.*

Combining Movements: "Cinquain" #2. Hold the infant and do the movements described in the cinquain as the teacher reads the poem. Remember to dance the infant through space, changing levels, speeds, direction and energy.

CREATING

Free Dancing/Improvising: "Props" #16. Using a large scarf or piece of material, pull the infant around the room, make shapes under the material, play tug-of-war, swing the infant, etc. Music: "Beautiful Day" - *Jump Children.*

COOLING DOWN

Goodbye Dance: Do a gentle, peaceful dance with your infant. Music: lullaby song.

LESSON FOR SENIORS

Length: 45-60 minutes   *Concept: Body Shapes*

WARMING-UP

Dance Exercises/Technique: Do 20 minutes of simple aerobic exercises that involve bending, stretching, swinging and twisting.

Introducing the Concept: BODY SHAPES: curved, twisted, angular and straight. See, say and do the words.

EXPLORING THE CONCEPT

Shaping: "Mirroring" #4 (variation)
Mirror the teacher's movements, dance away, mirror a partner's movements, dance away, your partner mirrors your movements, dance away. Music: selections from *James Galway's Greatest Hits* or "Slow and Fast" - *Feel of Music.*

DEVELOPING SKILLS

Developing Skills: Practice walking while making different shapes and movements with the arms. Give suggestions and ask for suggestions. Music: "Fisherman's Dream" - *Emerald.*

CREATING

Choreographing: "Cinquain" #5
Groups or individuals create dances to the cinquain under "Combining Movements" #5 or dancers may write their own cinquains. Dancers decide on beginning and ending shapes, create movement to describe the words in the poem and decide what other dance elements they will use in their dance to make it interesting.

COOLING DOWN

Sharing/Evaluating Choreography: Dancers show and discuss their studies.

LESSON FOR SENIORS

Length: 45-60 minutes   *Concept: Weight*

WARMING-UP

Dance Exercises/Technique: Do 20 minutes of simple aerobic exercises that involve stretching, bending, swinging and twisting movements.

Introducing the Concept: WEIGHT: strong, light. See, say and do the words.

EXPLORING THE CONCEPT

Exploring the Concept: "Loud and Soft #3
Explore moving strongly and lightly to loud and soft music. Discuss the different feelings evoked.
Music: "Soft and Loud" - *Feel of Music.*

Shaping: "Sculptor and Clay" #3
Mold each other into strong and light statues. Music: Japanese flute music. Share the finished statues with each other.

DEVELOPING SKILLS

Developing Skills: "Lunge/Tiptoe" #3
Practice lunging and tiptoeing. Music: "Annie's Song" - *Annie's Song.*

Combining Movements: "Cinquain" #4
Ask for suggestions for the third line of the cinquain, then let the dancers improvise their own movements as you read the poem.

CREATING

Free Dancing/Improvising: Play short selections of world music and have the dancers react with strong and light movements. Music: *Music from Distant Corners of the World.*

COOLING DOWN

Relaxing: Breathe deeply as you visualize floating on clouds or water.

LESSON ON VERBS AND ENERGY

Ages: 6-12   *Length: 30-45 minutes*

WARMING-UP

Introducing the Concept: ENERGY: sharp (sudden), smooth (sustained). Have the dancers see the words (written on the board), say the words, and try a few sharp and smooth movements. Discuss what makes a movement sharp (stopping the movement) and what makes a movement smooth (continuously moving).

Warm-up Activity: "Echo"
Dancers echo the teacher's sharp and smooth movements. The teacher moves for 4counts and then the dancers copy the movement for 4 counts. Music: "Echo" from *Rhythmically Moving.*

EXPLORING THE CONCEPT

Exploring the Concept: "Verbs"
"I am going to call out different verbs. Describe each verb through movement. Use your whole body and also try using different body parts. Do not use your voice. When the music pauses, freeze and wait for the next verb. Think about which verbs make you move smoothly and which make you move sharply."

   Some verb ideas: chop, paint, squeeze, poke, float, cough, swirl. Remind the dancers to use different body parts, not just arms and hands to describe the verbs. Music: any new age music without a strong beat or no music.

DEVELOPING SKILLS

Developing Skills: "Negative Space"
"Find a partner. One of you will move smoothly for 8counts creating a shape with a lot of negative space (empty space). The other dancer will make three sharp shapes, filling up the negative space in his/her partner's shape. You could fill up the space with one or more body parts. It might feel like poking holes in the empty spaces. Reverse roles."

   Music: use your voice. Count slowly for 8 counts, then clap sharply and count 1! 2! 3! Begin again. The skills being developed: visual and spatial awareness, cooperation, moving with contrasting energies, balance, coordination, problem-solving, creativity.

CREATING

Choreographing: Write the verbs used in "Exploring the Concept" on the board or let the dancers think of new verbs. Let the dancers suggest sharp or smooth vocal sounds to match the verbs. Divide the class into four or five groups. Assign each group the task of creating sharp sounds or smooth sounds. The sound should last about 15 seconds. Record each group's vocal score on tape. Have the class listen to the sound score and choose movements (either verbs previously used or new movements) to accompany the score. The dance might be chop, squeeze, swirl, poke, float or paint, shake, jiggle, swing, freeze. Play the dancers' sound score on the tape recorder as the dancers perform the dance.

   Variation: have the whole class think of five different sounds and five different verbs. Put the sounds and verbs together and let the whole class, or half the class at a time, perform the dance. You do not need to record the sound score. Music: the dancers' vocal score.

CONTINUED

LESSON ON VERBS AND ENERGY

COOLING DOWN

Sharing/Discussing: After watching each half perform the dance, discuss how the sounds supported the movements and how sharp and smooth movements made the dancers feel as they performed or watched. This could also be done in groups of 4-5 instead of as a whole class.

EXTENSION

Extend the activity by brainstorming more sounds, then think of verbs to accompany the sounds. You can also use the images of sharp and smooth to brainstorm verbs. When you have a long list of verbs, have the students write an action-packed short story using all the verbs on their list.

PART THREE

APPENDIXES

APPENDIX A

Assessment

Assessment in dance is essential if this art form is to become a basic part of public education. Learning occurs in dance and this learning can be assessed. Assessment provides information that is necessary if students are to continue to grow and develop. Assessment provides important information for the parents, the school and the community. Through assessment, students evaluate themselves, understanding what they know and what they need to know next.

In order for assessment to occur, there must first be clear learning outcomes, curriculum goals and appropriate assessment tools which are tied to the outcomes and goals. Learning outcomes are listed in "Why Learn Creative Dance." It is essential that all the learning outcomes (cognitive, affective, physical and social) be assessed. Curriculum goals and what is appropriate at certain stages of development are discussed in "Who Learns Creative Dance," "How Are Creative Dance Classes Structured," and "Movement."

Assessment tools can be designed in a variety of ways, when you have outcomes and goals firmly in place and the following ideas are taken into consideration.

> Assessment is linked to the curriculum goals and reporting indicates the student's progress toward these goals, discussing both strengths and weaknesses, and includes suggestions for progressing further toward these goals.

> Assessment is context dependent being specific to each student, taking into consideration their age, culture, and previous experience.

> Assessment is carried out on a formative (process) and summative (product) basis with many indicators of progress being used such as anecdotal comments, journals, videos, checklists and tests.

> Assessment consists of subjective evaluation based on objective criteria. The evaluator needs to have a good understanding of the learning outcomes (based on dance as an art form) in order for the assessment to be effective.

> Assessment needs to be a collaborative and friendly effort among the learner, peers and teacher. The learner should be aware of the outcomes and goals of the program and the assessment techniques. The assessments, all along the way, are shared with the learner to facilitate growth and development.

> (Adapted from the monograph *Assessment in the Fine Arts: Dance*, by Van Gyn and O'Neil.)

Assessment tools may be created in a variety of forms. When observing the process of acquiring dance skills and the product of the acquisition (skills is used in the broadest sense to include skills in all areas of learning), assessment might be in the form of anecdotal comments, conferences, journals, logs, notebooks, reports, checklists (created by a teacher and/or outside source), questionnaires (for teacher, student and parents), video tapes, critiques (by student, teacher, peers, and possibly a trained observer), or tests (teacher/student created and standardized). When a variety of assessment tools are utilized and gathered together to create an assessment portfolio, all parties involved will have a clear idea of a student's understanding and what the next step will be in the learning process.

Examples of possible assessment forms for your use are included on the next several pages. You will need to adapt them for your own situation but, hopefully, they will serve as a stimulus for developing your own assessment tools.

Below is an example of a skills checklist that a student, peer, or teacher could complete. Checklists can be used as a unit, quarterly, and/or yearly report. You might use a plus (+) for "consistently performs the skill" and a check (✔) for "performs the skill part of the time."

SKILLS CHECKLIST FOR UNIT ON SPACE

Name_____   Age_____   Grade_____

Dance Experience: Months_____   Years_____

Movement Skills

I can skip in two different directions
I can slide in a zigzag pathway
I can do three different turns in self space
I can do two different turns through general space
I can gallop leading with either leg in a curved pathway
I can jump in a pattern of forward, backward, side, side
I can use my upper body to draw curved pathways while using my lower body
      to move in a straight pathway
I can do a backward fall safely

Conceptual Skills

I can demonstrate correct alignment, using the elements of space to support me
I can move in three different pathways through space
I can demonstrate the difference between self space and general space
I can demonstrate the difference between size and level
I can demonstrate the six different directions
I can demonstrate the difference between single focus and multi-focus
I can use at least three different spatial elements while improvising
I can choreograph a study using an ABA form which clearly contrasts two spatial elements

Social Skills

I can gently mold a partner into a big and little shape
I can be a responsible leader when mirroring or shadowing
I can follow a leader's movements when mirroring or shadowing
I can work together with two other dancers to create a movement phrase

CONTINUED

Affective Skills

I have a good attitude in dance class
I work hard and try to do my best
I can express my feelings verbally
I can dance expressively

Cognitive Skills

I can spell the five different spatial concepts
I can describe the difference between level and size
I can name four self space movements and four general space movements

The form below could be completed by the teacher, peers, choreographer and a trained observer. The choreographer might use it throughout the rehearsal process to facilitate ongoing self-evaluation. The form can also be used by the students as they watch videos or live performances of professional choreographers and dance companies from the past and present. When using the form with young students, the teacher could go over the questions and elaborate on their meaning.

PERFORMANCE CRITIQUE

	Yes	Partially	No
Choreography			
1. Is the intent clear?	___	___	___
2. Is the form clear?	___	___	___
3. Is the form used effectively?	___	___	___
4. Is there unity?	___	___	___
5. Is there continuity?	___	___	___
6. Is there contrast?	___	___	___
7. Is there a climax?	___	___	___
8. Is the dance an appropriate length?	___	___	___
9. Is the space used effectively?	___	___	___
10. Are the dancers used effectively?	___	___	___
11. Does the music support the dance?	___	___	___

What dance elements are emphasized?

_____

What do you find most exciting or pleasing about this
  dance?

_____
_____

CONTINUED

	Yes	Partially	No

Performance

	Yes	Partially	No
1. Do the dancers execute the movements with clarity?	___	___	___
2. Are the dancers expressive?	___	___	___
3. Do the dancers show an understanding of timing/rhythm?	___	___	___
4. Do the dancers use correct focus?	___	___	___
5. Are the dancers working as an ensemble?	___	___	___

Technical Aspects (if not applicable write N/A)

	Yes	Partially	No
1. Are the costumes appropriate?	___	___	___
2. Is the lighting effective?	___	___	___
3. Is the set used effectively?	___	___	___
4. Is the prop used effectively?	___	___	___
5. Is the sound high quality?	___	___	___
6. Is the sound level appropriate?	___	___	___

Write a few sentences about how you felt after seeing this dance.

_____

_____

_____

The following is an example of some items that might be included on a written test. The test can be adapted to the student's reading and knowledge level.

UNIT TEST ON THE CONCEPT OF SPACE

Unscramble the following dance words:

irtecdoni   verucd   ellve   ndwo
yaahtpw   lapec   owl   socuf

Match the dance element with its descriptive words:

Level   self/general space
Pathway   single/multi
Place   forward/backward
Size   high/low
Direction   curved/straight/zigzag
Focus   big/little

Name four movements that allow you to travel through general space:

1._____   2._____   3._____   4._____

Name four movements that you do primarily in self space:

1._____   2._____   3._____   4._____

Put a T next to the true statements and an F next to the false statements.

The words big and high have the same meaning in dance.

When you use multi-focus you look at or see many things.

When you want to create a small shape you move your body parts far away from you.

You travel through space when you use general space.

When you move backward you always move in a straight pathway.

All your body parts must touch the ground when you move at a low level.

CONTINUED

347

Draw three different pathways and label them.

Remembering the videos shown in class,

Which culture dances primarily in self space? _____

Which culture utilizes primarily general space? _____

Write your own question about the concept of space and answer it.

The form below (which has been completed for one student) requires the teacher or trained observer to write descriptive comments about the student's knowledge and performance. The anecdotal comments can stand alone or, if necessary, a grade or point system can be given to each comment. This is only one example and can be adapted for your situation.

ANECDOTAL FORM

Student's Name   *Betsy Norman*

CONCEPTUAL SKILLS   *Understands and uses the dance vocabulary much of the time.*

MOVEMENT SKILLS   *Does not pick up skills easily but is able to do them adequately with practice.*

CREATIVE SKILLS   *Uses the dance elements very creatively when improvising but has trouble when organizing movement into a set piece.*

SOCIAL SKILLS   *Prefers to work alone or with a special friend but will work with other students when asked.*

VERBAL SKILLS   *Can verbalize the concepts studied to date. Enjoys participating in discussions.*

WRITTEN SKILLS   *Writes very brief comments in journal. Does not appear to like writing. Would rather be dancing.*

AUDIENCE SKILLS   *Loves to watch dancing. Very appreciative. Excellent at observation and evaluation.*

EXPRESSIVE SKILLS   *Enjoys sharing feelings through improvisation and discussion. Is very shy when working in group choreography.*

ATTITUDE   *Positive attitude, hard working and cheerful.*

OTHER COMMENTS   *This student has a good imagination and loves to improvise but needs to develop better group skills. I would like to see this student become more comfortable and sharing with a group.*

APPENDIX B

Teaching Academic Curriculum
Through the Kinesthetic Intelligence

Language Arts

1. **SPELLING/VOCABULARY:** Spell spelling or vocabulary words with letters formed using the whole body. Letters can be made on different levels, with varying size and with partners. Act out the meaning of the word with actions or a body shape. Write the words in space using different body parts as a pencil. Emphasize the vowel, silent letter, double letter, etc. by making those letters larger than the others. Always say each letter as you form or write it and say the word when you are finished.

2. **SCULPTOR AND CLAY:** Students sculpt each other into a shape that rhymes with a key word such as "might" (night, light, fight, tight, etc.). The class guesses the shapes and writes a list of rhyming words. Change roles. Repeat with different key words. Variation: instead of rhyming words have sculptors sculpt adjectives, verbs, emotions, occupations, transportation, antonyms, synonyms, homonyms, etc. OR have one person sculpt a letter and the other person think of an object beginning with that letter and sculpt the object: A is for airplane. It doesn't matter whether the students guess the shapes correctly. It is only important that they call out the type of word on which you are focusing (verbs, synonyms, compounds). This is a great way to brainstorm lists of words for creative writing because the visual sculptures stimulate many ideas.

3. **SYLLABLES/VOCABULARY:** Students put the same number of body parts on the floor or desk as the number of syllables in a word (watermelon -- four parts on desk). Think of an action for each syllable and do it as you say the word. The action may be the same for each syllable or different:

wa	ter	mel	on,		wa	ter	mel	on
jump—jump—jump—jump,					jump—turn—punch—stamp

Put groups of words together to form movement combinations. Say the syllables as accompaniment for the movement.

4. **PARTS OF SPEECH:** Pairs act out nouns and verbs or simple subjects and predicates: the noun dancer makes a frozen shape (tree) while the verb dancer does self space movement to describe the verb (falling). The class guesses the noun and verb. A quartet can create a longer subject and

predicate: number one is a frozen shape describing an adjective (huge), second is a noun shape (monster), third person is a moving verb shape (stomping), fourth is a moving adverb shape (quickly). The subject group might stand slightly apart from the predicate group. Example: fat robot walks slowly; tall candle flickers brightly, etc. Create even longer sentences with prepositional phrases (over the log). You could add more adjectives and adverbs. Also have students scramble their shapes, then the class must figure out the words and put them in the right order.

5. **PREPOSITIONS:** "Shape Museum" -- Have half the students make body sculptures and have the other half explore the sculptures using prepositions: move THROUGH the shapes, AROUND, UNDER, BESIDE, OVER, NEAR, FAR FROM, etc. When a dancer copies a statue, that statue comes alive and moves around the other statues.

6. **VOCABULARY:** Partners: one dancer follows the other dancer, copying his or her movement as they move through space together. When the music pauses, the teacher names a word such as "wide." The leader makes a wide shape and the follower has to make the opposite shape -- "narrow." Change leaders, dance through space, pause and try a new pair of antonyms such as over/under. The leader forms the shape of the word the teacher calls out and the follower has to think of the opposite word and forms that shape. Instead of antonyms, try compound words -- each dancer forms a root word, or homonyms (see/sea).

7. **OTHER IDEAS:** a) Create cinquains (five line poems) and perform them. Each dance element chapter contains a cinquain example. b) Putting dance words together into movement combinations helps develop sequencing, memory and ordering skills (walk, turn, stretch, melt). c) Form punctuation marks with body shapes and describe different sentences through movement: sentence ending in a period moves with plain, simple movement; sentence ending in a question mark moves with light, smooth, searching movement; sentence ending with an exclamation point moves with strong, sharp movement.

Mathematics

1. **STRETCH AND CURL SUMS:** Have the students think of two numbers that equal twelve (3, 9). Ask them to stretch into a big shape for three counts and curl back to a little shape for nine counts. Count as you stretch and curl. Discuss the size or length of the numbers (three is short, nine is long). Stretch and curl all the possible combinations and then try other sums. The children can really feel the length of the numbers.

2. **MATH IN PAIRS:** Give a math problem such as 4 + 3. One person in a pair puts four body parts on the floor. The other person puts three body parts on the floor. Together they count seven parts and then form the number seven with a body shape. Use fingers and toes plus other body parts when working with higher numbers. For subtraction (12 - 8), have the pair put a total of twelve parts on the floor. Then they remove eight parts and see that the answer is four parts left. They can form the number four with a body shape if desired. For multiplication (3 x 2), they would put three sets of two parts on the floor -- a set of elbows, a set of knees and a set of feet. They would count up the parts and form the number with a body shape. This activity is good for arm and shoulder strength along with practicing math skills.

3. **DIVISION:** Count the total number of people in your class (29). Have all the students dance around through general space. Pause the music, or give a signal, and ask dancers to get into groups of seven, forming a group statue. Count the number of statues. If there are students left over, they are the remainder. Write the problem on the board to reinforce the process: 29 divided by 7 = 4 with a remainder of 1. Try other divisors. Alter the total number of students and practice other division problems.

4. **16 COUNTS:** In pairs, one person dances in self space while the other dances in general space. The pairs dance for a specified number of counts determined by the math problem given by the teacher: 4 x 4 would be 16 counts of movement. Each time a math problem is given, the dancers reverse places (self and general space). Count out loud as the dancers move. Try many different operations. You might want to direct the movement by saying "9 + 4 with hopping movements," or "18 - 6 with strong movements."

5. **FRACTIONS:** "Dance 1/4 of your body, keeping 3/4 still. Dance with 2/4, dance with 3/4. Dance with 1/3, 2/3. Dance with 8/24 (1/3) of your body, 5/5 of your body (whole body)." Play lively music and pause it to call out a new fraction.

6. **GEOMETRY:** Form geometric shapes with body parts or props (stretchybands, elastic, string, streamers). Simple shapes can be formed by young dancers (circle, triangle, square), while more complicated shapes can be formed by older dancers (pentagon, parallelogram, equilateral triangle). Have trios form right triangles and ask the hypotenuse to dance away. Then ask the right angle dancers to form an acute angle and have the hypotenuse bisect the angle. Using the music for Seven Jumps, have the dancers dance during the music as they draw shapes and lines through space with their bodies. During the "hums," the dancers can form specified geometric shapes in groups.

Another idea is to give groups of students postulates. Have them act out the postulates and have the class guess them. For example: one and only one straight line may be drawn through any two distinct points.

Science

1. **MACHINES:** Each person makes a shape with one body part moving to describe a simple machine (pulley, wheel, screw, lever, etc.). The shapes connect one to another to form a big or small machine. Try adding sounds. Try a smooth machine and sharp machine, a fast and slow machine.

2. **ELECTRICITY:** a) Pairs demonstrate cause and effect -- touch partner's shoulder and partner moves. b) Groups demonstrate cause and effect through movement: blow up a balloon and it pops, push domino and all fall down, water flowing makes wheel move. c) Groups show how electric current works by forming with body shapes and movements a battery, wire, switch and bulb (or bell, vacuum, toaster, etc.). Groups might describe through movement a normal current, then an overloaded circuit and a loose connection and the effects.

3. **CINQUAIN:** Create a poem about a science concept or vocabulary word such as "magnet," "protozoa," "typhoon," etc. The concept must be described in only eleven words. This is an excellent way to synthesize information. Read the poem as the dancers perform it. Sounds

may be added when appropriate. Use this form:

noun	Typhoon
adjective, adjective	Swift, violent
verb, verb, verb	Crashing, smashing, lashing
four word sentence	Chinese for great wind
noun repeated or synonym	Hurricane

4. **BODY SYSTEMS:** Have groups create dances describing different systems of the body - respiratory, digestive, cardiovascular. Ask the students to show what happens to the systems when they become infected or drugs are used.

Social Studies

1. **MULTI-CULTURAL/MULTI-BODY PART:** "We are going to travel to four different countries. The first country is Ireland. What body part is most emphasized in Irish dancing? Yes, the feet! What element of dance is most emphasized? What do the feet do? Yes, speed! The feet dance fast! I am going to turn on Irish music. Let your feet dance quickly in self space and in general space. Your body is tall and straight, your arms are by your sides. Irish dancing is a little like American tap dance. Now, we are traveling to Japan. What body part is emphasized in Japanese dance? The arms and hands. What element of dance is emphasized? Flow. The arms move with free and bound flow. I will turn on music from Japan. Tell a story with your hands or imagine you are holding a fan or flowering branch as you dance in self space with your arms. Now we go to Russia. What body part is emphasized? The legs. What element is emphasized? Weight. Russian men dancers kick, squat and jump, with strong legs. I will turn on music from Russia while you carefully explore leg movements that help you change level. The last country we are going to visit is Africa. What body part is emphasized? The torso and pelvis. What element is emphasized? Rhythm. Listen to the many rhythms in the African music and move your torso and pelvis rhythmically. Let the movement of the rib cage move your arms. Let the movement of the pelvis initiate movement in your legs. Rather than just moving your legs and arms while keeping your torso still, start the movement in the center of the body and let it radiate out to the hands and feet."

Show pictures of dancers in costume from different countries. Use authentic music from the Nonesuch Explorer Series.

2. **MULTI-CULTURAL MIRROR:** After exploring movement from different countries as described above, group the students into duets, trios or quartets. "Choose a leader in your group. Stand behind your leader forming a pair, triangle or diamond shape (depending on how many in a group). I will play a short section of music from different countries. The leader will do movements based on our earlier explorations and the rest in the group will follow. When the music changes, turn to face another leader and mirror his or her movements." This activity will increase the students' movement vocabulary because they are getting new ideas from their peers.

3. **WORLD MUSIC:** Play short selections of music from many countries. Talk about the different rhythms and styles before or after the dancers have improvised movement to the music. How did the music make them move? Did they move in ways that were different from their normal movement patterns?

4. **FOLK DANCE:** After exploring other cultures through improvisation, teach folk dances from different countries. Use the resources listed in the Bibliography or invite parents or guest teachers to teach their native dances to your students. Show slides, films or photos of dancers in native dress. Bring in musical instruments if available.

5. **EASTERN AND WESTERN DANCE:** Show films or videos, available at libraries or universities, of dances from Asia and then ballet or modern dance from America or Western Europe. Discuss the differences with your students: Eastern dance is more grounded, primarily performed in self space, does not change levels, focuses on upper body and axial movements and dancers do not touch other dancers. Ballet and modern dancers use general space, change levels often, focus on leg movements and do a lot of partnering. After discussion, ask the dancers to explore movements to music from Asia that are similar to those seen on the video or talked about in discussion. Repeat with Western movements. Dancers might choreograph movement to a Haiku using primarily self space and arm movements. Then they might choreograph a Western folk or square dance to country music, focusing on general space, leg movements and partnering.

APPENDIX C

Exploring the Arts Through Dance

Exploring Visual Art Through Dance

1. **SHAPE:** a) Partners mold each other into shapes on different levels, in different directions, with variations in size, energy and weight. There are many variations of "Sculptor and Clay" described in the dance element chapters. Your students can mold real clay, make pipe cleaner shapes, or paper structures before or after shaping each other. b) Look in each chapter under "Shaping" for many more ideas relating to shape. Have your students draw the shapes created by bodies or draw shapes first and use the drawings as a stimulus for creating body shapes. c) Discuss the shapes in famous works of art and then create single or group statues that represent the shapes. How does a painting by Monet look different from a painting by Matisse? How do the shapes feel different when recreated with your body? d) Lie down in various shapes on large paper. Draw around the shapes and decorate the shapes with cloth, paper, paint, etc.

2. **LINE:** See the chapter on "Pathway" for many ways to integrate line and movement.

3. **TEXTURE:** Create rubbings of different textures or do weavings using different textures. Choose three textures such as sandpaper, silk and sponge and create a texture dance. Improvise sandpaper movements that are rough, sharp and quick. Improvise silky movements that are smooth, delicate and flowing. Improvise spongy movements that are bouncy and open. Now put the three textures into an order and create a dance in three sections. You could use the suite form so that section one is medium speed, section two is slow and section three is fast. Have small or large groups choreograph dances to share. They may add sound to each texture. After the dances are shown, let the students draw the textures and create art works based on the dances.

4. **COLOR:** a) Discuss how colors make you feel. Pair colors with movement words (red/sharp, blue/smooth, yellow/bouncy, black/strong) and create dances in ABA or suite form. Let the students decide on their own words. b) Talk about primary and secondary colors. Create watercolor washes mixing colors. Then have partners create a duet in which one dancer portrays the color yellow, the other portrays the color blue and together they portray the color green. Have different groups portray different primary and secondary colors. c) Look at works of art that have very different colors (Degas and Calder for example). Discuss the feelings evoked by these paintings and describe the feelings through movement. Have students create their own paintings, collages or drawings using color in different ways, before or after the movement.

5. **PATTERN:** Look at pictures, paintings, photos, quilts and cloth and discuss the different patterns in each. Is there a motif, how does the pattern repeat, is the pattern random, is there no

obvious pattern? Try to describe the pattern through movement either through shape or action. Give different groups different patterns and have them choreograph a dance describing their pattern. Ask the other dancers to draw the pattern as they watch the dances, then show the original pattern. Compare the original pattern to the newly created patterns motivated by the movement.

6. **SPACE:** a) Discuss the concept of negative space (empty space). Bring in examples of negative space in different art works. Have some dancers create shapes with a lot of negative space (large shapes with holes in them). Have other dancers fill up the negative space with a shape. Let the negative space dancers dance away and return to make a new shape over or around the small shape. Then the small shape dances away and the negative space shape is visible once more. Draw the designs created by the dancers. b) Create big human mobiles by connecting negative space shapes together with body part connections or props such as string, streamers, elastic, scarves, lycra strips, etc. Try to move the mobiles slightly. Look at Calder mobiles for ideas. Create your own mobiles out of materials instead of people.

7. **CRAFTS:** Make simple rhythm instruments and use them in dance class. Make masks and create a story dance or find a legend and recreate it through dance using the masks. Design wrapping paper by creating patterns from footprints and handprints (dip feet and hands in paint and dance on large pieces or rolls of paper). Create hats and crowns and use them in dances.

Exploring Drama Through Dance

1. **WARM-UPS:** Dance is an excellent way to warm up the actor physically and mentally. Try any of the "Quick Warm-up" ideas in the "Warming Up" Chapter. Activities that use partners are particularly good because they emphasize relationships and working together cooperatively. While warming up the body, add vocal sounds to warm up the voice.

2. **BODY PARTS:** Sometimes acting can get very cerebral and with young students turns into talking heads instead of talking bodies. The "Body Part" chapter has many activities that will help the actor to loosen up, become better acquainted with his or her body and feel more at ease moving through space. Explorations from other chapters will also help the actor feel more at ease moving through space, understand breath and rhythm and how to relate to others. Use the voice to create sounds to accompany the movement whenever appropriate.

3. **CHARACTERIZATION:** Exploring the dance elements will help characterization. Think of the character in terms of each element of dance and then emphasize particular elements to help define the character. Below are a few possibilities:

Place: Would the character move primarily in self space as someone who is pacing, waiting or watching? Would the character move through general space as someone who is searching, going to meet someone or on their way to somewhere?

Size: What size is the character? Making yourself small might connote a small child or old person. Making your body big might connote a bully or puffed-up ego. Making a narrow shape might work for a shy person, while a wide shape might help portray a proud person.

Level: On what level would your character move? A sleazy character might move low to the ground, a proud or haughty character would move on a high level and a timid person might move on a middle level.

Direction: Moving forward connotes aggression or sense of purpose. Moving backwards connotes fear or timidity. Moving side to side might connote nervousness or indecision.

Pathway: Moving in a straight pathway might indicate that your character was straightforward, honest and friendly. Moving on a zigzag path might mean your character was agitated, worried or sneaky. A curved pathway might indicate a dreamer or a lazy person.

Focus: A character with single focus might be direct, honest or aggressive. A character who shifts focus might be dishonest or nervous.

Speed: Moving quickly could indicate your character was worried, busy or nervous. Moving slowly might mean your character was tired, depressed or spaced-out.

Rhythm: Particular characters might have a special rhythm. A person with a wooden leg, a floozy, a drunkard or a monster would move with a special rhythm.

Energy: Sharp movements might indicate that your character was nervous, upset, angry, excited or clumsy. Smooth movements might indicate that your character was dreamy, sleepy, bored or graceful.

Weight: An aggressive, angry, proud or overbearing character might move strongly. A shy, ethereal, dreamy character might move lightly.

Flow: Bound flow would characterize someone who was angry, excited or up-tight. Free flow would characterize someone who was happy, open or mellow.

Body Parts: A hunchback or older person would accentuate the back. A flighty, nervous, timid or agitated character would accentuate the hands, arms and head. A sensual person would accentuate the pelvis. Someone drunk, militaristic, aggressive or confident would accentuate the legs. Accentuated shoulders might mean your character was unconfident or questioning.

Body Shapes: A proud or aggressive character would have a straight shape. A sick, anguished or cruel character would have a twisted shape. A round shape would indicate happiness, friendliness, jocularity. An angular shape would indicate meanness or nervousness.

Relationships: Standing far away from someone indicates anger or coldness. Near and around someone would be a sign of loving. Over someone would connote anger, aggression or dominance. Being under someone or something would indicate fear or timidity. Being between two people might connote confrontation or mediation. Being beside someone indicates support.

When you combine all the elements of your character, you will create a very strong, clear persona.

Exploring Music Through Dance

1. **SPEED:** See the chapter on "Speed" for many activities that relate to tempo and meter.

2. **RHYTHM:** See the chapter on "Rhythm" for a number of ways to explore rhythmic patterns and accent.

3. **INSTRUMENTS:** Each chapter has a section describing many different ways to combine rhythm instruments and dance.

4. **MUSIC:** Check the "Activity Music List" for songs that teach the concepts of speed and rhythm.

An Integrated Arts Activity

Divide your class into three to six groups. Give each group a large piece of chart paper and some felt tipped pens. One group will think of 4-5 sounds, then they will illustrate the sounds on the paper and finally create movement to accompany the picture and sounds (music, art, dance). The second group will put 4-5 movements together into a dance phrase, then they will create sounds to accompany the movement and finally draw the dance on the paper (dance, music, art). The third group will draw a design on the paper, then create movements to describe the design and finally make up a sound score to accompany the dance (art, dance, music).

When the students share their creations, let the audience guess which art form was the primary initiator. The primary initiator is usually the strongest form. If dance came first, the movement is usually very defined. If music came first, the sounds are unusual and distinct. If art came first, the design looks like an integrated work of art.

Talk about the elements of each art form that the students used in their pieces. If there are more than three groups, put the three art forms into other orders.

APPENDIX D

Props

Props can be very stimulating and motivating in creative dance classes but they can also be distracting. The first ten years that I taught creative dance I never used props. During the next ten years I have incorporated them into my dance classes with varying success.

Each class and age level responds differently to props. With young children, props can encourage more movement exploration and add excitement to a lesson. But young children sometimes become distracted by the prop and cease their movement exploration to stop and play with the prop. If this happens, I put the prop away for awhile or remind the children that the prop wants to dance, too. I have also discovered that the "Concept Exploration" part of the lesson is a good place to explore props because this is a structured activity. Sometimes the more structured you are with props, the better the results.

Older students can use props to expand their exploration of the movement elements or to add variety to their choreography. However, the movement possibilities of these students are sometimes stifled by adding an object they must manipulate. Structuring the prop activity is helpful in dealing with this problem. Another idea is to do the activity first with a prop and then without a prop. This often helps the student to better develop a specific movement concept.

When introducing a prop to a Free Dance/Improvisation, briefly demonstrate the many ways to manipulate the prop. Encourage your students to hold the prop on or with many different body parts, move the prop with different body parts, move around or on the prop, move the prop on different levels, in different directions. In other words, encourage your students to develop new ways of moving with the prop.

Use props sparingly. An overdose of props dilutes their magic. Use props to help develop and explore the dance concepts not as a focus themselves. Dance class is for learning about dance, not for playing with objects!

Virtually any object could become a prop for dance class. Listed below are some of my favorite props along with ways to explore them. In addition to these ideas, each concept chapter describes other ways to use props.

CARTONS

Empty milk cartons or egg cartons can be used to create leaping courses. Young children seem to need objects to leap over, while older students can leap over empty space. The cartons can be stacked to encourage leaps of different heights or placed side by side to encourage leaps of different widths. The cartons can be placed far apart or close together. They can be placed in lines, circles, semi-circles or scattered. Different sized milk cartons (pint, quart, gallon) can be used to emphasize the level and size of leaps.

WORD CARDS

Write all the dance vocabulary from the Dance Elements Chart on 5x7 index cards. Keep them in a card file categorized by the dance concept (Level, Size, etc.) so that they are accessible. I have put all the Space words on blue cards, the Time words on green cards, the Force words on yellow cards, Body words on orange, Locomotor on white and Nonlocomotor on salmon. This isn't necessary but it is a helpful visual aid. Use the cards to create movement combinations, explore the vocabulary, combine locomotor and nonlocomotor combinations and for choreography. I have made three sets of each word so that groups can use the cards simultaneously. You can laminate the cards for longer use but mine have lasted ten years without laminating.

STRETCHYBANDS

Make stretchybands out of stretchy jersey or lycra material. Cut foot wide pieces into 4, 5 and 6 foot lengths. 4 foot lengths are good for ages 2 - 9, 5 foot lengths for ages 10 - 15 and 6 foot lengths for adults. However, adults can use 4 foot lengths, also. Play around with the size and choose what works best for you. Sew the two ends together to form a loop and stitch around the edges loosely to help prevent tearing. Use these stretchybands to stretch into shapes, strengthen muscles and explore all the elements of dance.

SCARVES

The best scarf material is tricot chiffon. You can use one yard for each scarf or cut the 54 inch material in half to create two scarves. Of course, you can make small scarves, too, but the bigger ones are more fun. If you cannot find the tricot, choose a material that is light and has a lot of flow. Choose an interesting variety of colors if available -- black , white and deep purples, reds, blues and oranges as well as pastels. Use scarves to explore many elements -- smooth AND sharp, free flow AND bound flow, slow AND fast, etc.

PLASTIC FILM

Plastic film has a very different quality, texture and sound from the scarves and you get many more pieces for your money. You can punch, kick, toss, slash the plastic which is a great way to alleviate angry feelings. It is also terrific for floating, swaying, swinging and flying. It is wonderful for mirroring and "Magician and Zombie." The film is a tube. Cut it into 2 1/2 - 3 foot lengths. Then cut each length up the sides and you will have two pieces. You could cut long pieces (8 to 15 foot lengths) for special uses.

STREAMERS

Crepe paper streamers make a good prop unless young children put them in their mouths and they "bleed" all over their faces. Try white streamers for children who like to eat them! Tear the streamers in long enough lengths that make them fun to move, but not too long to trip on -- about 3 feet. Streamers only last two or three lessons but are fairly cheap. I only use the streamers occasionally, so I let the children take them to dance with at home.

BALLOONS

Balloons are a bother to blow up but are fun for special events or once a quarter. Buy good quality balloons and blow them up only three-quarters full. Soft balloons are less likely to pop and injure your students. Moving balloons with different body parts is wonderful for eye-hand coordination. Also encourage smooth floating movements while holding the balloon. Some parents feel very strongly about the safety of young children with balloons. By blowing them up only partially, I have never had a problem with popping. However, be sure to check with your parents before bringing out the balloons. Remember to explore the elements of dance with the balloons, not just toss them out for play time. Huge "balloons" can be made from the big white industrial garbage bags used by schools and businesses. Swoosh then open to capture air then bind them securely with rubber bands. They are very light and magical.

SPOTS

Spots may be made from foam carpet padding. Carpet stores will often give you remnants free of charge. Cut the padding into 12 inch circles (or any other desirable size or shape). Use these spots as self space markers, jumping pads, obstacles to leap over and dance around or places on which to make shapes.

CONES

Large traffic cones can often be purchased at hardware stores. Small traffic cones can be purchased through educational and physical education supply companies. Traffic cones can be used for obstacle courses, self space markers, line and place markers and objects to leap over.

RIBBON STICKS AND BALLS

With the rising popularity in rhythmic gymnastics, these props are easier to find than in the past. Children and adults enjoy using them for improvisation and choreography.

INSTRUMENTS

Collect rhythm instruments such as sticks, bells, shakers, tambourines, triangles, tone blocks and castanets. These can be made or purchased at educational supply stores, children's toy stores and folk music stores. Rhythm sticks can be made from wooden dowling. Cut 3/4 inch dowling into 10 inch lengths and sand the ends smooth. Make bells by stringing jingle bells on elastic and tying the ends in a knot. Certain pot lids make beautiful sounds when struck. Large plastic bottles make good drums when hit with a stick.

PARACHUTE

Parachutes can be found at Army and Navy surplus stores or educational supply stores. They come in different sizes. I prefer the larger sizes. Have your students dance on top of them, under them and around them. Ask them to make statues under the parachute which relate to the concept you are studying. Lift up the parachute and see the wonderful shape museum. Make a tent with the parachute and dance inside. Make a mountain and climb up the sides. Practice locomotor skills in a circular

Chuk'ems (left)
Chinese jump ropes
(below)

Material (above)
Spots (above, right)

Plastic (left)
Instruments (above)

364

pathway while holding the parachute. Create your own folk dances holding and moving the parachute. Pull young children around, as they sit on the chute, like a merry-go-round or back and forth like a sailboat. Remember to relate to the lesson's dance concept.

BENCHES

Old picnic benches work well. Make sure that they are sturdy, balanced and do not tip. Benches can be used as balance beams during leaping or obstacle courses. Dancers can also move under, over and around them in creative ways.

BEANBAGS

Beanbags of different sizes can be used when exploring weight and swings. They can be used to develop eye-hand coordination and balance.

CHINESE JUMP ROPES OR ELASTIC CIRCLES

You can buy Chinese jump ropes or make them by tying two ends of 1/2 inch elastic together to create a circle. Use the elastic as you would the stretchybands.

STRING/YARN

String and yarn may be used to make pathways on the floor. Challenge your students to move in different ways along the pathways. Ask them to make string designs on the floor then copy these designs with body shapes or movement. Have them toss the string in the air and let it fall where it will. Then challenge your students to copy the random shape that the tossed string makes. Create spider webs for dancers to move under, over, around and through. Strings can connect dancers together as they try to move cooperatively through space. Instead of string or yarn use thin, long scraps of lycra.

BAGS/TUBES

Make large bags and/or long tubes out of lycra, cotton jersey or tubular jersey. Let parents and toddlers explore the bags together. Have older students use them for choreography and improvisation. It is great fun to watch bodies making shapes and moving inside the bags and tubes!

MATERIAL

Collect large cloth remnants, old tablecloths or sheets. Use them in parent/infant/toddler/child classes for pulling young children around or as hammocks. Ask dancers to create magic shapes under the material which relate to the lesson concept. Have the other dancers try to guess the shape, remove the material and ask the dancers to copy the secret shape exactly. Form group statues or machines under the material, then remove the material and see the real shapes.

CHUK'EM

A chuk'em is a tube five feet long and two inches in diameter that is soft, flexible and will resume its basic shape. It is sort of like a big styrofoam dowl. The full length tube can be made into a circle connected by a small wooden dowl. The circles can be used as place markers, hoops or special spots and are a lot of fun to dance with. Each end of the long tube can also be put in a stand to create a bridge to crawl under, instead of using a bench. The chuk'em can be easily cut into different lengths for different uses. Short tubes can serve as connectors between dancers, instead of holding hands. This makes it fun to move in interesting ways without twisting arms and getting tangled or injured. Tubes of different lengths make a good prop for improvisation.

Dancers can balance the tubes on body parts, let them be extensions of arms, connect with other dancers, etc. Dancers can explore weight, using the tubes to pull and push apart from each other. Use the tubes as connections between different body parts for "Space Between." Can the dancers move together with the tube connecting their spines without letting the tube drop? Instead of leaping over cartons, leap over tubes of different lengths attached to stands. They can also be used as rhythm sticks and wands.

Be Creative!

Experiment with plastic and cardboard tubes, newspaper, masks, large rolls of paper, mylar ribbons, macrame rings with long ribbons tied to them, hats, costumes, pipe cleaners for creating shapes and whatever else comes to mind!

Prop Resource List

CHUK'EM
CHUK'EM Enterprise, Inc., 11080 Arroyo Beach Pl. SW, Seattle, WA 98146, 206-244-7049.

SCARVES
Dancing Colors, PO Box 61, Langley, WA 98260, 360- 221-5989 (Emily Day). Large collection of different sized scarves in fifteen different colors, fabrics from around the world and ribbon hoops.

PLASTIC FILM
Zim's, PO Box 7620, Salt Lake City, UT 84107. The film comes in twenty yard packages. The best colors are blue, red and yellow.

RIBBON STICKS, BALLS, CONES, CHUTES, etc.
Sportime, 1-800-283-5700.

Accompaniment for Dance Classes

ACCOMPANISTS

It is wonderful to have an accompanist for ages six through adult. A good accompanist can provide different rhythms, sounds and moods that provide motivation and support for exploration and skill development. An accompanist need not be a pianist. Any musician can accompany dance class with a little practice. Drums, wind, brass and string instruments can all be used for accompaniment. The best accompanist for creative dance is one who feels comfortable with improvisation.

Check your local music schools, universities, arts commissions and other dance programs for accompanists who work with dancers. Talk over your dance program, curriculum and lesson plan with the accompanist. It is important to have rapport, to work together so that the music and movement are integrated, not working against each other. Together you can build a strong, exciting program.

YOU AS ACCOMPANIST

If you are unable to afford or find an accompanist, you might buy some rhythm instruments and give it a try yourself. Different kinds of drums -- congo, tongue, tambour or claves, shakers, tambourines and triangles -- can be used to produce an underlying beat or rhythmic pattern. If you work in a public school, talk with a music specialist in your district. Ask for some help and ideas. With a little practice you will become more adept at accompaniment.

Your voice is also very important. Changing the tone, volume and rhythm of your voice will help support the changes in movement activities. Try to match the quality of your voice to the quality of the movement and the rhythm of your words to the rhythm of the steps or exercises you present.

RECORDED MUSIC

Recorded music is very useful when teaching infants through age six or seven because of the variety of activity records available for young children that incorporate movement. Of course, recorded music is necessary with older age groups when you do not have an accompanist.

If you are using tapes, it is most convenient to record single songs on ten minute cassettes. This way you will not have to spend time forwarding or reviewing long tapes to find the right selections. Ten minute cassettes can be ordered from Classic Cassettes of California, 1-800-678-1127 or Protape Northwest, 2412 2nd Ave., Seattle, WA, 206-441-8273.

Records can be more flexible than tapes because you can move the needle around and change the speed, if your player has speed control, but records do scratch and will soon be obsolete. Although CDs are more expensive, they offer the flexibility of records and the durability of tapes. Many CD players come with remote control devices that you can use as you move around the room to forward or review your music.

Buy a few recommended records, CDs or tapes to begin your collection. With New Age music the samplers are the best buys because they offer a selection of composers or selections from one composer. If possible, listen to the music before purchasing it. Slowly add to your collection as you find new, interesting, and useful music.

A good sound system is a must. If you have one with a turntable, tape and CD player this allows for the most flexibilty. Whatever you use, make sure the speakers provide enough volume for your space. If you travel from school to school invest in a quality portable system.

TYPES OF MUSIC

Using a variety of music in your creative dance classes will ensure success. Music appropriate to each age group and activity can be inspiring and supportive. Music that is boring or inappropriate will hinder your teaching. Music that has a strong, steady beat is excellent for the "Developing Skills" section of your lesson plan. Folk music works well for the "Combining Movements" section of the lesson plan because of its clear measures and repeating phrases. Music without a steady beat can be used as background for "Improvisation" and "Exploring the Concept" sections of the lesson plan.

Music that has clear changes in speed, volume or dynamics is very useful when teaching creative dance. The contrasts in the music will encourage the students to use contrasting dance elements in their explorations. Take time to find music that inspires you and supports the concepts you are teaching. When planning your lessons, try to include selections from several of the categories listed below.

Classical
Jazz
New Age
Country
Folk
Ethnic (African, Irish, Asian, etc.)
Rock
Popular
Musicals/Movies
Children's Songs (Hap Palmer, Buzz Glass, etc.)
Music for Dance Styles (Modern, Jazz, Ballet, Tap)

APPENDIX F

Instrumental and Activity Music List

Below are a few of my favorite composers and recordings. Other albums by the following artists are also worth looking into. The numbers listed below are for records but will lead you also to the tapes and CDs, if available.

Annie's Song. James Galway. RCA ARL1-3061
Music for composition, improvisation, exploration and locomotor skills. "Brian Boru's March" is soft/loud/soft. "Belfast Hornpipe" is good for locomotor movements. "Annie's Song" is good for free dancing.

Cinemagic. Dave Grusin. GRD-9547 (CD)
Music for explorations, free dancing and improvisations.

Deep Breakfast. Ray Lynch. RLLP-102
New age -- good background, light, bubbly music. Excellent for "Exploring the Concept," "Shaping" and "Free Dancing."

Dreams of Children. Shadowfax. WH-1038
Music for explorations and improvisations.

Emerald. Brewer, Rumbel, Tingstad. N 61011
Music for explorations, free dancing and improvisations. Also has a nice song in 3/4 meter for waltz run, etc.

The Essential Jean Michel Jarre. PRO LP 3
Electronic and synthesizer music for composition, improvisation, exploration.

Greatest Hits. James Galway. 7778 1-RC
An excellent selection of flute music for composition, improvisation and skill development.

Happy Hour. Hap Plamer. AR 716
A good selection of music for ages four through ten. A variety of rhythms and moods.

Hooked On Series.
Series of classic, jazz and movie songs. Each band has a variety of rhythms/moods but also a strong synthesizer beat which can get tiresome.

Movin'. Hap Palmer. AR 546
   A variety of upbeat and slow music, including a pause song.

Music for Creative Dance: Contrast and Continuum. Eric Chappelle. Ravenna Ventures, Seattle, WA, 206-527-7799 or NDA/AAHPERD, 1-800-321-0789.
   Instrumental music written especially for conceptual creative dance classes. Music with contrasts of fast/slow, sharp/smooth, strong/light, curved, straight/zigzag, etc. Plus continuous music in many different meters and rhythms. Excellent!!

The Nonesuch Explorer, Music from Distant Corners of the World. Nonesuch Records. H7-11 (two record set)
   Many different rhythms from different countries.   Wonderful for improvisation and cultural awareness.

Rhythmically Moving Series. Phyllis Weikart. High/Scope
   Record #1 has good rhythms and combination of fast and slow songs. Record #2 contains Seven Jumps, Doudlebska Polka and other useful folk dances. Others in the series are excellent folk dances for children and can be used for "Developing Skills" and "Combining Movements."

Solitude. Zamfir. Mercury 6313 238
   Very good for explorations and free dancing. "Inima" is a song which alternates slow and fast rhythms.

Suite for Flute and Jazz Piano. Claude Bolling. Columbia M33233
   Composition, improvisation, exploration.

Windham Hill Sampler '81. WH-1015
   A good variety of music for explorations, turning, sliding, etc.

More favorites: Kitaro, Bobby McFerrin, Windham Hill Samplers, Bochinche, David Sanborn, Vangelis, Narada Samplers, Nonesuch Explorer Series for Dances of the World.

Activity Songs to Use with Young Children

   On the following pages is a list of songs that can be used with young children. They work particularly well with ages 2-7, and infant and toddler classes. Most of the songs have words and describe different activities. The songs that are starred are instrumental. The instrumental songs work well with any age.
   Each element of dance is listed below. Under each element are the songs that I find helpful for exploring or reinforcing the element. The songs are listed on the left and the albums are listed on the right. A list of all the albums and their catalog numbers can be found at the very end of the list. The catalog numbers are for record albums, but many of the albums also can be found on tape and CDs. Any music store can help you order your selections.
   Remember, when you are using activity songs you need to offer your own suggestions for movement along with the voice on the music.
   Instrumental music is designated with an asterisk.

PLACE

"Sally"	Sally the Swinging Snake
"Surprise Song"	Walter the Waltzing Worm
"Moving Game"	Creative Movement & Rhythmic Exploration
"Slow and Fast" *	Feel of Music
"Soft and Loud" *	Feel of Music
"Together"	Feel of Music
"Seven Jumps" *	Rhythmically Moving 2
"Birdie Fly Down"	I'm Not Small
"Rockin' Hula"	Feelin' Free
"Play Your Instruments"	Play Your Instruments
"Wake Me, Shake Me"	Time After Time
"Inima" *	Solitude
"Baroque and Blues" *	Suite for Flute and Jazz Piano
"Javanaise" *	Suite for Flute and Jazz Piano
"Circle Your Way" *	Easy Does It

Any songs that have a verse and chorus, pauses , or two distinct changes in rhythm also work well for PLACE.

SIZE

"Soft and Loud" *	Feel of Music
"Slow and Fast" *	Feel of Music
"Make a Pretty Sound"	Homemade Band
"Haunted House "	Movin'
"Scales"	Feel of Music
"Seven Jumps" *	Rhythmically Moving 2
"Brian Boru's March" *	Annie's Song or Rhythmically Moving 1

LEVEL

"Move Around The Room"	Ideas, Thoughts and Feelings
"Building Bridges"	Ideas, Thoughts and Feelings
"Jump Jump Jump"	Dancing Words
"It's Just Fun"	Feelin' Free
"High and Low"	Learning Basic Skills Through Music Vocabulary
"Play"	Homemade Band
"Sammy"	Getting to Know Myself
"Scales"	Feel of Music
"Under the Stick"	Learning Basic Skills Through Music Vocabulary
"Something Special"	Sally the Swinging Snake
"Everything Has a Shape"	Sally the Swinging Snake

"A Tree Fell Down"   Easy Does It
"Soft and Loud"   Feel of Music
"Slow and Fast" *   Feel of Music
"Seven Jumps" *   Rhythmically Moving 2
"Five Beats to Each Measure"   Feel of Music -- change level on 1st beat

DIRECTION

"Let's Dance"   Learning Basic Skills Through Music, Vol. 2
"Left and Right"   Getting to Know Myself
"Sammy"   Getting to Know Myself
"Use Your Own Two Feet"   Jump Children
"Surprise Song" *   Walter the Waltzing Worm
"Slide Whistle Suite" *   Walter the Waltzing Worm
"Five Beats to Each Measure"   Feel of Music

    Any pause songs
    See songs under LOCOMOTOR.

PATHWAYS

"Sammy"   Getting to Know Myself
"How Are We Going?"   Learning Basic Skills Through Music Vocabulary
"Moving Game"   Creative Movement & Rhythmic Exploration
"How Many Ways"   Creative Movement & Rhythmic Exploration
"If My Feet Could Talk"   Toddler Time
"Way to Lead the Band"   Play Your Instruments/Make a Pretty Sound
"Genius of Course"   Walter the Waltzing Worm
"Surprise Song" *   Walter the Waltzing Worm
"Triangle, Circle and Square" Learning Basic Skills Through Music, Vol. 2
"Do a Little Dance"   Feel of Music
"Walk Around the Circle"   Learning Basic Skills Through Music Vocabulary
"Making Friends"   Ideas, Thoughts and Feelings

FOCUS

"Haunted House" *   Movin'
"Pause" *   Movin'
"Five Beats to Each Measure"   Feel of Music
"Dancing with a Stick"   Sally the Swinging Snake (use plastic)
"Do a Little Dance"   Feel of Music
"Echo" *   Rhythmically Moving #1

    Any pause songs, shadowing/mirroring songs or songs with sharp changes.

SPEED

"Slow and Fast" *	Feel of Music
"Song About Slow"	Walter the Waltzing Worm
"Walk Like a Cat"	Dancing Words
"The Toy Soldier"	Dancing Words
"Buzzing Bee"	Dancing Words
"Rocket"	Dancing Words
"Scales" *	Feel of Music
"Kye Kye Kule"	Hug the Earth
"Wiggy Wiggy Wiggles"	Sally the Swinging Snake
"Quickly and Quietly"	Feel of Music
"Shoes"	Dancing Words
"Tiger Hunt"	Having Fun with Ernie and Bert
"Seven Jumps" *	Rhythmically Moving 2
"Fjeskern" *	Rhythmically Moving 2
"Walking"	Come and See the Peppermint Tree
"Follow Me"	Come and See the Peppermint Tree
"Move Very Slowly"	It's About Time
"Move Very Quickly"	It's About Time
"Can You Feel the Tempo"	It's About Time

RHYTHM

"Ring Around"	Music Skills
"Way To Lead the Band"	Play Your Instruments/Make a Pretty Sound
"Got the Rhythm"	Hug the Earth
"Walking Notes"	Feel of Music
"Stop and Go"	Play Your Instruments
"Partners"	Learning Basic Skills Through Music, Vol. 2
"Five Beats to Each Measure"	Feel of Music
"Do a Little Dance"	Feel of Music
"Clap and Rest"	Feel of Music
"Rock and Roll Song"	Feel of Music
"3/4 Rag" *	Feel of Music
"Move and Rest"	Feel of Music
"Walter the Waltzing Worm"	Walter the Waltzing Worm
"Slide Whistle Suite" *	Walter the Waltzing Worm
"Surprise Song" *	Walter the Waltzing Worm
"Zippety Doo Dah" *	Fun for Toddlers
"Shoo Lie Loo"	Cloud Journeys
Duple and triple rhythms *	Music for Movement

ENERGY

"Flick a Fly"	Walter the Waltzing Worm
"Surprise Song" *	Walter the Waltzing Worm
"Swing, Shake..."	Walter the Waltzing Worm
"Slide Whistle Suite" *	Walter the Waltzing Worm
"Buzzing Bee"	Dancing Words
"Rocket"	Dancing Words
"Tummy Tango"	Kids in Motion
"Show Me"	Kids in Motion
"Slow and Fast" *	Feel of Music
"Rockin' Hula"	Feelin' Free
"Jibbety Jib"	Come and See the Peppermint Tree
"Be My Shadow" *	Fun Activities for Toddlers
"Zippety Doo Dah" *	Fun Activities for Toddlers

WEIGHT

"Soft and Loud" *	Feel of Music
"Rubberband Man"	Sally the Swinging Snake
"Flick a Fly"	Walter the Waltzing Worm
"Genius of Course"	Walter the Waltzing Worm
"Birdie Fly Down"	I'm Not Small
"Seven Jumps" *	Rhythmically Moving 2
"Touch the World"	Feel of Music
"Be a Bubble" *	Fun Activities for Toddlers

FLOW

"Rockin Hula"	Feelin' Free
"Astronauts and Robots" *	Let's Move and Learn

Pause songs
New Age music

BODY PARTS

"Bumpity Bump"	Feelin' Free
"Touch"	Getting to Know Myself
"Shake Something"	Getting to Know Myself
"Turn Around"	Getting to Know Myself
"Walter the Waltzing Worm"	Walter the Waltzing Worm
"What a Miracle"	Walter the Waltzing Worm

374

"Swing, Shake..."	Walter the Waltzing Worm
"Surprise Song" *	Walter the Waltzing Worm
"Something Special"	Sally the Swinging Snake
"Rubberband Man"	Sally the Swinging Snake
"Body Rock"	Kids in Motion
"Beanbag Boogie I and II"	Kids in Motion
"Rockin Hula"	Feelin' Free
"Triangle, Circle and Square"	Learning Basic Skills Through Music, Vo.l 2
"Beanbag" (use any prop)	Easy Does It
"If You're Happy"	Hug the Earth
"Clap Hands"	Circle Around or sing it yourself
"Move Around the Room"	Ideas, Thoughts and Feelings
"Building Bridges"	Ideas, Thoughts and Feelings
"Looby Loo"	Sing it yourself
"Hokey Pokey"	Circle Around or sing it yourself
"This Is the Way (we shake a leg)"	sing yourself
"Old MacDonald (had an arm)"	sing yourself
"Pause" *	Movin'

BODY SHAPES

"Everything Has a Shape"	Sally the Swinging Snake
"Touch"	Getting to Know Myself
"Tummy Tango"	Kids in Motion
"Triangle, Circle and Square"	Learning Basic Skills Through Music, Vol. 2
"How Many Ways"	Creative Movement & Rhythmic Exploration
"Pause" *	Movin'

BALANCE

"One Shoe"	Cloud Journeys
"Beanbag" (any prop)	Easy Does It
"Beanbag Boogie I and II"	Kids in Motion
"Everything Has a Shape"	Sally the Swinging Snake
"Seven Jumps" *	Rhythmically Moving 2
"Stop and Go"	Play Your Instruments

Any pause song

RELATIONSHIP

"Partners"	Learning Basic Skills Through Music, Vol. 2
"Making Friends"	Ideas, Thoughts and Feelings

"Circle Your Way" *	Easy Does It
"Touch the World"	Feel of Music
"Birdie Fly Down"	I'm Not Small
"Echo" *	Rhythmically Moving #1
"Mirror"	Dancing Words
"This Is What I Can Do"	Dancing Words
"Under the Stick"	Learning Basic Skills Through Music Vocabulary
"Tree Fell Down"	Easy Does It
"Dancing With a Stick"	Sally the Swinging Snake
"Shadow Dance"	Kids in Motion
"Follow Me" *	Fun Activities for Toddlers
"Be My Shadow" *	Fun Activities for Toddlers
"Follow Me"	Come and See the Peppermint Tree

LOCOMOTOR/NONLOCOMOTOR

"Walk Around the Circle"	Learning Basic Skills Through Music Vocabulary
"Slide Whistle Suite" *	Walter the Waltzing Worm
"Shoes"	Dancing Words
"Walk Like a Cat"	Dancing Words
"Skate"	Dancing Words
"Jump"	Dancing Words
"Here We Go Round the Circle"	Dancing Words
"Left and Right"	Getting to Know Myself
"It's Just Fun"	Feelin' Free
"Moving Game I and II"	Creative Movement & Rhythmic Exploration
"Sho Fly I"	On the Move
"Stop and Go"	Play Your Instruments
"Movement Rondo"	Time After Time
"Ring Around"	Music Skills
"Walking Notes"	Feel of Music
"Lead the Band"	Play Your Instruments
"All the Ways of Jumping"	Walter the Waltzing Worm
"Walter the Waltzing Worm"	Walter the Waltzing Worm (waltz run)
"Genius of Course"	Walter the Waltzing Worm (gallop, prance)
"Swing Shake..."	Walter the Waltzing Worm
"Sally"	Sally the Swinging Snake
"Wild and Wooly"	Tickly Toddle (gallop)
"Jump and Spin"	Come and See the Peppermint Tree
"Walking"	Come and See the Peppermint Tree
"One Shoe Hopping"	Cloud Journeys
"Sliding" *	Rhythmically Moving 1
"Funky Penguin" *	Movin'
"Jamaican Holiday" *	Movin'
Side 1 and 2 *	Happy Hour

376

FREE DANCE

"Feelin' Free"	Feelin' Free
"A Place in the Choir"	Hug the Earth
"Joy"	Feel of Music
"Rock and Roll Song"	Feel of Music
"Birdie Fly Down"	I'm Not Small
"Do a Little Dance"	Feel of Music
"Mango Walk"	Smorgasboard
"Let's Be Friends"	All of Us Will Shine
"Kids in Motion"	Kids in Motion
"Jump Children"	Jump Children
"Beautiful Day"	Jump Children
"Oh What a Miracle"	Walter the Waltzing Worm
"There Is a Fine Wind..."	All of Us Will Shine
"Wild and Wooly"	Tickly Toddle
"Magic Penny"	Cloud Journeys
"Birthday Song"	Cloud Journeys
Side 2 *	Pretend
Side 1 and 2 *	Happy Hour

INSTRUMENTS

"Play Your Instruments"	Play Your Instruments/Make a Pretty Sound
"Lead the Band"	Play Your Instruments/Make a Pretty Sound
"Put Your Instruments Away"	Play Your Instruments/Make a Pretty Sound
"Walking Notes"	Feel of Music
"Five Beats to Each Measure	Feel of Music
"Ring Around"	Music Skills
"Find a Way"	Ideas, Thoughts and Feelings
"Follow Along"	Ideas, Thoughts and Feelings

All songs on Homemade Band

REST/ALIGNMENT

"Time to Sleep"	Jump Children
"The Star"	Jump Children
"Sleepy Time"	Anne Murray Sings
"Stars Are the Windows"	Anne Murray Sings
"Lullaby Medley"	Anne Murray Sings
"Hobo's Lullaby"	Smorgasboard
"Sleepy Time Sea"	Tickly Toddle
"Imagination"	Having Fun With Ernie and Bert

"Quiet Time"	Time After Time
Side 2 *	Quiet Moments
Side 2	I'm Not Small
Side 1 and 2 *	Seagulls

PAUSE SONGS

"Pause" *	Movin'
"Freeze"	Kids in Motion
"Wildwood 2"	Homemade Band
"Making Friends"	Ideas, Thoughts and Feelings
"Zippety Doo Dah"	Fun for Toddlers
"Circle Your Way" *	Easy Does It
"Seven Jumps" *	Rhythmically Moving 2
"Shoo Fly II"	On the Move

ACTIVITY MUSIC LIST TITLES AND CATALOG NUMBERS

My favorite albums are indicated with an asterisk.

Hap Palmer Music

Creative Movement and Rhythmic Exploration AR 533

Easy Does It AR 581

Feel of Music AR 556   *

Feelin' Free AR 517

Getting to Know Myself AR 543

Happy Hour AR 716

Homemade Band AR 545   *

Ideas, Thoughts and Feelings AR 549

Learning Basic Skills Through Music, Vol. 2 AR 522

Learning Basic Skills Through Music Vocabulary AR 521

Movin' AR 546   *

Pretend AR 563

Sally the Swinging Snake AR 617

Seagulls AR 584

Tickly Toddle AR 597

Walter the Waltzing Worm AR 555

Other Music

All of Us Will Shine Tickle Tune Typhoon, Box 15153, Seattle, WA 98115

Anne Murray Sings CTW 79006

Circle Around. Tickle Tune Typhoon

Cloud Journeys B/B 111. Anne Barlin

Colors of My Rainbow MK 87-733

Come and See the Peppermint Tree DPT 101

Dancing Words AR 539. Buzz Glass *

Fun Activities for Toddlers KIM 2017

Having Fun With Ernie and Bert CC 25506

Hug the Earth. Tickle Tune Typhoon

I'm Not Small AR 547. Marcia Berman

It's 'Bout Time AR 88

Jump Children Rounder Records 8012. Marcy Marxer *

Kids in Motion Youngheart Records *

Let's Move and Learn. Human Kinetics Books. Rae Pica/Richard Gardzina

Music for Movement MLR 187

Music Skills MH 46

On The Move with Greg and Steve YR005R

Play Your Instruments and Make a Pretty Sound FC 7665. Ella Jenkins

Quiet Moments with Greg and Steve YR006R

Rhythmically Moving Series 1-4 High/Scope Press. Phyllis Weikart

Smorgasboard LFN 7902. Sharon, Lois and Bram

Time After Time AR 87

Toddler Time KIM 0815

Selection of Videos for Dance History

I enjoy showing videos to my classes (toddlers through adults) once a quarter. I talk a little about the dancers or choreographers and then relate the video selection to the day's dance concept. After I show the dance segment we create our own dance based on the concept and the ideas we saw in the video. For example, when exploring rhythm I might show the firecracker dance from *Holiday Inn.* Then we make up a dance with rhythm patterns and sharp sounds. The students love watching the videos and learning about professional dancers from the past and present. The videos listed below are available at most video rental stores or public libraries.

Holiday Inn - Fred Astaire (firecracker dance plus others)

Singin' in the Rain - Gene Kelly (several good dances)

Royal Wedding - Fred Astaire (dancing on the walls)

White Christmas - Bing Crosby and Danny Kaye (seasonal themes)

Court Jester - Danny Kaye (funny dance that speeds up)

Funny Face - Fred Astaire (beatnik dance plus others)

Oklahoma - choreography by Agnes DeMille (changed musical theatre forever by adding the element of ballet)

West Side Story - (jazz, men dancing, multi-cultural theme)

White Nights - Gregory Hines and Baryshnikov (tap and ballet)

Tap - Sammy Davis Jr, Gregory Hines and others

Fame, Footloose, Grease - Jazz, be-bop, breakdancing

Chorusline - Michael Bennett (good musical theatre dance but mature themes)

All That Jazz - Bob Fosse (good jazz dance but mature themes)

Nutcracker - Baryshnikov or Pacific Northwest Ballet

Catherine's Wheel - Twyla Tharp (modern)

Videotape the Arts and Entertainment Channel - Look for these names: Martha Graham, Paul Taylor, Alwin Nikolais, Merce Cunningham, Doris Humphrey, Alvin Ailey (modern); Rudolf Nureyev, Baryshnikov, Melissa Hayden, Cynthia Gregory, George Balanchine, Robert Joffery, (ballet); Jerome Robbins, Agnes DeMille (musicals and ballets); Fred Astaire, Gene Kelly, Ginger Rogers, Cyd Charisse (musicals).

You can read about these dancers in books on dance history listed in the Bibliography.

Classical and modern dance videos are available for sale from Princeton Book Company/Dance Horizons, PO Box 57, Pennington NJ 08534, 1-800-326-7149.

The National Dance Association offers for sale a series of videos, titled Dances of the World, that show authentic dances, costumes, and musicians from nine countries. Available from AAHPERD, 1900 Association Drive, Reston, VA 22091, 1-800-321-0789.

APPENDIX H

Bibliography

CREATIVE DANCE

Barlin, Anne. (1979). <u>Teaching Your Wings to Fly: The Nonspecialists Guide to Movement Activities for Young Children</u>. Santa Monica, CA: Goodyear.

Benzwie, Theresa. (1987). <u>A Moving Experience</u>. Tuscon, AZ: Zephyr Press.

Boorman, Joyce. (1969). <u>Creative Dance in The First Three Grades.</u> Ontario: Longman Canada Limited.

Boorman, Joyce. (1971). <u>Creative Dance in Grades Four to Six</u>. Ontario: Longman Canada Limited.

Joyce, Mary. (1980). <u>First Steps in Teaching Creative Dance</u> (2nd ed.) Palo Alto, CA: Mayfield Pub. Co.

Lloyd, Marcia. (1990). <u>Adventures in Creative Movement Activities: A Guide to Teaching.</u> Available through National Dance Association, AAHPERD, Reston, VA.

Russell, Joan. (1975). <u>Creative Movement and Dance for Children</u>. Boston: Plays.

Stinson, Sue. (1988). <u>Dance for Young Children: Finding the Magic in Movement</u>. Reston, VA: American Alliance for Health, Physical Education, Recreation and Dance.

MODERN DANCE AND CHOREOGRAPHY

Blom and Chaplin. (1988). <u>The Moment of Movement</u>. Pittsburgh, PA: University of Pittsburgh Press.

Cheney, Gay. (1989). <u>Basic Concepts in Modern Dance</u>. Pennington, NJ: Princeton Book Co.

Cohan, Robert. (1986). <u>The Dance Workshop: A Guide to the Fundamentals of Movement</u>. New York: Simon and Schuster.

Ellfeldt, Lois. (1967). <u>A Primer for Choreographers</u>. Palo Alto, CA: Mayfield Pub. Co.

Haselbach, Barbara. (1981). <u>Improvisation Dance Movement</u>. Magnamusic-Baton.

Humphrey, Doris. (1962). <u>The Art of Making Dances</u>. Pennington, NJ: Princeton Book Co.

Joyce, Mary. (1984). <u>Dance Technique for Children</u>. Palo Alto, CA: Mayfield Pub. Co.

Lockhart, Aileene and Pease, Esther. (1977). <u>Modern Dance: Building and Teaching Lessons</u> (5th ed.). Dubuque, IA: Wm. C. Brown Company Publishers.

Sherbon, Elizabeth. (1975). <u>On the Count of One: Modern Dance Methods</u>. Palo Alto, CA: Mayfield Pub. Co.

Shurr, Gertrude and Yocum, Rachael Dunaven. (1980). <u>Modern Dance Techniques and Teaching</u>. New York: Dance Horizons.

MISCELLANEOUS DANCE MATERIALS

Carr, Rachel. (1973). <u>Be a Frog, a Bird, or a Tree</u>. New York: Doubleday and Co. Yoga exercises for children.

Gardner, Howard. (1983). <u>Frames of Mind: The Theory of Multiple Intelligences</u>. New York: University Press.

Gaylean, Beverly-Colleene. (1983). <u>Mind Sight, Learning Through Imaging</u>. Santa Barbara, CA: Center for Integrative Learning. (Carried by Zephyr Press). A thorough book on the use of imagery in all subject areas.

Gilbert, Anne Green. (1977). <u>Teaching the Three R's Through Movement Experiences</u>. New York: Macmillan Pub. Co. Many ways to teach language arts, math, social studies, science and art through movement. Extensive annotated bibliography.

Harris, Jane A., Pittman, Anne M., and Waller, Marlys S. (1978). <u>Dance A While: Handbook of Folk, Square and Social Dance</u>. New York: Macmillan Publ. Co. (available from AAHPERD). Includes discussion of dance forms and instructions.

Nash, Grace. (1974). <u>Creative Approaches to Child Development with Music, Language and Movement</u>. New York: Alfred Publishing Co., Inc. Multi-arts explorations using Orff, Kodaly and Laban.

Schlaich, Joan and DuPont, Betty. (1988). <u>Dance: The Art of Production</u>. Reston, VA: National Dance Association.

Weikart, Phyllis. (1983). <u>Teaching Movement and Dance</u>. Ypsilanti, MI: High/Scope Press. Easy to use folk dance book.

Zirulnik, Ann, and Abeles, Jeanette (Eds.). (1985). <u>Resource List for Children's Dance</u>. Michigan Dance Association, 300 Bailey Street, Room 201, East Lansing, MI 48823. Sixty pages listing resources in books, records, films and other materials for children's dance.

DANCE FOR SPECIAL POPULATIONS

Beal, Rayma K. and Berryman-Miller, Sherrill. (1988) <u>Dance for the Older Adult</u>. Reston, VA: National Dance Association/AAHPERD.

Canner, Norma. (1975). <u>...and a time to dance</u>. Boston: Plays.

Gilbert, Debbie and Petroff, Joanne. Whistlestop, PO Box 20801, Seattle, WA 98102. Excellent lesson plans and materials for dance with special populations.

Levete, Gina. (1982). <u>No Handicap to Dance: Creative Improvisation for People With and Without Disabilities</u>. London: Souvenir Press.

HISTORY

Anderson, Jack. (1986). <u>Ballet and Modern Dance: A Concise History</u>. Pennington, NJ: Princeton Book Co. Publishers.

Au, Susan. (1988). <u>Ballet and Modern Dance</u>. New York: Thames and Hudson.

Chujoy, Anatole (Ed.). (1949). <u>The Dance Encyclopedia</u>. New York: A.S. Barnes.

HEALTH

Alter, Judy. (1983). <u>Surviving Exercise</u>. Boston: Houghton Mifflin.

Alter, Judy. (1986). <u>Stretch and Strengthen</u>. Boston: Houghton Mifflin.

Arnheim, Daniel. (1975). <u>Dance Injuries</u>. Pennington, NJ: Princeton Book Co. Publishers.

Elkind, David. (1981). <u>The Hurried Child</u>. Menlo Park, CA: Addison-Wesley Publishing Co. The causes and effects of stress on children.

Hendricks, Gay and Roberts, Thomas B. (1977). <u>The Second Centering Book</u>. Englewood Cliffs, NJ: Prentice-Hall Inc. Many excellent activities for dealing with emotions using centering and visualization.

CLASS MANAGEMENT

Long and Frye. <u>Making It Till Friday</u>. Pennington, NJ: Princeton Book Co. Publishers.

Dreikurs, Rudolph. (1968). <u>Psychology in the Classroom.</u> New York: Harper and Row.

Hendricks, Gay. (1981). <u>The Centered Teacher</u>. Englewood Cliffs, N.: Prentice-Hall Inc. Centering activities and a good section on discipline.

DANCE CURRICULUMS and ASSESSMENT

<u>A Guide to Curriculum Planning in Dance</u>. Wisconsin Department of Public Instruction, PO Box 7841, Madison, WI 53707-7841. 608-266-2188

<u>Dance Curricula Guidelines K-12</u>. National Dance Association, 1900 Association Drive, Reston, VA 22091

<u>Dance Education in the Vancouver Schools: K-12 Curriculum</u>. Vancouver School District No. 37, POB 8937, Vancouver, WA 98668-8937

Ross, M. (1986). <u>Assessment In Arts Education</u>. Elmsford, NY: Pergamon Press.

Van Gyn, Geraldine and Van Sant O'Neil, Donna. (1989). "Assessment of the Fine Arts: Dance" (monograph). University of Victoria, Victoria, BC, Canada.

Check with your state department of public instruction to see if your state has curriculum guidelines and/or assessment tools in dance or the fine and performing arts.